Social Accounting for Development Planning
with special reference to Sri Lanka

A Study prepared for the International Labour Office within the framework of the World Employment Programme

Social Accounting for Development Planning with special reference to Sri Lanka

GRAHAM PYATT

Senior Adviser, Development Research Centre,
World Bank, Washington DC, and

ALAN ROE

Senior Lecturer in Economics, University of Warwick

with
JEFFERY ROUND AND ROBERT LINDLEY
and based on work undertaken in association with
J.A.C. BROWN, PETER DAVIES, NEIL KARUNARATNE,
ROBERT MABRO, S. NARAPALASINGHAM,

with a Foreword by
RICHARD STONE

CAMBRIDGE UNIVERSITY PRESS
CAMBRIDGE
LONDON - NEW YORK - MELBOURNE

Published by the Syndics of the Cambridge University Press
The Pitt Building, Trumpington Street, Cambridge CB2 1RP
Bentley House, 200 Euston Road, London NW1 2DB
32 East 57th Street, New York, NY 10022, USA
296 Beaconsfield Parade, Middle Park, Melbourne 3206, Australia

First published 1977

Printed in Great Britain
at the University Printing House, Cambridge

Library of Congress Cataloguing in Publication Data

Pyatt, F. Graham.

Social accounting for development planning with
special reference to Sri Lanka.

Bibliography: p.
Includes index.
1. National income – Sri Lanka – Accounting.
2. Underdeveloped areas – National income – Accounting.
I. Roe, A.R., joint author. II. Title.
HC424.Z9157 1977 354′.549′3007231 76-30553

ISBN 0 521 21578 1

CONTENTS

TABLES

FIGURES

ABBREVIATIONS

BTN	Brussels Tariff Nomenclature
CBR	Central Bank of Ceylon, *Annual Report*
CR	Customs Department, *Trade Returns*
DCS	Department of Census and Statistics (Sri Lanka)
ERE	Ceylon Government, *Estimates of the Revenue and Expenditure of the Government of Ceylon*
IBRD	International Bank for Reconstruction and Development (World Bank)
ISIC	International Standard Industrial Classification
MPS	material product system
PMC	S. Narapalasingham. *On the Construction and Implementation of a Planning Model for Ceylon*, PhD Thesis of University of Bristol, 1970
SAM	social-accounting matrix
SES	Department of Census & Statistics, *Socio-Economic Survey, 1969/70*
SNA	(United Nations) System of National Accounts
UNDP	United Nations Development Project, Special Fund, *National Economic Planning and Programming Project Report*, Colombo 1968
UNSO	United Nations Statistical Office
WEP	World Employment Programme

PREFACE

This volume owes a great deal to a number of people, both individually and collectively. Its origins are in the work of the International Labour Office, Comprehensive Employment Strategy Mission, led by Professor Seers, which went to Sri Lanka at the invitation of the Government in 1971. That experience led to the view that progress in tackling the problems of employment creation and income distribution as integral components of development strategy was being held back by lack of a quantitative framework which embraced these questions alongside the conventional macroeconomic considerations of production, commodity balances, external transactions, etc. Accordingly, the invitation in 1973 from Mr Herbert Tennekoon, Governor of the Central Bank of Ceylon, to the ILO World Employment Programme Research Branch to send a team to address itself to these problems was both timely and welcome. This volume is based on the report of that team, and therefore owes its existence to Mr Tennekoon's initiative and to Dr Louis Emmerij, Director of World Employment Programme Research at that time.

The team which undertook the initial work comprised, in addition to ourselves:

Professor J.A.C. Brown, University of Oxford
Dr Neil Karunaratne, formerly Ministry of Industries, Colombo
Mr R.M. Lindley, University of Warwick
Mr R. Mabro, University of Oxford
Dr S. Narapalasingham, Ministry of Planning and Employment, Colombo
and Dr J.I. Round, University of Warwick

Our report was a team effort and essentially of joint authorship. It is because one of us was team leader, while the other took charge of editing the final drafts, that we emerge as prime movers in preparation of this present volume.

It is a pleasure to record thanks both to our team colleagues and to so many people in Sri Lanka for making the research mission possible. Our debt to Mr Tennekoon goes beyond the initial obligation for proposing the work since his active interest throughout has been critical. Equally, support from the ILO, and Louis Emmerij especially, was exceptional, and has seen us through to completion of this volume. Particular mention must also be made of Dr Lal Jayawardena, formerly Additional Permanent Secretary, Ministry of Planning and Employment, Colombo: he, together with Louis Emmerij, provided not only the initial impetus for the work, but also enthusiasm and encouragement to sustain it throughout.

The team was in Sri Lanka for six weeks and its task was essentially completed during that period and the subsequent two months. To accomplish this required considerable support and cooperation not only from individuals already mentioned. Dr W. Rasaputram, Director of Economic Research in the Central Bank of Ceylon, Mr R.D.K.J. Arthanayeka, Secretary to the Governor, and Mr Victor Dissanayake, Protocol Officer, made every facility available to us, not least the expert cooperation of Mr Rajah Christopher and the secretarial assistance of Mr Dharmawansa.

Professor H.A. de S. Gunasekera, Secretary, Ministry of Planning and Employment gave us opportunity to discuss our work with him and allowed the release of Dr S. Narapalasingham to join the team in the UK after its return here, to be a coauthor of the report. This was of enormous value to us. We are also most grateful to Mr Leelananda de Silva, Senior Assistant Secretary, Ministry of Planning and Employment, for all he did for us; and to Mr L.N. Perera, Deputy Director of the Department of Census and Statistics and Mr W.S.M. Fernando, Statistician, for their active cooperation and provision of clerical assistance. More generally we were able to have a number of interesting exchanges with members of the Plan Implementation Division of the Ministry and must particularly thank Messrs D. Nesiah and S. Selvaratnam and the UN advisers attached to the Ministry, notably Dr Jitindra Modi and Mr R.K. Srivastava.

An opportunity to present our ideas was provided by Mr T.B. Subasinghe, Minister of Industries and Scientific Affairs and we enjoyed considerable cooperation from him and his colleagues, not least Mr L.N. Bandaranaike, Additional Secretary of the Ministry, Mr C. Abeysekera, Director of Public Corporations, Mr J. Somasunderam, Deputy Director, Small-Scale and Rural Industries Department, and Mr U. Godamunne, Statistical Officer within the Ministry. We owe a particular debt to the Minister and the Industrial Development Board for the release of Dr N. Karunaratne to join the team in the UK to be a joint-author of the final report. Our debt to the Board goes beyond this and in particular we must thank the former Chairman, Mr M. Wijenaike, for his interest and support not least in providing valuable library facilities and research assistance, and for making Dr Karunaratne's time available to us. We must also thank Mr N. de Mel, Director of the Technical Services Agency of the Board for his help.

In addition to the help we received in depth from the Central Bank, Ministry of Planning and Employment, Ministry of Industries and the Industrial Development Board, there are many others who gave their time and encouragement to our work. In this context we must thank particularly:

Mr M. Senanayake,
Deputy Prime Minister and Minister of Irrigation, Power and Highways
Dr N.M. Perera,
Minister of Finance
Dr Gamani Corea,
formerly Deputy Governor, Central Bank
Dr Doric Souza,
Secretary, Ministry of Plantation Industries
Mr K.H.J. Wijedasa,
Director of Agricultural Development
Dr Shelton Kodikara,
President, University of Ceylon, Peradeniya
Mr C. Wijenaike,
Chairman, Planters Association

Mr L.W. Perera,
Chairman, Nuwara Eliya Planters Association
Mr A.M.S. Perera,
Secretary, Planters Association
Mr T.A. Gunawardena,
Government Agent, Polonnaruwa
Mr A.P.B. Manamperi,
Government Agent, Anuradhapura
Mr V.E. Karunaratne,
Deputy Commissioner of Labour
Dr Beatrice V. de Mel,
Medical Research Institute
And there are many others whose help and assistance was invaluable. Not least the Warwick University Library which put up with considerable inconvenience to forward this work and Bela Balassa kindly read a late draft of this book and made a number of most helpful comments.

The present volume owes a great deal to Robert Lindley and Jeffery Round for further work and substantial editorial help. This is acknowledged by their status as subsidiary authors of this book. Peter Davies and Geoffrey Tyler have provided research assistance, as have Shail Jain, Jane Nolan and Zaitu Virji. Shirley Hail and Anne McKenna have typed the various drafts and, much more, have coordinated this undertaking from its early origins through to completion. All of which serves to underline the team nature of the study.

There is a final acknowledgement to make, to Professor Richard Stone, which goes far beyond our thanks to him for agreeing to write the Foreword. As architect of the UN System of National Accounts and instigator, in association with Professor Brown, of the Cambridge Growth Project, we must thank them both, in our respective proportions, for having guided our earliest efforts in research and for the framework of concepts and ideas which are the basis of the work in this volume. In particular, we hope that the extent to which our work within the UN conceptual scheme is unorthodox will not disguise its intellectual antecedent in the work begun, under Stone, in Cambridge in 1959.

What, then, have we tried to achieve in this volume? First, we have attempted, by demonstration to the contrary, to answer critics of the present state of macro-economic statistics on two questions. One concerns whether the UN standardised system is irrelevant to developing countries. The other is whether it is impractical. On relevance our approach is to show that the questions of concern with respect to employment and income distribution can be included in the standard framework for analysing growth: to do this calls for an extension, not a rejection, of the system. On practicality, the fact that we have been able to obtain numbers without any new primary data collection indicates that much can be made of existing sources. Of course, we remain open to the suggestion that Sri Lanka is a special case. However, our 'feel' for this is: 'Not so', and earlier work on the UK social accounts, on regional accounts for Wales, and subsequent efforts in Swaziland strengthen this view.

Beyond these considerations our main concern has been to develop a tool for policy determination in Sri Lanka. In this regard it is open to us to give focus to the essentially neutral formats of standardised data systems, and we have chosen to rearrange entries in the Social Accounting Matrix to give emphasis to the factorial and personal income distributions. Reactions suggest that the element of psychological novelty that this creates is well worth while. For, while there is no accepted model of the development process there is, on a growing front, a general recognition that distribution and growth are not independent issues, but rather are aspects of a single process. And it is essential to see them as such if policy is to be articulated so as to avoid or compromise the potential trade-offs.

Some policy analyses based on our data are set out in Chapters 4 to 6 and others are outlined elsewhere. However, we have by no means exhausted the possibilities and much remains for subsequent work. Meanwhile it is important to note that our work with secondary data sources is constrained by the classifications imposed at the primary stage. On a number of issues analysis is frustrated by these classifications: for example, duality cannot be analysed properly when production data are available only on a principal product basis, since this begs important issues about the forms of organisation of the production processes. It is for such reasons that we are critical of the mechanistic and conformist approach adopted in the macroeconomic field in most countries: and this sterility makes an interesting contrast with the flexibility enjoyed in the field of social statistics with reference, for example, to classifications by housing or nutritional standards, and not least with respect to social class itself.

No doubt issues such as these will go on being debated for a long time. But meanwhile there is a lack of communication between statisticians and economists in most countries, rich and poor alike, which is not helped by purist approaches by the former or a preference among the latter to make subjective judgements on the basis of 'insight' – often complaining, meanwhile, about 'inadequate' data. If this volume could be a step towards bringing these factions together in working towards quantitative policy analysis, the efforts that went into it would be amply rewarded.

Graham Pyatt
Alan Roe

FOREWORD

BY PROFESSOR RICHARD STONE

1 The development of economic data systems

> 'If to be well apprized of the true State and Condition of a Nation, Especially in the Two maine Articles of it's People, and Wealth, be a Piece of Politicall Knowledge, of all others, and at all times, the most usefull, and Necessary; Than surely . . . Such a Knowledge of our own Nation must be of the Highest concern: But since the attaining thereof (how necessary and disireable soever) is next to impossible, We must Content our selves with such near approaches to it as the Grounds We have to go upon will enable us to make.'

Thus, nearly three hundred years ago, wrote one of the greatest of the Political Arithmeticians, Gregory King, in the preface to his *Naturall and Politicall Observations and Conclusions upon the State and Condition of England* (1696). Most readers who open the present work will agree that a knowledge of the people and wealth of a country is essential for understanding and good government; and when they have read it will immediately recognise that its authors have been struggling with the same problem as that with which Gregory King was concerned. I do not say this because this book is about Sri Lanka, a country which many may suppose not to possess a very highly developed statistical system. The problem is a perfectly general one which has exercised even the most developed countries over the past thirty or forty years, a period during which sustained efforts have been made all over the world to convert such economic data as happened to be available into a complete and coherent system of national accounts.

Much of the work of the Political Arithmeticians is surprisingly modern in tone; for instance, King's estimates of economic magnitudes for 1688, set out in his *Naturall and Politicall Observations*, can be recast, as shown by Deane (1955), in the form of five balancing accounts which in the past generation has become so familiar. Moreover, King's interests and general outlook have much in common with those of the authors of this book and of many other applied economists and econometricians of the present day. All study the world we live in; all are concerned with public policy and would like to see some quantitative information applied to it; and all realise that in such work it is useless to restrict oneself to any particular discipline. In a complex situation in which the forces of demography, ecology, economics and sociology interact, it is senseless to ignore three of these subjects because one's own early professional training happens to have been in the fourth.

If I am right in thinking that there is a remarkable affinity between the general approach of many social scientists today and a small, gifted group writing three hundred years ago, it seems reasonable to ask: what happened in between? In particular, why was it that the kind of work done by King, Davenant, Graunt and Petty seems to have died with their generation and to have taken a very long time to pick up? I wish I knew; as it is I can only conjecture a few factors that may have been at work. First, the men I have mentioned were rarely teachers and, if they were (Petty was for a time professor of anatomy at Oxford and professor of music at Gresham College, London), did not teach the subject that here concerns us, so that there were no disciples to keep alive an interest in their work. Second, the almost complete lack of data would have been discouraging to all but the ablest and most imaginative and these are always thin on the ground. Third, economic thought all over Europe became directed to the theoretical systematisation of economic connections, an attitude which led to the political economists of the classical school, who seem to have been less interested in observing economic life than in making inferences from a few primary assumptions. Finally, the prevailing, if never unchallenged, philosophy of *laissez-faire* can hardly have done much to encourage the establishment of comprehensive data systems. Throughout the eighteenth century the need for information on specific topics was recognised, but the proper regulation of wider issues of economic and social policy was more a matter of precept than of statistics, as readers of Studenski's admirable *The Income of Nations* (1958) will know.

Great improvements took place in economic and social statistics in nineteenth-century Britain. Excellent compilations were made by such writers as McCulloch (1837) and Porter (1843); and the importance of connections was emphasised by many writers, for example Newmarch (1869). On the whole, the note seems to have been steady progress towards limited objectives, one of the more extensive of which was the estimation of the national income. Baxter (1868), who made one of the best estimates of the century, concerned himself not only with the distribution of income by size but also with its distribution over the major regions of the British Isles: England and Wales, Scotland and Ireland. But even here the synthetic vision of the Political Arithmeticians was absent; perhaps because the data were at the same time too many to encourage bold attempts and too few to permit estimates which could stand up to contemporary criticism.

Over the next two generations further improvements took place, more national income estimates were compiled and new sources of information, such as the first British census of production in 1907, made their appearance. Measures of output and expenditure as well as of income began to be made in a number of countries. And in the late 1930s it was recognised independently by a number of economists that the various estimates could be combined and related within an accounting framework, thus restoring at least as far as purely economic magnitudes were concerned, the synthetic vision of the Political Arithmeticians.

This development was not merely the outcome of improved statistics. The economic malaise of the 1920s and the shock of the great depression set conventional precepts at a discount and the factual study of economic conditions at a premium. Writers as different in their approach as Keynes (1936) and Tinbergen (1937, 1939*a* and 1939*b*) stressed the connections between macroeconomic variables and stimulated the search for a framework within which these variables could be related and which could be filled in with numerical estimates. Before very long the national accounts emerged in answer to this challenge.

In the United States, Copeland (1935, 1937) emphasised the accounting aspect of contemporary work on national income statistics. In England, Clark

(1937) compiled statistics of income, output, expenditure, savings, investment and foreign trade, though he did not set them out in an accounting framework. In Palestine, Gruenbaum (Gaathon) (1941) devised an accounting framework for his estimates of national income and outlay. In Holland, van Cleef (1941a, b) developed a system of national book-keeping. In Britain the official estimates of national income and expenditure, UK Treasury (1941–), were presented from the outset in an accounting framework. About that time the term 'social accounting' was coined by Hicks (1942). In 1944, official talks were held in Washington with the object of bringing more closely into line the statistics of national income and expenditure in Britain, Canada and the United States. One of the topics discussed at these meetings was a system of social accounts which could be used as a framework for the whole range of economic statistics. A report of these discussions is given by Denison (1947).

At the end of 1945, a subcommittee appointed by the Committee of Statistical Experts of the League of Nations met at Princeton to discuss the problems arising in the measurement of the national income and in the construction of social accounts. In their report, published as UN (1947), this group recommended that the estimation of the national income be set within a social accounting framework and designed a system of *pro forma* accounts 'for the whole economic system or for major sectors of it', believing such accounts to be 'of great utility in practical economic analysis and . . . also capable of statistical estimation'. This report and its appendix can perhaps be regarded as the first handbook of social accounting.

At the beginning of the 1950s, the newly established Organisation for European Economic Co-operation drew up a standard system of national accounts, published first as OEEC (1950) and then, more fully, as OEEC (1952). This was followed shortly afterwards by the first version of the United Nations' system (SNA for short), published as UNSO (1953). From the outset the proposals made by the two organisations were conceptually very similar though they differed slightly in details of presentation. They were republished with minor revisions in 1958 and 1960 respectively and at this point became virtually identical.

By the end of the 1950s national accounting had spread to all regions of the world and an immense amount of work has been done on a wide range of specialised topics within this general field. Accordingly, a feeling developed in the early 1960s that there was need for a major revision in which such matters as industrial interdependence, flows of funds and balance sheets would be integrated into the national accounts. This work was organised by the Statistical Office of the United Nations and the new SNA appeared as UNSO (1968).

While the scope of the SNA was greatly increased in the new version, there were still a number of topics, referred to in UNSO (1968, paras. 1.83–1.98, pp. 14–16), which were left over for future treatment. One of these, of central interest in this book, relates to the distribution of income, consumption and wealth. This forms the subject of a separate set of proposals made by the Statistical Office of the United Nations to which reference will be made in the next section.

2 The special features of the present system

National accounting systems can be built up from two points of view, the general or the particular; though whichever line is followed the ultimate purpose is the same: to provide a data base for economic analysis and policy.

Systems established by international organisations, like the SNA rather naturally start from a general point of view. Analytical interests and policy problems vary from country to country and so there is little point in attempting to highlight particular interests or problems. What is needed is a systematic and coherent framework which can accommodate the main bodies of data, such as intermediate product flows, final demands, flows of funds and so on, needed for a statistical description of the functioning of an economy. Publications describing such systems can be considered best-practice or, since compromises are inevitable, at least good-practice manuals: there is a place for everything generally considered important, no attempt is made to find room for information which no-one collects or wants to collect, and the user is left free to put his emphasis where he pleases and to leave some parts of the system completely aggregated while other parts are elaborated in detail.

By contrast, the framework described in this book has been devised from a particular point of view: to provide a data base for the kind of economic analysis and policy considered by the authors to be of particular relevance in the present conditions of Sri Lanka. Their point of view, however, is shared by many in rich and poor countries alike; and so this book is of far more general interest than it would be if it were just another arrangement of national accounts statistics or a selection of data designed exclusively for a single country.

The way the authors have set about the achievement of their particular aim has been to rearrange and extend the framework of the SNA so as to ensure that it can be used to analyse questions relating to employment and the distribution of income. The rearrangement is designed to highlight the receipt of factor incomes and their disbursement over various spending institutions; and the extension is designed to divide the household sector into a number of groups distinguished by location (urban, rural), organisation (estates and other rural) and income.

The first modification, the rearrangement, is straightforward. The entries in a set of accounts can be presented in a matrix in which, by convention, the receipts appear in the rows and the payments in the columns; and in which, reflecting the fact that accounts balance, each row sum is equal to the corresponding column sum. To take a very simple example, let us suppose that the original system contains two types of account of which the first has two members and the second one. Then we might write out its transactions matrix, $\mathbf{A}^*$ say, in the form

$$\mathbf{A}^* = \left[\begin{array}{cc:c} a_{11} & a_{12} & a_{13} \\ a_{21} & a_{22} & a_{23} \\ \hdashline a_{31} & a_{32} & a_{33} \end{array}\right] \qquad (1)$$

where the dotted lines serve to partition the matrix and thus separate the two types of account. If we wish to bring the third account in $\mathbf{A}^*$ into the first position we can do this by submitting $\mathbf{A}^*$ to an orthogonal transformation based on a permutation matrix, $\mathbf{P}$ say. In this example, $\mathbf{P}$ takes the form

$$\mathbf{P} = \begin{bmatrix} 0 & 0 & 1 \\ 1 & 0 & 0 \\ 0 & 1 & 0 \end{bmatrix} \qquad (2)$$

and the rearranged matrix, $\mathbf{A}$ say, is given by

$$
\mathbf{A} = \mathbf{P}\,\mathbf{A}^*\,\mathbf{P}^{-1}
$$

$$
= \begin{bmatrix} 0 & 0 & 1 \\ 1 & 0 & 0 \\ 0 & 1 & 0 \end{bmatrix} \begin{bmatrix} a_{11} & a_{12} & a_{13} \\ a_{21} & a_{22} & a_{23} \\ a_{31} & a_{32} & a_{33} \end{bmatrix} \begin{bmatrix} 0 & 1 & 0 \\ 0 & 0 & 1 \\ 1 & 0 & 0 \end{bmatrix}
$$

$$
= \left[\begin{array}{c:cc} a_{33} & a_{31} & a_{32} \\ \hdashline a_{13} & a_{11} & a_{12} \\ a_{23} & a_{21} & a_{22} \end{array}\right] \tag{3}
$$

where the dotted lines again serve to separate the two types of account.

Rearranging a system of accounts does not change it in any fundamental respect, it simply encourages a different way of looking at it. The same cannot be said of the second modification, the extension. Although the SNA distinguishes compensation of employees from other forms of factor income and, indeed, contains a considerable amount of information about types of income payment, all households are aggregated into a single sector. This being so, the SNA as it stands can throw no light on the distribution of income among households or on the probable effects of any proposal for its redistribution. But as I said at the end of the preceding section, this does not mean that the whole subject has been overlooked by the Statistical Office of the United Nations; rather, it is a reflection of historical developments in this area of statistics. Comprehensive data on the distribution of income are notoriously difficult to obtain and to fit into a wider framework. Studies based on partial information, such as the earnings of male workers in full-time employment, suggest that at any rate these partial distributions remain stable over long periods of time. And until recently, much more interest centred on production and growth than on consumption and equality.

For such reasons as these, questions of distribution are not dealt with in the SNA. However, as is mentioned in UNSO (1968, para. 1.87, p. 14), the Statistical Office was engaged at the time in preparing an integrated system of statistics of the distribution of income, consumption and wealth which at the *macro* level fits completely both into the SNA and into the MPS (see UNSO (1971)) and at the *micro* level is complementary to these two systems. The latest documents on the subject are UNSO (1972, 1974).

Meanwhile the authors of this book are to be congratulated on their initiative in grasping firmly the nettle of distribution and in demonstrating the flexibility of the SNA and its applicability to developing countries.

3 Consistency and adjustment

The filling in of a national accounting framework reveals endless statistical difficulties which come to light only gradually and cannot all be resolved immediately. Data are always incomplete and rarely consistent; different bodies of statistics are often collected by a variety of agencies which do not all make use of an agreed set of definitions and classifications; different methods of collection give rise to sampling and other errors of many kinds. In such a situation, an intimate knowledge of the available statistics is not enough; a strategy and a certain amount of courage are also needed. The strategy is required in order to extract the best possible quantitative description of the economy from the statistical data available. Of course, there may be so few data and what there are may be of such poor quality that very little can be done; but this is not the normal case and much is lost if we are not willing to compare statistics from different sources and adjust them so as to bring about a consistent and therefore usable description of the economic process. The courage is required because the methods that must be adopted run counter to the professional statistician's ingrained dislike of tampering with basic data even when it is obvious that not all these data can be correct.

The strategy adopted in this book can be outlined as follows. First, the data available from different sources are confronted with one another within the accounting framework; this step shows how far they are consistent. Second, a view is taken of the reliability of the different sources. In doing this, it has to be recognised that a generally reliable source may in certain respects be inaccurate: for instance, it is usually found that expenditures on alcohol and tobacco are systematically underestimated in household budget enquiries. Finally, accepting provisionally the more reliable sources as accurate, an attempt is made to meet the arithmetic and accounting constraints of the social accounting matrix by adjusting the estimates contained in what are deemed to be the less reliable sources. It may, however, prove impossible to do this in a plausible way, in which case it is necessary to reconsider the supposedly reliable sources. In practice, a certain amount of iteration between earlier and later stages cannot be avoided but the aim remains the same throughout, namely to adjust what are believed to be the weaker estimates and preserve as far as possible those believed to be the stronger.

This is a laborious method calling for a great deal of information and judgement. It must not be supposed that the resulting estimates are accurate simply because they are consistent; but if our judgements are at all correct, such estimates will be an improvement on the inconsistent set of data with which we started and provide a firmer basis for analysis than it could provide.

Since this method represents an attempt to use subjective judgements about the reliability of initial estimates, it seems reasonable to ask whether still better results could not be obtained by applying a formal, mathematical treatment rather than *ad hoc* manipulations to our subjective assessment of reliability. It is not surprising that in their pioneering study the present authors did not adopt such a treatment but, if their strategy for handling inconsistent data comes to be generally adopted, there are a number of reasons why a formal treatment might prove desirable.

In the first place, initial estimates are never wholly accurate though we may believe some of them to be so reliable that we should not wish to change them; if we do hold this belief, we should give the estimate in question a variance of zero, remove it from the set of variables to be adjusted and add it to the set of constraining constants. In the second place, we can sometimes recognise covariances, as when two estimates must sum to a known total which may not be recorded in the social accounting matrix. In the third place, the trial and error method which I have described, apart from being time-consuming, would probably be influenced in practice by the order in which the adjustments were made. And, finally, the people responsible for the adjustments would be likely to change from time to time and it would be desirable to preserve some unity of treatment in spite of such changes.

The means now to be described of adjusting observations subject to constraints are well-known in the natural sciences and were suggested many years ago, in Stone, Champernowne and Meade (1942), as a possible method of adjusting social accounting estimates. The method requires that we formulate the constraints which are satisfied by the true values and that we form a variance matrix of the complete set of initial estimates. The adjustment procedure can then be formalised as follows.

Consider a vector, $\mathbf{x}^*$ say, (of type $\nu \times 1$) which contains unbiased estimates of the elements of another vector, $\mathbf{x}$ say, of true values. Suppose that the elements of $\mathbf{x}$ are subject to μ independent linear constraints, that is

$$\mathbf{G}\,\mathbf{x} = \mathbf{h} \tag{4}$$

where $\mathbf{G}$, the constraint matrix, is of type $\mu \times \nu$ and rank μ; and $\mathbf{h}$, a vector of known constants, is of type $\mu \times 1$. Let $\mathbf{V}^*$, of order ν and rank greater than μ, denote the variance matrix of the elements of $\mathbf{x}^*$; and assume that any constraints satisfied by $\mathbf{x}^*$ are linearly independent of (4). Then the best linear unbiased estimator, $\mathbf{x}^{**}$ say, of $\mathbf{x}$ is given by

$$\mathbf{x}^{**} = \mathbf{x}^* - \mathbf{V}^*\mathbf{G}'\,(\mathbf{G}\,\mathbf{V}^*\,\mathbf{G}')^{-1}\quad(\mathbf{G}\,\mathbf{x}^* - \mathbf{h}) \tag{5}$$

from which it can be seen that the elements of $\mathbf{V}^*$ need only be approximated up to a scalar multiplier, since any such multiplier will disappear in the matrix product $\mathbf{V}^*\mathbf{G}'\,(\mathbf{G}\,\mathbf{V}^*\,\mathbf{G}')^{-1}$. The variance matrix, $\mathbf{V}^{**}$ say, of $\mathbf{x}^{**}$, the vector of adjusted estimates, is given by

$$\mathbf{V}^{**} = \mathbf{V}^* - \mathbf{V}^*\,\mathbf{G}'\,(\mathbf{G}\,\mathbf{V}^*\,\mathbf{G}')^{-1}\,\mathbf{G}\,\mathbf{V}^* \tag{6}$$

The variance matrix, $\mathbf{V}^{**}$, of the final estimates which satisfy all the constraints differs from $\mathbf{V}^*$, which relates to the initial estimates, in that it takes into account the constraints of the system as well as the initial impressions of the investigator.

Provided we are careful to include only independent constraints, the formation of the constraint matrix raises no problems. If, as in this book, we are concerned with the entries in a set of accounts expressed in money terms, the constraints are of three kinds. First, the true entries are single-valued, so that if we have estimates of one of these entries from two sources, there will be two elements in $\mathbf{x}$ and a constraint expressing the fact that their difference is zero. Second, in any row (or column) of the matrix, the elements in that row (or column) must sum to the corresponding row (or column) total. And, third, accounts balance, that is to say any row total is equal to the corresponding column total.

The formation of the variance matrix of the initial estimates is an altogether more difficult and uncertain enterprise since it can only be based on the subjective impressions of the investigator. In some cases it will be possible to calculate sampling errors, but these are not the only errors to be considered, and in many cases it will not be possible to calculate even this component of error. However, there is no need to despair. By working with various sources of data, statisticians are usually able to form impressions of their relative soundness, and so the adjusted estimates, as well as being consistent, are likely to be an improvement on the original ones. It is often said that there is no point in applying mathematics to inaccurate data; but this is by no means generally true and is quite beside the point in the present context.

How, then, should we set about constructing a variance matrix for the entries in a set of social accounts? It is virtually impossible to give a prescription which is generally valid since so much depends on particular circumstances, but one way to make a start might be, as attempted in Stone ed. (1953–70), to quantify the relative reliability of (*a*) our sources and (*b*) the individual estimates within each source, bearing in mind that some of these estimates may be positively or negatively correlated. In so doing we might assume, in the absence of evidence to the contrary, that all estimates from a given source had the same relative reliability, implying variances proportional to the squares of the estimates.

In practice the number of estimates, ν, is likely to be large and so it is necessary to consider the computing aspect of the method. There are three points to be made. First, as can be seen from (5), the matrix to be inverted is of the order of the number of constraints, μ, and not of order ν. Second, as shown in Stone (1970, XIV), it is often possible to partition the constraints and carry out the adjustment in stages, thus reducing the largest matrix to be inverted to the number of constraints in the largest subset. Third, it may be possible to adopt a hierarchical approach, first adjusting the entries in a summary set of national accounts and then adjusting subsets of estimates to these controlling totals.

As can be seen, the method is not a mechanical one, imposing some arbitrary rule of adjustment on the initial estimates, but a means of using the impressions of the investigator systematically to make improvements. It can be extended to deal with the problem of adjusting a series of matrices to allow for autocorrelated, systematic and proportional errors. I shall not discuss these extensions but will now give a constructed numerical example which illustrates how the adjustments are made and how, in suitable circumstances, the method can be used to provide indirect estimates of items that cannot be estimated directly.

Consider a closed economy without capital, in which there is one factor of production, labour, two types of households and two branches of production. The true entries in the five accounts of this system, which are unknown and for all practical purposes unknowable, can be set out as shown in Table A.

Table A *A social-accounting matrix: the true entries*

	Labour	Households		Production		Total
Labour	0	x_{12}	x_{13}	x_{14}	x_{15}	$x_{1.}$
Households	x_{21}	0	0	0	0	$x_{2.}$
	x_{31}	0	0	0	0	$x_{3.}$
Production	0	x_{42}	x_{43}	0	x_{45}	$x_{4.}$
	0	x_{52}	x_{53}	x_{54}	0	$x_{5.}$
Total	$x_{.1}$	$x_{.2}$	$x_{.3}$	$x_{.4}$	$x_{.5}$	

Following the usual convention, incomings are shown in the rows and outgoings are shown in the columns; for instance, the labour income received from the two types of household and from the two branches of production is shown in the first row, and the disbursement of this income to the two types of household is shown in the first column.

For the purpose of filling in this table, three hypothetical sources of data are available, which in Table B will be denoted by the prefixes *a*, *b* and *c*.

Source *a* consists of collections of official statistics believed to be relatively reliable. Two of the items in Table B are based on them. Thus the total of row 1, ${}_a x^*_{1.}$, is derived from a detailed earnings enquiry which, however, being mainly concerned with occupations, does not provide the classification by sources of income required for the entries in row 1. And the second item of consumption of the first type of household, ${}_a x^*_{52}$, is based on tax statistics, thus avoiding a

Table B *A social-accounting matrix: the initial estimates*

	Labour	Households		Production		Total
Labour	0	${}_cx^*_{12}$	${}_cx^*_{13}$	${}_bx^*_{14}$	${}_bx^*_{15}$	${}_ax^*_{1\cdot}$
Households	..	0	0	0	0	..
	..	0	0	0	0	..
Production	0	${}_cx^*_{42}$	${}_cx^*_{43}$	0	${}_bx^*_{45}$	${}_bx^*_{4\cdot}$
	0	${}_ax^*_{52}$	${}_cx^*_{53}$	${}_bx^*_{54}$	0	${}_bx^*_{5\cdot}$
Total	..	..	..	..	..	

wholly inadequate estimate derivable from source *c*. By contrast, the second item of consumption of the second type of household, x_{53}, although produced by the same branch of production as produces x_{52}, has a different commodity mix and can therefore be reliably estimated from source *c*. This situation may not seem very likely in practice but can be accepted in a simple example, since the true situation could be handled by a further disaggregation of commodities.

Source *b* can be thought of as an all-embracing census of production. But it is not an entirely coherent source since the questions asked relate to specific topics and, like most actual censuses, do not require establishments to provide a balanced statement of their inputs and outputs. Thus, while we can obtain output estimates, ${}_bx^*_{4\cdot}$ and ${}_bx^*_{5\cdot}$, these do not necessarily agree with the corresponding input totals, and so no estimates of $x_{\cdot 4}$ and $x_{\cdot 5}$ are shown in Table B.

Source *c* is a household expenditure survey and, like many such surveys, either does not ask questions about income for fear of biasing the answers to questions about expenditure, or yields estimates of income which are palpably much too low and therefore unusable. As a consequence, there are no estimates of the income received by the two types of household although there is an estimate of total income paid out, ${}_ax^*_{1\cdot}$, which does not agree, however, with the components derivable from sources *b* and *c*.

If we put all these initial estimates together we reach the familiar situation: an incomplete and inconsistent social accounting matrix. The numerical values of these estimates, corresponding to the symbols in Table B, are set out in Table C.

Table C *A social-accounting matrix: the numerical values of the initial estimates*

	Labour	Households		Production		Total
Labour	0	15	3	130	80	220
Households	..	0	0	0	0	..
	..	0	0	0	0	..
Production	0	15	130	0	20	190
	0	25	40	55	0	105
Total	..	..	..	..	..	

Apart from the zeros, there are thirteen numbers in Table C and these are linked by five constraints. Three of these require that the incoming entries in the accounts for labour and the two branches of production should sum to total incomings in each case; and the remaining two require that the sum of the incoming entries in the two production accounts should equal the sum of the corresponding outgoing entries. Thus **G** in (4) takes the value

$$\mathbf{G} = \begin{bmatrix} 1 & 1 & 1 & 1 & -1 & 0 & 0 & 0 & 0 & 0 & 0 & 0 & 0 \\ 0 & 0 & 0 & 0 & 0 & 1 & 1 & 1 & -1 & 0 & 0 & 0 & 0 \\ 0 & 0 & 0 & 0 & 0 & 0 & 0 & 0 & 0 & 1 & 1 & 1 & -1 \\ 0 & 0 & -1 & 0 & 0 & 1 & 1 & 1 & 0 & 0 & -1 & 0 & 0 \\ 0 & 0 & 0 & -1 & 0 & 0 & 0 & -1 & 0 & 1 & 1 & 1 & 0 \end{bmatrix} \tag{7}$$

and **h** in (4) takes the value

$$\mathbf{h} = \{0 \quad 0 \quad 0 \quad 0 \quad 0\} \tag{8}$$

so that the term $(\mathbf{G\,x}^* - \mathbf{h})$ in (5) is given by

$$(\mathbf{G\,x}^* - \mathbf{h}) = \{8 \quad -25 \quad 15 \quad -20 \quad 20\} \tag{9}$$

In constructing the initial estimate of the variance matrix, $\mathbf{V}^*$, I have assumed: (i) that the relative reliabilities of the three sources, a, b and c, are in the ratios 1 : 2 : 4; (ii) that within each source the dispersion of an estimate is proportional to its size; and (iii) that all covariances are zero. As a consequence of (iii), $\mathbf{V}^*$ is a diagonal matrix with its diagonal elements proportional to a vector, $\mathbf{v}^*$ say, given by

$$\begin{aligned} \mathbf{v}^* = \{ & 36.0 \quad 1.44 \quad 676.0 \quad 256.0 \quad 484.0 \quad 36.0 \quad 2704.0 \\ & 16.0 \quad 1444.0 \quad 6.25 \quad 256.0 \quad 121.0 \quad 441.0 \} \end{aligned} \tag{10}$$

By forming the vector, $\mathbf{x}^*$, of initial estimates from the numbers in Table C and by substituting this, together with (7), (9) and (10), into (5) we can calculate the vector, $\mathbf{x}^{**}$, of the corresponding final estimates. These are set out in Table D.

Table D *A social-accounting matrix: the final estimates corresponding to the initial estimates in Table C*

	Labour	Households		Production		Total
Labour	0	14.46	2.98	124.33	85.42	227.19
Households	. .	0	0	0	0	. .
	. .	0	0	0	0	. .
Production	0	15.13	139.70	0	20.63	175.46
	0	24.76	30.16	51.13	0	106.05
Total	. .	. .	. .	. .	. .	. .

The numbers in Table D, unlike those in Table C, satisfy the five independent constraints imposed on the initial estimates. But Table D is still not complete, because we did not have initial estimates of all the entries in Table A. At the same time we did not use all the independent constraints connecting the full set of entries in Table A.

By using these additional constraints we can complete Table D. In this example the procedure is so straightforward that there is no need to write it down formally: since the entries in Table D satisfy the constraints connecting the initial estimates, we can equate the column totals for the labour account and the two production accounts to the corresponding row totals. There were no constraints on the two household accounts but since everything they receive or pay for comes from the three balanced accounts, their total receipts are equal to their total payments and so we can equate their total incomes to their total expenditures. The complete set of final estimates thus obtained is set out in Table E.

Table E *A social-accounting matrix: the complete set of final estimates*

	Labour	Households		Production		Total
Labour	0	14.46	2.98	124.33	85.42	227.19
Households	54.35	0	0	0	0	54.35
	172.84	0	0	0	0	172.84
Production	0	15.13	139.70	0	20.63	175.46
	0	24.76	30.16	51.13	0	106.05
Total	227.19	54.35	172.84	175.46	106.05	

Thus in the end we obtain a completely balanced matrix in which the initial estimates are adjusted and indirect estimates are provided for the entries not directly estimated initially.

It remains only to set out the variance matrix, $\mathbf{V}^{**}$, corresponding to the adjusted initial estimates given in Table E. This matrix takes the form

$$\mathbf{V}^{**} = \begin{bmatrix} 34.73 & -0.05 & -13.95 & -3.64 & 17.09 & -0.18 & -13.87 & 0.26 & -13.80 & -0.08 & -3.44 & 0.15 & -3.38 \\ -0.05 & 1.44 & -0.56 & -0.15 & 0.68 & -0.01 & -0.55 & 0.01 & -0.55 & -0.00 & -0.14 & 0.01 & -0.14 \\ -13.95 & -0.56 & 256.76 & -54.73 & 187.52 & 2.86 & 214.58 & 4.05 & 221.49 & -0.37 & -15.04 & -35.27 & -50.68 \\ -3.64 & -0.15 & -54.73 & 107.38 & 48.88 & -0.18 & -13.68 & -7.75 & -21.61 & 1.59 & 64.93 & 33.11 & 99.63 \\ 17.09 & 0.68 & 187.52 & 48.88 & 254.18 & 2.48 & 186.48 & -3.44 & 185.52 & 1.13 & 46.31 & -2.00 & 45.44 \\ -0.18 & -0.01 & 2.86 & -0.18 & 2.48 & 35.58 & -31.92 & -0.12 & 3.54 & -0.02 & -0.96 & 0.68 & -0.30 \\ -13.87 & -0.55 & 214.58 & -13.68 & 186.48 & -31.92 & 306.44 & -8.88 & 265.64 & -1.75 & -71.86 & 51.06 & -22.55 \\ 0.26 & 0.01 & 4.05 & -7.75 & -3.44 & -0.12 & -8.88 & 15.35 & 6.35 & 0.13 & 5.16 & 2.31 & 7.60 \\ -13.80 & -0.55 & 221.49 & -21.61 & 185.52 & 3.54 & 265.64 & 6.35 & 275.53 & -1.65 & -67.65 & 54.05 & -15.26 \\ -0.08 & -0.00 & -0.37 & 1.59 & 1.13 & -0.02 & -1.75 & 0.13 & -1.65 & 6.17 & -3.18 & -1.28 & 1.71 \\ -3.44 & -0.14 & -15.04 & 64.93 & 46.31 & -0.96 & -71.86 & 5.16 & -67.65 & -3.18 & 125.89 & -52.61 & 70.09 \\ 0.15 & 0.01 & -35.27 & 33.11 & -2.00 & 0.68 & 51.06 & 2.31 & 54.05 & -1.28 & -52.61 & 89.32 & 35.42 \\ -3.38 & -0.14 & -50.68 & 99.63 & 45.44 & -0.30 & -22.55 & 7.60 & -15.26 & 1.71 & 70.09 & 35.42 & 107.22 \end{bmatrix} \qquad (11)$$

By construction, $\mathbf{V}^{*}$ in this example is a diagonal matrix, and the off-diagonal covariances in $\mathbf{V}^{**}$ arise as a consequence of the constraints. Neither matrix can tell us anything about the absolute accuracy of the estimates but it is interesting to compare the diagonal elements of (11) with the corresponding numbers in (10), which are the diagonal elements of $\mathbf{V}^{*}$. From this comparison we see that the variances of the final estimates are never greater than those of the initial estimates and in many cases are strikingly smaller. Thus it would seem that if we have some confidence in our original assessment of relative reliability, our final estimates are not only consistent but also more accurate, which is only to be expected since they are based on more information.

4 Demographic and social influences

So far my comments have related to the purely statistical aspect of this book. As the authors themselves make clear, this is only the first part of their work on the economy of Sri Lanka. The second, of which they give a few samples in the later chapters, will be concerned with analysis; and will deal with such matters as the structure of protection, the impact of the tax system on the distribution of income and the supply and demand for different kinds of labour. Such subjects as these are obviously important from a social as well as from an economic point of view. For instance, a productive system needs a number of skills acquired in the middle or upper ranges of the educational system, and production will be held back, or actually halted, if these skills are not available in sufficient quantities. Conversely, disappointment and frustration will arise if the productive system does not absorb the quantity of skills supplied by the educational system. In this as in so many other cases we ought to have in mind the social as well as the economic consequences which may follow from any given policy.

The recognition of such issues, which is in line with the general point of view expressed in this book, implies that many of the analyses we should like to see would benefit from a full and systematic presentation of social and demographic data and an explicit description of their links with economic data. This, given the present state of social and demographic statistics, is more easily said than done. Information exists, of course, and has long existed about many of the characteristics of human beings: their age and sex, their marital status, their family attachments, their education, their occupation, their medical and criminal records and so on. But this information, even in those countries where it is most abundant, is not integrated and does not form a system as does information on production, consumption, accumulation, foreign trade, prices, taxes and so on, when organised within the framework of the national accounts.

The reasons for attempting integration, however, are as strong in the one case as in the other. An integrated system helps to identify the data required for the analyses we want to make and to check that these data are consistent. For example, the demand for a place in a university depends on a complex of factors such as type of school, personal ability, family background, home locality and job opportunities; thus if we want to make useful projections of desired university capacity, we should combine data on education, on socio-economic status, on geographical distribution and on employment. As things stand now in most countries, such data come from four different, non-communicating statistical spheres, each with its own circumscribed aims and its own taxonomic conventions. As a result, any attempt to combine them will be at best inaccurate and at worst impossible.

The formulation of an integrated system of social and demographic statistics such as I am advocating has two distinct aspects: the taxonomic and the analytical. On the taxonomic side, the classifications appropriate to such a system are partly personal (age, sex, educational qualifications, occupation, health record, etc.), partly familial (family size, social class, income group, place of residence, race, religion, etc.) and partly institutional (school, industry, hospital, etc.). Given a set of unifying taxonomic criteria, these classifications can be combined to form composite categories, or states, the combinations depending on which aspect of life we are interested in analysing. Examples of states are: being aged 17, attending secondary school and preparing for advanced-level examinations; being aged 30 and working in a textile factory as a secretary; being aged 70 and receiving treatment in a geriatric hospital.

On the analytical side, the core of the system is a standard framework for presenting data on human stocks and flows. This framework takes the form of an accounting matrix similar to the standard input–output matrix of economics, but in which the unit of account is the human being instead of the rupee or pound or franc. In this matrix the opening and closing population stock vectors, classified by appropriate socio-demographic categories, are connected by the population flows that take place during the interval. This framework, besides being extremely flexible in that it can accommodate data on any aspect of social life we may wish to study, lends itself to a great variety of analytical uses.

Furthermore, it enables us to relate socio-demographic variables to economic variables: on the one hand to costs, such as the costs of educating people in different parts of the educational system or of treating patients in different hospitals; and on the other hand to benefits, such as scholarships and sickness compensation or, more broadly, the economic advantages of education and health. A condition for being able to make such connections in detail is, again, the use of common classifications; for instance, we should need a conformable classification of educational categories both in recording student flows and in recording educational costs.

Although this is not the place in which to describe the whole system in detail, the information with which it is concerned seems to me so relevant to the topics in which the authors of this book are interested that a short description of the standard framework and of some of the models which can be based on it may be of interest.

The framework itself is given in symbolic form in Table F. As shown, it relates to something called 'our country' but it could equally well relate to a larger or smaller region. What numerical data we fill it with will depend, as I said, on our analytical needs.

Table F *A demographic matrix connecting the opening and closing stocks of year θ with the flows during year θ*

State at new year θ / State at new year $\theta + 1$	Outside world	Our country: opening states	Closing stocks
Outside world	α	d'	
Our country: closing states	b	S	Λn
Opening stocks		n'	

The symbols in Table F have the following meanings:

α a scalar, denotes the total number of individuals who both enter and leave 'our country' in the course of year θ and so are not recorded in either the opening or the closing stock of that year. An example is a baby born during the year who dies before the end of it.

b a column vector, denotes the new entrants into 'our country', namely the births and immigrations of year θ, who survive to the end of the year. Individuals in this group are recorded in the closing stock but not in the opening stock.

d′ a row vector (the prime superscript indicates transposition), denotes the leavers from 'our country', namely the deaths and emigrations of year θ. Individuals in this group appear in the opening stock but not in the closing stock.

S a square matrix, denotes the survivors in 'our country' through year θ, and these are recorded in both the opening and the closing stock. They are classified by their opening states in the columns and by their closing states in the rows.

n′ a row vector, denotes the opening stock in each state.

Λn a column vector, denotes the closing stock in each state. The symbol Λ denotes the shift operator defined by the relationship $\Lambda^\tau \mathbf{n}(\theta) \equiv \mathbf{n}(\tau + \theta)$.

This scheme can be explained as follows. Let us begin with the row vector $\mathbf{n}'$, the elements of which are the numbers of people in our country who are in different states, or categories, at the beginning of an interval, say a year. These people will either die or emigrate in the year, in which case they will be recorded in the row vector $\mathbf{d}'$, or they will survive in our country to the end of the year, in which case they will be recorded in the matrix **S**. If we look at a column of **S** we shall see in what numbers the survivors from a given initial state have remained in that state or moved to other states in the course of the year. If we look at a row of **S** we shall see in what numbers the survivors in a given final state have remained in that state or moved to it from other states in the course of the year. The elements of the vector **b** are the numbers entering our country, whether by birth or immigration, in the course of the year, classified by their final state. If we add the elements of **b** to the corresponding row sums of **S**, we obtain the vector of closing stocks $\Lambda\mathbf{n}$.

This scheme provides a basis for a model of the social process represented by the classifications used to define the states of the system. Thus we have just seen that

$$\Lambda\mathbf{n} \equiv \mathbf{S}\mathbf{i} + \mathbf{b} \tag{12}$$

where **i** denotes the unit vector, so that **Si** denotes the row sums of **S**. If we derive a coefficient matrix (**C** say, usually referred to as a matrix of transition proportions) by dividing the elements of each column of **S** by the corresponding element of **n** (that is, form

$$\mathbf{C} = \mathbf{S}\hat{\mathbf{n}}^{-1} \tag{13}$$

where $\hat{\mathbf{n}}^{-1}$ denotes a diagonal matrix formed from the reciprocals of the elements of **n**) then on substitution for **S** from (13) into (12) we obtain

$$\Lambda\mathbf{n} = \mathbf{C}\mathbf{n} + \mathbf{b} \tag{14}$$

indicating that the closing stock vector is equal to the vector of new entrants plus the opening stock vector transformed by the matrix **C**. If we are dealing with a population in stationary equilibrium, so that $\Lambda\mathbf{n} = \mathbf{n}$, then (14) becomes

$$\begin{aligned} \mathbf{n} &= \mathbf{C}\mathbf{n} + \mathbf{b} \\ &(\mathbf{I} - \mathbf{C})^{-1}\mathbf{b} \end{aligned} \tag{15}$$

which has the appearance of the equation of an open Leontief model. Indeed it has a similar interpretation, since $(\mathbf{I} - \mathbf{C})^{-1}$ is a matrix multiplier which transforms the new-entry vector, **b**, into the population vector, **n**. Further, if **C** can be interpreted as a probability matrix, then the process given by (15) can be regarded as an absorbing Markov chain with $(\mathbf{I} - \mathbf{C})^{-1}$ as the fundamental matrix. Many developments of this simple model are given in Stone (1973).

Equations (14) and (15) are clearly quantity equations connecting stocks and new entrants. From input–output analysis we should expect to find a corresponding price (or cost) equation based on **C**′, the transpose of **C**. This indeed exists and, taking education as an example, can be formulated as follows.

Let the educational costs of a year spent in each state be represented by the elements of a vector, **m** say, so that there will be positive entries for elements representing educational states and zero entries for elements representing other states. Then, assuming **m** to be constant, the vector of accumulated costs, **k** say, is given by

$$\begin{aligned} \mathbf{k} &= \mathbf{m} + \mathbf{C}'\mathbf{m} + \mathbf{C}'^2\mathbf{m} + \ldots \\ &= \mathbf{m} + \mathbf{C}'\mathbf{k} \qquad (16) \\ &= (\mathbf{I} - \mathbf{C}')^{-1}\mathbf{m} \end{aligned}$$

which is the price analogue of (15) above. If we combine (15) and (16) we can see that

$$\begin{aligned} \mathbf{m}'\mathbf{n} &= \mathbf{k}'(\mathbf{I} - \mathbf{C})(\mathbf{I} - \mathbf{C})^{-1}\mathbf{b} \\ &= \mathbf{k}'\mathbf{b} \end{aligned} \qquad (17)$$

that is to say, for the simplest case of a population in stationary equilibrium in which the unit costs in each educational state are constant, this year's total expenditure on education, **m′n** is equal to the total future cost of educating this year's new entrants, **k′b**.

What I have said in this section is only an indication of what can be done with a properly coordinated system of statistics. A full description of its possibilities will be found in a report recently published by the United Nations, *Towards a System of Social and Demographic Statistics*, UNSO (1975). Like the SNA, this system is developed from a general point of view, it being recognised that different countries have different problems and also different capacities for collecting and processing data. The report considers a number of areas into which the study of society can be divided, such as population growth and movement, family and household groupings, education, participation in economic activity, health and medical care and many others; and for each area makes suggestions about the data to be collected, the classifications to be used and the social indicators to be constructed. And it concludes with a series of numerical examples of possible analyses including applications to the process of income formation and the distribution of incomes (UNSO, 1975, XXV B).

5 Epilogue

In conclusion, what of priorities and the future? Priorities are a matter for policy makers and analysts in individual countries and I have nothing to contribute on this score. But there is one general point. The data base described in this book is well suited to the kind of structural analysis for which it was designed. But it could also contribute to other forms of model and, in particular, to a model of the conventional type directed primarily to the productive aspects of the economic process. The importance of the distributive aspects is not a reason for neglecting production, particularly in poor countries where there cannot be much to redistribute unless production can be substantially increased. For this purpose it would probably be necessary to add a time dimension to many of the entries in the social accounting matrix. In some areas this should present little difficulty since many series, such as the national accounts, have been compiled regularly for many years. But there are probably some areas where past data are only available for one or more isolated years; and even some, especially if we move further into the socio-demographic field, where there are no processed statistics though there may be a certain amount of basic data. Whatever the actual situation, many interesting problems of statistical organisation are likely to be encountered.

But perhaps this is not the moment at which to contemplate such questions. Rather, for the time being we should await the outcome of the second, analytical phase of the authors' work since this will give us some indication of the output that can be obtained from the input described in this book.

1
The general background

1 Introduction

It is only in the last three decades that the majority of economists and politicians in the developed world have come to attach high priority to the economic advancement of those countries which are variously classified as 'underdeveloped', 'developing', 'emerging', or 'less-developed'. Previously these countries were generally seen in colonial or neo-colonial terms as contributing to the economic well-being of the metropolitan countries and having only a relatively modest claim to any economic progress unconnected with that role. The policies and approaches which have replaced this colonial mentality have undergone many changes in the thirty years since the Second World War and have been the subject of much controversy. But successful as they have undoubtedly been in a number of respects, they have left the typical developing country of the 1970s with a substantial legacy of outstanding problems. In particular, many years of active development policy have not succeeded in reducing the incidence of absolute, let alone relative poverty in some countries. This policy has not cured, and has probably contributed to, the continuance of enormous discrepancies in living standards within particular countries; to problems of underemployment, and unemployment; to severe imbalances between urban and rural life; and to many other related difficulties.

Against this background there is now an increasingly articulate call for a 'New Economic Order' from the developing countries, demanding that development policy should be set in an international framework which is as much 'of' the poorer nations as it is 'for' them. While changes in the international context within which the poorer countries are trying to develop are of major importance, it remains the case that the internal policies which they pursue and which are urged on them have been, and will be in future, equally important in determining the successes and failures of development efforts. In this respect, while we lack a full understanding of how the various contemporary problems have come about, it seems that a common factor running through many of them has been a commitment to economic growth as the prime objective of development strategy throughout much of the post-war period. This was not necessarily because economic growth was universally seen as a legitimate end in itself, but in part at least because it was widely believed that growth was a necessary condition for the achievement of other objectives such as the elimination of poverty and unemployment. Tragically, while it may have been a necessary condition and remains so, it has not proved to be a sufficient strategy for realising these basic goals.

To take just one example: in relation to the objective of fuller employment,

Morawetz (1974), after a thorough survey of the issues, was able to conclude only that:

> the conflict between output and employment is rather more complex than is often supposed. Further theoretical and applied research is needed to elucidate the circumstances in which the two objectives do not conflict, to describe the exact parameter of the trade-off in cases where they do conflict, and to suggest the relative weights that should be given to current and future output and employment.*

*See Morawetz (1974), p. 502.

In the present state of knowledge, similar non-committal conclusions are necessary in relation to the link between growth, on the one hand, and distributional objectives with respect to income and the elimination of poverty on the other. It follows that there is an urgent need for further study and research into the nature of these linkages both at the theoretical and the empirical level.

The present study is intended as a contribution towards reaching this better understanding. Based on knowledge of the issues that face policy makers in developing countries, and of the research which is directed towards helping them, our concern is the design and implementation of a macroeconomic information system which can (*a*) make the best possible use of available data by bringing it together in a coherent picture of the economy which describes what is happening in the relevant dimensions of production, distribution, trade and accumulation; and (*b*) point up the need for refinement in data collection and tabulation from the point of view of perceiving how policies and fate might impinge on the various facets of the economic system. Thus we are concerned with a tool to aid policy makers in evaluating, quantitatively, the impact of alternative action on a variety of objectives, and so permit them to form a statistical view of the nature of the trade-offs between objectives which might be implied.

This study relates mainly to Sri Lanka (formerly Ceylon) and is to be seen, therefore, in the first instance as a specific attempt to realise the intent of our research in terms of the problems of that country. At the same time, the research on Sri Lanka can be regarded as a prototype case-study to demonstrate a methodology which we believe to be capable of application to most developing countries and which has been applied subsequently to a small African economy, namely Swaziland.† If policy makers in both developed and underdeveloped countries are serious in their publicly stated intentions to pursue development strategies embracing objectives far broader than economic growth, then data systems of the type which we present in this volume will become increasingly necessary as a basis for rational policy formulation.

†The report on this work, Pyatt and associates (1975) has not been published.

The methodology we discuss is predominantly statistical and unashamedly so, since there can be little doubt that one of the main failings of the methodology for decision making (including 'economic planning') in developing countries has been its neglect of the need for an appropriate information system to support the decision-making process. In some countries this failing has been a matter of organisation within statistical offices leading to decision makers operating independently and in apparent ignorance of the mutually interactive nature of their respective roles. In other situations statistical development has been starved of resources, perhaps because vested interests have had no particular wish for decision making to become more quantitative and objective.

Our starting point is the opinion that a high degree of integration of economic decision making and statistical development is always desirable, and that the statistics available in developing countries are rarely so bad as to support the counter-opinion that the involvement of statistical information is more likely to mislead the decision maker than to guide him towards a correct decision. It is certainly true that in all countries there are individual sets of economic statistics which are highly inaccurate or internally inconsistent. Sri Lanka is no exception, and some of the particular problems there are discussed in Chapter 2. However, since there is no such thing as completely accurate data, except perhaps in relation to the most micro of phenomena, the only sensible approach to statistics is to regard each piece of data as being subject to varying degrees of inaccuracy. This in turn implies that it is quite legitimate to amend individual pieces of data within limits set by some assessment of the extent of their inaccuracy, provided that there is some acceptable method for making the adjustment. Hopefully, this same approach will also indicate areas where the data are too inaccurate to be used at all. Unfortunately, the literature on planning and development, as well as that on technical statistics, has paid only scant attention to this point, with the result that an excessively high proportion of decisions seem to be made without reference to underlying facts which could easily be made available; or alternatively are made by reference to statistical 'facts' which could easily be improved by confronting them with related statistics.

Above all, the developing countries, and those who would advise them, often seem characterised by what might be termed 'statistical pessimism' – the view that the accuracy of existing data is so bad as to make it unusable, and that the obstacles in the way of organising usable statistics and in reasonable time are something close to being insuperable. We hope that our study, if it achieves nothing else, will by demonstration temper this pessimistic view.

In brief then, our study draws its justification from the growing acceptance of the fact that the numerous objectives of developing countries cannot sensibly be subsumed into the single objective of faster growth of GDP or GNP. It has two main aims. The first is to suggest a framework for economic statistics which is capable of informing economic policy formulation in a situation where the objectives of policy go beyond the simple question of growth. The second aim is to demonstrate the possibilities of utilising sets of data which might otherwise be regarded as virtually useless, by incorporating them into this framework in such a way that the nature of their inaccuracies are revealed by confrontation with related data sets. The demonstration is carried out in relation to Sri Lanka and so, in pursuing our main aims, we also hope to have achieved a third, namely that of presenting an accurate portrait of the economy of Sri Lanka in 1970 and the interaction between its various sectors, institutions, and objectives.

The background to this study in terms of the evolution of development policy, development theory, the attitudes of international bodies and so on, is fairly lengthy and not easily summarised in a few pages. However, in the remainder of this chapter and in Chapter 2, we attempt to indicate the more important aspects of this background in an effort to convey a fuller impression of the role of the present volume. In the rest of this chapter we expand on the points already made about the limitations of post-war development strategies (Section 2); discuss the role of international initiatives in relation to statistical development (Section 3); summarise the more important manifestations of the changing international climate regarding development strategy (Section 4); and, finally (Section 5), identify some theoretical and empirical aspects of the relationship between growth and other objectives which have recently been researched. Chapter 2 is wholly given over to an analysis of the recent evolution of the Sri Lankan economy and to an identification of the specific conflicts between objectives which our data framework ought to try to identify. Chapter 3 introduces the structure of the data system which we have prepared, presents aggregated figures from this system for 1970 and examines the nature of the classifications used in the disaggregated system. In Chapters 4 to 6 we attempt to give a flavour of the analytical usefulness of the system by examining quantitatively a number of issues such as investment strategy, protection policy and resource allocation, and the distributional consequences of fiscal policy. These chapters anticipate more thorough analysis of these and other issues which will form part of our subsequent work. Chapter 7 incorporates some brief remarks about the further quantitative analysis of employment and distributional issues which might be expected to emerge on the basis of this volume, as well as some remaining statistical problems.

The detail on the methods used to compile the rather large data system which underlies our work naturally occupies a substantial part of this volume. However, we have relegated discussion of this methodology to an appendix (Appendix 1), so as to permit the reader to learn about the system and what it looks like in broad terms, followed by some illustrations of its analytical possibilities without, at this stage, having to embrace all the statistical detail. Nevertheless we would stress that the methods described in Statistical Appendix 1 represent the substantive contribution of this volume. Finally, Statistical Appendix 2 discusses one of the 'physical' tables underlying the main system, the Manpower Matrix.

2 Some aspects of post-war development experience

It is no doubt dangerous to attempt to summarise the development experience of the one hundred and thirty odd countries which comprise the so-called 'third world' since the very attempt implies an homogeneity of these countries which is at least partly illusory. As Professor Bauer is fond of pointing out,* the 'developing' countries are normally defined negatively – as all countries in the world less the handful of rich industrial countries – an approach to definition which introduces a tendency to seek for similarities in order to justify the notion that the label has some meaning.† However, though the countries themselves undoubtedly do differ, their development experience may nevertheless be similar if only because that experience is partly shaped by policies towards them of the rich nations which fall into the error of defining the developing countries negatively, and pay inadequate attention to the real differences which do exist. In addition, the 'developing nations' have to some extent accepted the label which has been chosen, perhaps erroneously, to group them together, and as a result have determined their own policies partly in imitation of other developing countries and partly by mutual agreement or supposedly common objectives.* For these and other reasons there is some consistency of experience as between countries which it is reasonable to try to summarise.

*See, for example, Bauer (1971), p. 19.

†In this study we will normally use the label 'developing' though in doing so we have no intention of implying that 'development' is the inescapable fate of the countries concerned, nor that the development which they do experience is always 'desirable'.

*A good example is the apparent willingness of groups of developing countries to form common policies in relation to particular primary commodities even though the interests of some individual countries in relation to these commodities are diametrically opposed.

The view of the early fifties – traceable intellectually to the Harrod–Domar model of the growth process – that growth was merely a matter of increasing the part of GDP devoted to investment, possibly by means of a higher domestic savings rate, but more probably by foreign aid, was soon shown to be excessively naive. At an early date it became apparent that an increase in the availability of capital funds to a poor country was not a sufficient condition for the use of these funds for productive investment. Indeed, the restricted domestic markets and duality of the developing countries, combined with acute shortages and rigidities of supply of such fundamental resources as skilled manpower, combined to invalidate the Harrod–Domar assumption that the capital–output ratio would stay constant in the face of a higher savings ratio.

The failure of the Harrod–Domar solution in its most naive form led on to the remarkably unanimous view that, if effective absorption of new capital was impeded by resource bottlenecks, then governments should organise themselves to eliminate those bottlenecks by some form of economic planning. Though there was an opposing point of view, represented most forcefully, perhaps, in the writings of Bauer, the proliferation of development plans during the past twenty years is adequate testimony to the relative impotence of this competing view, at least as far as its influence on practical policy is concerned.

Although integrated development plans for non-developing countries can be traced back to the early years of this century, it is only since the Second World War that there has been near-universal acceptance of the axiomatic need for developing countries to attempt to control their economic futures by planning. In his major study of planning, Albert Waterson (1966), identified some 780 national plans, 602 of which related to developing countries outside the Soviet bloc and 753 of which had been introduced since 1945. Since 1966, most of the 183 countries involved in this orgy of planning will have written two more plan documents, so that the total of post war plan documents for developing countries will by now be in excess of 1000.

Although this incredible volume of planning activity can be partly traced to the failure of the naive development models referred to earlier, it also owes a good deal to the institutional circumstances of the post-war years and especially the international acceptance of foreign aid as a crucial ingredient of successful development. As one of the conditions of giving aid, aid donors have required some evaluation of the effects of aid both on the economy of the recipient countries and on their own balance of payments. The existence of some document analysing the expected future development of the recipient economy and the interaction of its various sectors has proved to be a convenient basis for conducting this evaluation. Thus the institutional emergence of foreign aid and the preparation of comprehensive plans are intimately connected. The most clear-cut example of this link is represented by the 1961 establishment of The Charter of the Alliance for Progress, which is said to have directly led to the establishment of planning agencies in nine Latin American countries where formerly none existed.* Other examples abound, and nearly all aid agencies, whether bilateral or multilateral, have placed their authority behind the argument in favour of planning.

*See Waterson (1966), p. 36.

The strong link between foreign aid and planning is the obvious explanation of the paradoxical advocacy of planning for the developing countries by rich nations such as West Germany and the USA which have been slow to accept the benefits of planning in relation to their own economies. It is also the first of several explanations why so many of the planning exercises referred to above have failed to come anywhere near to achieving their stated objectives. It is quite clear that many development plans are written with the sole objective of qualifying for foreign aid and that their existence implies absolutely nothing about a commitment to plan in any normally accepted sense of the word. Waterson refers to plans for Brazil and Ghana, for example, which were prepared in a matter of a few weeks and with little or no reference to the ministries and agencies who were supposedly responsible for implementation of the plan.† The need to keep at least one wary eye on the aid donor is also a reason why some plans appear to omit, or to be purposefully vague about, some of the major aims of government, while emphasising lesser objectives which are unlikely to offend the sensitivity of donor governments. It seems probable that one should discount the seriousness of a large number of published plan documents for these and related reasons.

†Waterson (1966), p. 146.

However, even allowing for this factor, the degree of success of economic planning in achieving what should be its fundamental objective – namely an improvement in living standards, and especially of those sectors of society suffering poverty in its most extreme forms – has been disappointing. There are many reasons for this, but one of the more important has been the failure of the planning machinery to translate what we have termed the 'fundamental' objective into specific operational objectives, and thence into quantifiable form as 'targets'. It is only if this translation can be made that it becomes possible to identify relevant policy instruments and to evaluate their possible impact on the specified targets and thence on the underlying development objectives. This important aspect of the planning operation seems to have gone wrong for a number of reasons and we need to devote a few paragraphs to it since it is crucial to an understanding of the rationale behind this present study.

First, planning has often gone wrong because, while accepting the fundamental objective of improving living standards, many plans have also embraced numerous other specific objectives which have not been explicitly linked to the fundamental objective and may even have been inconsistent with it. For example, it is not unheard of for plans to include balance of payments equilibrium and a stable currency among the objectives of the planning operation. The failure to preserve a coherence between the fundamental objective of development policy and the more specific operational objectives and strategies obviously creates problems at a subsequent stage when these objectives in some way have to be quantified as targets of policy. That the failure is so widespread is not surprising since the incorporation in a plan of a multifarious list of objectives, even though they may be inconsistent both with each other and with the fundamental aim of planning, is an obvious way of side-stepping the problems posed by a lack of consensus about appropriate strategy which might postpone or completely preclude the publication of a plan document. Nonetheless, there is no escaping the obvious truth that this ploy severely reduces the possibility that the plan can achieve any real improvement in the general standard of living.

A second reason why the planning operation often seems to go wrong at the stage of specifying objectives and targets is that one of the specific operational objectives or strategies which might be implied by the primary objective of improved living standards has been allowed to predominate, so that ends and means are inverted. Thus Waterson (1966) writes:*

*Waterson (1966), p. 145.

> Although there may be a variety of other basic objectives the ultimate objective of national development in most countries is to raise the level of living of all people in the country through expanded output and use of consumer goods and services for education, health and cultural activities. For almost all less developed countries, this requires an acceleration in the rate of economic growth to provide higher per capita incomes.

From here it is an easy (but treacherous) step to the view that an increase in the size of the economic cake will lead to an improvement in material prosperity for everyone, and is therefore preferable to a policy of helping the deprived by redistributing a cake of something like fixed size. There are two possible errors in this view. The first is that the distribution of an expanding cake is not independent of the methods used to expand it; and that, as we shall see later, the methods adopted by many developing countries since the war have involved a bias in the direction of less equality of distribution. The second is that while a larger cake may increase the absolute material well-being of even the lowest income groups, it is at least arguable that the proper objective of policy ought to be an improvement in the relative position of these groups. Post-war development policy has patently failed to achieve this in all but a few cases.

Whether the assumption of a link between living standards in general and GDP growth is erroneous or true is a matter upon which theoretical analysis and statistical enquiry can both shed some light.* We refer to studies in both of these areas in the final section of this chapter. Meanwhile we can simply state that the prejudice that this assumption is not necessarily valid underlies the work in this volume. Our view is that much depends on the form which redistribution takes and the institutional framework, both economic and political.

*It is relevant to note that the vast majority of development plans of the 1950s and 1960s had faster growth of GDP as their main operational objective. A notable exception was the Ceylon Ten-Year Plan (1959), which gives emphasis to the need to create employment opportunities.

The perversion of the fundamental objective by its translation into, and deposition by, growth of GDP has implications for the evolution of the institutional framework for policies as well as for the policies themselves. To the extent that what happens in practice depends on the chosen objective, to allow growth in national income to usurp the position of growing living standards as the single objective leads to a situation in which the institutions of society may be ill-conditioned for implementing the policies which could do most to achieve progress.

At this point in the argument it is worth emphasising the obvious fact that the objectives which dominate in practice are *a fortiori* the objectives of those with political power. However, the question we are concerned with is not, in the first instance, what those objectives should be, but rather that, given that the objectives relate to the standards of living of different groups in society, how can a quantitative macroeconomic description of the society be established which will capture this dimension of living standards and hence be a useful tool in designing policies which are addressed directly to it.

A third factor which is relevant to this discussion is the potential contradiction that, while the ostensible aim of planning is invariably a general rise in living standards, it is quite clear that the pursuit of this aim must involve an increase in frugality. Thus Gunnar Myrdal writes:†

†Myrdal (1956), p. 64.

> There is no other road to economic development than a forceful rise of the part of national income which is with-held from consumption and devoted to investments, and this implies a policy of utmost austerity – independently of whether the increased savings are engendered through high levels of profits or through increased taxation . . . This frugality, which must be applied to the level of living of the masses of the people for the simple reason that they are the masses.

But this is not really the strong contradiction which ardent opponents of planning, such as Bauer, have asserted,* since it is readily resolved by arguing that the austerity of the present is merely the price to pay for the enhanced prosperity of the future. However, one must go some of the way with Professor Bauer since, when defining operational objectives and translating these into targets, planners do tend to regard the need for an intertemporal redistribution of income as being axiomatic, even though this impinges unfavourably upon the prospects for achievement of the ultimate objective in the shorter term. This being the case, it is surprising that development plans have paid so little regard to a quantification of the distribution of the short term sacrifices of living standards and to the nature of the trade-off between current and future income. It is as though in translating the ultimate objective of development into its major operational objective, namely growth of GDP, the primacy of the former over the latter has been mysteriously destroyed. This, at least, is the implication of the apparent attempts of many development plans to maximise the amount of intertemporal income redistribution in favour of the future.

*See Bauer (1971), p. 73.

So there are at least three aspects to the explanation of why the specification of the targets of policy might have failed to properly reflect the underlying development objectives from which these targets are supposed to derive. Let us now look in more detail at some of these targets and the way in which they have been pursued in the post-war years.

The first point to note in this context is that once economic growth has been accepted (perhaps wrongly) as a valid way of attaining development aims, industrialisation appears (cf. Lewis (1954) and Ranis and Fei (1966)) as a natural route to faster growth. This is because of the generally higher productivity levels characteristic of industrial, as opposed to primary, activities and the implication that income per head can be increased by shifting resources into industrial activities. It is a view encouraged by the inescapable conclusion from both time-series and cross-section statistical studies that the share of industry in both output and employment totals does increase as income per capita increases.* Politically, a higher degree of industrialisation has a great attraction to the developing countries since it symbolises the escape from colonial subservience and the 'hewer of wood' and 'drawer of water' type of role. Thus a higher level of industrial output has invariably been established as one of the prime policy targets of developing countries.

*This fact is well documented in Chenery and Syrquin (1975), for example.

There is of course nothing wrong with this target as such, but unfortunately the method of pursuing it since the war has typically produced effects which have run counter to the ultimate objectives of a general rise in living standards. In particular, the overriding emphasis on 'import substitution' – the establishment of industry geared to supplying the domestic market – has had serious adverse effects on both income distribution and employment levels.

The main distortions involved in the process of import substitution are by now well known through the writings of Prebish (1964), Little, Scitovsky and Scott (1970) and several others, and it is therefore only necessary to present a brief summary. First and foremost the basic inefficiency of industry in its early stages, combined with the small scale of operation to which the limited size of domestic markets normally condemn it, means that levels of protection have to be extremely high in order to ensure viability. Average levels of effective protection of manufacturing industries currently stand at well over 100 per cent in many parts of SE Asia and Latin America, and cases where the value added of particular industries is negative if calculated at world prices are by no means unheard of. (Chapter 6 cites some examples from Sri Lanka.) Furthermore, tariff rates and the related gamut of administrative controls, such as import licensing, impinge unevenly on different industries with the tendency being to afford higher protection to the consumer goods which are capable of production within the developing countries, and far lower protection to capital goods.† This obviously lowers the relative price of capital and so provides an inducement to labour-saving techniques.

†As argued by Johnson (1967).

As well as conferring high potential profits on industry, protection provides a crucial source of revenue for government and is a device for assisting balance of payments equilibrium without the need to resort to devaluation of the currency. However, the devaluation alternative would raise the incomes of agricultural producers who sell their output on world markets at prices fixed in foreign currency terms, and would lower the cost of living of this same group by lowering the costs of otherwise protected consumption goods. In short the benefits of protection have only accrued to industry and to the government as a result of what is effectively a tax on the agricultural sector, i.e. on the sector which in most developing countries embraces the majority of those in lower income groups. This is perhaps the most important manifestation of Professor Myrdal's observation previously quoted:* 'frugality, which must be applied to the level of living of the masses of the people for the simple reason that they are the masses.'

*See p. 7 above.

The potentially high industrial profits implied by protection also imply a high rate of return on capital, which exacerbates the bias towards capital intensity referred to earlier. This bias has been reinforced by the need for the industrialisation process to rely on equipment from developed countries which reflects their high opportunity cost of labour in terms of capital, rather than the far lower opportunity cost applying in the developing world. It is also reinforced by the prevalence of foreign aid policies which are tied to purchases of capital equipment, by prematurely high wages in industrial sector activities, and possibly by government subsidisation in relation to interest payments. Typically, the sum total of these various biases against higher employment levels, at least in the short term, is substantial.

Finally, and this is especially true in South East Asia, including Sri Lanka, the industrialisation strategies which have been followed have generated enormous problems of underutilisation of capacity. This is partly because of the high industrial profits conferred by protection and the possibilities of earning reasonable profits on the basis of a relatively low degree of utilisation of capacity. It is partly due to the more liberal attitude applied to the importation of capital goods as compared with raw materials and semi-finished products. Finally, it owes a good deal to the bureaucratic inefficiencies and delays, to say nothing of corruption, associated with the issuing of import licences. But, however it arises, contemplation of this excess capacity conjures up the tragic picture of low income households, especially in the agricultural sector, being taxed to help finance the acquisition of capital equipment which then stands idle. It represents a major indictment of the industrialisation strategies pursued by a large number of developing countries in the past twenty years.

These biases against the agricultural sector and against fuller employment can be seen as indictments of the policies of the developing countries themselves. It is important that we also note that similar indictments can be, and have been, directed against the policies of developed countries. These are not our principal concern since we are dealing with methods of improving policy in the developing nations. However, it is true that the general decline of protectionism engineered in the post-war years under the auspices of GATT has not applied as fully to agricultural commodities and to manufactures of special interest to developing countries, such as cotton textiles, as it has in other areas. In addition, it is clear that the remaining levels of industrial protection in the rich nations represent an important reason for the high emphasis attached to an import substitution strategy. A more liberal trading attitude on the part of the rich countries could have many of the same results on income distribution and employment as would some retraction from the commitment to import substitution on the part of most developing nations.*

*We would not wish to suggest that this commitment is relevant to all developing countries. Thus, for example, South Korea and Taiwan have both pursued relatively export oriented industrialisation policies while Tanzania and Communist China have given prime emphasis to agricultural development.

While policies towards industry have certainly contributed to many of the contemporary problems of developing countries, it has to be conceded that there are other, and less controllable causes as well. As Morawetz (1974) has reminded us in his recent survey article, if the manufacturing sector employed 20 per cent of the labour force, it would need to expand at 15 per cent per annum merely to absorb the increment to a labour force growing at 3 per cent, even in the absence of any productivity improvements. This is an enormous task made even more weighty by the extent to which the rate of expansion of labour force participation is increased. And, of course, it is the case that there was a significant expansion of the rate of population increase in most developing countries after the war; an expansion which happened to be particularly dramatic in Sri Lanka and which was having serious labour force implications by the early 1960s. Even in the absence of ill-advised industrialisation strategies, this factor alone would have caused severe problems of underemployment, and therefore poverty, for the developing countries of the 1970s.

There are a number of additional factors which are extremely important in particular contexts but which cannot be explored at all fully in this brief survey. They include the as yet little explored possibility that policies within the agricultural sector have exacerbated distributional and employment problems by discriminating in favour of commercial, modern and capital intensive agriculture to the detriment of small-scale and labour-intensive agriculture.* This view has recently been examined by Thorbecke and Dambe. Secondly, as we will discuss more fully in the Sri Lankan context in the next chapter, the wrong emphasis in education policies has contributed a structural dimension to the unemployment problem among the highly educated. Thirdly, there is the very common urban bias involved in wages policy and infrastructural development which in some cases has had the effect of moving formerly disguised unemployment in the agricultural sector to the towns. And so we could go on. But whatever the reasons (and generalisations in relation to them can only go so far), it is not surprising that as a result of the various forces at work improvements in living standards during the past thirty years have not been universal, and in many respects the problem of poverty has got worse rather than better.†

*It is interesting that this accords with one of the results of the Adelman and Morris (1971) study of the determinants of income distribution discussed in the final section of this chapter.

†A considerable amount of evidence on this issue is adduced in a recent study by Chenery *et al.* (1974).

To summarise the discussion so far, the era represented by the last thirty years has seen the almost universal acceptance of the need for development planning, partly, though not entirely, because the era has also witnessed the emergence of foreign development aid as a major international institution. Any judgement of the record of development during this period based on the standard indicator of growth of GDP per capita can only conclude that it has been enormously successful in comparison with any other historical period; growth rates of the order of 5 per cent per annum or above, are now relatively common. And yet even casual study of many individual countries readily indicates that acute poverty lingers on, the unemployment problem gets bigger, and there really is not much evidence of the general rise in living standards which economic growth is supposed to bring in its train. Improvements in prosperity seem confined to particular groups in society, to particular regions, to particular localities (normally urban rather than rural) and to particular sectors. In this section we have attempted to identify some of the failings of development strategy and planning procedures which underly this asymmetry of experience. In the next section we examine how international statistical policy has reflected this experience.

3 International statistical development and the role of data

The post-war commitment to development planning and other forms of government intervention in the economies of developing countries have brought in their wake a need for a considerably expanded base of economic data with which to inform the policies involved in this intervention. The manner in which the international community has responded to this need is discussed in some detail in Professor Stone's foreword to this volume and it is clear that the response has been impressive. Indeed, the outpouring of macroeconomic data, including substantial sectoral detail, from the developing countries has been on the same scale as the flood of development plans referred to earlier. The UN *Yearbook of National Account Statistics*,* for example, now incorporates macroeconomic data for some 150 countries, most of which are in the category of developing countries.

*UN Statistical Office (Annual).

Yet, despite this apparent success, there is considerable disquiet about the relevance and usefulness of a good deal of these data in terms of their ability to assist the pursuit of the central objectives of the countries concerned. Thus, for example, in a recent ILO paper on development strategy for the Second Development Decade, Professor Hans Singer commented as follows:*

> International efforts might be made to gear all data systems – such as measurement of GNP, measurement of impact of government expenditure, beneficiaries of investment programmes, and so on – to these new targets. This applies especially to the data systems maintained or supported by the United Nations. It will, of course, be objected that the data would not be available to monitor these new targets† immediately; but this objection has been raised for the past ten years and we are in danger of continuing in an endless vicious circle in which the absence of data leads to the setting of wrong targets, and the setting of wrong targets leads to the collection of the wrong data. The time has come to make the break, and, given the will, this can be done. Once it is generally realised that much of the data now collected (such as GNP growth as conventionally measured, or export growth which includes the internal transactions of multinational enterprises operating in developing countries) are irrelevant to development (the purpose of which is to reduce and eliminate poverty), it becomes clear that this sort of data collection could be discontinued in order to switch resources to obtaining more relevant data.

*International Labour Office (1975), p. 83.

†Targets which are discussed briefly in the next section.

The disquiet about the relevance and usefulness of data has a number of aspects in addition to those emphasised by Singer. First, there is the frequently voiced argument that despite the enormous expansion in the availability of data for developing countries, the statistical documentation for these countries is often poor in terms of the reliability of those data which do exist. In short, although too slow to meet the expanding need for data, statistical outputs which have been possible are too inaccurate to be useful. If we accept the view that there is no such thing as a completely accurate piece of data, this point must relate to the issue of whether the degree of inaccuracy of particular data is such as to make them unusable. Further, it is inevitable that in the process of confronting the large data needs of a highly interventionist government policy with the small resource base, especially of suitable manpower, of the 'average' developing country, the data which emerge will probably be less accurate than they would be in a rich country.

Thus to take the view which is sometimes held, that the quantitative analysis of potential policies must be delayed until the statistics needed to inform those policies have been improved, is naive. Better statistics must regrettably be viewed as something of a luxury good produced partly as the result of economic 'development' rather than as its precursor. It follows that developing countries must learn to adapt to the idea of getting the most that they can from those statistics which are already available or which can be collected without enormous additional utilisation of scarce resources. The opportunity cost of improved data collection is considerable and the episode recounted by Waterson* in which 70 staff devoted more than a year to a thorough (15 volume) statistical diagnosis of the Uruguayan economy, is something which cannot, and probably should not, be repeated in most countries.

*Waterson (1966), p. 184.

The comments of the previous paragraph may appear to come very close to saying that any statistics are better than no statistics, but in fact this is not the message. Indeed, the taking of decisions on the basis of statistics which are transparently meaningless is clearly an extremely dangerous thing to do. Rather, the message is that statistical resources should be reorganised (and no doubt added to where possible) to make existing statistics usable in a way that they have not been usable in the past. The textbooks on statistics adopted in developing countries should be rewritten to incorporate chapters on the techniques for using incomplete and otherwise imperfect data.* For it is a fact that much economic decision making in poor countries will have to continue to rely on data which, in one way or another are inadequate, and much effort needs to be devoted to showing how this is to be done. This view, while not without its advocates in the post-war years, has received relatively little support, and the more normal approach of development economists to statistics has been to bemoan, or even ridicule, the inadequacies and to advise expenditure of funds to relieve those of the inadequacies which are the most irritating from the viewpoint of their own particular areas of work. In our view this approach is not very helpful since it ignores the reality of the information problem in poor countries, and merely leads ultimately to the recommendation that more scarce resources be devoted to work on statistics.

*We have incorporated some suggestions along these lines in Appendix 1, and work is in hand with formal techniques of the type discussed in Section 3 of the Foreword to this volume.

A second aspect of the disquiet concerning post-war progress in the statistical field in the developing world relates to the role of the international agencies and their advocacy of standardised data systems. A very large amount of the increased post-war availability of macroeconomic data referred to earlier is due to the efforts of the United Nations and other international agencies in producing manuals explaining the sort of data which are 'needed', the classifications which are appropriate and the methods of collection. These same agencies have also contributed by supplying technical assistance personnel to help carry through their recommendations, and by their requirements for macroeconomic planning, and hence data, which have been built into their foreign-aid agreements. The UN System of National Accounts (SNA, for short), first produced in 1952 and last revised in 1968,† has been a particularly important influence in this respect. And yet there is no doubt that many see the SNA as a monolithic, excessively ambitious, dogmatic structure which 'requires' developing countries to produce data in which they have no analytical interest, using classifications and conventions which are quite inappropriate to their circumstances, and so on.

†UNSO (1968).

In our view, even a cursory look at the original conception and content of the SNA reveals the unfairness of this type of criticism. The strength of the SNA structure lies in the inherent flexibility of its approach to classification and aggregation, and this is such as to permit it to embrace many of the distinguishing characteristics of the developing countries. Certainly, there are several interesting demonstrations of this point, including the modified input–output system of Dudley Seers,* and the system for West Indian plantation-type economies developed by Kari Levitt.† The first of these, in particular, is a good example of Professor Stone's earlier point in relation to the SNA, that* 'the user is left free to put his emphasis where he pleases and to leave some parts of the system completely aggregated while other parts are elaborated in detail'.

*See, Seers (1961).

†Levitt (1973).

*See p. xix, above.

But it is true that demonstrations of the Seers type, which show the value of a comprehensive macro-data system to developing economies, are relatively few and far between, and also clear that the SNA structure has been disappointing as far as its impact on analytical work in these countries is concerned. It may be that this deficiency could be solved by more and better demonstrations of the type detailed in this volume, but in our view the major initiative for improvement must come from the international agencies themselves. In this context, let us consider the competing demands placed upon statistical offices in developing countries by international agencies on the one hand, and internal economists, planners, etc. on the other.

The demands of the former group will normally be specific, biased in favour of international comparability, supported by the provision of technical assistance personnel whose career progression is dependent upon the international agency set-up, and will probably emanate from statisticians. By contrast, it is clear that the statistician in developing countries often sees the demands placed upon him by his own economists as unreasonable in the sense that they appear to imply scant recognition of the difficulties of generating the required information, to allow insufficient time, and to be generally naive from a statistical point of view. This reflects the fundamentally different working style of the statistician as compared with the economist in a developing country; the one working meticulously, and often in difficult conditions, towards the preparation of the best possible estimates, the other pressured towards relatively quick decisions and anxious to lay his hands on any data which can inform those decisions. Regrettable as this conflict is, whenever it exists, it helps to bias the other conflict, between foreign and domestic demands on the statistician, in the direction of resolution in favour of the former. The result is one which our relatively limited experience indicates to be fairly common. The statistical office spends a disproportionate amount of time serving the needs of international comparability. The domestic users of data despair of their statisticians and either stop expressing to them their own needs for data, or establish their own data collection arrangement.*

*For some examples of this from Sri Lanka see Chapter 2, and for some brief comments about the situation in India see Mitra (1963).

In those cases where the situation described in the previous paragraph applies, it would be grossly unfair to lay the entire blame for this on the international agencies. However, it is clear that they are an important part of the scenario and an improvement in the quality of their assistance to statistical services should certainly involve a greater emphasis than at present on the preparation of data systems which are relevant to specific countries and to specific problems within them, even though this implies a partial abandonment of the requirements of international comparability. Experience indicates that this development will not easily occur autonomously. In addition they must place their authority behind the fuller integration of statistical work into the decision-making process, although once again this may imply some retraction from the aim of international consistency and some compromise of the purity of statistics as an independent discipline.

A change of emphasis is also required in another sense as well. The SNA is a product of the planning age and has a specific planning model underlying it. In the same way that the fundamental aim of planning, namely a generalised improvement in living standards, appears to have been lost sight of relative to proximate, but less important objectives (notably growth of GDP) so too does the statistical framework supporting it appear to be geared to this set of lesser objectives. The main reflection of this, so far as implementation of the SNA is concerned, is in the enormous emphasis which seems to be attached to getting 'right' the major accounting aggregates such as GDP, GNP and so on. As Mitra has put it:†

†Mitra (1963).

> In retrospect, it can be doubted whether the efforts made by the United Nations Statistical Office and the Technical Assistance Administration in the course of the past fifteen years to improve statistics in the underdeveloped countries have led to entirely desirable consequences. For reasons of prestige, many of these nations have felt compelled to con-

> centrate their statistical estimates to compilation of such global estimates as those of national income, capital formation and savings. When an expert, under the auspices of the UN, has gone to a country on a short term assignment, pressure has been brought upon him to help the local statisticians in assembling glamorous macroeconomic estimates. Fashion has thus pushed necessity aside. As a result, development of basic statistics such as data on production, prices, population movements, growth and distribution of labour force has been on the whole neglected.

Mitra's point is clearly in accord with our own, but he too fails to incorporate in his list of neglected basic statistics a reference to what must surely be the most fundamental of economic statistics, namely those describing living standards of different categories of families and their movement over time.

To return to Hans Singer's recent paper on the Second Development Decade, he argues that:*

> there is, of course, no harm (if resources permit) in continuing to undertake the conventional GNP calculations in order to find out whether conventional GNP growth is higher or lower than before. But this should be considered a mere academic exercise – to answer the question whether or not there has been a 'trade-off' – and of no particular importance for a development strategy. For such a strategy only socially weighted GNP figures can be of real relevance.

*International Labour Office (1975), p. 84.

The fundamental criticism of the SNA in this context relates to its extremely aggregative approach to the household sector. This is not because the original conception of the system was unaware of distributional questions but because at the time (of the 1968 revision), work on these questions was relegated to a separate compartment. To quote the 1968, SNA document:†

> The Statistical Office is engaged in preparing an integrated system of statistics of the distribution of income, consumption and wealth which at the macro level fits completely into the SNA (and also into the MPS), and at the micro level is complementary to the two systems.

†UNSO (1968), p. 1.87.

Unfortunately, this work has been a long time in coming to fruition, even now it appears to be very little known as compared with the SNA and there appear to have been few, if any, attempts to demonstrate, at the level of practical statistics, that it can be fully integrated into the national accounts presentation of the SNA. Our work in Sri Lanka involves a partial demonstration of this integration but also indicates that there are the most extreme difficulties in carrying it through, not least because of the large biases which are invariably present in data derived (as distributional data normally must be), from household surveys. Nonetheless, it is fundamental to our view that this integration of 'separate' data sets must be made if we are to make progress in quantifying the impact of potential policies on distributional objectives.[1]

It can also be noted that the analytical as opposed to the statistical applications of the SNA have thus far been largely confined to developed economies and, in particular, to the UK.[2] This no doubt reflects the fact that Stone is the chief architect of the SNA and that the first social accounting matrix (SAM) as we know it was produced in the course of the Cambridge Growth Project which he directed with Alan Brown. This first SAM was the empirical counterpart of the earliest Cambridge Growth Model.[3] The present SNA data system and associated model have evolved from these origins and in this sense are not rooted in the problems and perspectives of developing countries.[4] For this reason, as well as showing the sort of statistical framework which might feasibly be adopted by

1 Further demonstration of this point is contained in the work of Altimer (1975) which shows huge discrepancies for wages as between income surveys and national accounts in a number of Latin American countries.

2 A notable exception, on which our own work relies heavily, is Narapalasingham (1970).

3 See Cambridge, Department of Applied Economics (1962–) for details of this early work.

4 Narapalasingham's work is not independent of its Cambridge origin any more than our own. (Narapalasingham was a student there at one time.) His research wa[s] undertaken under Brown's direction.

developing countries, it is obviously of importance to demonstrate the analytical uses for a developing country to which this framework might be put. We have made a start on the analytical aspects of our own work in Chapters 4 to 6 of this present volume, which presents some analysis of policy issues for the Sri Lankan economy as viewed through the data framework.

At this juncture a point of emphasis needs to be made. This is simply that we see statistics as an input into informed opinion and as a means of making better policy decisions. The case for statistics as a purely descriptive historical record is an extremely limited one. Thus our concern to see the available data put together in a consistent macroeconomic framework is not simply because each separate piece of information gains in quality by the many implicit tests for and attempts to achieve consistency that are inevitably involved. This is only a part. For the rest, the point is that the complete (albeit relatively crude) picture which emerges generates psychological novelty by virtue of showing how one aspect of the economy relates to another. Thus, for example, the network of facts leading from the commodity composition of imports to the distribution of income over households, once displayed, makes it possible to recognise the implications for living standards of tariff and quota policy. Of course, to bring out these implications requires more by way of analysis than the basic data. But the data are an important part of the total picture and the point at which we choose to begin. We make this choice not least because having the data is suggestive of policies, or of policy implications, which might well otherwise be missed.

Finally, while the above discussion focuses on the developing countries of the world, many of the points, especially those relating to the consistency of statistics and the insulation, more or less, of statistics from policy formulation, are not issues on which the developed countries have a particularly good record.* However, their comparative wealth of resources in terms of administrative and professional cadres makes it less important in some respects that they should use these resources efficiently. Moreover, the developed societies are changing less quickly *a fortiori* and there is less urgency in human terms attached to solving some of their internal, distributional questions. The problems in the developing world are at once more pressing and, with respect to sorting our their macroeconomic data systems, more easily resolved. Accordingly, something can be done with relatively little effort to provide a tool for working more effectively on the real issues. At least, that is our hope in having undertaken this study.

*For a detailed discussion of the British Government Statistical Service and some of the problems it has had, see UK, House of Commons, 1966. A more general discussion of statistics in relation to a developed country is in Pyatt (1968).

4 The emerging international consensus

International opinion is rapidly coming to accept the reality that an emphasis on economic growth has failed the developing countries in many of the ways described in Section 2 above. The purpose of this section is to review briefly a couple of the more important manifestations of the new consensus which bear closely on our own research.

The action which most clearly symbolises the emergence of the new international viewpoint was the approval in 1970 by the General Assembly of the United Nations of a strategy for the Second Development Decade which attached great importance to many objectives of economic policy which had formerly been relegated to subsidiary status or completely ignored. Most importantly it recognised that the ultimate objective of development is the well-being of the individual, of all individuals, and that the persistence of 'undue privileges, extremes of wealth and social injustices' may well be inconsistent with the achievement of this objective. In accord with this, it placed its full support behind policies, whether of the developed or the developing countries, designed to increase the proportion of the working population in employment and to reduce the incidence of unemployment and underemployment. The policies in question were broadly defined to cover monetary, fiscal, trade, technology and research policies with a good deal of emphasis given to rural development and public expenditure projects.

The two international agencies which have taken up this new emphasis with the most vigour are the International Labour Office (ILO) and the World Bank (IBRD). The former, which for many years has placed its support behind the case for fuller employment as an objective of development in its own right, has recently strengthened this commitment considerably through the medium of the World Employment Programme (WEP) which it inspired. The WEP which was launched in 1970 has involved a major programme of research over a wide field related to employment generation and technical assistance as well as an ambitious series of large-scale and comprehensive employment missions (to Colombia, Sri Lanka, Iran, Kenya, the Dominican Republic, the Philippines and the Sudan to date). These missions have been concerned with the development of a comprehensive employment oriented development strategy for each of the particular countries concerned, and, at the same time, with the generation of conclusions about causes and appropriate solutions for employment and related problems which have a wider relevance. In a recent, and fairly searching, appraisal of the missions' work* it was concluded that they have already made four major contributions to an understanding of the employment problem, namely:

*See International Labour Office (1973).

(i) they have recognised, and confirmed, the comprehensive nature of the employment problem and the policies needed to cope with it; employment had been recognised as 'part of the wider problem of development and transformation, and in particular as part of the problem of poverty and income distribution and the whole social situation in the countries concerned';†

†ILO, ibid., p. 6.

(ii) they have improved understanding of the various dimensions of unemployment and underemployment;

(iii) they have recognised a number of structural imbalances of importance to the problem, notably those of an educational and regional nature;

(iv) and they have evolved a new and unconventional view of the role of the so-called 'informal' urban sector, and, to a lesser extent, of traditional agriculture in the process of economic and social development.

The participation in the comprehensive employment missions of the WEP by staff of all the major UN agencies (ILO, FAO, UNESCO, WHO, UNIDO, UNICEF, and UNCTAD) as well as the World Bank, the IMF and GATT, is testimony to the importance which the international community now attaches to the objectives embodied both in the WEP and the strategy for the Second Development Decade more generally.

However, there is a serious difficulty in all this, in that the exploration of distributional issues must be heavily quantitative in nature. The question of how the demands for labour of different types will respond to different possible development strategies is one which requires quantitative knowledge of the employment structure of different production activities and how these will evolve. To explore the question of the probable impact of income redistribution on employment, one needs this information again, but also information on the demand patterns of different household income groups as well as the import content of these demands. To analyse income distribution one needs quantitative information about how the distribution arises; whether from the pre-existing distribution of asset ownership, from the returns to these assets, from the structure of government taxation or transfer payments or from some other cause. Equally, to analyse the causes of locational inequalities in employment and income possibilities, including those involved in the urban/rural distinction, one needs detailed information about the production structure of each locality, its links with employment structure, demand patterns and so on. As the WEP comprehensive employment missions, not surprisingly, have confirmed, it is impossible to approach the employment/income distribution range of issues in anything other than a macroeconomic context.

This the missions have clearly recognised. As the summary of the meeting called to evaluate them puts it:*

> the mission reports are comprehensive not just in the sense that a conventional development plan is comprehensive in covering all sectors, but in the sense of viewing employment as a part of the problem of development and development as a societal process rather than just a movement of certain key economic aggregates. This aspect of the mission report comes close to work that has been going on elsewhere in the UN system in search of a 'unified approach to development'.

*International Labour Office (1973).

What the missions have been less quick to do is check their specific recommendations against the macroeconomic relationships which their own theoretical arguments would suggest to be important. In particular, they have been slow to reflect their remarks about the comprehensive and macro nature of the problem by using data in a macro and comprehensive fashion. Indeed, this has been accepted as one of the four major failings of the programme of missions. Erik Thorbecke has expressed this in the following terms:

> Probably the greatest conceptual shortcoming of all the reports is the lack of a macroeconomic consistency framework. This is particularly important when it is accepted that an employment strategy can only be formulated in the context of a comprehensive development strategy. . . . it can be argued that a disaggregated framework is necessary in order to obtain mutually consistent projections of output and employment. However, anyone who has ever attempted to build such a consistency model realises the number of relative arbitrary assumptions which have to be made and the relatively dubious quality of much of the statistical information on which the quantitative framework must, of necessity, be based. Notwithstanding these qualifications many questions can be answered – albeit approximately – within such a framework which could not be answered with any degree of confidence within a partial equilibrium framework.†

†International Labour Office (1973), p. 70.

To the extent that this criticism has been accepted by the agencies involved in the WEP, and in conjunction with their commitment to the aims of the Second Development Decade, it should represent an important pressure for the development of data systems which are more relevant to the real problems of the developing countries than those systems which the international agencies currently support.

The work reported in this volume is one response to the criticism. It is a limited response in the sense that the definition of the framework precludes examination of some of the questions which may arise in this area. However, this limitation is not in the nature of things; it is merely a reflection of the fact that ours is a prototype study designed to indicate what is possible, and not the last word in the statistical development which the new international consensus obviously requires. We are firmly wedded to the view that the SNA represents a sound basis for this development, subject to it putting more emphasis on the living standards of different household categories and the emergence of an implementation programme based less heavily on the needs of international comparability. On the question of whether this form of re-emphasis is likely to be consistent with continued use of a standard set of concepts and definitions across developing countries, we are inclined to agree with Bell and Duloy that this is an empirical matter:*

> What is needed is a pilot study, covering perhaps half a dozen countries, which would subject concepts and methods to a severe test and, if the results were encouraging, provide the basis for a standard frame. But lest anyone be pessimistic about the possibilities, it is worth recalling the debates in the 1950s about whether a standard system of national accounts could be developed. The real question is not whether it is possible but whether the gains from compatibility and international pressure to compile the data would outweigh the possible losses from over-standardization of concepts and priorities.

*See Chenery *et al.* (1974), p. 240.

In endorsing this view we hope that the present study may have some role as a preliminary exploration of the issues.

5 Theory and research

Although it is not central to the purpose of this volume, the growing theoretical and empirical literature on the link between growth and other possible objectives of development policy is clearly of relevance in advising the type of data which policy makers may or may not require. Accordingly this final section of our introduction provides a brief summary of some important aspects of this literature. For the most part we concentrate on income distribution as an alternative objective to growth, although a good deal of what is said applies equally to the employment objective to which we turn at the end of the section.

At the theoretical level, one of the key arguments is that stemming back at least as far as Adam Smith, that different classes of society have different tendencies to consume rather than accumulate, and that any redistribution of 'revenue' between classes would therefore change the overall savings rate and therefore growth. Contemporary models of the growth process continue to draw on Smith's distinction between the savings performance of different classes, although his view of the profligacy of the landlord class receives little contemporary support. One development of Smith's basic idea is the view that inflation tends to redistribute income in favour of profits and away from wages, and so it is also a method of increasing the growth rate.† Another incorporates the Keynesian notion of a negative correlation between income and the marginal propensity to consume. This clearly permits differences in aggregate savings rates to be related, not to economic classes as in Smith, but to different income groups, and thereby leads to the familiar conclusion that a more even income distribution, in this sense, will slow capital accumulation and therefore economic growth. Against this is the converse argument that has little relevance for most developing countries, that if growth is slowed by a shortage of aggregate demand then a redistribution of income towards the lower income groups will help.

†This has been argued by Thirlwall and Barton (1971), for example.

If one accepts the Keynesian viewpoint of the effects of income redistribution on savings as the dominant argument in the controversy about the relationship between the living standards of current and future periods then one is left with a simple trade-off in living standards over time. Even in this relatively simple case, there is a need, as already noted, for economists and statisticians to do more than at present to calculate the reductions of present living standards resulting from attempts to increase the growth rate. Clearly, at some point the present day costs of faster growth must surely prove unacceptable.

But all this assumes that redistribution would decrease savings. In fact the evidence is far from being unambiguous on the point. And even if it were not, the situation is almost certainly more complex than this since domestic savings are not the only constraint on development: and it is clear that an income redistribution may react on other constraints in quite a different fashion. Perhaps most important in this context is the argument also stemming from demand theory,* that the propensity to consume different items varies between income groups with the consequence that income distribution influences the balance of payments to the extent that total supplies of some consumption goods rely more heavily on imports than others. More specifically, it is argued that the goods which carry a relatively high weight in the budgets of the higher income groups will involve a relatively high import content. Thus, to the extent that the balance of payments constraint is binding, redistribution to the lower income groups will ease that constraint and contribute to a faster growth rate. This sort of mechanism has been explored in a number of studies, recent contributions including those by Pyatt *et al.* (1973) and by Paukert, Maton and Skolka (1974). In the latter study, which relates to the Philippines, it was found that redistribution towards greater equality would increase the level of GDP and thus, in spite of a lowering of the import content of GDP would raise the absolute level of imports. Data for Sri Lanka which bear further on this issue but produce different conclusions are examined in Chapter 5.

*Paukert (1973) cites a large number of antecedents for this viewpoint.

A related point is as follows. To the extent that a redistribution of income changes the pattern of output demand, it will also change the pattern of demand for those factors which produce the relevant outputs. In particular, it is often argued that a redistribution of income towards the lower income groups will raise the demand for labour intensive commodities and so increase the employment of labour relative to capital. To the extent that this happens there may well be engendered a cumulative mechanism since the increased employment will produce income for the lower parts of the income distribution. Both the level and the rate of growth of GDP are increased (provided that the savings rate is maintained), since it is clear that the process involves a reduction in the average capital–output ratio. So once again, growth and a more equitable income distribution are shown to be consistent objectives of policy rather than contradictory ones. To refer once again to the study by Paukert *et al.* (1974), it was shown there that any one of the hypothetical redistribution policies led to significant increases in employment, to a lower degree of capital intensity of production and to a lower capital–output ratio. But yet again the empirical evidence is not unambiguous. Other studies point to the offsetting reduction in the demand for services as a result of redistribution, leading to the conclusion that redistribution may have only a limited impact on the demand for labour.

The study by Paukert and his associates is an excellent example of quantitative research into the mechanisms linking the various targets and objectives of the developing countries. It is one of the advantages of the data system which we have compiled for Sri Lanka that it is ideally suited to servicing the data needs of this type of applied research. In the absence of such research it is difficult to say, in any particular situation, whether growth and a more equitable income distribution will be complementary or competitive objectives of policy. It is also the case that partial models of the type referred to here can be misleading. Income distribution influences demand and hence output. But at the same time output influences employment and hence income distribution. Analysis of such two-way causal links is not easy and the subject is treated at length in a study by Pyatt and Thorbecke (forthcoming).

The ambiguity remains when we move from analysis to the purely statistical approach of correlating inequality and GDP for different countries. This story begins with an essay written twenty years ago by Simon Kuznets in which he advanced the proposition that* 'in the early phases of industrialisation in the underdeveloped countries, income inequality will tend to widen before the levelling forces become strong enough first to stabilise and then reduce income inequalities'.

*See Kuznets (1955).

Since this proposition depended on the extremely limited data on income distribution then available, it has turned out to be rather inspired in so far as subsequent work involving much fuller cross-section coverage of countries has largely verified Kuznets' original insight.† In particular, a recent paper by Paukert involving comparison of 56 countries reaches, among others, the following conclusion:*

†See, for example, Oshima (1962), Paukert (1974), and Chenery *et al.* (1974).

*Paukert (1973), p. 121.

> the differences in income distribution between the developed and developing countries are not as important as the pattern of income distribution which is typical for particular levels of development. The data presented in this article supports the hypothesis expressed but not fully tested by Kuznets and Oshima that with economic development, income inequality tends to increase, then become stable and then decrease. These data clearly show that there is an increase in inequality as countries progress from below the $100 level to the $101–200 level and beyond. They establish that the peak of inequality is reached on attainment of the level of development and the structural pattern characterised by the countries which in the neighbourhood of 1965 had a GDP per capita in the $201–500 range.

Paukert found that his conclusion about the non-linearity of the relationship between GDP and income distribution applied to all of the various measures of distribution with which he experimented.

The question arises as to whether these cross-country correlations should be interpreted as having any causal relevance to particular countries. The most influential case against such interpretation of the strong relationship found by Kuznets and others is that presented in a recent study by Adelman and Morris (1971). Their starting point is the view that many non-economic factors intercede between the economic ones to help determine both the factoral distribution of income and, from there, the size distribution of income by households. Such factors might include non-market norms for wages attributable to a colonial influence or a powerful traditional elite, the degree of political participation by the principal economic and social groupings in the country, and so on. Using the methodology of their earlier study on social and political factors in economic growth (Adelman and Morris (1967)), they put numerical values on a large number of political and social variables as well as some economic variables including GDP, and proceed to study the relationship between these variables and various measures of inequality in 44 developing countries. Their most controversial conclusion is that the level of GNP per capita is of relatively minor importance as an explanation of income distribution differences between countries as compared with several of the other variables which they examined. Since their study preceded that of Paukert (1973) and involved evidence from a far larger sample of countries than any previous study, it was necessary to attach a good deal of credence to this conclusion.

However, the statistical methods used by Adelman and Morris (1971), on the one hand, and Paukert (1973), on the other, are different and this alone may be a partial explanation of their differing results. Paukert himself has suggested that Adelman and Morris, by imposing a linear form on a relationship which other evidence shows to be non-linear, may have biased their results against the Kuznets hypothesis. The acid test of this point of view, namely the re-estimation of the Adelman and Morris results allowing GDP to exert its influence in a non-linear fashion, remains to be done.

Emphasis on this one technical point should not cause us to ignore the rather long list of further conclusions which emerge from the Adelman and Morris study. These conclusions throw a good deal of light on possible determinants of income distribution, and it is important that we attempt to at least summarise the more important of these.

First, if we look at measures of inequality using the share of income of the lowest 20 per cent or 60 per cent of the income distribution, then the major determinant of inequality would appear to be the degree of socioeconomic and technical dualism. The more dualistic the economy, the greater the inequalities. Secondly, if we measure inequality by reference to the share of income of the top percentiles of the income distribution, then the abundance or otherwise of natural resources enters as a major determinant of inequality. Other factors which correlate positively with inequalities as measured in this way are the degree of development of human resources (broadly indicated by school enrolment rates) and the extent of government participation in the economy (indicated by the share of government investment in total investment). Other factors which appear as important influences on one or other of the Adelman and Morris measures of inequality are the methods of agricultural organisation (with emphasis on small farming being associated with rather less inequality than larger-scale methods), the degree of social mobility (the greater this is the lower the inequality) and the degree of cultural and ethnic homogeneity (the greater this is the lower the inequality).

All of this gives considerable food for thought. Some of the significant variables listed above are positively correlated with GDP and so their effect on distribution can be translated to give a familiar GDP–distribution trade-off. But for many of the variables the correlation with GDP will be weak and so, to the extent that we accept the Adelman and Morris results, we have to be prepared to entertain and examine trade-offs which are relatively unfamiliar. For example, attempts to improve the educational system, to increase the degree of government participation in the economy and to allow a freer role for foreign investment, all seem to have potentially unfavourable implications for income distribution if the observed correlations are taken literally. This represents a challenge and implies a large number of difficulties for the task of designing an information framework to examine distributional questions. The relationships which Adelman and Morris suggest are not simple, nor are they independent of each other. But to the extent that they may exist, they obviously need to receive some reflection in any set of data established for this purpose.

When we move on to consider the relationship between output, or output growth, and employment a number of variants of the relationships already discussed need to be introduced. For example, there is the familiar hypothesis that a reduction of employment resulting from the adoption of a more capital-intensive technique may increase savings and therefore speed the growth rate. Secondly, there is a suggestion that capital-intensive methods may generate a faster rate of technical progress, and hence a faster rate of economic growth, than labour-intensive methods. And, as a final example, there is the interesting suggestion that small-scale firms are faced by factor prices which more nearly accord with scarcity prices than those facing large firms and so are more likely to adopt labour-intensive techniques.* These and other aspects of the employment–growth trade-off have been exhaustively summarised recently by Morawetz (1974), and we can do little better than refer the reader to this source with a reminder about Morawetz' inability to draw any general conclusion about whether these two objectives conflict or complement each other. Again these conclusions represent a considerable challenge to anyone who would attempt to design a data system to examine employment issues.

*See IBRD (1973).

It needs to be emphasised at this point that the above discussion makes no claim to be exhaustive of the many issues which obviously arise, and some which are only vaguely perceived, as a result of making questions of living standards and their distribution the focal point of concern about development. Our concern here is simply to establish that this reorientation brings into prominence a wide range of issues involving relationships within and interrelationships between different facets of economic and social structure. Accordingly, a consistent, disaggregated macroeconomic information framework is an essential part of monitoring what is relevant as well as a necessary starting point for the design of policies. It is for these reasons that we feel our framework for Sri Lanka might be of much wider interest. Meanwhile, many of the arguments about how one set of variables may be influencing another are given much fuller treatment in the forthcoming volume by Pyatt and Thorbecke, which was referred to previously, than we have felt to be necessary here.†

†An overview of this work is published as Pyatt and Thorbecke (1976).

2
The Sri Lanka background

1 Social welfare

Having identified the broad international background into which our work fits, we now turn to the specific economy which has been the focus of much of our actual statistical work to date, namely Sri Lanka. Having accepted the view that appropriate data systems must, to a degree, be country specific, it is clearly important to indicate those specific problems and institutional circumstances of the country which our data is designed to elucidate, even though some of these circumstances may apply more generally. While the bulk of the Chapter is concerned with economic problems, Section 5 provides a brief discussion of some specific statistical difficulties.

In the bald terms of travelogue, the Republic of Sri Lanka (formerly Ceylon) has a population of approximately 13 million. It is an island with a land area of 25332 square miles, which is approximately one quarter the size of the UK. The mountainous central southern part of the island (3000–7000 feet) is surrounded by an upland belt which in turn is surrounded by a coastal plain around the island but much narrower in the West and South than in the North. Proximity to the equator implies a continuously high temperature at least in the coastal regions. Sri Lanka is believed to have been colonised from Southern India in about 540 BC, and an impressive succession of Sinhalese rulers held sway over the island for well over 2000 years thereafter. The Portuguese conquered part of the island in the early part of the sixteenth century giving way to the Dutch in 1640 who in turn gave way to the British in the eighteenth century. The island regained its independence in 1948.*

*See Ceylon, Department of Census and Statistics (1969).

Sri Lanka is certainly one of the more heavily documented and researched of the developing economies of the world. Some would attribute this to the charm and hospitality of its people, and the beauty of its physical geography. However, it also owes a good deal to the inherent interest, and even uniqueness, of many of the economic problems of the country. Thus the preface to a recent book on the population problem of Sri Lanka suggests that:†

†Jones and Selvaratnam (1972).

> Ceylon has been a forerunner for the countries of Southern Asia in many matters related to social and economic development. First of all, it experienced a dramatic decline in mortality in the late 1940s, a decline heralding an upsurge in rates of population growth that has already doubled Ceylon's population since that time. The other countries of Southern Asia quickly followed suit and the resulting increase in numbers during the past two decades is unprecedented in the history of mankind.

> . . . Ceylon has also been a forerunner in the provision of social welfare services. The system of free education and health services and consumer subsidies is unmatched anywhere in the region. Successive governments have shown over the years a commendable concern for the welfare of the country's poorer citizens. And yet the provision of so many free services has become a severe strain upon the economy.
>
> Ceylon has also unfortunately, been a forerunner in a less desirable area: it has developed a severe foreign exchange problem, of the kind that is likely to become increasingly widespread in Southern Asia during the 1970s. The symptoms are falling prices for its main export products, slow increases in the volume of exports, and a decline in foreign exchange reserves to dangerous levels. The inevitable adjustment is recourse to severe import controls.

And there is yet a fourth sense, not listed by Jones and Selvaratnam, in which Sri Lanka has been a forerunner, namely in the nature and scale of its employment problem.

The extent of Sri Lanka's uniqueness can be seen when one compares its expenditures on social welfare, education and health with that of other Asian countries. In a paper by Lotz (1970), it is shown that in the period 1962–65, 25 per cent of government expenditure was on education and health, and 32.6 per cent on social welfare; making a total of 57.6 per cent of total government expenditure (15.5 per cent of GDP) being allocated to welfare programmes. By comparison, Thailand expended 27.9 per cent, Malaysia 24.4 per cent and India only 18.1 per cent of their budgets upon welfare programmes. In other words Sri Lanka spent proportionately at least twice as much as her neighbours upon welfare services.

The record of social progress in Sri Lanka since the war has been impressive, especially in the light of the rapid acceleration in population growth resulting mainly from the malaria eradication campaign in the late 1940s. In the space of less than two years the death rate fell from 20 per thousand to 13 per thousand, causing population growth to accelerate to something near to 3 per cent per annum, with the result that population is currently over 10 per cent higher than it would have been in the absence of the campaign.*

*Jones and Selvaratnam (1972).

The first major aspect of social policy in Sri Lanka has been the commitment to a completely free educational system, first introduced in the 1940s. Since then there has been a rapid expansion of the educational sector which has taken the numbers of pupils in schools up to two and three quarter million (20 per cent of total population), the number of University students to over 16 000 as compared with only 1000 in 1946, and reduced illiteracy to very low levels.† Annual current expenditure on education now amounts to nearly Rs 600 million, which is approximately 15 per cent of total government current spending.* As indicated in the Lotz (1970) study previously referred to, this is an extremely high proportion for a country of Sri Lanka's relative poverty.

†Source: International Labour Office (1971).

*Although a small amount of private education remains, this has been severely curtailed since the withdrawal of government aid from the private schools in 1961.

Health expenditure has also reached very high levels (currently 8 per cent of recurrent expenditure), and the Sri Lanka health service is generally regarded as one of the best in Asia. For example, in 1965, the number of hospital beds in Sri Lanka was equal to 1 per 328 people as compared with 1889 in India, 1756 in Thailand, 1338 in Burma and 1218 in Indonesia. Of the Asian countries for which data are available, only Singapore and Taiwan appeared to have more favourable ratios. Similarly, Sri Lanka is exceptional in the developing world in that virtually all births are professionally supervised. The health programme has had a continuing and significant impact upon mortality rates going beyond the dramatic improvements achieved during the malaria eradication campaign in the mid 1940s.* For example, between 1944 and 1955, the crude death rate and the infant mortality rate were both halved while the maternal mortality rate was cut by two thirds. An important point is that since most health facilities are provided free by the government and have an even geographical spread, it is clear that health service benefits, as with educational benefits, accrue in a relatively egalitarian manner.†

The third and major component of Sri Lanka's rather exceptional social welfare programme is the large scale subsidisation of certain major food items, notably rice. The rice ration was first introduced in 1942 (though price controls were introduced three years earlier), because of concern about possible curtailment of imported supplies which then, as now, accounted for a significant proportion of domestic consumption. The ration was set at two measures of rice per person per week, one of which was supplied at a subsidised price, and one free. Although the economic justification for continuing the subsidisation of rice had ended by the late 1940s, political factors have ensured its continuance, albeit with many modifications, to the present day. The major determinants of the budgetary cost of the rice subsidy to the government have been the rapid growth of population (since every child over the age of one receives a ration), and the world price of paddy which became a particularly inflationary element after 1972 with the price rising from £36 per ton to something approaching £180 in the space of two years. In spite of substantial cuts in the quantum of the ration in 1973, this last price increase has contributed to a near tripling of the cost of the subsidy to the government during the period since 1970. The need to minimise this cost has meant that for most of the post-war years the government has preferred to buy imported rice which, at the official exchange rate, has involved a lower rupee cost than the locally produced alternative. It has also held down the guaranteed price for locally produced rice at a level giving only a very weak incentive to increased production. The dangers of this type of policy were always apparent but they have been underlined very forcefully by the dramatic escalation of the import price of the past few years.

Other foodstuffs have been brought under ration from time to time. Currently these other commodities include dhal, chillies, coriander, cumin seed and maldive fish. In addition, the Food Commissioner, who administers the rationing scheme, has the sole right to import certain foodstuffs, the most important of which are flour and sugar, and can control the resale price of these items. The prices of these items are not necessarily subsidised, and until the early 1970s sugar, in particular, was resold at a price which yielded a significant profit to the Food Commissioner. Indeed, in the 1960s profits on the resale of foodstuffs financed as much as 50 per cent of the rice subsidy but once again there was a dramatic change in the situation in the early 1970s, and this percentage has now fallen below zero.

Overall the prevailing purchase and distribution arrangements for foodstuffs represent an enormous burden on the government budget. The food subsidy is currently (1974) about equal to the sum of expenditures on education and health combined, i.e. about 20 per cent of government recurrent expenditure and equivalent to 60 per cent of government capital expenditure.

It has to be recognised that the extremely comprehensive social welfare programme briefly described in the preceding paragraphs has been, and remains a major contributory factor to the quality of life of the average Sri Lankan, not least because of its effect on child mortality (now only 50 per 1000 live births as

*It is estimated that the incidence of malaria in Sri Lanka fell from 40.4 per cent of the population in 1946 to 0.005 per cent in 1960. Most of this improvement occurred in the 1940s.

†Jones and Selvaratnam (1972).

compared to 140 in 1945), and the overall mortality rate which continued to decline slowly but significantly after the dramatic improvement associated with the malaria campaign. It has also played an important role in making Sri Lanka a relatively egalitarian society. In a recent study of income distribution by Paukert, the Gini coefficient for Sri Lanka came out at 0.440, while that for developing countries as a whole was found to have a value of 0.467.* This is only a small difference. However, in Paukert's analysis the comparison is based on personal incomes *before* tax and takes no account of the impact on real incomes of the Government's exceptionally high expenditures on social welfare.† Since the benefits of those expenditures accrue in a strongly egalitarian manner, their incorporation into an inter-country comparison of income equality would certainly show Sri Lanka in an extremely favourable light.*

*See Paukert (1973).

†A calculation of income distribution allowing for these benefits is made by Dr Lal Jayawardena in Chenery *et al.* (1974). See also Codippily (1974).

*There is also a good deal of evidence that the equality of income distribution has increased markedly during the past two decades. See Karunatilake (1971).

Without denying these advantages, it must also be recognised that the strain which this social welfare programme imposes on both the government budget position and the balance of payments is enormous, has been rising, especially since 1972, and is increasingly recognised as being impossible to sustain in the long term. The evolution of the position in relation to the government budget is shown in Table 2.1. It can be seen that the recurrent deficit is now equal to approximately half of total recurrent spending and about equal to the total of welfare spending. A similar point can be made by reference to an analysis by Samarasinghe (1973) of the elasticity of total revenues and expenditures over the period 1950–69. Whereas the income elasticity of expenditure exceeded unity in fifteen of these twenty years, the corresponding elasticity of revenue did so in only seven years. The result of all this has been a significant fall in the proportion of total expenditures financed by tax revenue (from over 100 per cent in 1953/54 to 64 per cent by 1970). Over the same period, the contribution

Table 2.1 *Welfare expenditures in the government budget 1955–74.*†

†Source: Karunatilake, (1975).

Year	(1) Recurrent spending in total (Rs million)	(2) Welfare expenditure (Rs million)	(3) (2) ÷ (1) (per cent)	(4) Government recurrent deficit (Rs million)	(5) (4) ÷ (2) (per cent)
1955/56	891.8	325.1	36.5	−40.0	12.3
1956/57	1110.0	368.0	33.2	−228.0	61.9
1957/58	1054.8	417.2	39.6	−249.0	59.7
1958/59	1280.2	511.4	40.0	−446.0	87.2
1959/60	1366.7	598.6	43.8	−448.0	81.6
1960/61	1485.5	651.2	43.8	−509.0	76.8
1961/62	1512.7	651.3	43.1	−501.0	76.9
1962/63	1520.3	666.3	43.8	−439.0	65.9
1963/64	1737.5	826.3	47.6	−519.0	62.8
1964/65	1896.3	736.4	38.8	−520.0	70.6
1965/66	2019.5	756.2	37.5	−682.0	90.2
1966/67	2129.2	702.1	33.0	−723.0	102.9
1967/68	2363.2	858.2	36.3	−850.0	99.0
1968/69	2668.4	926.2	34.7	−947.0	102.2
1969/70	3032.0	1015.6	33.5	−1150.0	113.3
1970/71	3174.2	1245.9	39.3	−1327.0	106.5
(1971/72)*	(4263.1)	(1565.2)	(36.7)	(−1707.0)	(109.0)
1973	3876.8	1395.6	36.3	−1414.0	104.2
1974	3990.3	1644.5	41.2	−1982.0	120.5

*Data for a 15 month period

of foreign aid has increased from about 2 per cent of expenditure to about 10 per cent, which is similar to the amount of government borrowing from the Central Bank. The story acquired an additional and serious dimension in about 1969–70 when the Government resorted to heavy use of short-term suppliers credits. With rising interest rates this has imposed an ever increasing burden on finances, and it was estimated that interest payments in 1974 would total over Rs 600 million. This is three times as great as the corresponding total for 1968/69 and equal to about 80 per cent of the food subsidy bill.

As one response to this deteriorating situation, cuts in the food subsidy were implemented in October 1973.* However, as already noted, these have not caused any net reduction in the Government's food bill because of the sharp rises in the import prices of several basic foodstuffs which occurred at about the same time. Unfortunately and inevitably the cuts in rationed food, combined with the sharp price rises of many non-rationed items, have severely affected the real living standards of most working-class families: it is quite clear that money-wage increases have not been large enough to compensate. So, for perhaps the first time since the war, malnutrition has emerged as a problem for Sri Lanka, especially in the estates sector.†

*The free rice ration was reduced from 2 lbs a head per week to 1 lb; wheat flour was rationed and the price increased by 50 per cent; and a sugar ration was also reduced.

†See UK Department of Trade (1975).

2 The employment problem

Reference has already been made to the effect of the post-war health programme on the rate of population increase. This, combined with the slow growth of output during substantial parts of the period has led to a severe and worsening problem of open and disguised unemployment. The high level of expenditures on education have compounded this problem by giving it a structural dimension in the sense that a severe imbalance between the supply and demand of relatively highly educated manpower is now increasingly apparent.

Although the comparability over time of different sources of information about the size of the employment is suspect,* it would seem to be indisputable that aggregate employment since 1946 has been growing far less rapidly than population; perhaps at a little over 1 per cent as compared with nearly 3 per cent for population. Even allowing for the decline in the proportion of total population in the working age groups of 10 to 64 years, a decline which obviously adds to the strain on the social services referred to above, the growth of employment has been too slow. Thus the proportion of the employed labour force to the population of working age fell from about 56 per cent in 1946 to 50 per cent in 1968,† while unemployment is currently about 800 000 or 18 per cent of the labour force.* Although there are many factors behind the inability of employment to grow in line with population, it is significant that the proportion of population engaged in agricultural activity actually rose during the period 1946–68, while the proportion of the population which could be described as urbanised barely changed.†

*For example in the 1946 Population Census the 'employed' were defined to include employers, employees, own account workers and the temporarily unemployed, but to exclude unpaid family workers and those seeking employment for the first time. In the 1953 Census, unpaid family workers were included.

†Provisional result of the 1971 Census.

*Central Bank of Ceylon, *The Determinants of Labour Force Participation in Sri Lanka*, 1973.

†Jones and Selvaratnam (1970).

The picture to emerge from all this shows an increasingly well-educated labour force, looking more and more to non-agricultural forms of employment but being faced with the marked inability of the economy to generate appropriate jobs at anything like the required rate. It was this structural imbalance in the labour market which was the main focus of the report of the World Employment Programme Comprehensive Employment Mission of 1971.* The imbalance has several aspects and arises 'because the opportunities for additional work occur at the wrong season or in the wrong place, require special skills compared with what the various types of labour can offer, or carry lower income status than people will accept.'†

*ILO (1971).

†*op. cit.*, p. 21.

The increasing educational level of the labour force is shown in the following table adapted from the mission report. Comparing the first two and the last columns, one can clearly see that the proportion experiencing higher levels of educational attainment has been increasing during the last twenty years. Table 2.3, also abstracted from the same report, indicates the enormity of the open unemployment among the young and its correlation with higher levels of educational achievement (defined here as 'O' level or better). This latter table clearly shows that unemployment rates among the lower age groups are very much larger for those with higher educational qualifications; and considerably so for females in comparison with males. A further tendency, not brought out in this table, is for the unemployment rates of the well qualified to be greater in rural than in urban areas.

The mission report also draws attention to the special problem of the labour force on the tea and rubber estates. Ever since the introduction of plantation agriculture into Sri Lanka in the middle of the nineteenth century, the labour demand in this sector of the economy has been largely met by the importation of migrant labour from southern India. Although there have been reverse flows,

Table 2.2 *Distribution of the non-estate labour force by education and age, 1969/70 (per cent)*

Education \ Age group	15–24	25–34	35–44	45–54	55–59
No schooling	5.1	5.9	15.0	14.6	18.6
Primary, grades 1–5	31.3	32.0	40.8	45.1	46.8
Middle, grades 6–10	45.6	39.6	32.3	30.8	27.6
Passed 'O' level	16.5	19.3	11.0	8.9	6.4
Passed 'A' level and above	1.5	3.2	0.9	0.6	0.6
Total	100.0	100.0	100.0	100.0	100.0

Source: International Labour Office (1971)

Table 2.3 *Those searching for work by age and sex, with or without GCE 'O' level qualifications, as percentage of active labour force*

Age group	Males		Females		Total	
	No 'O' levels	'O' level +	No 'O' levels	'O' level +	No 'O' levels	'O' level +
15–19	39	81	34	98	38	92
20–24	23	54	32	76	25	64
25–34	5	8	10	38	6	17
35–44	1	5	4	8	1	–
45–54	1	–	2	–	1	–
55–59	–	–	8	–	1	–
Total	11	21	16	53	12	32

Source: International Labour Office (1971)

the number of southern Indian estate workers in Sri Lanka exceeded 600 000 by 1945 and now totals about 680 000. There are severe restrictions on the mobility of these workers, imposed not only by language difficulties but also by a denial of permits to work outside the estates and ineligibility for public sector employment. These difficulties have a background in ambiguities over nationality. When given the opportunity to indicate nationality preference, the estate families were split as between those choosing Indian nationality and those choosing Sri Lankan. Moreover, checking the qualifications of many individuals for Sri Lankan nationality has proved to be a major administrative problem. Meanwhile there is a constructive dialogue between the Governments of India and Sri Lanka being conducted in what, for both of them, are difficult circumstances. These include the fact that while the estate population has been growing recently at about 2 per cent per annum the output of the plantation sector has been sluggish, so that unemployment among estate workers has inevitably risen rapidly. Open unemployment among estate workers is now at a level in excess of 50 000 persons, of whom 90 per cent are aged between 15 and 19 years. In addition, it is clear that the austerity of the past few years has affected the estates population particularly badly. In the absence of integration of parts of this population into the rest of the economy, or of migration back to southern India, these economic problems seem virtually intractable.

There are two further aspects of the employment position in Sri Lanka which deserve mention and which also make the problem less tractable. First, a good deal of unemployment would appear to be voluntary in the sense that vacancies do exist in some occupations in sufficient numbers to absorb part of the unemployment. Probably the most important reason for this is that the aspirations of those out of work, especially the young, cause them to eschew many of the jobs which are available as being inadequate in terms of the income, the security, the conditions of work and the status which those jobs offer. Thus in the Labour Force Survey of 1968, while 68 per cent of those unemployed between the ages of 15 and 24 who did not have the 'O' level qualifications were willing to take any employment, the corresponding proportion of those with 'O' levels was only 21 per cent.* Secondly, the generous provision of social welfare benefits has the effect of lowering the search costs of those who are out of a job but seeking one. Thus the length of time for which the out-of-work are prepared to wait for the right job to appear can often be quite long, given that the potential gain, net of search costs, is large. This gain is further affected by the very low incomes associated with the jobs which are immediately available, and by the fear of accepting a 'sub-standard' occupation and then being permanently associated with it. The WEP Mission Report also suggested that the attitudes of parents to their children's employment was such as to make them willing to carry part of the cost of job search. This being the case the unemployment rates will tend to be higher among children of higher income families. But, by the same token, these same children will have a greater possibility of ultimately obtaining the more remunerative jobs. In this way, income inequalities become self perpetuating.

*See International Labour Office (1971), p. 33.

The picture that emerges is one in which the Sri Lanka people are obtaining distinct benefits from the welfare programme in the form of subsidised food, good health services and universal free education. This has contributed to an increasing population among whom the national income must be shared, and also to an increase in the proportion of the population to which large welfare payments need or will need to be made. Education has exacerbated this problem by the false expectations which it has engendered and by the imbalances between the supply of, and demand for particular skills to which it has contributed.

3 The external position

The broader background to the critical economic situation of the past few years is, of course, that Sri Lanka is an example *par excellence* of an export economy heavily dependent on a limited range of agricultural export commodities.* Tea, rubber and coconut products typically account for well over 90 per cent of Sri Lanka's earnings from commodity exports and the prices and production of these three commodities are obviously of fundamental importance for the behaviour of the economy. Since the war the fortunes of the three major crops taken together have gone through three phases. The first of these was the Korean War commodity boom when the price of rubber, in particular, rose dramatically. The second, beginning in about 1955 was the steady downward trend of both tea and rubber prices. The third and last phase begins in about 1972 with significant increases in the prices of all three commodities, but more than offset by increases in import prices.

*A detailed description of the history of these and other export commodities in Sri Lanka is included in Snodgrass (1966).

The Korean War commodity boom was the main reason for the improvement of fortunes in 1950 and 1951, with the richer nations stockpiling products such as rubber which they feared would become in short supply as they had done during the Second World War. Unfortunately for Sri Lanka, by 1952 the boom was at an end and prices began to fall interrupted only by the temporary emergence of a tea boom which took prices to a peak in 1955. In many respects these booms came at an ideal time for Sri Lanka which had only been independent since 1948 and had only had a fully independent currency since 1950. It was a golden opportunity to put the economy onto a new and more diversified basis by the development of import substitutes, and to generally lessen dependence upon the three major export commodities. In the event this opportunity was not taken. Instead, import restrictions were relaxed with the result that many non-essential goods flooded in and the opportunity for building a buffer which could be used to dampen the economic effects of fluctuating commodity prices was lost.

In consequence, Sri Lanka was rather badly placed to withstand the foreign exchange difficulties of the second phase when export prices fell by over 20 per cent and import prices rose about 40 per cent, thereby causing a massive deterioration of the terms of trade. Since export volume came nowhere near to compensating for the decline in price, export earnings stagnated until 1965 as did real incomes.† During this period the structure of total demand shifted dramatically away from exports as can be seen from Table 2.4. The share of exports in GNP fell from over 34 per cent in 1959 to less than 18 per cent by 1973. As the table also shows, the corresponding adjustments in demand structure associated with this decline were somewhat erratic, with the share of capital formation, for example, falling significantly until 1964, and then rising subsequently. The main feature of the adjustment to a reduced export share is the dramatic fall in the share of imports from 37 per cent of GNP in 1959 to 19 per cent in 1973. This reflects the increasingly comprehensive gamut of measures to restrict imports; measures including import licensing introduced in 1962 and progressively made more restrictive, quota restrictions, including a virtual ban on imports of certain luxury goods (notably cars), higher tariff barriers, devaluation in 1967 and again, partially, with the introduction of a dual exchange rate, in 1968, and so on.

†The value of exports attained in 1955 was not surpassed until 1965 and the values achieved in 1966, 1967 and 1969 were all lower than the 1955 level.

While these controls have obviously been successful in restraining imports in the aggregate, they have also caused a substantial deterioration in consumption standards and, perhaps more important, by restricting the availability of intermediate inputs have often represented a major impediment to more rapid industrialisation. Thus in the decade following the introduction of import controls,

Table 2.4 *Gross national product, exports, imports and gross domestic capital formation at current factor cost prices (Rs million)*

	(1) GNP	(2) Exports	(3) Exports as % of GNP (1) ÷ (2)	(4) Gross domestic capital formation	(5) Gross domestic capital formation as % of GNP (1) ÷ (5)	(6) Imports	(7) Imports as % of GNP (1) ÷ (2)
1959	5893	2016	34.2	1113	18.9	2176	36.9
1962	6503	1971	30.3	1080	16.6	2070	31.8
1964	7291	1937	26.6	1113	15.3	2102	28.8
1967	8265	1847	22.4	1377	16.7	2106	25.5
1970	11562	2244	19.4	2555	22.1	2521	21.8
1973	15155	2716	17.9	2630	17.4	2851	18.8

Source: Ceylon, Central Bank *Annual Reports.*

manufacturing increased its share of GNP only fractionally despite the incentives associated with very much higher levels of protection. Sri Lanka, in common with many other countries in the developing world, now suffers from chronic underutilisation of manufacturing capacity as well as the delays, inefficiencies and corruption associated with a comprehensive system of administrative restrictions.

In the last phase, beginning in about 1972, there has been a significant rise in the prices of Sri Lanka's main export commodities as illustrated in Figure 2.1. Unfortunately however it has been rapidly followed by huge rises in the prices of 'essential' imports such as oil, sugar and rice which implies considerable rises in Sri Lanka's import bill so demonstrating yet again that Sri Lanka's prosperity is inextricably tied up with world commodity prices.

The ambitious programme of social welfare interacts with the balance of payments position in a number of ways. First, by depressing the incentives for

Figure 2.1a External trade, value and volume of exports (1948 = 100).

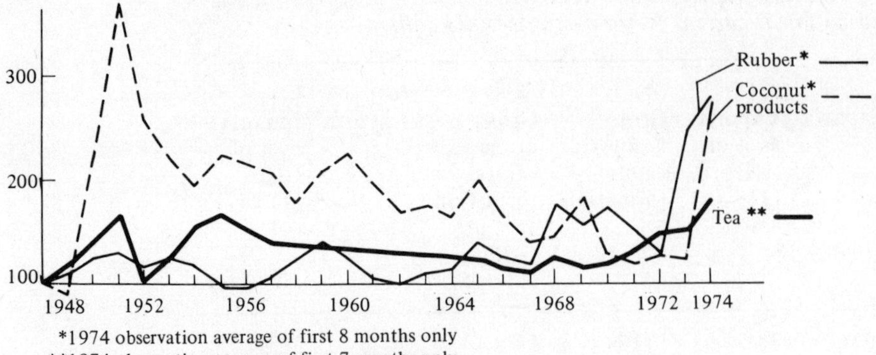

Figure 2.1b Export prices of major commodities (1948 = 100). Source: Central Bank of Ceylon, *Annual report.*

increased food production, it has contributed to the emergence of a very large import bill for basic foodstuffs. For example, Rs 1800 million was spent on imports of rice, sugar and flour in 1974; this is approximately 40 per cent of the total import bill. Secondly, by diverting investment expenditures into projects with long construction periods and low productive returns, e.g. schools, it has slowed the expansion of manufacturing output, and not least, of that part of manufacturing output such as textiles which could have substituted for some part of the high imports of basic consumer goods. This latter effect has been seriously compounded by the restrictions on industrial output forced by the need to impose severe import restrictions. Finally, by boosting real incomes, the welfare programme has generated an 'artificially' high level of demand for consumer goods which has inevitably reacted back on the balance of payments. In short, the external position has been adversely affected by both demand and supply influences stemming from the programme of social welfare.

The overall trade balance has now been severely in deficit for several years, with an especially severe deficit (over Rs 700 million) appearing in 1969. Sri Lanka now has an extremely weak foreign reserve position and has moved heavily into debt with short-term credits meeting almost half of the foreign exchange gap in the last two years for which data are available. The detailed record of the balance of payments for the past two decades is set down in Table 2.5 below. Despite the significant improvement in export earnings since 1972, the resources gap has continued to widen and, with world interest rates at a high level, the financing of this gap has proved increasingly expensive as well as problematic.

It is clear that the balance of payments position is likely to represent a serious impediment to satisfactory pursuit of full employment objects. The ILO World Employment Programme Mission estimated that a full employment target for 1985 would require employment growth of 3.5 per cent per annum till 1985. Assuming a 2.5 per cent growth of productivity, this implies a growth rate of output of 6.0 per cent which was reckoned to imply a growth rate of imports of between 4.0 and 4.5 per cent per annum and total imports in 1985 of Rs 5000 million (at 1968 prices).* The calculation then proceeded as given below.

If one allows for the change in world prices away from 1968 levels then the residual requirement for non-traditional exports is increased both by the oil-price increases (raising imports in current prices), and the poor prospects for the world tea price.† It seems probable that full employment combined with external

*We pass over the point that these calculations can only be properly carried out using the sort of disaggregation which we have attempted. These readily reveal that the output growth required by a given growth of employment depends critically on where the employment growth is expected to occur.

†Recent estimates suggest that tea exports of Rs 1500 in 1968 current prices could only be achieved given the most optimistic assumptions about the world demand and supply position.

	Rs million
Exports required to give small surplus in 1985	5100
Traditional exports (assuming maximum probable fall in their share from 90 percent to 70 percent) of which*	3570
Coconuts = 1000 +	
Rubber = 1000 +	
Required tea exports = 1500 maximum	
Balance = Required non-traditional exports (as compared with approximately 250 in 1968)	1530

*See ILO (1971), p. 63.

Table 2.5 *Balance of payments, 1950–73 (Rs million)*

Year	Trade balance (i)	Total goods and services (ii)	Total current account (iii)	Non-monetary capital* (iv)	Basic balance (iii) + (iv)
1950	239	206	137	−22	+115
1951	238	116	89	−41	+48
1952	−397	−342	−446	25	−421
1953	−138	−113	−158	−39	−197
1954	340	349	306	21	+327
1955	415	384	323	−49	+274
1956	196	137	82	−11	+71
1957	−95	−156	−195	−15	−210
1958	−89	−130	−153	19	−134
1959	−185	−196	−208	21	−187
1960	−210	−242	−220	15	−205
1961	−87	−105	−94	37	−57
1962	−143	−146	−140	37	−103
1963	−161	−182	−168	84	−84
1964	−193	−200	−160	−1	−161
1965	−13	18	59	16	+75
1966	−344	−327	−290	119	−171
1967	−335	−310	−288	168	−120
1968	−380	−370	−355	217	−142
1969	−746	−836	−797	265	−532
1970	−316	−420	−350	180	−170
1971	−287	−301	−216	380	+166
1972	−255	−270	−196	255	+59
1973	−299	−246	−161	184	+23
1974	−1227	−1151	−899	248	−651

*Non-monetary capital = Direct investment and other private investment (long and short) + central government loans received.
n.b. excludes central government short-term liabilities.
Source: Ceylon, Central Bank, *Annual Report.*

balance would require something like a tenfold expansion of non-traditional exports by 1980.

The external payments position has necessitated a number of changes in Sri Lanka's exchange rate regime in recent years. From 1949, when the Ceylonese rupee became an independent currency, until November 1967, the rupee was fixed in terms of sterling at the rate of £1 to Rs 13.3. Following the UK devaluation in 1967, the rupee devalued by 20 per cent which implied an effective devaluation against sterling of 7 per cent. May 1968 saw the introduction of Foreign Exchange Entitlement Certificates (FEECs), which essentially impose a dual exchange rate system designed as an incentive to non-traditional exporters. Under this system the official rate was left unchanged but the FEEC rate which was applicable to a clearly defined range of transactions was set at 44 per cent lower (raised to 55 per cent in 1969). In November 1971, at the time of the Smithsonian agreement, the sterling par value of the rupee was abandoned and the rate was pegged to the dollar, a move which implied some appreciation against sterling. However, when the pound sterling began to float in June 1972, it was decided that the rupee should once again be pegged to sterling, but now at a rate of £1 to Rs 15.6. This position has remained broadly unchanged except that the FEEC rate was increased to 65 per cent in November 1972.

4 Industrialisation

Despite the constraints on faster industrial development caused by a restricted availability of intermediate inputs, there was in fact some considerable expansion of industrial capacity in the period following the tightening of import restrictions at the end of the 1950s. Thus more than 400 new industrial firms were established in the private sector between 1961 and 1963, and industrial employment rose by some 30 per cent. There are now nearly 2000 industrial firms in the private sector and these employ about 75 000 persons, or about 5 per cent of total employment. Well over half of all firms are small-scale units employing less than 100 workers and the contribution to total production of the largest 10 per cent of firms is something of the order of 85 per cent.

From the outset during the Second World War Sri Lanka's industrialisation has involved a substantial role for the public sector, especially in those areas where the scale of investment involved was thought to be too large to be dealt with by the private sector. Factories were set up during the war to manufacture plywood, leather, ceramics, glass and a number of other products, some of which ceased production at the end of the war when increased competition demonstrated their inherent lack of viability. Cement and paper factories were established in the early 1950s and in the mid 1950s powers were taken to establish state enterprises as semi-autonomous corporations. By 1963 there were fourteen state industrial corporations in operation and this number had increased to twenty-one by 1967 and to twenty-five by 1972.

In line with the basic reason for establishing state corporations, the government has granted monopoly status to those such as cement, tyres and steel – where the scale of investment required is particularly large. In other cases such as textiles, leather and ceramics, the state corporation coexists and competes with private enterprises. Though the performances of many of the state enterprises has been much criticised,* the majority are now profitable (although often with a very low rate of return on capital), and it is clear that they are a permanent feature of the country's institutional arrangements. Their output is currently about Rs 2000 million, or well over half of private manufacturing output and they employ about 48 000 people.

*See Karunatilake (1971), Chapter 9, for example.

The role of the foreign investor in the industrialisation process is subject to several constraints which were defined in detail in a 1966 white paper.† Broadly, foreign investment was welcomed, would be free from any form of expropriation or discriminatory treatment, and would qualify for various tax concessions. However, a preference was stated for joint venture arrangements involving some local capital or, where a scheme was initially financed entirely from overseas sources,

†Ceylon Ministry of Planning and Economic Affairs, (1966).

for the progressive transfer of some part of the capital to local interests. The screening of applications from would-be foreign investors is conducted by the inter-ministerial Foreign Investment Approvals Committee which appears to pay particular attention to the employment and export potential of applicants and to the scope for using local raw materials. It is now anticipated, following the 1976 Budget Speech of Mr Felix Dias Bandaranaike, that a new Foreign Investment Guarantee Law will be drafted which will be rather more liberal than that which currently exists.

5 Data availability and organisation in Sri Lanka

From many points of view Sri Lanka has cause to be proud of the statistical documentation of economic and social phenomena which she has managed to build up over the years. In the extremely thorough statistical appendix to his own book on the country, Professor Snodgrass even goes so far as to say:* 'The body of economic statistics available for Ceylon must certainly rank as one of the most complete and accurate in the world for a country of such low per capita income.' Specially worthy of mention is the fact that more or less consistent National Accounts data are available back to 1945, and that trade data on the main agricultural commodities are available from as early as 1860.

*Snodgrass (1966), p. 300.

And yet there are many aspects of statistical development in Sri Lanka in the past two decades which give cause for concern and there is little doubt that Sri Lanka gives a good example of many of the statistical problems discussed more generally in the previous chapter. In particular, a good many of the available statistics are not readily usable, for one reason or another, in planning or policy formulation. Many data which are published are clearly inconsistent with other published data. In several cases two or more sets of data relating to the same phenomenon give strikingly different results, there are serious gaps in the availability of data and substantial delays in their production.

The situation in relation to the National Accounts is a major example of some of these points and therefore worth describing. In 1952, the director of the Department of Census and Statistics instituted a system of national accounts based mainly on his own ideas but influenced also by an early set of accounts produced by B.B. Das Gupta. This system, which was subsequently applied to all years back to 1947, has been used with certain modifications ever since with the results being published in the annual *Statistical Abstract of Ceylon*.† However, a problem arose in 1958 when the Central Bank began to discharge its statutory obligation of preparing an economic review of the previous year. It soon became clear that the national accounts produced by the Department of Census and Statistics became available far too late to be usable for this purpose and, in addition, were insufficiently detailed in many respects. Eventually the Central Bank began to produce its own estimates and publish them in the *Central Bank Report*. In general, the Central Bank estimates are better in that they have been quicker to remove the more significant weaknesses of the earlier system, they incorporate more sectoral detail and are available more quickly. However, for the user of statistics, the coexistence of two sets of national accounts data is a source of considerable confusion, not least because the two estimates often display significantly different trends from one year to the next. It is not possible to fully document the discrepancies between the two sets of data but Tables 2.6 and 2.7 below give the flavour of the problem.

†Though it is noteworthy that these results are published in the UN *Yearbook of National Account Statistics*, long before they appear in the Ceylon Department of Census and Statistics *Statistical Abstract*.

The problem is compounded by the availability of yet more estimates from the Ministry of Planning and Economic Affairs, prepared in connection with plan

Table 2.6 *Gross national product at current factor cost (Rs million)*

	1963	1964	1965	1966	1967	1968	1969	1970	1971
DCS estimate	6563	6940	7082	7317	7842	9363			
Central bank estimate	6797	7291	7484	7705	8265	7876	10748	11618	11828
Discrepancy (%)	3.6	5.1	5.3	5.4	5.5				

Table 2.7 *Value added by sector, 1968 (Rs million)*

	(1) Central Bank Estimate	(2) DCS Estimate	Excess of (2) over (1) %
Agriculture, forestry, hunting and fishing	3691	3877	5.0
Mining and quarrying	47	69	46.8
Manufacturing	1121	1086	−3.1
Construction	522	625	19.7
Electricity, gas, water	16	53	231.3
Transport, storage and communications	939	936	0.3
Wholesale and retail trade	1421	1208	−15.0
Banking, insurance and real estate	139	139	–
Ownership of dwellings	333	259	−22.2
Public administration and defence	474	475	0.2
Services	1227	1264	3.0
Total gross domestic product	9930	9991	0.6

formulation. The waste of resources and confusion associated with this duplication of work is considerable and the case for an integration of effort is overwhelming.*

Similar problems of duplication apply in relation to several other important categories of economic data, notably data on trade, manufacturing output and employment. Trade statistics are produced both by the Customs Department (which publishes information both monthly and annually), and by the Balance of Payments Division of the Central Bank which bases its estimates on the records of actual payments and receipts. The discrepancies between these two sources of data are considerable as Table 2.8 clearly indicates, and are too large to be explained solely by lags in payment or receipt of goods. And again the problem is compounded by data from a third source, since the Food Commissioner produces estimates of imports of rice, flour and sugar which do not agree with the other two sources. For example, in 1970 the Food Commissioner recorded 11 per cent more rice, 14 per cent less flour and 11 per cent less sugar than the Customs Department.

*This case has been made in some detail by a subgroup of the World Employment Programme Mission. See ILO (1971a).

Table 2.8 *Merchandise imports (c.i.f.), 1958–68 (Rs million)*

	(1) Customs Department estimate	(2) Central Bank estimate	Excess of (2) over (1) %
1958	1717	1713	–0.2
1959	2005	1958	–2.3
1960	1960	2006	2.4
1961	1703	1794	5.3
1962	1660	1906	14.8
1963	1490	1869	25.4
1964	1975	1960	–0.7
1965	1474	1922	30.4
1966	2028	2018	–0.5
1967	1738	1985	14.2
1968	2173	2341	7.7

Source: *Statistical Abstract of Ceylon*, various years, but for example, 1970, Table 163; and *Central Bank of Ceylon Report*, 1971, Table 47.

In the field of industrial statistics, more or less independent estimates are produced by the Department of Census and Statistics, the Central Bank and the Ministry of Industries. However, since neither the definitions nor the sampling frames of the various surveys used to generate these estimates are consistent, they are difficult to compare, and the discrepancies in the results are large. An indication of the orders of magnitude of these discrepancies is shown in Table 2.9 below.

As a final example of the duplication of effort, we can note that separate

Table 2.9 *Industrial output in selected industries, 1970 (Rs million)*

	(1) Ministry of Industries	(2) Central Bank estimate	Excess of (1) over (2) %
Food, beverages and tobacco	629	685	8.9
Spinning, weaving and finishing of textiles	137	173	26.3
Manufacture of wood	23	21	–8.7
Manufacture of paper products	60	65	8.3
Petroleum and coal products	198	191	–3.5
Chemical products	148	159	7.4
Iron and steel basic industries	51	39	–24.5
Electrical machinery	62	88	41.9
Other machinery	126	71	–43.6
Other metal products	80	97	21.3

Source: Central Bank, *Annual Report*, 1971, Table II(b)2; and Ministry of Industries, *Statistics of Industrial Production*, 1968–70 (mimeographed).

employment data are published by the Department of Census and Statistics, the Central Bank and the Department of Labour. In this area, as in the others mentioned above, there is a degree of cooperation in data collection between the agencies involved but this stops far short of the use of common sampling frames and definitions, and comparison of the different results is extremely difficult.

As well as those criticisms relating to inconsistencies between different data sources and duplication of effort, there are many other criticisms which can and have been levied at statistical organisation in Sri Lanka. First of all there is the familiar problem of gaps in the data; gaps which are especially serious in the areas of agricultural land use, small-scale industry, construction and other forms of investment. Secondly, statistical work in Sri Lanka, as in many other countries, can be criticised for its compartmentalisation of individual data sets and its failure to knit these together into a comprehensive and consistent macro framework. Such an integration of presently unrelated statistics would be a powerful influence for the acceptance of a standard set of definitions by different agencies, and would make the data far more valuable from a user's point of view. However, this improvement will not take place autonomously: there are after all some good historical reasons for individual agencies having to establish their own initiatives in data collection. Some administrative action is therefore required to bring about the greater coordination of data.

This need was recognised by the Statistical Policy Group of the WEP Mission which, among other things, recommended a degree of centralisation of statistical collection at the DCS, the maintenance of central mailing lists or registers of statistical units to be used by all data collecting agencies, DCS scrutiny of all statistical questionnaires before issuance and so on.* If implemented, these recommendations would significantly ease the task of preparing the type of data framework described in the rest of this volume, as well as increasing its reliability at a number of crucial points. Meanwhile, the presence of gaps and inconsistencies in the economic data – not only of Sri Lanka but of many other developing countries as well – provides the rationale and justification for the experiments in data manipulation which are fully documented in the Statistical Appendix to the present volume.

*See ILO (1971a) for detailed recommendations by the group.

6 Summary and conclusions

Sri Lanka's record of social progress during the post-war years has been extremely impressive and has undoubtedly contributed to a quality of life for the average citizen which is better than that which can be found in countries at a comparable stage of development. However, the social welfare programme has contributed to the emergence of a number of increasingly severe economic problems, particularly in the sphere of government finance and the balance of payments. This fact combined with world economic conditions, and especially rising food prices and interest rates, has forced a contraction in the scale of government welfare payments in the past two years and severe cuts in living standards. The programme of food subsidisation, and the heavy protectionism deemed necessary as a result of the serious balance of payments position have contributed to the disappointing rate of expansion of food production and industrial output respectively. In turn, the sluggishness of output in conjunction with a large-scale educational programme have caused a serious and worsening employment problem.

One can anticipate that the next few years must see significant changes in many aspects of Sri Lankan economic policy. This will require both a thorough assessment of the manner in which existing policies have interacted with the obvious problems of the moment, as well as some analysis of the likely impact of new policies on these problems. While statistical material exists in Sri Lanka to facilitate this analysis, its use involves numerous problems, not least of inconsistencies between different sources and inadequate documentation of the links between the various dimensions of the economic problem. This volume addresses itself to the problem of improving this statistical information system with a view to easing the task of analysis of policy choices which is so clearly necessary.

3

An overview of the data scheme and some problems of classification

1 Introduction

Having discussed the background to our work at some length, the statistical information system which we have compiled for Sri Lanka is now introduced in the present chapter. The chapter is in five sections following this introduction. In the next section we begin to define our data framework, showing explicitly how it relates to standard national income information, and to inter-industry and other transactions of a 'transfer' nature. This discussion begins with a closed economy, and is then extended to cover trade and other external transactions. At this point we arrive at a social accounting matrix (SAM) presentation of data which bears a close relationship to the aggregated UN SNA,* except for some refocusing of emphasis on the distributional aspects of the system.†

*See UNSO (1968).

†This system is in fact quite general in the sense that by appropriate re-arrangement of rows and columns and disaggregation, it could yield most of the 'alternatives' to the SNA which have been mooted including, for example, the Seers' modified input–output system which has been used in Zambia, Ghana and elsewhere.

Then in Section 3, we consider some of the most important deficiencies of our aggregate system, and in Section 4 introduce a quantified version of this aggregate system for Sri Lanka. Section 5 concerns itself with the crucial issue of appropriate disaggregation and classification, paying particular attention to the compromises between the 'ideal' and the 'practically possible' which were necessary in the Sri Lankan context. It is at this point where adherence to general prescriptions has to end and statistical work must proceed with a clear view about those issues which are likely to be in the arena of debate. We therefore regard this as a crucial, and potentially contentious part of our work. Finally, in Section 6, we present a partially disaggregated data system for Sri Lanka. As noted earlier, the full detail about the compilation of our fully disaggregated system is relegated to Statistical Appendices.

2 The basic structure

Historically the design of a statistical information system as a social accounting matrix has evolved from the combination of two ideas; the matrix presentation of national income accounts, reflecting the Keynesian model of the market for goods and services, and the input–output model of the structural interdependence of production in the economy. The Keynesian model divides economic activity into three categories: production; income and expenditure; and accumulation. Table 3.1 shows these aspects of a *closed* economy in a simple social accounting matrix (SAM) framework which serves to illustrate two basic rules for understanding such matrices. These are

(i) for every row there is a corresponding column and the system is complete only if the corresponding row and column totals are identical;

Table 3.1 *An aggregated social-accounting matrix (SAM)*

			Production accounts		Institutions accounts		
			Production activities 1	Factors of production 2	Current 3	Capital 4	Total (excluding transfers)
1	Production accounts	Production activities	*	0	Consumption expenditure	Investment expenditure	Final demand
2	Production accounts	Factors of production	Value added	0	0	0	National product
3	Institutions accounts	Current	0	Factor payments	*	0	National income
4	Institutions accounts	Capital	0	0	Savings	*	Savings
5		Total (excluding transfers)	Domestic product	National income	National expendi-	Investment	

(ii) every entry is a receipt when read in its row context and an expenditure from the point of view of its column. The description of social accounting matrices as single entry accounts derives from this rule.

In Table 3.1 the production accounts are divided as between the accounts of production activities, which generate value added; and factors of production, which provide primary services employed by production activities. Column 1 of the table shows the cost structure of production activities. The first element is shown as an asterisk. It represents money flows from production activities to production activities. It is therefore a transfer payment between production activities and as such does not enter into national income. The second item in the column is value added by production activities, which goes as a payment to the factors of production, i.e. to capital, labour and other resources. Production activities have no transactions with institutions as such, so all other items in the column are zero. The column total (excluding transfer payments) is therefore the sum of value added in production activities, i.e. the domestic product.

The second row of Table 3.1 shows that value added is the sole source of income of the factors of production. The second column shows how this is paid out: it goes to the current account of institutions, i.e. to households, companies and government. Institutions are defined as having the legal right of ownership. Accordingly only they can accumulate and only they can provide the services of factors of production. Since they provide the factor services, they receive value added in the form of factor payments, i.e. wages, salaries, rent and profit.

Column 3 shows how institutions spend the national income. For the most part they buy goods and services provided by production activities for consumption. What they don't spend in this way by definition they save, subject only to the complication of transfers between them (again shown as an asterisk) which we ignore in national accounts because they net out to zero.

Finally, because institutions are the only bodies with the legal right of ownership, only they can save and accumulate. There may be capital transfers between them (known as flow-of-funds), but these net to zero. Total savings must be spent, therefore, on capital goods. Thus, in row and column 4 savings equal investment expenditure, which represents a further source of income for the production activities which provide the capital goods.

In contrast with the national income accounts, the input–output model of the structural interdependence of production in an economy has an information system such as that shown in Table 3.2, which is again restricted to the simple case of a closed economy. As is immediately obvious from the table, it is not a regular (square) SAM format but rather an inverted 'L' shape concerned only with two alternative ways of accounting for the gross outputs of production activities. From the revenue, or demand, point of view and therefore reading across the row, gross output comes from inter-industry transactions and final demand. The latter is simply consumption and investment expenditure while the former is the set of transfer payments between production activities which were ignored in the SAM presentation of Table 3.1. Accordingly the information in the row of Table 3.2 is the same as that in row 1 of Table 3.1 except that the inter-industry transfers are no longer omitted. The column of Table 3.2 has exactly the same relationship with the first column of Table 3.1. It follows at once that the two information systems can be combined by including inter-industry transfers in Table 3.1. Because these lie on a diagonal of Table 3.1 they do not upset the balance of rows and columns in that table. These same remarks apply equally to other transfers so that we may generalise Table 3.1 further by making both current and capital transfers between institutions explicit in the table as well as transfers between production activities. This leads to the SAM format in Table 3.3 which, like Table 3.1, has the property that each row sum is the same as the corresponding column sum.

It is obvious that Table 3.3 contains more information than Table 3.1. The question is whether this information is useful. The answer is 'no' if we are interested only in national income because in that context the inter-industry and inter-institutional transfers net out. However, input–output analysis is not directed towards identifying the size of aggregates but is concerned with the relative size and interdependence of different sorts of production: it helps to answer questions posed at the disaggregated level, not the aggregate level. For example, it asks what must be the structure of production in relation to a given

Table 3.2 *An aggregated input–output system*

	Production	Final demand	Total
Production	Inter-industry transactions	Consumption plus investment	Gross outputs
Factors of production	Value added		
Total	Gross outputs		

Table 3.3 *An aggregated social-accounting matrix embracing input–output transactions*

			Production accounts		Institutions accounts	
			Production activities 1	Factors of production 2	Current 3	Capital 4
1	Production accounts	Production activities	Inter-industry transactions	0	Consumption expenditure	Investment expenditure
2		Factors of production	Value added	0	0	0
3	Institutions accounts	Current	0	Factor payments	Current transfers	0
4		Capital	0	0	Savings	Capital transfers

structure of final demand, and what will be the pattern of prices given the primary (or value-added) costs of each production activity. Similarly, current transfers between institutions give information on their relative incomes, while capital transfers reflect the structure of savings and investment. These structural/distributional questions are irrelevant to a concern for national income aggregates. However, they are obviously of great interest from the point of view of understanding how any economy works. Hence the extra information in Table 3.3 is of considerable value.

Just how much more is learned by adoption of a SAM framework in which transfers appear explicitly will depend crucially on the systems of classification and disaggregation which are employed. Thus inter-industry transactions give details of the dependence of one industry on another for its raw materials. This will yield a very crude picture of interdependence if only three production activities, say, Agriculture, Industry and Services are distinguished. But even this is better than no disaggregation at all. At the inter-industry level it would at least tell us the extent to which industry in an economy processes domestic agricultural output and hence something about the linkages in the economy. In the context of Table 3.3 it would also mean that the generation of value added by sector of origin would be shown.

The fifth section of this chapter discusses the disaggregations and classifications adopted in our Sri Lanka work and the reasons for them. Meanwhile, it can be noted that the issues involved in choice of classifications for the different accounts in Table 3.3 are not entirely separable. For example, the disaggregation of factors of production interacts with that for production activities in row 2, column 1. If there are x factors and y activities, then the entry 'value added' must in fact be interpreted as an $x \times y$ table (or sub-matrix) showing how much income each factor gets from each activity. The richness of this detail from the point of view of policy analysis will depend on the insights into factor markets which can be obtained by suitable choice of the respective x- and y-classifications. Crucial from this point of view is the classification of institutions which is adopted. The view of income distribution which is obtained from Table 3.3 is defined by the relative incomes of the different sub-categories of institutions which are distinguished in any empirical study. It is the interaction of this disaggregation of institutions with other disaggregations which provides our basis for analysing the causes and effects of inequality.

A data framework such as that defined above as Table 3.3 underlies most of the macroeconomic information systems which have been devised since the war, including the SNA, and is the basis of our own work. However, for our purposes it is lacking on two counts, both of which relate to the way in which the information is arranged, and therefore to its psychological impact, rather than to the actual information content. The first unsatisfactory aspect of Table 3.3 is that it emphasises production rather than incomes and income distribution. While granting that the production activities of an economy are its engine room, it does not necessarily follow that these should be given the limelight in the display of a picture of the economy. On the contrary, there is every reason to make prominent in the display the things in which we are most interested: specifically, the way in which the results of economic activity are distributed. The engine room should be available for inspection, but at least some will not wish to be exposed to it and remain content simply to know that it is there. The second respect in which Table 3.3 is unsatisfactory is that for all its technical elegance it is something of a mess. There is no pattern to its zero and non-zero entries and the sense that economists feel of a cascade of transactions making up the circular flow of money and resources is not captured. Table 3.4 is an attempt to overcome these aesthetic objections by rearrangement of rows and columns and the inclusion of income receipts by different types of factors, and then by institutions, in the primary position in the matrix at the top left-hand corner.

A point to note about Table 3.4 is that the format is much more nearly symmetric than Table 3.3. In particular the bottom right-hand square (i.e., ignoring row 1 and column 1) is both symmetric and triangular with all the transfers of the economy along its diagonal. Indeed the format would be completely symmetric if we placed the first row 'Factors of Production' at the end after 'Production Activities' but left the column order unchanged.*

*In fact the row 'Factors of production' belongs equally in either location because this is the essence of the circular flow of payments.

So far the discussion has been entirely in terms of a closed economy but it is reasonably easy to extend the framework of Table 3.4 to embrace the added complexities of an open economy. Conceptually it would be possible to repeat the matrix shown in Table 3.4 a further three times so as to give the picture which, in its most aggregated form is shown in Table 3.5. Each of the four blocks of Table 3.5 could contain the same detail as shown in Table 3.4. However, since this complete picture would be extremely demanding on data and would show many transactions of limited relevance from the point of view of the study of an individual economy, it is normal to suppress many aspects of it. In particular, the whole of the south-east quadrant would normally be omitted, factor payments between Domestic and Rest of the world sectors would often be shown on a net basis, and the columns of the north-east matrix and the rows of the south-west matrix would often be aggregated together. These procedures yield a SAM having the appearance of Table 3.6.

It is a matrix in the form of Table 3.6 which we have tried to complete for Sri Lanka and so it is as well to make sure that the meaning of each row and column

Table 3.4 *A rearrangement of the social-accounting matrix of Table 3.3*

			Factors of production	Institutions accounts		Production activities	Totals
				Current	Capital		
			1	2	3	4	5
1	Factors of production		0	0	0	Value added	Factor incomes
2	Institutions accounts	Current	Factor payments	Current transfers	0	0	Institutions incomes
3	Institutions accounts	Capital	0	Savings	Capital transfers	0	Acquisition of funds
4	Production activities		0	Consumption Expenditure	Investment Expenditure	Inter-industry Transactions	Gross outputs
5	Totals		Factor incomes	Institutions Expenditures	Allocation of funds	Gross outputs	

Table 3.5 *A highly aggregated social-accounting matrix for an open economy*

Domestic sector receipts from domestic sectors	Domestic sector receipts from rest of world
Rest of world receipts from domestic sectors	Rest of world receipts from rest of world

n.b. All receipts are also expenditures when read in the context of their respective columns rather than that of their rows.

is quite clear. This is as follows:

Row 1 Factors of production receive incomes from the various production activities for provision of factor services. Thus at the intersection of row 1 with column 5 we have the distribution of income between factors. Depending on the disaggregation of factors which is adopted this will show the income of labour (of different kinds), i.e., wages, profits as a return on capital, and rental incomes of natural resources (such as land and mineral rights); and, at the intersection with column 4, its dependence on the structure of production. The intersection with column 6 shows the factor incomes received from abroad.

Col. 1 The factor incomes are paid out to the providers of factor services. For

Table 3.6 *An aggregated social-accounting matrix for an open economy*

		(1)	(2) Institutions accounts	(3)	(4)	(5)	(6)	(7)
		Factors of production	Current a/c	Capital a/c	Production activities	Total domestic = 1+2+3+4	Rest of world	Grand total = 5+6
(1)	Factors of production	0	0	0	Value added payments to factors	Allocation of GDP by factors	Net factor income received from abroad	Incomes of the factors of production
(2)	Institutions accounts: Current	Allocation of factorial incomes to institutions	Current domestic transfers	0	0	Incomes of domestic institutions before transfers	Net non-factor income from abroad	Incomes of domestic institutions after foreign transfers
(3)	Institutions accounts: Capital	0	Savings	Capital domestic transfers	0	Aggregate domestic savings	Net capital received from abroad	Aggregate savings
(4)	Production activities	0	Consumer expenditure on domestically produced goods	Investment expenditure on domestically produced goods	Inter-industry transactions	Aggregate domestic demand	Exports	Aggregate demand = gross outputs
(5)	Total domestic = 1+2+3+4	Incomes of the factors of production	Domestic expenditure of income by institutions	Investment expenditure on domestically produced goods	Expenditures by activities on domestic goods and services	–	Total foreign exchange	–
(6)	Rest of world	0	Imports of consumer goods	Imports of capital goods	Imports of intermediate goods	Imports	–	Imports
(7)	Grand total	Incomes of the factors of production	Incomes of domestic institutions after foreign transfers	Aggregate investment	Total costs = gross outputs	–	Total foreign exchange receipts	–

example, agricultural wages would go to rural households if they are one of the sub-groups in the classification of institutions. Similarly industrial wages will go to urban households, and rental incomes to those institutions which own natural resources. The institution Government receives the profits of state owned corporations, etc.

Row 2 The primary source of income for institutions is from factor services, as explained above. In addition, there are transfers between them: taxes paid to government; profits distributed by companies to shareholders (households); subsidies paid out by government to the poor and needy. Aggregating all sources of income in the row we get the total income of each institution, and in particular the personal income distribution between different types of household. The sub-total in column 5 shows the same distribution but excluding factor incomes from abroad.

Col. 2 Institutions pay out some of their incomes as transfers as just discussed in relation to row 2. For the rest they either save their income or spend it on consumer goods which can be either domestically produced or imported. The savings represent a transfer to their capital account. Consumption of domestically produced goods implies a demand on production activities which receive revenue in exchange for consumer goods.

Row 3 Institutions acquire capital funds in the first instance from their own savings. Beyond this there is a transfer or flow of funds between them through the savings institutions and capital markets. The total of funds available to the economy as a whole is increased by capital receipts from the Rest of the world at the intersection with column 6.

Col. 3 The funds acquired by each institution are in part transferred to other institutions as described above. Beyond this they are spent on capital goods supplied either by domestic production activities or by imports.

Row 4 Production activities receive money from sale of consumer goods, capital goods, and exports. They also receive revenue from sales to other production activities of intermediate goods. Together these revenues make up the total sales or gross outputs of each of the production activities, i.e. of agriculture, industry, trade, transport, etc.

Col. 4 The sales revenue of each production activity is taken up in part by purchases of raw materials which may be either domestically produced or imported. The remainder of production costs takes the form of value added which is paid out to the factors of production in the form of wages to different types of labour, as rents on land and other natural resources, and as profits as the reward of capital.

Row 6 The total imports into the economy are allocated between the three broad categories of use, namely final consumption, capital formation and further use in production.

Col. 6 The total receipts from the rest of the world are detailed with the major item receipts from exports of goods and non-factor services, shown at the intersection of column 6 and row 4.

3 Some outstanding issues

Before turning to numerical results for Sri Lanka, there are three aspects of the basic structure set out above which we would hope to improve upon in subsequent work. First, the information system is defined entirely in *flow* terms and gives no recognition to *stock* concepts, unlike the SNA which does do this explicitly. Thus, while our structure is able to indicate the nature of the distribution of income and some of its determinants through the detailed classifications which are adopted, it conveys no information about the distribution of asset ownership or wealth except insofar as the latter underlies some of the flows, particularly those from factors to institutions shown in row 2, column 1. This is a major limitation since differences between, say, rural and urban households in levels of wealth are presumably a major influence upon the differences in income which they receive in any particular period. This failure to treat the wealth explicitly inevitably masks consideration of policies which would attack an unacceptable income distribution by the redistribution of assets. Equally, it circumscribes analysis of the macro implications of policies or other developments in the economy, which operate by way of influencing the ownership of, or returns on, particular types of wealth. To give but one example, if we wished to examine the effects on the production structure, and therefore on factor payments and employment of forced saving *via* a National Provident Fund scheme, we would need information about the nature of the diversion of savings which this might imply, and the location of the effects of this diversion. This in turn would imply information about total wealth, and its distribution across particular assets among those households subject to the forced saving. In the absence of this information, we cannot claim that any analysis which we conduct using our framework is fully comprehensive.

At this stage the defence for this major omission is quite simply that it is extremely difficult on the basis of presently available information, certainly for Sri Lanka, to compile the necessary data. There are few countries in the world that have comprehensively documented the wealth of the personal sector, even in total, and probably none that have disaggregated this information so as to show the wealth of particular categories of household. In some cases it might not be meaningful to do so; in cases, for example, where the economic power and income associated with assets, such as land, is attached to traditional rights and not to ownership in any legally identifiable sense. But in most cases the failure to produce these data probably reflects a fundamental lack of concern about distributional questions and therefore about even the most fundamental determinants of distribution. This is something which one can expect the new climate of international opinion to change. Meanwhile, we can note that the effect of wealth ownership on income is not only a matter of wealth in the form of tangible and financial assets but normally also has a good deal to do with the wealth of an individual in the form of his inherited abilities, social position and training. Many of the income inequalities found in developing countries stem from a 'disproportionately' high return to particular types of education: an information system relevant to examining distributional questions ought ideally to document this sort of relationship. However, the statistical questions involved are clearly enormous and we have made no attempt to get on terms with them in this present study except insofar as translating from factor incomes to the incomes of institutions as required by the flow from column 1 into row 2 of our framework requires, implicitly, an underlying statement of who owns and provides the services of the various factors of production.

Secondly, the information system of Table 3.6, being defined entirely in terms of money flows, makes no reference to the physical volume of goods and factors which underlie them. It is of course possible to place the inter-industry matrix on a physical basis provided that relative prices of the outputs of the separately distinguished production activities can be calculated. However, these relativities are difficult to determine, not least because of the non-homogeneity of output within a given activity, and the resulting ambiguities about the price per unit of such outputs. This, of course, is no more nor less than a familiar index-number problem. Meanwhile there are two other areas of the matrix where it seems important to get behind the money value of transactions and look at the implications in terms of physical volume. The first is in the general area of factor payments by activities, where an analysis of employment problems clearly requires the identification of a matrix of the physical labour demands of particular industries as well as the money payments associated with these demands. We have made an attempt to extend the basic framework as described above in this way, and some aspects of the issues involved in doing so are discussed in Appendix 2. The second of these areas is that of consumption spending: poverty, and one of its most severe manifestations, namely malnutrition, are ultimately not defined in terms of so many rupees too little expenditure on particular items but in terms of inadequate *physical* intake of these items. The consumption vectors, and especially the elements in this which relate to food, therefore need an interpretation in terms of physical units as well as money values. We have not been able to proceed far with this translation in the present study but regard it as a matter of importance that attempts should be made to do so.

Finally, and rather less fundamentally, the structure defined in Table 3.6 fails to draw the SNA distinction between production activities and the commodities which they produce. Thus the technology underlying the inter-industry relationships of this structure has to be defined in terms of production activities (or industries), rather than commodities, and there is no reflection of the fact that the same industry may produce several commodities each of which has a different input structure. We regard this as a relatively minor deficiency of the present structure if only because it can fairly easily be put right. This has been demonstrated, at least to our own satisfaction, in subsequent work on Swaziland, where the industry/commodity distinction was employed.*

*See Pyatt and associates (1975).

4 The aggregated Sri Lanka matrix

Table 3.7 presents a highly aggregated version of the 1970 data framework for Sri Lanka, arranged in essentially the same format as Table 3.6 but with two modifications. The first of these is to subdivide the current account for institutions into households, companies and government. This same disaggregation was not possible for the capital account so that the latter is labelled as a Combined capital account. An implication of this is that there is no requirement to show details of the flow of funds between households, companies and government. Current transfers between these institutions are shown, however. The second modification is that sub-totals for domestic transactions are not shown in Table 3.7. It would, of course, be easy to do so. Table 3.8 is a schematic version of Table 3.7 which can be referred to for an interpretation of the latter to complement the picture of Sri Lanka in 1970, based on Table 3.7, which is set out in the remainder of this section.

The National Income (GNP) or Sri Lanka in 1970 was 11 360 (i.e., Rs 11 360m.) in current prices and is shown as the sum of row (1) of Table 3.7. Subject to a few minor differences discussed in the Statistical Appendix, this is the same figure as the total shown in the *Central Bank Report.*† Reading along row (1), it can be seen that this was made up of 100 of wages and salaries paid by households (to domestic servants), 1275 of wages and salaries paid by government to its employees and 10 098 of wages, salaries, profits and rent paid by what we term production activities and which are defined fully below.* The remaining item of *minus* 113 is the net factor payments to the rest of the world, the main component of which is the repatriated profits of overseas companies operating in Sri Lanka.

†See Ceylon, Central Bank (1972), Table 1.

*It would of course have been legitimate to treat the wages and salaries of domestic servants and government employees identically with other factor payments and establish appropriate production accounts for these activities. However, following convention, we have not done this on the grounds that the gross outputs of these two activities are identical to factor payments.

Table 3.7 *Social-accounting matrix for Sri Lanka, 1970 (full aggregation)*

		(1)	(2)	(3)	(4)	(5)	(6)	(7)	
			Institutions current accounts						
		Factors of production	Firms	Household	Government	Combined capital§ account	Production activities	Rest of world (current)	Totals (Rs million)
(1)	Factors of production			100	1275		10 098	–113	11 360
(2)	Institutions current accounts: Firms	1575			294				1869
(3)	Institutions current accounts: Households	9785	644		248			18	10 698
(4)	Institutions current accounts: Government	–	376	567*	104	313	856	130	2346
(5)	Combined capital account §		833	1339	42‡			425	2640
(6)	Production activities			7601	302	1962	4358	2113	16 336
(7)	Rest of world (current)		16	1091	79†	364	1024		2573
	Totals (Rs million)	11 360	1869	10 698	2346	2640	16 336	2573	

* Includes indirect taxes on consumption expenditure
† Includes imports and current transfers to rest of world
‡ Not exactly accurate because of rounding errors
§ Includes rest of world capital account

Table 3.8 *Social-accounting matrix for Sri Lanka in schematic form*

		(1) Factors of Production	(2) Institutions current accounts: Firms	(3) Household	(4) Government	(5) Combined capital account	(6) Production activities	(7) Rest of world (current)	Total
(1)	Factors of production			Value added by domestic servants	Value added in government		Value added in production (residual)	Net factor incomes from abroad	Total factor incomes
(2)	Institutions current accounts: Firms	Gross profits			Government transfers to firms				Total current receipts – firms
(3)	Institutions current accounts: Households	Wages, salaries and unincorporated business profits	Distributed profits		Government transfers to households			Transfers from rest of world	Total current receipts – household
(4)	Institutions current accounts: Government		Firm transfers to government	Household transfers to government*	Indirect taxes on government expenditure	Indirect taxes on investment	Indirect taxes on production	Export duties and FEEC's on exports	Total current receipts – government
(5)	Combined capital		Savings of firms (residual)	Savings of households (residual)	Savings of government (residual)			Balance of payments deficit (residual)	Total capital receipts
(6)	Production activities			Consumer expenditure on domestic goods	Government expenditure on domestic goods	Sales/purchases of domestic capital goods	Inter-industry transactions	Export of goods and services	Gross output
(7)	Rest of world (current)		Transfers to rest of world	Consumers expenditure on imports	Government imports and transfers overseas	Imports of investment goods	Imports of intermediate goods		Total current payments abroad
(8)	Total	Total factor incomes	Total expenditure by firms	Total household expenditure	Total government expenditure	Total capital payments	Total cost of production	Total current receipts from abroad	

* Includes indirect taxes on consumption expenditures

Reading down column (1), we see that 9785 of total GNP was received as incomes by households and so, by implication, comprised wages and salaries *plus* the profits of unincorporated business. The balance of 1575 constituted the profits of companies, both private and public.

Column (6) shows the cost structure of production. From the column total we see that the total costs of production, including profits (and therefore the value of production also), summed to 16 336. This was made up of 10 098 of wages, salaries and profits, 856 of indirect taxes paid to government, 4358 of material inputs from other production activities and 1024 of raw materials and semifinished products imported from the rest of the world.

Row (6) shows the various uses of total production. 7601 constituted consumption goods sold to households, 302 constituted goods sold for government current uses, 1962 were capital goods including stock accumulation, 4358 were sold to other productive activities for further processing and 2113 went for export. The various uses of output described in row (6) are all valued at producer prices. The values can be adjusted on to a consumers' price basis by adding the appropriate indirect taxes which are incorporated in row (4).

Column (7) shows the sources of foreign exchange earnings. 2243 derived from sales of exports of which 2113 was the value received by export producers and 130 was the net indirect taxes on exports paid to government. This 130 comprises 327 of export duties and 197 of FEEC *rebates* to exporters. Finally, there is a receipt of 18 of remittances from the rest of the world by households and the payment (negative entry) of 113 of profits. Row (7) shows the current uses of foreign exchange, of which easily the most important is imports of goods and services. Imports totalled 2521 of which 1091 were consumption goods purchased by households, 42 were imports used for government current purposes, 364 were capital goods and 1024 were materials and products purchased by productive sectors. The remaining entries in row (7) sum to 52, of which 16 is a transfer payment by firms and 36 is a transfer payment by the government. It will be noted that the sum of the receipts are less than the sum of the payments, implying a balance of payments deficit. This deficit is the 425 shown at the intersection of column (7) and row (5); that is, it is shown as a net receipt from the rest of the world available to finance capital payments.

Having described the entries in the first account of the table and the last two accounts, we can move into the central part of the table and discuss the current accounts of domestic institutions plus the combined capital account shown in rows and columns (2) to (5) inclusive. Beginning with firms, we have already seen that the main source of funds is profits of 1575. Reading along row (2), it is recorded that firms also receive 294 of transfer payments from government, giving them total current funds of 1869. Looking down the column, 376 of this is paid either as direct taxation or as current transfers to government, 644 is distributed profits and 16 is transferred to the rest of the world. This leaves firms with a balance of savings of 833, which is shown as being paid to the consolidated capital account.

Households have already been shown as receiving incomes from the factor accounts of 9785. In row (3), we can see that this is supplemented by transfer payments by government of 248, distributed profits of 644 and remittances from the rest of the world of 18, giving total household income of 10 698. The entries in column (3) record how this income was used. 100 went to pay the wages of domestic servants, 567 was used to make tax and transfer payments to government, 7601 was used to acquire domestically produced goods and services and 1091 was used to purchase imported consumption goods. As already noted both of these last two items are valued at producer prices; the indirect taxes and subsidies which constitute the difference between producer and consumer prices are included, along with direct taxation, in the 567 of payments to government.

The balance of total household incomes after deducting the various expenditure items is household savings. It amounts to 1339 and is shown as being paid into the household capital account.

The last of the three institutions accounts shown in Table 3.7 is that of the government. The current receipts of government are shown in row (4) and constitute 376 of tax and transfer payments by firms, 567 of tax and transfer payments by households, 104 of transfers within government, 313 of indirect taxation on imported capital goods, 856 of indirect taxation on production and 130 of indirect taxation on imports. These various sources of income sum to 2346. Column (4) provides a statement of the various uses of this income. 1275 was used for the payment of wages and salaries to civil servants, 294 plus 248 went as transfer payments to firms and households respectively, 104 as transfers within government mainly between local and central government. 302 was used to acquire domestic goods and services and 43 was used to acquire imports. The balance of the item at the intersection with row (7) is transfer payments to the rest of the world of 36. The receipts listed exceed the expenditure by the 42 of government savings shown at the intersection of row (5) and column (4).

The combined capital account shows total payments (in the columns) and receipts (in the rows) of 2640. The total outlays on capital formation, including imported capital goods and indirect taxes, was financed by the savings of firms, households and government totalling 2214, and the balance of payments deficit of 425. This reflects the familiar *ex post* identity between aggregate savings and aggregate investment but says nothing about the manner in which the capital expenditures of *individual* sectors were financed either by their own savings or by capital transfers including lending/borrowing. To obtain such detail we would need to have separate capital accounts for each institution in place of the combined capital account employed here.

5 Disaggregation and problems of classification

The various aggregates described in the preceding section are of some interest in their own right and not least because they include some of the more familiar aggregates from national accounting usage. However, we must clearly move to a more disaggregated picture if we are going to throw light on the things that really interest us such as living standards of different household groups and the effect on these of production structure and so on. But while the various accounts which should be incorporated into the basic structure, and upon which this chapter has so far concentrated, are well established and fairly uncontroversial, the question of the appropriate disaggregation of these accounts is potentially far more contentious and is certainly not capable of being defined uniquely. It is at the point of determining appropriate disaggregations where some value judgements inevitably enter. At this same point it can be argued that the generalised prescriptions of international schema start to fall down, while the lack of available data forces certain compromises, with what might otherwise be ideal. Finally, it is at this point where a clear understanding of the possible uses of the data starts to become necessary.

We can begin the discussion of our approach to disaggregation in the specific Sri Lankan context by summarising, in Table 3.9, the details of the disaggregations which were ultimately adopted. It remains then to set down the reasons for choosing these various classifications in the remainder of this section. It will

Table 3.9 *Classifications*

(*A*) Production activities	(*B*) Institutions	(*C*) Consumption commodities	(*D*) Factors of production	
1 Tea 2 Rubber 3 Coconuts 4 Paddy 5 Livestock 6 Fishing 7 Logging and firewood 8 Other agriculture 9 Mining and quarrying 10a Rice milling 10b Flour milling 11 Dairy products 12 Bread 13 Other bakery products 14 Carbonated beverages 15 Desiccated coconut 16 Other processed food 17 Distilling 18 Tobacco 19 Textiles 20 Wood products 21 Paper 22 Leather 23 Rubber 24 Chemicals 25 Oils and fats 26 Coconut fibre and yarn 27 Petroleum and coal 28 Structural clay products 29 Ceramics 30 Cement 31 Basic metals 32 Light engineering 33 Transport equipment 34 Machinery, other equipment 35 Other manufacturing 36 Construction 37 Electricity 38 Road passenger transport 39 Rail transport 40a Wholesale trade 40b Retail trade 40c Other transport 41a Communication 41b Hotels and restaurants 41c Professional services 41d Dwellings 41e Other services	Private corporations Public corporations *Urban households* Rs 0–200 Rs 200–399 Rs 400–599 Rs 600–799 Rs 800–999 Rs 1000+ *Rural households* Rs 0–200 Rs 200–399 Rs 400–599 Rs 600–799 Rs 800–999 Rs 1000+ *Estate households* Rs 0–200 Rs 200–399 Rs 400–599 Rs 600–799 Rs 800–999 Rs 1000+ *Government* (column entries) Civil administration Defence Education Health Housing and other Social services Agriculture, irrigation and land development Roads and highways Other economic services Local government expenditure Current transfer payments *Government* (row entries) Direct taxes Export taxes Import duties Government food profits Profits of state enterprises Other indirect taxes /subsidies FEEC receipts Other current receipts Local government	Rationed rice Outside ration rice Wheat flour Other grains and cereals Condiments Pulses Coconuts Vegetables, fruits and other nuts Meat Fish Milk and milk products Oils, fats including butter Tea Sugar Other food and beverages Meals away from home Toddy Other alcoholic beverages Traditional tobacco Modern tobacco Clothing and footwear Rent, rates and water charges Fuel and light Consumer durables Household operation (services) Household operation (goods) Personal care and health Transport and communications Recreation Miscellaneous	**Employee labour** *Urban sector* Professional, technical and related workers Administrative, executive and managerial workers Clerical workers Sales workers Agricultural workers Miners, quarrymen and related workers Transport and communication workers Craftsmen, production process workers and labourers Service, sports and recreation workers *Rural sector* Professional, technical and related workers Administrative, executive and managerial workers Clerical workers Sales workers Agricultural workers Miners, quarrymen and related workers Transport and communication workers Craftsmen, production process workers and labourers Service, sports and recreation workers *Estates sector* Professional, technical and related workers Administrative, executive and managerial workers Clerical workers Sales workers Agricultural workers Miners, quarrymen and related workers Transport and communication workers Craftsmen, production process workers and labourers Service, sports and recreation workers	**Self-employed** *Urban sector* Professional, technical and related workers Administrative, executive and managerial workers Clerical workers Sales workers Agricultural workers Miners, quarrymen and related workers Craftsmen, production process workers, and labourers Transport and communication workers Service, sports and recreation workers *Rural sector* Professional, technical and related workers Administrative, executive and managerial workers Clerical workers Sales workers Agricultural workers Miners, quarrymen and related workers Transport and communication workers Craftsmen, production process workers and labourers Service, sports and recreation workers *Estates sector* Professional, technical and related workers Administrative, executive and managerial workers Clerical workers Sales workers Agricultural workers Miners, quarrymen and related workers Transport and communication workers Craftsmen, production process workers and labourers Service, sports and recreation workers. **Private housing** **Private corporate capital** **Public corporate capital**

be seen that these reasons are a mix of views about what is the 'ideal' classification, given the likely uses of the data, and of statistical expediency in terms of what data were fairly readily available. This last factor acquired particular importance in our work since we had neither time nor resources to carry out any collection of new data or systematic retabulation of data previously collected.

While the classifications we have been obliged to use may fall some way short of the ideal, the amount of detail we were ultimately able to incorporate goes a long way towards it from many points of view. Thus Table 3.9 implies that the full SAM described in Appendix 1 has well over 100 rows and columns of consistent data in the format of Tables 3.7 and 3.8. This then provides a number of detailed insights into the economy of Sri Lanka, some of which are discussed in the remaining Chapters. It is relevant to point out that these insights could have been more sharply focused if time and resources had allowed us to look into some alternative classification systems. As it is, some compromises were inevitable as explained in the remainder of this section.

5.1 The classification of production activities

Since most of our work on the input–output section of the data framework was based on an original study by Dr S. Narapalasingham (1970), our classification of production sectors was heavily based on his, though with slightly more disaggregation where this seemed feasible. Broadly, Narapalasingham identifies 41 production groups of which numbers 1 to 8 are agricultural but include some processing, 10 to 35 are manufacturing, and 38 to 41 produce services. The classification is completed by Mining and quarrying (Sector 9), Construction (36), and the generation and transmission of Electricity (37). Narapalasingham's classification is based on the International Standard Industrial Classification (ISIC) though with some aggregation where the quality of the available data and the relative unimportance of the items seemed to justify it. Beyond this we have separated Rice milling from Flour milling (Sector 10 in Narapalasingham's classification), disaggregated the Trade and Transport sectors (Sector 40) and the Communication and Services sectors (Sector 41). However, to retain comparability with the Narapalasingham study we have retained his numbering system, using small Roman letters to indicate the sub-divisions which have been introduced by us. One broad feature of the Narapalasingham classification which we have retained is that subsidiary products of individual sectors have been allocated, wherever possible, to the industries in which they are the principal products. To the extent that this procedure has been successful it takes care of the failure, referred to earlier, to draw the SNA distinction between commodity accounts and industry accounts.

A main guiding principle in any production classification is to define a separate category for any activity which is reasonably large, or likely to become large, provided also that it has a distinct input structure, or is distinguished in some other significant way from other activities. However, aggregation of activities is justified whenever organisational arrangements are such as to cause two or more activities to take place in fixed proportions. In Sri Lanka the output of the tea industry (Sector 1) involves a vertical integration of two activities, the growing of the green leaves and their processing into black tea. This justifies our definition of only one sector for tea instead of two. Similarly, and by the same sort of reasoning, the production of crude rubber latex is combined with its subsequent processing into crepe or sheets, in Sector 2. However, in the case of coconut where the further processing of the basic output can take a number of different forms which do *not* necessarily relate to each other in fixed proportions, separate processing sectors such as Coconut fibre and yarn (Sector 26) needed to be defined. Another example is the omission of toddy from Sector 17, namely Distilling. The reasoning here is that since toddy is obtained by the fermentation of sap from coconut trees it is more appropriately classified with fresh coconuts in Sector 3. Rice and flour milling were ultimately separated because of the significantly different proportion of raw inputs supplied by foreign sources in the two cases.

In these and various other ways the standard ISIC was amended to fit the particular circumstances of Sri Lanka. However, this process was clearly compromised at a number of points by the inadequacy of the available statistics. Thus, for example, the classification makes no provision for the value of coconut trees used for construction, the use of coconut husks as fertilisers, the paddy straw used for animal feedstuffs, and the value of cow dung used as fertiliser. In addition the textile sector has perforce to accommodate spinning, weaving, knitting and so on, even though these activities almost certainly do not proceed in fixed proportions.

5.2 *The classification of institutions*

5.2.1 *Households*

Since the study of living standards and their determination is central to our whole exercise, the classification of institutions, and especially institutions within the household sector, is of critical importance and therefore warrants a rather thorough treatment. In particular, if we are interested in planning for redistribution as well as growth it is clear that a disaggregation of households into groups is only useful if the groups which are identified are liable to be affected differently by growth or if there is some scope for redistribution between them. It is especially desirable that the classification should separately identify those groups which might be of particular concern for policy, for example, the very poor or the landless labourer. However, it is not enough simply to separate out these 'target' groups as they have been called, since policies to deal with them must inevitably have implications for other groups as well. Accordingly we need an exhaustive classification of households which identifies groups of special concern for policy and with respect to which the effects of policy are identifiable. In short, it is important to have a comprehensive household classification which includes target groups as one, but not the only, part.

In fact, we can identify three main criteria in classifying households, the first of which is a regional distinction including what is often the fundamental dichotomy in developing countries, namely that between urban and rural areas. If we wish to put any quantitative substance to the concept of duality this is the easiest way to do it. It is also meaningful in the sense that the mass of the poor are normally to be found in rural areas: the difference between urban and rural per capita income is often large and is usually a major dimension of inequality which reflects other important aspects of duality.

The second potentially important criterion for disaggregating households is based on sociological factors in situations where religious or social differences make for differences in economic circumstances. In the Sri Lankan context, the most important household group which warrants a separate category in our classification according to this criterion are households of the southern Indian estate workers. They are different from other rural households in that they speak another language, regarding southern India as home even though they may have been born in Sri Lanka. They have little political power and are excluded from most factor markets: they generally have few ties with the rest of the economy.

Clearly, then, there is a good case for regarding these households as a separate group within the population because they clearly do raise separate problems in terms of the design and administration of policies. In this particular case, we are fortunate in that the sociological distinction coincides with a geographical one and also because available data permits its implementation. Accordingly, we have distinguished separately Urban, Rural and Estate households, using the label 'rural' to apply to those non-urban households which are also non-estate.

Finally, our disaggregation of households requires an economic criterion and the obvious one to choose is difference in wealth. However, wealth as a criterion variable presents a number of difficulties in drawing the line between different groups of households, and in making the distinctions it is necessary to have in mind the statistical difficulties of gathering and analysing data. There are a few things that might be done. For example, the grouping of rural households may not be too difficult on the basis of land ownership, e.g. size of land-holding, and perhaps also the nature of tenancy, e.g. share-croppers may need to be separately shown. However, beyond this, and especially when we turn to the urban areas, the feasibility of distinguishing households by wealth on the basis of data presently available in Sri Lanka is extremely low. Thus in our work so far we have abandoned wealth as the economic criterion for grouping households and used *income* instead.

An approach based on income is not without its problems either, since nearly all available published data on incomes in Sri Lanka relates to the distribution of income by *household* rather than by *individual*. In our view this method of classification is only of limited usefulness if one is concerned with the welfare implications of any given income distribution. The main problem is that a large household may be placed into a high income category simply because that household contains a relatively large number of income earners, even though the average income of each member of that household, and therefore its standard of living, may be low. Similarly, the present system of classification allows households in which the average income of each household member is high to be placed in a relatively low income category. The nature of the problem is illustrated by Table 3.10 which is based on data extracted from the 1969/70 *Socio-Economic Survey*. It is clear from the table that household size becomes an important 'determinant' of income distribution when it is defined by household rather than by individual. This factor severely impedes meaningful analysis. It could, of course, be overcome by extensive retabulation of the basic data. But this was not a possibility available to us given our resources.

Table 3.10 *Income distribution by household and household size*

Income group (Rs per month)	Percentage of households having more than 5 members	Average household size (no.)
100 and below	20.4	3.9
100–199	38.8	5.1
200–399	57.8	6.2
400–599	71.7	7.2
600–799	71.8	7.5
800–999	75.1	7.5
1000 and above	76.4	7.7

5.2.2 *Government expenditures and revenues*

Beginning with government *current* expenditures, the first disaggregation in our work is into expenditures on goods and services on the one hand, and transfer payments on the other. This distinction is well established in economic analysis. Its importance from the point of view of studying the impact on the economy of government expenditures is clear: while the first category of expenditures generates direct demands on resources, the second is primarily redistributional. Within each of the two broad categories of expenditures we attempted some further disaggregation by 'purpose'. This leads to the complete classification shown in Table 3.9. The main criterion here is that a separate category should be established for any expenditure item which is large, is likely to become large, or, if small has some strategic importance or is otherwise politically sensitive. Our classification broadly reflects this principle.

A similar principle applies to *capital* expenditures of government where an additional factor is the widely different cost structures of different categories of capital formation (certainly in Sri Lanka and probably elsewhere, too). We were able to produce some disaggregated capital expenditure accounts for government based on the work of Narapalasingham (1970) and the United Nations Development Project (1970). However, in accordance with our decision to restrict ourselves to a single capital account, this disaggregation was not used in the SAM itself.

The classification of government revenues is virtually self-explanatory. However, it should be noted that the Indirect tax/subsidy item includes the rice subsidy, while the profits of the non-autonomous state commercial activities, including the Food Commissioner, are treated as though they were indirect taxes. This is because where the government has a monopoly in a particular activity, a price change has the same impact on government revenues and the price of the commodities affected as would a change in the indirect taxation of those commodities. It is therefore logical to define the profits of these activities as indirect taxes. However, it should be stressed that this practice is not followed in the case of the autonomous state enterprises since in these cases the government has no power to determine the use to be made of profits.

A number of other interesting disaggregations of government revenue are possible but have not been attempted by us. For example, a proposal for a new system of National Accounts in Trinidad* involves the separation of certain tax receipts into taxes payable assuming no concessions, rebates, etc. and into the value of the concessions. This is interesting in that it allows detailed studies of the incidence of fiscal *concessions*, whereas the detail in our present system only permits detailed study of the incidence of tax payments.

*See Levitt (1973).

5.3 *The classification of consumption commodities*

Our estimates of private consumers' expenditure were taken in two stages. We first estimated the expenditure by households on various categories of goods and services such as food, clothing, fuel and light and so on. At the second stage we broke each of these expenditures down by identifying both source of supply (whether domestic, in which case we tried to identify the particular production activity doing the supplying, or imports), and the indirect tax element in the price of each commodity. We had a good deal of flexibility about the classification involved at the first of these stages since the basic source of data, namely the 1969/70 *Socio-Economic Survey*,† identifies 164 categories of expenditure of which food items account for 107, liquor and tobacco account for 8, non-durable goods and services account for 48.

†Ceylon, Department of Census and Statistics (1971/72).

Some aggregation was necessary merely in order to make the tables at all manageable. In fact we aggregated the 164 categories into 30, of which 16 related to food expenditure (accounting for 55 per cent of recorded expenditure) and 4 related to alcohol and tobacco (5 per cent of expenditure). Within the food expenditure group we detailed certain items of special interest to Sri Lanka, e.g. rationed versus non-rationed rice, wheat flour, coconuts, sugar; and grouped the remainder conventionally into groups such as meat, fish and so on. Within tobacco we split 'traditional' (beedi, cigars, chewing tobacco) from 'modern' (factory made). The remaining groups have been arranged to keep goods distinct from services. Broadly we tried to work at about the same level of aggregation as the tables published in the *Central Bank Report*,* but to preserve a little more detail where this seemed specially relevant to the problems of Sri Lanka.

*See Ceylon, Central Bank (1972), Table 10.

5.4 The classification of factors of production

Our disaggregation of value-added payments to factors is collected into five separate factor accounts in the first instance, followed by an occupational and vocational disaggregation of the two of these which involve labour. Hence we have:

1 Employee labour
2 Self-employment
3 Private housing
4 Private corporate capital
5 Public corporate capital

The returns to self-employment, in which category we include own-account workers and employers in receipt of unincorporated business net income, comprise returns to labour services, to entrepreneurial activities, and to the deployment of capital owned by the self-employed. Since there are considerable conceptual problems associated with distinguishing between returns to labour and returns to capital in the total income of this group of the population, and since there is insufficient data on the ownership of assets in Sri Lanka for us to attempt a calculation of returns to non-corporate capital employed in each production activity, we have adopted this composite factor in preference to splitting it into labour and capital elements.

The factor called private housing receives all the value added of the production activity 41d, 'Dwellings'. It is subsequently distributed to households and private corporations in the form of net rental value on owner-occupied dwellings, as free housing as a factor payment, and net rent on private rented accommodation.

The two corporate capital factors receive surpluses on the operations of private and public corporations. A glaring data deficiency which undermines our confidence in the factor payments figure is the lack of independent estimates of the return to private corporate capital. As we explain in the Statistical Appendix, our initial estimate of this item is merely the residual after subtracting all other factor payments from the value-added figures. In the light of the practical difficulties, we have made no attempt to subdivide private capital according to whether it is owned domestically or by foreigners. However, we obviously recognise the analytical usefulness of the distinction.

Beyond this, the further disaggregation of the employee labour and self-employment by location and by occupation involved several broad principles and constraints which it is worth discussing in some detail. First, it is clear that different technologies within a given production activity require different combinations of skills and capital equipment and lend themselves to alternative forms of market organisations. Thus not only is it important to identify various occupational groups within labour, but it is also desirable to distinguish the conditions under which employment takes place; for example, whether or not current technologies allow ease of entry and have thrown up extensive unincorporated business sectors characterised by a proliferation of own-account workers and small employers.* In this case our compromise has been in having to use the same occupational structure for both employee and self-employed labour.

*Alternative disaggregations, data permitting, of the employed could relate to size of establishment by employment or capital asset valuation, etc.

Secondly, the proportion of people in wage employment, i.e. receiving a wage for their labour rather than a price for their product, is of great relevance when considering policies to aid redistribution by interfering in labour and product markets. Adopting a statistical framework which distinguishes the incomes accruing to these different groups of people within each production activity (together with the 'physical' tables which underlie the flows of income in the framework) helps to monitor, for example, how benefits from promoting the small-scale sector in the various industries are distributed among the various categories of employment and self-employment.

Thirdly, in relating educational and employment policies one needs a framework which enables the calculation of 'benchmark' demands for different skills contingent on the expansion of different production activities. Whether one dares to adopt fixed coefficients, thereby turning the descriptive framework into the simplest of demand models, is a question for model building. Here we suggest that the minimum that should be contained in a quantitative view of this part of the economy is a measure of the income flows relating to the different skills which are actually engaged in production. We recognise that with alternative technologies and labour-market conditions, substitution possibilities in the short- and medium-run *could* have led to a different cost and employment structure for each production activity. The least we can do is to record what in fact occurred through occupational categories of relevance to policy. It is unfortunate therefore that we were obliged to keep to the occupational categories separately distinguished in the *Socio-Economic Survey*. While they in fact follow the International occupation and skill classification, their relevance to policy – e.g. education and vocational training – is very tenuous. However, an advantage of our procedure is that it allows occupational categories to be combined in the factor classification with the distinction of employment status between 'employee' and 'self-employment' and with the geographical distribution as between urban, rural and estate households. In effect, therefore, we are able to distinguish 9 × 2 × 3 = 54 different types of labour within our factor classification.

6 A partially disaggregated version of the Sri Lanka matrix

Finally, in this chapter, we present a disaggregated version of the SAM introduced in the previous sections. This is set down in Table 3.11 which contains six factor accounts, five accounts for institutions, twelve production activities and, as before, one account for the rest of the world. The nature of the reaggregation from Table 3.9 is shown below. For completeness, the bottom part of Table 3.11 also shows the physical volume of employment which production activities generate in each of nine employment categories.

Although still in a semi-aggregated format, the data of Table 3.11 reveal a good deal about the structure of the Sri Lanka economy. Beginning with the totals of the first six rows (the factor account rows) of the matrix, we see that of the total factor incomes of 11 360, approximately half takes the form of wages and salaries, while 44 per cent is accounted for by profits.† The largest share (57 per cent) of the wage and salary bill accrues to rural labour while urban and estate households receive 30 per cent and 13 per cent respectively.

†See pp. 158–62 of Appendix 1 for details of the method used to construct this part of the data set.

Looking at the sources of factor incomes as revealed by the entries in the first six rows, we can see that urban labour draws about 31 per cent of its wage and salary receipts from government employment while the corresponding figures for rural and estate households are 23 per cent and 1 per cent respectively. By contrast, the estate sector draws over 86 per cent of its income from the tea and rubber sectors alone, as compared with the urban sector where only about 1 per cent of wage and salary income depends on these two major export commodities. Among other things the table also reveals the heavy dependence (23 per cent) of rural labour incomes on paddy production, the importance of the trade and transport sector to both rural and urban labour incomes and the importance to total profits of the trade and transport, construction and other agriculture sectors.

Turning to the first six columns of the table, we see the manner in which the *factor* incomes already discussed, accrue to various *institutional* sectors. Urban households draw labour incomes of 1673, but this is increased by 137 (or 8 per cent) as a result of the ownership of housing services and by 662 (or 40 per cent) as the result of receiving a share of the profits of unincorporated businesses. In total the basic labour income of urban households is increased by 48 per cent as a result of the ownership of non-labour factors. By contrast, and as a reflection of the manner of organisation of the rural sector, the rural-labour incomes are increased by over 105 per cent when account is taken of receipts of income from non-labour services, and especially the profits from unincorporated businesses. Estate-labour incomes, however, are increased by only a modest 9 per cent, once again revealing the high degree of separateness of estate incomes from the rest of the economy.

If we move along the rows of the table representing Institutional current accounts, we can see that there are two major sources of institutional income other than those already discussed, namely receipts of distributed corporate profits and transfer payments of various kinds from the government. The factor-income receipts of urban, rural and estate households are increased by 21 per cent, 2.4 per cent and 1.7 per cent respectively as a result of adding these two categories of receipt. The enormous discrepancy between the urban and other sectors largely arises from the strong urban bias in the ownership of incorporated capital but is not entirely due to this, and our figures suggest that the urban sector also fares disproportionately well when it comes to receipt of government transfers. On the other hand, the table also reveals another side of this coin since urban sectors pay out some 25 per cent of their factor-income receipts (i.e. before transfers), in the form of direct and indirect taxes, as compared with only 3 per cent and 0.5 per cent respectively for rural and estate households.* These comparisons are rather interesting since they suggest that the effect of a progressive tax system is such as to roughly cancel out the income gain to urban households associated with its disproportionate share in the ownership of corporate capital.

*See the government row in the block of the table relating to Institutions Current Accounts, and refer to pp. 162–6 of Appendix 1.

If we bring together the various income receipts and transfers so far discussed, we arrive at the distribution of income before tax by institutional category. This can be read off from the totals shown at the end of rows (or columns) 7–10 inclusive and in percentage form is as shown below. Allowing for tax payments, the shares for urban, rural and estate households become 22.0 per cent, 55.9 per cent and 6.6 per cent respectively.

The savings propensities of the six institutional sectors which the table identifies can be calculated by comparing the appropriate entries in the row of the Combined capital account with the income totals just discussed. In fact, in

Table 3.11 *Aggregated social-accounts matrix and manpower matrix for Sri Lanka, 1970 (Rs million)*

		Factors of production						Institutions current accounts					
		Urban labour	Rural labour	Estate labour	Housing	Public capital	Private capital	Firms	Households – urban	Households – rural	Households – estate	Government	Combined capital account
Factors of production	Urban labour								38			523	
	Rural labour									56		742	
	Estate labour										6	10	
	Housing												
	Public capital												
	Private capital												
Institutions current accounts	Firms				135	175	1266					294	
	Households – urban	1673			137		662	434				91	
	Households – rural		3184		330		3026	203				151	
	Households – estate			711	31		30	7				6	
	Government							376	368	195	4	104	313
Combined capital account								833	520	808	11	43	
Production activity	Tea								14	56	6	2	–55
	Rubber												25
	Coconut								52	207	30	4	29
	Paddy												49
	Other agriculture								350	988	138	16	
	Agricultural processing								275	1065	138	26	90
	Mining								2	6	1		
	Traditional industry								209	569	79	7	58
	Modern industry								132	335	33	59	17
	Construction											92	1595
	Trade and transport								402	1078	142	89	154
	Services								435	799	60	7	
Rest of world								16	207	741	143	79	364
Total		1673	3184	711	633	175	4985	1869	3004	6903	791	2346	2640

Employment category	Professi
	Manag
	Cle
	Agricu
	M
	Tran
	Se
Total employ	

Tea	Rubber	Coconut	Paddy	Other agriculture	Agricultural processing	Mining	Traditional industry	Modern industry	Construction	Trade and transport	Services	Rest of world	Total		
Production activity															
12	4	11	28	115	32	4	103	84	55	454	210		1673	Urban labour	Factors of production
49	84	86	719	366	54	16	177	66	107	494	168		3184	Rural labour	
22	92	22		12	10		1	1	4	17	13		711	Estate labour	
											633		633	Housing	
				–12	16	3	10	67	19		72		175	Public capital	
2	141	410	231	1095	141	61	145	441	863	1468	100	–113	4985	Private capital	
													1869	Firms	Institutions current accounts
												6	3004	Households – urban	
												6	6902	Households – rural	
												6	791	Households – estate	
33	4	14	5	19	80	2	263	154	76	130	76	130	2346	Government	
													425	Combined capital account	
											2	839	864	Tea	Production activity
							8					341	374	Rubber	
					247						6	2	577	Coconut	
			70		1012			2					1133	Paddy	
1	1			95	31	2	62	2	5		39	106	1846	Other agriculture	
				11	34		187	1			40	152	2019	Agricultural processing	
							2	3	74		1	19	108	Mining	
5				19	19		96	29	102	47	5	92	1346	Traditional industry	
2	24	9	35	50	24	9	36	329	137	127	31	72	1541	Modern industry	
						1			161	10	47		1906	Construction	
5	11	9	8	23	116	6	113	138	222	137	62	210	2975	Trade and transport	
5	2	6	9	1	4			1	6	17	14	280	1647	Services	
5	12	10	29	53	199	3	143	223	74	74	128		2573	Rest of world	
4	374	577	1133	1846	2019	108	1346	1541	1906	2975	1647	2573		Total	

Tea	Rubber	Coconut	Paddy	Other agriculture	Agricultural processing	Mining	Traditional industry	Modern industry	Construction	Trade and transport	Services	Rest of world	Total		
	–	–	1	1	1	–	1	3	4	4	27		41	Professional	Employment category
	1	1	–	–	2	1	3	2	1	16	5		33	Managerial	
	1	–	–	2	1	–	5	8	3	42	23		90	Clerical	
	1	–	1	1	5	1	4	3	1	226	22		266	Sales	
	186	45	714	273	34	–	5	3	–	3	–		1851	Agricultural	
	–	–	–	–	–	12	–	–	–	–	–		12	Miners	
	–	–	2	–	1	–	1	2	3	104	4		118	Transport	
	2	1	1	8	32	8	244	57	102	63	33		556	Craft	
	1	3	–	2	4	–	2	2	2	8	114		144	Service	
	19	51	719	288	81	21	266	78	116	464	228		3111	Total employment	

	per cent
Firms	14.9
Urban households	23.9
Rural households	54.9
Estate households	6.3

1970 the average propensities to save were 44.6 per cent, 17.3 per cent, 11.7 per cent, 1.4 per cent and 1.8 per cent for firms, urban, rural, and estate households, and government respectively. In spite of the lower savings propensity of rural, as compared with urban households the former are more important in absolute terms supplying nearly 31 per cent of the total capital funds as compared with 20 per cent from urban households, 32 per cent from firms and only 2 per cent from government and estate households combined.* The balance of capital funds (15 per cent of the total), was accounted for by a foreign capital inflow.

*See Stage 8 of Appendix 1 for a discussion of the difficulties of an accurate quantification of institutional savings.

In parallel with the discussion of differences in savings propensities as between sectors, the data of Table 3.11 also permits comparisons of the differential propensities to consume the outputs of the various production sectors. However, since this is a matter which is taken up at some length in Chapter 6, we can pass over this and proceed directly to a discussion of output and production structure. The totals of the twelve rows and columns labelled Production activity, permit an immediate identification of the sectoral contributions to total gross output of 16 336 as shown in Table 3.7.† It is of some interest that despite their obviously critical role in the economy, the traditional export sectors of tea and rubber account for only 8 per cent of total gross output as compared with about 24 per cent for the other agriculture and agricultural processing combined, 28 per cent for trade, transport and services and about 18 per cent for industry. The distinguishing feature of these sectors is that virtually all of their output (99.8 per cent in the case of tea, and 97.9 per cent in the case of rubber), is accounted for by *final* demands (principally exports) whereas most other sectors rely to a larger extent on induced demands arising from outputs in other sectors. Thus, trade and transport which is the most important sector in terms of gross output in Table 3.11, depends to the extent of 30 per cent on other Sri Lankan sectors for its sales. After tea and rubber, the sector most heavily dependent on exporting is mining where nearly 18 per cent of output goes for exporting.*

†See pp. 136–42 of Appendix 1 for details of the method used to calculate sectoral gross outputs.

*See Appendix 1 pp. 126–7 for details of the estimation of exports.

In similar fashion, the production block of the table reveals the differential dependence of the various sectors on other final demands. For example, if we examine the entries relating to consumption demand, we can see that the sectors 'other agriculture' and 'agricultural processing' are critically dependent on this category of demand with the degree of dependence being 80 per cent and 73 per cent respectively. The contrast between traditional and modern industry is also worthy of note in that the former draws 64 per cent of its gross revenues from consumption as compared with only 32 per cent for the latter. Although the former is a far more intensive employer of labour than the latter, the comparison is of interest in pointing out the need for an employment-oriented development strategy to take due account of the need for increased consumption to supply the demand to sustain expanding outputs in the most labour-oriented sector.

As we attempt to bring out in relation to the fully disaggregated system in the following chapter, few sectors depend heavily on intermediate demands from any other single sector. The main exception to this is paddy production which, of necessity, depends heavily on demands from the agricultural processing sector and thence on consumption.

Turning to the columns of the block of the matrix relating to Production activities, we can examine the cost structure of the various sectors. One important distinguishing feature on the cost side relates to the income creating power of a sector as measured by the share of factor incomes in total gross output. The traditional sectors of tea, rubber and coconut do well on this point with factor income to gross output ratios of 68 per cent, 85 per cent and 92 per cent respectively. The industrial sectors, on the other hand, carry much lower values for this ratio but, by implication, have far more substantial linkages to other sectors of the economy. Of course, this is particularly true with the agricultural processing sector where only 13 per cent of the costs of production are represented in factor incomes.

Given the information already discussed about the passage of factor incomes to various institutional sectors, it is an easy matter to translate the comparison of sectors from a *factor* income creating viewpoint, to a comparison from the viewpoint of *institutional* income creation. Thus, for example, it is very straightforward to see how much additional gross output in any sector is necessary in order to produce one additional unit of income in the hands of, say, rural households. This, and related exercises are carried out in depth in Chapter 4.

Another valuable piece of information which emerges more or less directly from an examination of the Table 3.11 detail on production activities, concerns the import content of total costs.* The numbers indicate that the three industrial sectors, namely modern industry, traditional industry and agricultural processing, all have import shares in total costs of 10 per cent or higher as compared with the norm for the agricultural sectors of about 3 per cent. Tea production is a rather surprising exception to this general pattern with an import ratio of about 10 per cent.

*See Appendix 1 pp. 128–30 for details of method.

As a final illustration of the information contained within the moneyflows part of Table 3.11, we can examine the row and column relating to the rest of the world. The row shows that, of total imports of 2573, 42 per cent are used for consumption purposes, 14 per cent for investment purposes, and about 40 per cent for intermediate purposes. The column shows that, of total export receipts of 2148 (2573 − 425), 55 per cent are due to tea and rubber and only 8 per cent are due to traditional and modern industry. This is a characteristic of the economic structure which Sri Lankan policy is designed to change, but as our earlier analysis has shown, success in this policy involves complicated feedbacks to income creation, and distribution which may not be wholly desirable.

Finally, and briefly, the above description of money flows can be linked to the physical employment characteristics of the production system as shown at the bottom of Table 3.11. This indicates that paddy production is the largest employer of labour followed by tea and trade and transport. The row totals show, not surprisingly, that agricultural workers are easily the most important employment category. Of more interest is the comparison of the employment and gross output totals for each production activity. This reveals that one thousand jobs implies Rs 1.4 million of gross output in tea, Rs 2.0 million in rubber and Rs 1.6 million in paddy production. It is of particular interest to note that the corresponding figures for traditional and modern industry respectively are Rs 1.5 million and Rs 19.8 million. Even though one may not believe in the absolute constancy over time of these figures, the difference between them is sufficiently great to confirm the obvious importance of the *structure* of production in any employment-oriented strategy.

The analysis of this chapter has hopefully demonstrated the very considerable information about an economy which is contained within the social accounting system which we propose, even when this is defined in a relatively aggregative form. In the next three chapters, we draw on the fully disaggregated system and attempt to provide an idea of the analytical possibilities which are implicit in this system.

4

Income distribution and input–output: some preliminary analysis

1 Introduction

The main purpose of this volume is to make the case for developing particular types of macro data framework and to demonstrate the methodology needed in practice to do so. For us the analytical follow-up to this statistical work is only now beginning,* but it is the analytical work which will ultimately have to justify the data exercises. It is important, therefore, even at this early stage, that we attempt to give a flavour of the analytical insights which might emerge from working with the data base that our statistical efforts have been designed to establish. Accordingly, in this and the next two chapters the data from our full social-accounting matrix is used to describe and analyse some features of the Sri Lankan economy with special reference to the factors influencing income distribution and employment.

*Under the umbrella of a two-year project financed by the SSRC and directed by Alan Roe.

Since analysis, and even description, normally imply some underlying 'model' of the economy, a few preliminary comments about our attitude to the relationship between data and models are in order at this point. Underlying every model is an implicit data system, and every data system implies a *class* of economic models. Thus, by compiling a particular SAM we have inevitably restricted ourselves to the class of models implied by it. In this context it is worth recalling that one of our objectives has been to demonstrate that a macro data system could be constructed despite the inadequacy of much of the primary information. To carry through this demonstration we have had to make our illustration of classification schemes and definition of variables consistent with the data which currently exist. By so doing we are locked into a particular type of model even though our approach might be more valuable if it was not so restricted. For example, available data on production are classified under the assumption that technology is related to the product group. An alternative view is that, relative to an important set of issues, production should be classified not simply according to type of commodity but also with reference to the organisation of the production process, e.g. as household production activities, unincorporated businesses, corporate capitalism and state enterprise. However, to have illustrated the use of this alternative classification we would have needed to reclassify the primary data, and this option was not open to us. But such an option is available to a developing country in relation to future data collection and tabulation. And it is an option which can be recommended within our framework if interest attaches to analysis which calls for such a taxonomy.

So, the implicit models of the analyses which follow are all conditioned by the data constraints which are binding on us. In addition, they are mostly linear models and imply fixed coefficients. Though we are obviously aware of the deficiencies of a fixed-coefficient approach, we would defend its use here on the grounds that we are still at the stage of trying to elicit information about directions of effect and broad orders of magnitude rather than aspire to any greater precision. In fact greater precision generally implies non-linear models and will usually require additional data to that which is included in our SAM framework, such as data on elasticities of substitution in production or consumption. Non-linear models therefore detract attention from SAM data to a degree. In avoiding such a diversion we must be content to work with fixed-coefficient, linear models in the knowledge that they are well tried and a proven means of obtaining a first cut at orders of magnitude in relation to many problems.*

*Detailed techniques for working with non-linear models in a SAM framework – and some of the pros and cons of doing so – are discussed in Pyatt and Thorbecke (forthcoming).

A final introductory point relates to the fact that the data with which we are working relates to 1970 and is thus already several years out of date. While this is obviously of concern to us we would make the point once again that our purpose in this volume is not so much to advise contemporary policymaking in Sri Lanka but rather to indicate how data needed to inform policy can be collated and manipulated. The choice of a year to use in this demonstration is of relatively minor importance except insofar as it has bearing on how quickly data can be collated and made available. We are well aware of the very real difficulties of producing timely data in countries like Sri Lanka, and recognise that it would be a difficult task to produce a fully up to date version of the data matrix which we are proposing on a regular basis. But at the same time we would argue that it is far less difficult once procedures for handling incomplete data, such as those discussed in Appendix 1, are accepted as legitimate statistical practice. For the moment we are regarding problems of updating our matrix as part of our future work and meanwhile can report that a recent study in Swaziland has reinforced our experience with respect to the timeliness with which available raw data can be processed into a SAM format. Against this background we proceed in the remainder of this chapter, and in the two chapters following, to explore the usefulness of a SAM on the assumption that it can be assembled for a date which is near enough to the present to be of use for the policymaker.

The division of topics between these chapters is that, in the remainder of this chapter, we address ourselves to an exploration of how our data system can help to identify the impact of sectoral expansion on different targets of policy such as output growth, employment, the income of particular household groups, and so on. Chapter 5 is more descriptive and examines the evidence we have adduced on the differential consumption patterns of different income groups. Given that different consumption patterns imply different degrees of import dependence and labour intensity (if the goods are produced domestically), this provides us with a basis for quantifying the balance of payments and employment consequences of any proposed scheme for redistributing income. In conjunction with the later work on the price raising effects of indirect taxation, it also permits us to quantify the redistributional consequences of this taxation. Chapter 6 then concentrates on the impact on both resource allocation and income distribution of fiscal policy. We look first at how the data system permits identification of the impact of the tax system, including the dual exchange rate system, on the incentives for different categories of exports. We then show how the data framework can be used to calculate the levels of effective protection applying to particular sectors, and thereby indicate how the allocation of resources is distorted by prevailing levels of protection. Finally, we look at the implications of the present tax system on the structure of prices as a first step in an analysis of the income distributional consequences of indirect taxation.

2 Input–output structure of the accounts

In Chapter 3 it has been pointed out that the basic information needed for input–output analysis is contained within our social accounting matrix framework. Also, it was argued subsequently that in order to analyse income distribution within a macroeconomic setting it is necessary to disaggregate households in a manner analogous to the disaggregation of production structure which underlies input–output analysis. In this chapter, then, we present empirical results on these aspects of our accounts and show how they permit a generalisation of input–output to cover not only the structure of production but also the factorial distribution of income and its distribution across household types.

There are two main reasons for choosing this initial illustration of our accounting framework and the data therein. The first is that the exercise serves to illustrate the structure of the system and the circular flow of income as discussed in Chapter 3. Not least it becomes clear that the framework is ideally suited to multiplier analysis of the effect of exogenous injections into the economy, such as increased export demand, on outputs, employment and incomes, with each of these being disaggregated according to the classification system embodied in the social accounts.

A second reason for choosing this exercise as an initial illustration is that it is a natural extension of previous work on two fronts. One of these refers to earlier modelling work in Iran.* In this study an attempt was made to capture the two-way linkages whereby (i) income distribution affects final demand, and hence the structure of production; and (ii) the structure of production influences factor demands and hence the structure of income distribution. In the Iran study there were no explicit accounts for the factors of production so that the routing of this second linkage via these accounts had to be an implicit one. One consequence of this is that employment effects could not be fully integrated into the analysis. Since factor accounts do appear explicitly in the present framework, it is natural to re-examine this earlier work in the light of this innovation.

*See Pyatt *et al.* (1972) or Blitzer, Clark and Taylor (1975), Chapter 5.

While our own earlier work lacked factor accounts, previous studies in Sri Lanka had fallen short on the treatment of income distribution. This should not be taken as a criticism however. Foundations laid in data collection and reconciliation† were built on by our collaborator in the present study, S. Narapalasingham, who constructed a dynamic input–output model of the Sri Lankan economy.* His work was based on that of the Cambridge Growth Project which in turn pioneered social accounting in the form which is now established as the UN SNA.† Narapalasingham's was a pioneering effort which shared with its antecedents a treatment of institutions which did not disaggregate the household sector. However, within this restriction, Narapalasingham was perhaps first in the field to explore empirically how a change in income distribution might affect production structure, i.e. the first of the two links discussed above. Not least, then, in view of the interest in these questions in Sri Lanka the initial illustration of our social-accounting matrix relates to the interdependence of production structure and income distribution.

†By Abdul Meguid and Lal Jayawardena as part of a UNDP Planning Project.

*S. Narapalasingham (1970).

†See Cambridge, Department of Applied Economics (1962–).

Table 4.1 sets out the basic structure of our social-accounting matrix for present purposes. The three main sets of accounts which interest us are for factors, institutions (current accounts) and activities. Within these are six factors of production and six institutions, including three different household types: urban, rural and estate households. These and other details have been given in Table 3.9 which sets out the classifications in full. Also shown there are the 48 production activities distinguished in the full study. This number is raised to 50 for the present analysis by treating domestic service and public administration as

Table 4.1 *Schematic social-accounting matrix*

		Expenditures				
		Factors	Institutions	Activities	Other accounts	Total
Receipts	Factors	0	0	$T_{1.3}$	$T_{1.4}$	t_1
	Institutions	$T_{2.1}$	$T_{2.2}$	0	$T_{2.4}$	t_2
	Activities	0	$T_{3.2}$	$T_{3.3}$	$T_{3.4}$	t_3
	Other accounts	0	$T_{4.2}$	$T_{4.3}$	$T_{4.4}$	t_4
	Total	t_1'	t_2'	t_3'	t_4'	

additional production activities rather than as direct factor payments to value added by institutions. All other accounts are collected together as a fourth block in the schema of Table 4.1. These are accounts for indirect taxes; the combined capital account for domestic institutions; and a combined current and capital account for the rest of the world.

From this description it will be apparent that some rearrangement of data is necessary to arrive at the format of Table 4.1. But this is valuable in that it simplifies the structure of interrelations within the accounts to expose essentials, and also serves to illustrate once more our view that accounts should be arranged in the way that is most constructive for the task to hand.

In Table 4.1 the notation $\mathbf{T}_{i.j}$ is used to represent the matrix of transactions which are receipts of the *i*th set of accounts resulting from expenditures by the *j*th set. Thus $\mathbf{T}_{1.3}$ is a 6 X 50 matrix showing how each of the six factors of production derives incomes from each of the 50 production activities. Numerically this sub-matrix is obtained from Appendix 1, Table A41a. This is indicated in Table 4.2, which shows schematically the data sources in the statistical appendix that provide an empirical illustration of the schema in Table 4.1.

Having explained the sources of data for Table 4.1 we can now proceed to their analysis. A first step towards this is to note that the symmetry of the table preserves the basic identity of row and column totals which are denoted (in row-sum notation) by the vectors $\mathbf{t}_1$ to $\mathbf{t}_4$. The normalisation of a transactions matrix $\mathbf{T}_{i.j}$ by the vector $\mathbf{t}_j$ will be denoted by $\mathbf{A}_{i.j}$ where

$$\mathbf{A}_{i.j} = \mathbf{T}_{i.j}\hat{\mathbf{t}}_j^{-1} \tag{4.1}$$

Thus $\mathbf{A}_{i.j}$ is obtained from $\mathbf{T}_{i.j}$ by dividing elements of the latter by the sum of the column in which they appear. We shall adopt this treatment for All $\mathbf{T}_{i.j}$s in each of the first three columns of Table 4.1. Doing so implies that the accounting constraints across rows can be expressed as

$$\begin{bmatrix} \mathbf{t}_1 \\ \mathbf{t}_2 \\ \mathbf{t}_3 \\ \mathbf{t}_4 \end{bmatrix} = \begin{bmatrix} 0 & 0 & \mathbf{A}_{1.3} \\ \mathbf{A}_{2.1} & \mathbf{A}_{2.2} & 0 \\ 0 & \mathbf{A}_{3.2} & \mathbf{A}_{3.3} \\ 0 & \mathbf{A}_{4.2} & \mathbf{A}_{4.3} \end{bmatrix} \begin{bmatrix} \mathbf{t}_1 \\ \mathbf{t}_2 \\ \mathbf{t}_3 \end{bmatrix} + \begin{bmatrix} \mathbf{x}_1 \\ \mathbf{x}_2 \\ \mathbf{x}_3 \\ \mathbf{x}_4 \end{bmatrix} \tag{4.2}$$

where $\mathbf{x}_i$ is the vector of row sums of the sub-matrix $\mathbf{T}_{i.4}$ for each i = 1, 2, 3, 4.

Table 4.2 *Data sources for empirical illustration of the accounts schema in Table 4.1*

		Expenditures				
		Factors	Institutions	Production activities	Other	Total
Receipts	Factors			Source for $T_{1.3}$: A.41A	Source for $T_{1.4}$: A.40	Source for t_1: A.40
	Institutions	Source for $T_{2.1}$: A.40	Source for $T_{2.2}$: A.40 A.14 A.25		Source for $T_{2.4}$: A.40 A.14 A.25	Source for t_2: A.40 A.14 A.25
	Production activities		Source for $T_{3.2}$: A.16	Source for $T_{3.3}$: A.16	Source for $T_{3.4}$: A.16	Source for t_3: A.16
	Other		Source for $T_{4.2}$: A.40 A.14 A.25	Source for $T_{4.3}$: A.16 A.14 A.25	Source for $T_{4.4}$: A.40 A.14 A.25	Source for t_4: A.40, A.14, A.25 A.16
	Total	t_1'	t_2'	t_3'	t_4'	

Subsequent analysis assumes that each of the $\mathbf{x}_i$s is an exogenous set of numbers, and that each of the $\mathbf{A}_{i.j}$ matrices in equation (4.2) has constant elements. This latter assumption is returned to later. Meanwhile, combining these two sets of assumptions implies that values of $\mathbf{t}_1$ to $\mathbf{t}_4$ can always be obtained from any assumed values of $\mathbf{x}_1$ to $\mathbf{x}_4$. And the mathematics of this can be expressed as

$$\begin{bmatrix} \mathbf{t}_1 \\ \mathbf{t}_2 \\ \mathbf{t}_3 \end{bmatrix} = \begin{bmatrix} 0 & 0 & \mathbf{A}_{1.3} \\ \mathbf{A}_{2.1} & \mathbf{A}_{2.2} & 0 \\ 0 & \mathbf{A}_{3.2} & \mathbf{A}_{3.3} \end{bmatrix} \begin{bmatrix} \mathbf{t}_1 \\ \mathbf{t}_2 \\ \mathbf{t}_3 \end{bmatrix} + \begin{bmatrix} \mathbf{x}_1 \\ \mathbf{x}_2 \\ \mathbf{x}_3 \end{bmatrix} \tag{4.3}$$

and

$$\mathbf{t}_4 = \mathbf{A}_{4.2}\mathbf{t}_2 + \mathbf{A}_{4.3}\mathbf{t}_3 + \mathbf{x}_4 \tag{4.4}$$

Equation (4.4) above shows how the balance of the fourth set of accounts can be derived once $\mathbf{t}_2$ and $\mathbf{t}_3$ are known, that is, once the first three sets of accounts are balanced. This residual balance equation is not of further interest to us. We can therefore concentrate on equation (4.3) which can now be written as

$$\mathbf{t} = \mathbf{A}\mathbf{t} + \mathbf{x} \tag{4.5}$$

so that

$$\mathbf{t} = (\mathbf{I} - \mathbf{A})^{-1}\,\mathbf{x} \tag{4.6}$$

These last two results show how $\mathbf{t}$ (i.e. $\mathbf{t}_1$, $\mathbf{t}_2$ and $\mathbf{t}_3$) can be derived from $\mathbf{x}$ (i.e. $\mathbf{x}_1$, $\mathbf{x}_2$ and $\mathbf{x}_3$), through a generalised inverse $(\mathbf{I} - \mathbf{A})^{-1}$. This is a strictly analogous procedure to that followed in conventional input–output analysis which is concerned with the determination of $\mathbf{t}_3$ only. From equation (4.3) it is apparent that

$$\mathbf{t}_3 = \mathbf{A}_{3.3}\mathbf{t}_3 + (\mathbf{A}_{3.2}\mathbf{t}_2 + \mathbf{x}_3) \tag{4.7}$$

so that

$$t_3 = (I - A_{3.3})^{-1} (A_{3.2}t_2 + x_3) \tag{4.8}$$

Equation (4.8) is a part of our system and therefore completely consistent with it. It is also the end of the story in the simplest form of input–output analysis since the latter assumes that $A_{3.2}t_2$ is exogenous. Thus, in this simplest approach t_3 (the level and structure of output) is derived through the inverse $(I - A_{3.3})^{-1}$ of direct and indirect commodity requirements on the basis of assumed demands on activities from other accounts. From (4.8) an obvious extension is to decompose these assumed demands and to allow for a part of them, $A_{3.2}t_2$, to be determined simultaneously with t_3. This part depends on t_2, i.e. on the level and distribution of income across institutions. Accordingly, we are considering a system in which output structure and income distribution are determined simultaneously, as opposed to one which treats them as separable.

3 Decomposition of the generalised inverse

The preceding discussion, and in particular equation (4.6), shows that the simultaneous determination of factor and institution incomes and production levels can simply be regarded as a generalised problem in input–output analysis, given appropriate definition of the matrix **A**. However, it also follows from the subsequent discussion of how this links to conventional input–output analysis that it may be useful to decompose the generalised inverse $(I - A)^{-1}$ into contributory parts which reflect the different mechanisms at work within it, resulting from the interconnections within the system. This is the approach pursued in this section. From it we conclude that it is useful to write $(I - A)^{-1}$ as

$$(I - A)^{-1} = M = M_3 M_2 M_1 \tag{4.9}$$

where the notation **M** is used to indicate a multiplier matrix in the sense that all its elements are greater than (or equal to) the corresponding elements of an identity matrix.

The aggregate multiplier matrix, **M**, shows how an increase in any element of **x** will increase the corresponding element of **t** by at least the same amount, and may also have indirect effects on other elements of **t**. The right-hand side of equation (4.9) states that these aggregate multipliers can be decomposed into three separate multipliers. M_1 and M_2 are referred to as being 'own-effects' multipliers, as opposed to M_3 which collects together cross-effects. The distinction between M_1 and M_2 is as follows. A change in an element in the vector x_i of **x** will influence t_i for two sets of reasons. One is that there may be transfers within the ith set of accounts so that, for example, an increase in demand on a production sector will cause it to increase its demand on another production sector. A second example is that increased income for companies from an exogenous source will result in increased income for government through profits taxation. Such multiplier processes which operate within a set of accounts can be referred to as 'own direct effects' or 'own transfer effects'. These contrast with M_2 which collects together 'own indirect effects' which arise from the fact that an increase in the elements of x_i will affect t_i via other accounts. Thus an increase in demand on a production activity will cause it to hire more factors. This will raise incomes in the factor accounts which will in turn raise incomes in the institution accounts. These latter accounts will spend some of the increased income, and in doing so will raise demand on the production accounts beyond the level of the initial increase which came from an exogenous source. Finally, the multipliers $\mathbf{M}_3$ record cross effects, i.e. the impact of an increase in elements of $\mathbf{x}_i$ on $\mathbf{t}_j$ for $j \neq i$.

To establish the existence and properties of these multiplier effects requires manipulation of equation (4.3). This can start most easily with the own direct effects, $\mathbf{M}_1$, which depend on transfers within a particular set of accounts. Some slight rearrangement of equation (4.3) allows us to write it as

$$\begin{bmatrix} \mathbf{t}_1 \\ \mathbf{t}_2 \\ \mathbf{t}_3 \end{bmatrix} = \begin{bmatrix} 0 & 0 & 0 \\ 0 & \mathbf{A}_{2.2} & 0 \\ 0 & 0 & \mathbf{A}_{3.3} \end{bmatrix} \begin{bmatrix} \mathbf{t}_1 \\ \mathbf{t}_2 \\ \mathbf{t}_3 \end{bmatrix} + \begin{bmatrix} 0 & 0 & \mathbf{A}_{1.3} \\ \mathbf{A}_{2.1} & 0 & 0 \\ 0 & \mathbf{A}_{3.2} & 0 \end{bmatrix} \begin{bmatrix} \mathbf{t}_1 \\ \mathbf{t}_2 \\ \mathbf{t}_3 \end{bmatrix} + \begin{bmatrix} \mathbf{x}_1 \\ \mathbf{x}_2 \\ \mathbf{x}_3 \end{bmatrix} \tag{4.10}$$

The basic operation involved here is to separate out the diagonal elements of $\mathbf{A}$ (i.e. $\mathbf{A}_{2.2}$ and $\mathbf{A}_{3.3}$) from the other non-zero elements.

Moving the first term on the right hand of (4.10) over the left, it is then natural to define a matrix $\mathbf{M}_1$ where

$$\mathbf{M}_1 = \begin{bmatrix} \mathbf{I} & 0 & 0 \\ 0 & (\mathbf{I} - \mathbf{A}_{2.2})^{-1} & 0 \\ 0 & 0 & (\mathbf{I} - \mathbf{A}_{3.3})^{-1} \end{bmatrix} \tag{4.11}$$

from which equation (4.10) can be re-expressed as

$$\mathbf{t} = \mathbf{M}_1 \begin{bmatrix} 0 & 0 & \mathbf{A}_{1.3} \\ \mathbf{A}_{2.1} & 0 & 0 \\ 0 & \mathbf{A}_{3.2} & 0 \end{bmatrix} \mathbf{t} + \mathbf{M}_1 \mathbf{x} \tag{4.12}$$

Equation (4.11) defines the multiplier matrix $\mathbf{M}_1$ introduced in equation (4.9). This definition shows that it captures the impact of interindustry dependence on the conventional input–output sense via the inverse $(\mathbf{I} - \mathbf{A}_{3.3})^{-1}$. Indeed equation (4.8) is contained in equation (4.12). This is clearly seen when the latter is written extensively as

$$\begin{bmatrix} \mathbf{t}_1 \\ \mathbf{t}_2 \\ \mathbf{t}_3 \end{bmatrix} = \begin{bmatrix} \mathbf{I} & 0 & 0 \\ 0 & (\mathbf{I} - \mathbf{A}_{2.2})^{-1} & 0 \\ 0 & 0 & (\mathbf{I} - \mathbf{A}_{3.3})^{-1} \end{bmatrix} \times \left\{ \begin{bmatrix} 0 & 0 & \mathbf{A}_{1.3} \\ \mathbf{A}_{2.1} & 0 & 0 \\ 0 & \mathbf{A}_{3.2} & 0 \end{bmatrix} \begin{bmatrix} \mathbf{t}_1 \\ \mathbf{t}_2 \\ \mathbf{t}_3 \end{bmatrix} + \begin{bmatrix} \mathbf{x}_1 \\ \mathbf{x}_2 \\ \mathbf{x}_3 \end{bmatrix} \right\} \tag{4.13}$$

The equation (4.8) is now easily extracted from the expression for $\mathbf{t}_3$ in equation (4.13). At the same time it can be noted that symmetric treatment of the institutions accounts leads to the novelty of having the multiplier matrix $(\mathbf{I} - \mathbf{A}_{2.2})^{-1}$ in the system.

The result (4.12) can be written as

$$\mathbf{t} = \mathbf{A}^* \mathbf{t} + \mathbf{M}_1 \mathbf{x} \tag{4.14}$$

where the matrix $\mathbf{A}^*$ is defined as

$$\mathbf{M}_1 \begin{bmatrix} 0 & 0 & \mathbf{A}_{1.3} \\ \mathbf{A}_{2.1} & 0 & 0 \\ 0 & \mathbf{A}_{3.2} & 0 \end{bmatrix}$$

A point to emphasise is that $\mathbf{A}^*$ has zeros on its diagonals: the importance of diagonal elements of $\mathbf{A}$ is taken care of by the multiplier matrix $\mathbf{M}_1$. This means that, apart from $\mathbf{M}_1$, all other multiplier effects must be due to the connectedness of different accounts in the system as a whole. This will be discussed shortly. Meanwhile it should be noted that the procedures assume that $\mathbf{M}_1$ exists. From (4.11) this requires the existence of the Leontief inverse $(\mathbf{I}-\mathbf{A}_{3.3})^{-1}$ and of $(\mathbf{I}-\mathbf{A}_{2.2})^{-1}$. The necessary conditions needed are weaker than with respect to $(\mathbf{I}-\mathbf{A})^{-1}$ and present no problems in practice. Assuming they are satisfied, $(\mathbf{I}-\mathbf{A}_{\mathrm{i.i}})^{-1}$ can be written as

$$(\mathbf{I}-\mathbf{A}_{\mathrm{i.i}})^{-1} = \mathbf{I} + \mathbf{A}_{\mathrm{i.i}} + \mathbf{A}_{\mathrm{i.i}}^{2} + \mathbf{A}_{\mathrm{i.i}}^{3} + \ldots \tag{4.15}$$

which must be greater than $\mathbf{I}$ since all elements of $\mathbf{A}_{\mathrm{i.i}}$ are positive. Hence $\mathbf{M}_1$ exists and is a multiplier matrix.

Turning now to the effects which depend on connections between the accounts it can be noted that from equation (4.14)

$$\mathbf{t} = (\mathbf{I}-\mathbf{A}^*)^{-1}\,\mathbf{M}_1\mathbf{x} \tag{4.16}$$

assuming that the inverse $(\mathbf{I}-\mathbf{A}^*)^{-1}$ exists. Again this assumption is quite reasonable, and we can write

$$(\mathbf{I}-\mathbf{A}^*)^{-1} = \mathbf{I} + \mathbf{A}^* + \mathbf{A}^{*2} + \mathbf{A}^{*3} + \ldots \tag{4.17}$$

$$= (\mathbf{I} + \mathbf{A}^* + \mathbf{A}^{*2})\,(\mathbf{I} + \mathbf{A}^{*3} + \mathbf{A}^{*6} + \ldots \tag{4.18}$$

$$= (\mathbf{I} + \mathbf{A}^* + \mathbf{A}^{*2})\,(\mathbf{I} - \mathbf{A}^{*3})^{-1} \tag{4.19}$$

The second of the two matrices on the right hand side of this equation is our definition of $\mathbf{M}_2$, and the first of the pair is $\mathbf{M}_3$. From (4.18) it is apparent that both these matrices are indeed multiplier matrices.

The decomposition (4.19) may seem to be somewhat arbitrary since it is generally true that

$$(\mathbf{I}-\mathbf{A}^*)^{-1} = (\mathbf{I} + \mathbf{A}^* + \ldots + \mathbf{A}^{*k-1})\,(\mathbf{I}-\mathbf{A}^{*k})^{-1} \tag{4.20}$$

However, the choice of $k = 3$ in (4.19) is appropriate in the present case because we are dealing with a system of three accounts: factors, institutions and activities. If the system was extended, e.g. by adding commodity accounts, then $k = 4$ would be the appropriate choice.

The significance of $k = 3$ in the present case is seen most easily by considering the successive terms $\mathbf{A}^*$, $\mathbf{A}^{*2}$ and $\mathbf{A}^{*3}$ which appear in (4.19). Writing $\mathbf{A}^*$ as

$$\mathbf{A}^* = \begin{bmatrix} 0 & 0 & \mathbf{A}^*_{1.3} \\ \mathbf{A}^*_{2.1} & 0 & 0 \\ 0 & \mathbf{A}^*_{3.2} & 0 \end{bmatrix} \tag{4.21}$$

it follows that

$$\mathbf{A}^{*2} = \begin{bmatrix} 0 & \mathbf{A}^*_{1.3}\,\mathbf{A}^*_{3.2} & 0 \\ 0 & 0 & \mathbf{A}^*_{2.1}\,\mathbf{A}^*_{1.3} \\ \mathbf{A}^*_{3.2}\,\mathbf{A}^*_{2.1} & 0 & 0 \end{bmatrix} \tag{4.22}$$

and

$$\mathbf{A}^{*3} = \begin{bmatrix} \mathbf{A}^*_{1.3}\,\mathbf{A}^*_{3.2}\,\mathbf{A}^*_{2.1} & 0 & 0 \\ 0 & \mathbf{A}^*_{2.1}\,\mathbf{A}^*_{1.3}\,\mathbf{A}^*_{3.2} & 0 \\ 0 & 0 & \mathbf{A}^*_{3.2}\,\mathbf{A}^*_{2.1}\,\mathbf{A}^*_{1.3} \end{bmatrix} \tag{4.23}$$

Thus $\mathbf{A}^{*3}$ is a block diagonal matrix and therefore so is $\mathbf{M}_2$. The elements of this matrix show the multipliers that result from tracing an initial impact from its source through the system and back to the account from which it started. Since we have a system of three accounts here, getting back to source requires three steps.*

The fact that $\mathbf{M}_2$ is block diagonal implies that it captures only the effects of $\mathbf{x}_i$ on $\mathbf{t}_i$. Cross effects can be derived from $\mathbf{M}_3$ which, from (4.21) and (4.22), is given by

$$\mathbf{M}_3 = \begin{bmatrix} \mathbf{I} & \mathbf{A}^*_{1.3}\,\mathbf{A}^*_{3.2} & \mathbf{A}^*_{1.3} \\ \mathbf{A}^*_{2.1} & \mathbf{I} & \mathbf{A}^*_{2.1}\,\mathbf{A}^*_{1.3} \\ \mathbf{A}^*_{3.2}\,\mathbf{A}^*_{2.1} & \mathbf{A}^*_{3.2} & \mathbf{I} \end{bmatrix} \tag{4.24}$$

*The interested reader can note that the accounts would be spurious if it was impossible to return to source. In fact the non-zero entries of $\mathbf{A}^*$ must correspond to a permutation matrix. In the present case, (4.21) corresponds to the permutation matrix given by Stone as equation (2) in his foreword to this volume.

Tables 4.3 to 4.7 give some empirical results from applying the above analysis to our Sri Lanka data. They do not cover a complete calibration of the four matrices $\mathbf{M}_1$, $\mathbf{M}_2$, $\mathbf{M}_3$ and $\mathbf{M}$ since each of these has 62 rows and columns and the full results are therefore somewhat overwhelming. Accordingly, we have selected some of the potentially more interesting sub-matrices for presentation and discussion.

The submatrices which form the diagonal of the matrix $\mathbf{M}$ are shown in Tables 4.3 to 4.5. The first of these, denoted $\mathbf{M}(1,1)$ shows the full multiplier effect of an exogenous increase in the income of a particular factor on that factor and all others. These multipliers include both direct and indirect effects. They show, for example, that a unit exogenous increase in income for rural labour results in an overall increase of 1.36 units in rural labour income, i.e. the specific multiplier is 1.36. However other factors also receive increased income as a result of the one exogenous increase, notably 'other private capital' which benefits to the extent of 0.87.

Table 4.3 has a number of interesting features. Particularly worthy of note are the low multipliers for estate labour and public capital: these factors benefit relatively little from increased demand for other factors (see the rows of the table relating to these two factors). It can also be noted that increased demand for the factor 'public capital' is of relatively little benefit in generating derived demand for other factors (see the column for public capital).

Because the first sub-matrices on the diagonals of $\mathbf{M}_1$ and $\mathbf{M}_3$ are both identity matrices, it follows that $\mathbf{M}(1,1)$ is equal to the leading element on the main diagonal of $\mathbf{M}_2$. Hence,

$$\mathbf{M}(1,1) = \mathbf{M}_2(1,1) \tag{4.25}$$

as noted in the title of Table 4.3. This implies that the numbers in that table

Table 4.3 *Components of the multiplier matrices* $\mathbf{M}(1,1) = \mathbf{M}_2(1,1)$

			Factors of Production					
			Labour			Capital		
			Urban	Rural	Estate	Housing	Other private	Public
Factors of production	Labour	Urban	1.20	0.19	0.19	0.19	0.18	0.08
		Rural	0.36	1.36	0.38	0.35	0.34	0.12
		Estate	0.03	0.03	1.04	0.03	0.03	0.01
	Capital	Housing	0.16	0.14	0.13	1.14	0.13	0.02
		Other private	0.77	0.87	0.96	0.77	1.76	0.13
		Public	0.02	0.02	0.02	0.02	0.02	1.00

derive solely from own indirect effects, i.e. from an exogenous increase in income of a factor resulting in further increases in factor incomes via the effects of the initial increase working through the other accounts and back to source.

In contrast, own indirect effects are not the only contribution to the income multipliers for institutions. In addition there are 'own direct (or transfer) effects' and these are shown as

$$\mathbf{M}_1(2,2) = (\mathbf{I} - \mathbf{A}_{2.2})^{-1} \tag{4.26}$$

in Table 4.4 as the lower of the two numbers in each cell. Generally these transfer effects are quite small: the largest elements refer to the impact of increased income for private companies on the incomes of urban households (0.31) and government (0.23).

When own indirect and direct effects are combined (to form $\mathbf{M}(2,2)$) we obtain the full income multipliers for institutions shown by the upper number in each cell of Table 4.4. The most prominent feature here is, perhaps, the contrast between rural and estate households. Indeed it is interesting to note that rural households gain more than estate households from an exogenous increase in income for the latter (see the column relating to estate households). They also have the same relationship with government, and benefit considerably from other exogenous income increases that originate with urban households or private companies. However, when interpreting these results it should be remembered that a multiplier increase for rural households should be divided by the total income of rural households to obtain the proportionate change in rural incomes. Redistribution will then be in favour of rural households as opposed to, say, urban households, only if the proportionate change is greater for the former than the latter.

Table 4.5 gives the final element in the diagonal of $\mathbf{M}$ (i.e. $\mathbf{M}(3,3)$) as the first figure in each cell, together with the conventional Leontief inverse,

$$\mathbf{M}_1(3,3) = (\mathbf{I} - \mathbf{A}_{3.3})^{-1} \tag{4.27}$$

Table 4.4 *Components of the multiplier matrices* **M**(2,2) *and* $\mathbf{M}_1$(2,2)

		Institutions					
		Households			Companies		
		Urban	Rural	Estate	Private	Public	Government
Institutions: Households	Urban	1.41 / 1.01	0.42 / *	0.43 / *	0.61 / 0.31	0.12 / 0.01	0.67 / 0.05
	Rural	0.97 / 0.01	2.01 / 1.00	1.08 / *	0.81 / 0.16	0.23 / 0.01	1.29 / 0.07
	Estate	0.04 / *	0.05 / *	1.05 / 1.00	0.03 / 0.01	0.01 / *	0.05 / *
Institutions: Companies	Private	0.24 / *	0.26 / *	0.28 / *	1.15 / 1.01	0.04 / *	0.24 / 0.03
	Public	0.04 / 0.01	0.03 / *	0.03 / *	0.04 / 0.02	1.03 / 1.02	0.14 / 0.11
Institutions: Government		0.21 / 0.10	0.14 / 0.02	0.13 / *	0.30 / 0.23	0.21 / 0.19	1.16 / 1.03

* = Less than 0.005.
The elements of **M**(2,2) are the upper entries while the elements of $\mathbf{M}_1$ (2,2) are the lower entries in each cell.

which is provided by the second of each pair of cell numbers. The full details in this table are presented primarily to enable readers to pursue calculations of their own design. For present purposes some of the main points emerge from Table 4.6 which sets out statistics of off-diagonal elements of the table in frequency distribution form.

With reference to Table 4.6 it is clear from the large number of zero and negligible numbers in the Leontief inverse that the direct interdependence of industries in Sri Lanka is limited. However, once indirect effects are taken into account, over 80 per cent of the elements are recorded as 0.01 or larger. This, then, gives a sense of magnitude to the general expectation that allowing for indirect effects enhances the interdependence within the economy.

Examination of Table 4.5 reveals that most of the larger elements in **M**(3,3) occur in relatively few rows: row 4, Paddy; row 8, Other agriculture; row 10a, Rice and grinding mills; row 16, Other processed foods; row 40a, Wholesale trade; row 40b, Retail trade; row 40c, Other transport; and row 41d, Dwellings. Thus the table suggests that the generalised effect of increased demand on any productive sector is to raise demand for the basic necessities of food, shelter and the activities most closely associated with them.

The final set of results to be presented refer to the full multiplier effects of increased demand for the products of each of the fifty production activities on factor incomes (**M**(1,3)) and on institution incomes (**M**(2,3)). These are shown in Table 4.7. In reading the table it should be noted that since these results refer to off-diagonal partitions of **M**, there is no reason, a priori, why any element of the table should exceed unity.*

*It can also be noted that some elements in the rows for public capital and public companies are negative. This reflects the observed losses of state enterprises in some activities in the base year.

Table 4.5 *Components of the multiplier matrices:* **M**(3,3) *and* $\mathbf{M}_1$(3,3)

PRODUCTION ACTIVITY

	1 Tea	2 Rubber	3 Coconuts	4 Paddy	5 Livestock	6 Fishing	7 Logging and firewood	8 Other agriculture	9 Mining and quarrying	10a Rice milling	10b Flour milling	11 Dairy products	12 Bread	13 Other bakery products	14 Carbonated beverages	15 Desiccated coconut	16 Other processed food	17 Distilling	18 Tobacco	19 Textiles	20 Wood products	21 Paper	22 Leather	23 Rubber	24 Chemicals
1 Tea	1.02 1.00	0.02 0	0.02 0	0.02 0	0.02 0	0.02 0	0.02 0	0.02 0	0.02 0	0.02 0	0.01 0	0.01 0	0.01 0	0.01 0	0.01 0	0.01 0	* 0	0.01 0	0.01 0	0.01 0	0.02 0	0.01 0	0.01 0	0.01 0	0.01 0
2 Rubber	* *	1.00 1.00	* 0	* 0	* 0	* 0	* 0	* 0	* *	* *	* 0	* *	* *	* *	* 0	* *	* 0	* *	* *	* *	* *	* *	0.01 *	0.15 0.15	* *
3 Coconuts	0.08 *	0.09 *	1.09 1.00	0.08 *	0.13 0.05	0.09 0	0.08 0	0.08 *	0.08 0	0.08 *	0.05 0	0.05 0.01	0.03 *	0.11 0.05	0.06 0	0.95 0.86	0.02 0.01	0.09 0.02	0.04 *	0.04 *	0.08 *	0.06 *	0.08 0.01	0.07 *	0.10 0.05
4 Paddy	0.21 *	0.22 *	0.22 0	1.27 1.07	0.20 0	0.22 0	0.21 0	0.20 0	0.20 0	1.18 0.97	0.12 0	0.08 0	0.08 0	0.14 0	0.15 0	0.21 *	0.01 0	0.18 0	0.10 *	0.10 *	0.21 0	0.16 0.01	0.17 *	0.16 *	0.14 *
5 Livestock	0.05 0	0.05 0	0.05 0	0.05 0	1.05 1.00	0.06 0	0.05 0	0.05 0	0.05 0	0.05 *	0.03 0	0.25 0.23	0.02 0	0.04 0	0.04 0	0.05 0	* *	0.05 0	0.03 0	0.03 0	0.05 0	0.04 0	0.23 0.18	0.05 *	0.04 0
6 Fishing	0.05 0	0.05 0	0.05 0	0.05 0	0.05 *	1.06 1.00	0.06 0	0.05 0	0.05 0	0.05 0	0.03 0	0.02 0	0.02 0	0.04 0	0.04 0	0.05 0	0.01 *	0.05 *	0.03 *	0.03 0	0.05 0	0.04 0	0.04 0	0.04 0	0.04 0
7 Logging and fire-wood	0.03 0.01	0.02 *	0.02 0	0.02 0	0.02 0	0.02 0	1.02 1.00	0.02 0	0.04 0.02	0.02 0	0.01 0	0.01 0	0.02 0.02	0.01 *	0.02 *	0.02 *	* 0	0.02 0	0.01 0	0.01 *	0.10 0.08	0.02 *	0.02 *	0.02 *	0.02 *
8 Other agriculture	0.22 *	0.23 *	0.22 0	0.21 0	0.21 *	0.23 0	0.22 0	1.30 1.09	0.21 *	0.21 *	0.13 0	0.09 *	0.09 0	0.16 0.01	0.16 0	0.22 *	0.01 0	0.19 0	0.19 0.09	0.11 *	0.24 0.02	0.17 0.01	0.18 *	0.17 *	0.15 *
9 Mining and quarrying	* *	* *	* 0	* 0	* 0	* 0	* 0	* 0	1.00 1.00	* *	* 0	* 0	* 0	* *	* *	* *	* 0	* 0	* *	* *	* *	0.01 0.01	* *	* *	* *
10a Rice milling	0.22 0	0.23 0	0.22 0	0.21 0	0.20 0	0.22 0	0.22 0	0.21 0	0.20 0	1.21 1.00	0.13 0	0.09 0	0.08 0	0.14 0	0.16 0	0.22 0	0.01 0	0.19 0	0.10 0	0.10 0	0.21 0	0.15 0	0.17 0	0.16 0	0.14 0
10b Flour milling	0.01 0	0.01 0	0.01 0	0.01 0	0.01 0	0.01 0	0.01 0	0.01 0	* 0	* 0	1.00 1.00	* 0	0.04 0.04	* 0	* 0	0.01 0	* 0	* 0	* 0	* 0	0.01 0	* 0	* 0	* 0	* 0
11 Dairy products	0.01 0	0.02 0	0.02 0	0.01 0	0.01 0	0.02 0	0.02 0	0.01 0	0.01 0	0.01 0	0.01 0	1.01 1.00	0.01 0	0.01 0	0.01 0	0.02 0	* 0	0.01 0	0.01 0	0.01 0	0.02 0	0.01 0	0.01 0	0.01 0	0.01 0
12 Bread	0.03 0	0.04 0	0.04 0	0.04 0	0.04 0	0.04 0	0.04 0	0.04 0	0.04 0	0.04 0	0.02 0	0.02 0	1.02 1.00	0.03 0	0.03 0	0.04 0	* 0	0.04 0	0.02 0	0.02 0	0.04 0	0.03 0	0.03 0	0.03 0	0.03 0
13 Other bakery products	0.01 0	0.01 0	0.03 0	0.01 0	0.01 0	0.02 0	0.02 0	0.01 0	0.01 0	0.01 0	0.01 0	0.01 0	0.01 0	1.02 1.00	0.02 0	0.02 0	0.02 0	0.02 0	0.02 0	0.02 0	0.02 0	0.02 0	0.02 0	0.01 0	0.01 0
14 Carbonated beverages	* 0	* 0	* 0	* 0	* 0	* 0	* 0	* 0	* 0	* 0	* 0	* 0	* 0	* 0	1.00 1.00	* 0	* 0	* 0	* 0	* 0	* 0	* 0	* 0	* 0	* 0
15 Desiccated coco-nut	0.03 *	0.03 *	0.03 *	0.03 *	0.09 0.07	0.03 0	0.02 0	0.03 *	0.02 0	0.02 *	0.01 0	0.02 0.01	0.01 *	0.08 0.06	0.02 0	1.02 1.00	0.01 *	0.02 *	0.01 *	0.01 *	0.02 *	0.02 *	0.03 0.01	0.02 *	0.0 0.0
16 Other processed food	0.17 0	0.22 0	0.24 0	0.24 0	0.27 0.04	0.25 0	0.25 0	0.23 0	0.23 0	0.23 0	0.14 0	0.10 0.01	0.10 0.01	0.16 0	0.17 0	0.24 0	1.01 1.00	0.23 0.02	0.11 0	0.12 0	0.24 0	0.16 0	0.20 0.01	0.17 *	0.1 *
17 Distilling	0.02 0	0.02 *	0.02 0	0.01 *	0.01 0	0.02 0	0.02 0	0.01 *	0.01 0	0.01 *	0.01 0	0.01 0	0.01 *	0.01 0	0.01 0	0.02 0	* 0	1.44 1.42	0.01 0	0.01 0	0.02 0	0.01 *	0.01 *	0.01 *	0.0 0.0
18 Tobacco	0.08 0	0.09 0	0.09 0	0.09 0	0.09 0	0.09 0	0.09 0	0.08 0	0.08 0	0.08 0	0.05 0	0.03 0	0.03 0	0.06 0	0.06 0	0.09 0	* 0	0.05 0	1.04 1.00	0.04 0	0.09 0	0.06 0	0.07 0	0.07 0	0.0 0
19 Textiles	0.06 *	0.06 0	0.06 0	0.05 0	0.05 0	0.06 0	0.06 0	0.05 0	0.05 *	0.05 0	0.03 0	0.02 0	0.02 *	0.04 *	0.04 *	0.06 *	* 0	0.05 *	0.03 0	1.09 1.06	0.06 *	0.04 *	0.05 *	0.04 *	0.0 *
20 Wood products	0.04 0.02	0.02 *	0.02 *	0.02 *	0.02 *	0.02 *	0.02 *	0.02 *	0.02 *	0.02 *	0.01 *	0.01 *	0.01 *	0.01 *	0.02 *	0.02 *	* *	0.02 *	0.01 *	0.02 *	1.36 1.34	0.02 *	0.02 *	0.02 *	0.0 0.0
21 Paper	0.05 0.03	0.04 0.01	0.02 *	0.03 *	0.02 *	0.03 *	0.02 0	0.03 0	0.02 *	0.03 *	0.01 *	0.01 *	0.01 *	0.02 *	0.02 *	0.03 *	* *	0.02 *	0.02 0.01	0.02 0.01	0.03 *	1.07 1.06	0.05 0.03	0.06 0.04	0.0 0.0
22 Leather	0.01 0	0.01 0	0.01 0	0.01 0	0.01 0	0.01 0	0.01 0	0.01 *	0.01 0	0.01 *	0.01 0	* 0	* 0	0.01 *	0.01 0	0.01 0	* 0	0.01 0	* 0	* 0	0.01 *	0.01 0	1.19 1.18	0.03 0.02	0.0 0
23 Rubber	0.01 *	0.01 *	0.01 *	0.01 *	0.01 *	0.01 *	0.01 *	0.01 *	0.01 *	0.01 *	0.01 0	* *	* *	0.01 *	0.01 *	0.01 *	* *	0.01 *	0.01 *	0.01 *	0.01 *	0.01 *	0.06 0.05	1.01 1.00	0.0 *
24 Chemicals	0.06 0.02	0.07 0.03	0.06 0.01	0.08 0.03	0.05 *	0.05 *	0.05 *	0.09 0.04	0.04 *	0.08 0.03	0.03 0	0.02 *	0.03 0.01	0.03 *	0.04 *	0.06 0.01	* *	0.04 *	0.02 *	0.03 0.01	0.05 *	0.06 0.02	0.07 0.03	0.08 0.04	1.(1.(
25 Oils and fats	0.03 *	0.03 *	0.03 *	0.03 *	0.10 0.07	0.03 0	0.03 0	0.03 *	0.03 0	0.03 *	0.02 0	0.03 0.02	0.01 *	0.07 0.06	0.02 0	0.03 *	0.01 0.01	0.03 *	0.01 *	0.01 *	0.03 *	0.02 *	0.04 0.02	0.03 *	0. 0.
26 Coconut fibre and yarn	0 0	0 0	0 0	0 0	0 0	0 0	0 0	0 0	0 0	0 0	0 0	0 0	0 0	0 0	0 0	0 0	0 0	0 0	0 0	0 0	0 0	0 0	0 0	0 0	0 0
27 Petroleum and coal	0.07 0.02	0.06 0.02	0.05 *	0.05 *	0.05 *	0.07 0.02	0.05 *	0.05 *	0.07 0.03	0.06 0.01	0.03 *	0.02 *	0.02 *	0.04 0.01	0.04 *	0.06 0.01	* *	0.05 *	0.02 *	0.03 *	0.07 0.02	0.06 0.02	0.05 0.01	0.10 0.06	0. 0.
28 Structural clay products	* 0	* 0	* 0	* 0	* 0	* 0	* 0	* 0	* *	* 0	* 0	* 0	* 0	* 0	* 0	* 0	* 0	* 0	* 0	* 0	* 0	* 0	* 0	* 0	* 0
29 Ceramics	* *	* 0	* 0	* 0	* 0	* 0	* 0	* 0	* *	* 0	* 0	* 0	* 0	0.02 0.01	* 0	* 0	* 0	* 0	* 0	* 0	0.01 0.01	* 0	* 0	* 0	* *
30 Cement	* *	* 0	* 0	* 0	* 0	* 0	* 0	* 0	* *	* 0	* 0	* 0	* 0	* 0	* 0	* 0	* 0	* 0	* 0	* 0	* 0	* 0	* 0	* 0	* 0
31 Basic metals	0.01 *	0.01 *	0.01 *	0.01 *	* *	0.01 *	0.01 *	* *	* *	* *	* 0	* *	* *	0.01 *	0.01 0.01	0.01 *	* 0	* *	* *	* *	0.01 *	0.01 *	0.01 *	* *	0. *
32 Light engineering	0.10 0.04	0.09 0.03	0.07 0.01	0.07 *	0.06 *	0.07 *	0.08 0.02	0.07 *	0.11 0.05	0.07 0.01	0.04 *	0.04 0.02	0.03 *	0.11 0.06	0.13 0.08	0.07 0.01	* *	0.06 *	0.04 0.01	0.05 0.02	0.07 0.01	0.08 0.03	0.08 0.03	0.06 0.01	0. 0.
33 Transport equip-ment	* *	0.01 *	0.01 *	0.01 0	* 0	0.01 *	0.01 *	0.01 0	* *	* *	* 0	* *	* 0	* *	* *	0.01 *	* 0	* 0	* *	* *	0.01 *	* *	* *	* *	* *

The elements of **M**(3,3) are the upper entries in each cell, while the elements of $\mathbf{M}_1$ (3,3) are the lower entries.

25 Oils and fats	26 Coconut fibre and yarn	27 Petroleum and coal	28 Structural clay products	29 Ceramics	30 Cement	31 Basic metals	32 Light engineering	33 Transport equipment	34 Machinery, other equipment	35 Other manufacturing	36 Construction	37 Electricity	38 Road passenger transport	39 Rail transport	40a Wholesale trade	40b Retail trade	40c Other transport	41a Communication	41b Hotels and restaurants	41c Professional services	41d Dwellings	41e Other services	Domestic services	Public administration	
0.02	0.02	0.01	0.02	0.01	0.01	0.01	0.01	0.01	0.01	0.01	0.01	0.01	0.02	0.02	0.01	0.02	0.02	0.02	0.02	0.02	0.02	0.01	0.02	0.02	1 Tea
0	0	0	0	0	*	0	0	0	0	0	0	0	0	0	0	0	0	0	*	0	0	0	0	0	
*	*	*	*	*	*	*	*	*	*	*	*	*	0.01	*	*	*	0.01	*	*	*	*	*	*	*	2 Rubber
*	*	*	*	*	*	*	*	*	*	*	*	*	*	*	0	0	*	*	*	*	0	*	0	0	
0.84	0.23	0.06	0.09	0.06	0.04	0.03	0.05	0.04	0.06	0.07	0.08	0.06	0.08	0.08	0.08	0.08	0.08	0.08	0.11	0.08	0.08	0.04	0.09	0.09	3 Coconuts
0.75	0.14	0	0	0	*	0	*	*	0	*	*	0	*	*	0	0	*	0	0.03	*	0	*	0	0	
0.21	0.22	0.14	0.22	0.14	0.11	0.08	0.14	0.09	0.14	0.17	0.19	0.16	0.20	0.19	0.19	0.20	0.20	0.21	0.26	0.20	0.20	0.11	0.23	0.22	4 Paddy
*	0	0	0	0	*	0	0	0	*	*	0	0	*	*	0	*	0	*	0.07	*	0	*	0	0	
0.05	0.05	0.04	0.05	0.04	0.03	0.02	0.03	0.03	0.04	0.04	0.05	0.04	0.05	0.05	0.05	0.05	0.05	0.05	0.07	0.05	0.05	0.03	0.06	0.06	5 Livestock
0	0	0	0	0	0	0	0	*	0	0	0	0	*	0	0	0	*	0	0.02	0	0	0	0	0	
0.05	0.06	0.04	0.06	0.04	0.03	0.02	0.04	0.02	0.04	0.04	0.05	0.04	0.05	0.05	0.05	0.05	0.05	0.05	0.07	0.05	0.05	0.03	0.06	0.06	6 Fishing
0	0	0	0	0	0	0	0	0	0	0	0	0	0	0	0	0	0	0	0.02	0	0	0	0	0	
0.02	0.02	0.01	0.07	0.02	0.01	0.01	0.01	0.02	0.02	0.02	0.03	0.02	0.02	0.02	0.02	0.02	0.02	0.02	0.07	0.02	0.02	0.01	0.02	0.02	7 Logging and firewood
*	0	*	0.05	*	*	*	*	0.01	*	*	0.01	0	*	*	*	0	*	*	0.05	*	*	*	0	0	
0.22	0.23	0.15	0.23	0.15	0.11	0.08	0.14	0.10	0.15	0.18	0.20	0.17	0.21	0.20	0.20	0.21	0.21	0.22	0.30	0.21	0.22	0.12	0.24	0.24	8 Other agriculture
*	0	0	0	0	*	0	*	*	*	*	*	0	*	*	*	*	0	*	0.10	*	*	*	0	0	
*	*	*	0.05	0.07	0.16	0.02	*	*	*	0.03	0.05	*	*	0.01	*	*	*	*	0.01	*	0.01	*	*	*	9 Mining and quarrying
*	0	*	0.05	0.07	0.16	0.01	*	*	*	0.02	0.04	*	*	*	*	*	*	*	0.01	*	*	*	0	0	
0.22	0.23	0.14	0.22	0.15	0.11	0.08	0.14	0.09	0.15	0.18	0.19	0.16	0.20	0.20	0.19	0.20	0.20	0.21	0.26	0.20	0.21	0.11	0.23	0.23	10a Rice milling
0	0	0	0	0	0	0	0	0	0	0	0	0	0	0	0	0	0	0	0.07	0	0	0	0	0	
0.01	0.01	*	0.01	*	*	*	*	*	*	*	*	*	*	*	*	*	*	0.01	0.03	*	0.01	*	0.01	0.01	10b Flour milling
0	0	0	0	0	0	0	0	0	0	0	0	0	0	0	0	0	0	0	0.02	0	0	0	0	0	
0.02	0.02	0.01	0.02	0.01	0.01	*	0.01	0.01	0.01	0.01	0.01	0.01	0.02	0.01	0.01	0.01	0.02	0.02	0.02	0.01	0.02	0.01	0.02	0.02	11 Dairy products
0	0	0	0	0	0	0	0	0	0	0	0	0	0	0	0	0	0	0	0.01	0	0	0	0	0	
0.04	0.04	0.03	0.04	0.03	0.02	0.02	0.03	0.02	0.03	0.03	0.04	0.03	0.04	0.04	0.04	0.04	0.04	0.04	0.05	0.04	0.04	0.02	0.05	0.05	12 Bread
0	0	0	0	0	0	0	0	0	0	0	0	0	0	0	0	0	0	0	0.02	0	0	0	0	0	
0.02	0.02	0.01	0.02	0.01	0.01	0.01	0.01	0.01	0.01	0.01	0.01	0.01	0.01	0.01	0.01	0.01	0.01	0.02	0.02	0.01	0.01	0.01	0.02	0.02	13 Other bakery products
0	0	0	0	0	0	0	0	0	0	0	0	0	0	0	0	0	0	0	0.01	0	0	0	0	0	
*	*	*	*	*	*	*	*	*	*	*	*	*	*	*	*	*	*	*	0.02	*	*	*	*	*	14 Carbonated beverages
0	0	0	0	0	0	0	0	0	0	0	0	0	0	0	0	0	0	0	0.02	0	0	0	0	0	
.90	0.03	0.02	0.03	0.02	0.01	0.01	0.02	0.01	0.02	0.02	0.02	0.02	0.02	0.02	0.02	0.02	0.02	0.02	0.02	0.03	0.02	0.01	0.03	0.03	15 Desiccated coconut
.27	*	0	0	0	*	0	*	*	0	*	*	0	*	*	0	0	*	0	*	*	0	*	0	0	
.24	0.25	0.15	0.25	0.17	0.12	0.09	0.15	0.10	0.16	0.19	0.22	0.18	0.23	0.22	0.21	0.22	0.22	0.23	0.27	0.22	0.23	0.13	0.25	0.25	16 Other processed food
	0	0	0	0	0	0	0	*	0	0	0	0	0	0	0	0	0	0	0.06	0	0	0	0	0	
.02	0.02	0.01	0.02	0.01	0.01	0.01	0.01	0.01	0.01	0.01	0.01	0.01	0.01	0.01	0.01	0.01	0.01	0.02	0.01	0.01	0.01	0.01	0.02	0.02	17 Distilling
	0	0	0	0	0	0	0	*	0	*	0	0	0	0	0	0	0	*	*	*	0	0	0	0	
.09	0.09	0.06	0.09	0.06	0.04	0.03	0.06	0.04	0.06	0.07	0.08	0.07	0.08	0.08	0.08	0.08	0.08	0.09	0.08	0.08	0.08	0.05	0.09	0.09	18 Tobacco
	0	0	0	0	0	0	0	0	0	0	0	0	0	0	0	0	0	0	0	0	0	0	0	0	
.06	0.06	0.04	0.06	0.04	0.04	0.02	0.04	0.02	0.04	0.05	0.05	0.04	0.05	0.05	0.05	0.05	0.05	0.06	0.07	0.05	0.06	0.03	0.06	0.06	19 Textiles
	0	*	*	*	0.01	0	*	*	*	*	*	*	*	*	*	0	0	*	0.02	*	0	0	0	0	
02	0.02	0.01	0.02	0.01	0.01	0.01	0.02	0.12	0.02	0.05	0.03	0.02	0.02	0.02	0.03	0.02	0.02	0.02	0.02	0.02	0.02	0.01	0.02	0.02	20 Wood products
	*	*	*	*	*	*	0.01	0.10	*	0.04	0.06	*	*	*	0.01	*	*	*	*	*	*	*	0	0	
03	0.03	0.02	0.03	0.02	0.02	0.01	0.02	0.01	0.05	0.08	0.02	0.02	0.03	0.03	0.02	0.03	0.03	0.04	0.03	0.03	0.02	0.02	0.03	0.03	21 Paper
	*	*	*	*	0.01	*	*	*	0.03	0.06	*	*	0.01	0.01	*	0.01	*	0.02	0.01	*	0	0.01	0	0	
01	0.01	0.01	0.01	0.01	*	*	0.01	0.03	0.01	0.01	0.01	0.01	0.01	0.01	0.01	0.01	0.01	0.01	0.01	0.01	0.01	*	0.01	0.01	22 Leather
	0	0	0	0	*	0	*	0.02	0	*	*	0	*	*	0	0	*	0	*	0	*	0	0	0	
01	0.01	0.01	0.01	0.01	0.01	*	0.01	0.03	0.01	0.01	0.01	0.01	0.05	0.01	0.01	0.01	0.05	0.01	0.01	0.01	0.01	0.01	0.01	0.01	23 Rubber
	*	*	*	*	*	*	*	0.02	*	*	*	*	0.04	*	*	*	0.04	*	*	*	*	*	0	0	
06	0.05	0.03	0.05	0.03	0.03	0.02	0.04	0.04	0.03	0.07	0.05	0.04	0.05	0.05	0.04	0.05	0.05	0.05	0.05	0.09	0.05	0.03	0.05	0.05	24 Chemicals
01	*	*	*	*	*	*	0.01	0.02	*	0.03	0.01	*	*	*	*	*	*	*	0.01	0.05	*	*	0	0	
04	0.03	0.02	0.03	0.02	0.01	0.01	0.02	0.01	0.02	0.02	0.03	0.02	0.03	0.03	0.03	0.03	0.03	0.03	0.03	0.03	0.03	0.02	0.03	0.03	25 Oils and fats
01	*	*	0	0	*	0	*	*	0	*	*	0	*	*	*	0	*	0	*	*	0	*	0	0	
	1.02	0	0	0	0	0	0	0	0	0	0	0	0	0	0	0	0	0	0	0	0	0	0	0	26 Coconut fibre and yarn
	1.02	0	0	0	0	0	0	0	0	0	0	0	0	0	0	0	0	0	0	0	0	0	0	0	
)7	0.14	2.68	0.12	0.13	0.06	0.07	0.04	0.03	0.08	0.05	0.06	0.06	0.14	0.09	0.06	0.05	0.07	0.05	0.06	0.06	0.05	0.03	0.05	0.05	27 Petroleum and coal
)2	0.09	2.65	0.07	0.10	0.03	0.05	0.01	0.01	0.04	0.01	0.01	0.02	0.10	0.04	0.01	*	0.02	*	0.02	0.01	*	0.01	0	0	
	*	*	1.00	*	*	*	*	*	*	*	0.02	*	*	*	*	*	*	*	*	*	*	*	*	*	28 Structural clay products
	0	0	1.00	0	0	0	0	0	0	0	0.02	0	0	*	0	0	0	*	0	*	*	*	0	0	
	*	*	*	1.00	*	*	*	*	*	*	0.01	*	*	*	*	*	*	*	0.01	0.01	*	*	*	*	29 Ceramics
	0	0	0	1.00	0	0	0	*	0	*	0.01	0	0	*	0	0	0	*	*	*	*	*	0	0	
	*	*	*	*	1.18	*	*	*	*	*	0.07	*	*	*	*	*	*	*	*	*	0.01	*	*	*	30 Cement
	0	0	0	*	1.18	0	0	0	0	0	0.07	0	0	*	0	0	0	*	0	*	*	*	0	0	
1	0.01	0.01	0.01	*	0.01	1.01	0.08	0.02	0.03	0.01	0.02	0.01	0.01	0.01	0.01	*	0.01	0.01	0.01	*	0.01	*	0.01	0.01	31 Basic metals
	*	*	*	*	0.01	1.01	0.08	0.02	0.03	0.01	0.02	*	0.01	0.01	*	*	*	*	*	*	*	*	0	0	
7	0.09	0.08	0.07	0.05	0.15	0.12	1.12	0.06	0.05	0.14	0.12	0.12	0.15	0.13	0.07	0.07	0.11	0.07	0.07	0.07	0.07	0.04	0.07	0.07	32 Light engineering
1	0.02	0.04	0.01	0.01	0.11	0.09	1.08	0.03	0.01	0.09	0.06	0.07	0.09	0.07	0.01	*	0.05	0.01	0.01	*	*	*	0	0	
	0.01	*	0.01	*	*	*	0.02	1.00	*	0.01	0.01	*	0.01	0.01	*	*	0.01	0.01	*	*	0.01	*	0.01	0.01	33 Transport equipment
	*	*	*	*	*	*	0.01	1.00	*	*	*	*	*	*	*	*	*	*	*	0	0	*	0	0	

Table 4.5 (*continued from pages 78 and 79*)

PRODUCTION ACTIVITY

	1 Tea	2 Rubber	3 Coconuts	4 Paddy	5 Livestock	6 Fishing	7 Logging and firewood	8 Other agriculture	9 Mining and quarrying	10a Rice milling	10b Flour milling	11 Dairy products	12 Bread	13 Other bakery products	14 Carbonated beverages	15 Desiccated coconut	16 Other processed food	17 Distilling	18 Tobacco	19 Textiles	20 Wood products	21 Paper	22 Leather	23 Rubber	24 Chemicals
34 Machinery, other equipment	* 0	* 0	* 0	* 0	* 0	* 0	* 0	* 0	* 0	* 0	* 0	* 0	* 0	* 0	* 0	* 0	* 0	* 0	* 0	* 0	* 0	* 0	* 0	* 0	* 0
35 Other manufacturing	0.01 *	0.01 *	0.01 *	0.01 0	0.01 0	0.01 0	0.01 0	0.01 0	0.01 *	0.01 *	* 0	* 0	* *	0.01 *	0.01 *	0.01 *	* 0	0.01 *	* 0	* *	0.01 *	0.01 *	0.01 *	0.01 *	0.01 *
36 Construction	0.01 *	0.02 *	0.02 *	0.02 *	0.02 0	0.02 *	0.02 0	0.02 0	0.03 0.01	0.02 *	0.01 0	0.01 0	0.01 0	0.01 *	0.01 0	0.02 *	* 0	0.02 0	0.01 0	0.01 0	0.02 *	0.01 *	0.01 *	0.02 *	0.01 *
37 Electricity	0.02 0.01	0.02 *	0.01 *	0.01 *	0.01 *	0.02 *	0.02 *	0.01 *	0.04 0.03	0.02 *	0.01 *	0.02 0.01	0.01 *	0.03 0.02	0.08 0.07	0.02 *	* *	0.01 *	0.01 *	0.02 0.01	0.02 0.01	0.03 0.01	0.04 0.03	0.03 0.02	0.02 0.01
38 Road passenger transport	0.06 *	0.07 *	0.07 *	0.07 *	0.07 0	0.08 0	0.07 0	0.07 0	0.07 0	0.07 *	0.04 0	0.03 0	0.03 0	0.05 0	0.06 0	0.07 *	* 0	0.07 0	0.03 0	0.04 0	0.07 0	0.05 0	0.06 0	0.06 0	0.05 0
39 Rail transport	0.03 0.01	0.03 *	0.03 0	0.03 0	0.02 0	0.03 0	0.03 0	0.02 0	0.04 0.02	0.04 0.01	0.02 0	0.01 0	0.01 0	0.02 *	0.02 0	0.03 *	* 0	0.02 0	0.01 0	0.01 *	0.03 0.01	0.02 *	0.02 *	0.02 *	0.02 *
40a Wholesale trade	0.09 0.04	0.08 0.04	0.07 0.01	0.06 0.01	0.07 0.02	0.07 0.01	0.07 0.01	0.06 0.01	0.09 0.04	0.08 0.02	0.06 0.03	0.06 0.03	0.09 0.07	0.14 0.10	0.12 0.08	0.15 0.09	0.01 0.01	0.09 0.04	0.06 0.03	0.08 0.06	0.21 0.15	0.09 0.05	0.13 0.08	0.11 0.07	0.12 0.08
40b Retail trade	0.16 0	0.17 0	0.16 0	0.16 0	0.15 0	0.17 0	0.16 0	0.15 0	0.15 0	0.15 0	0.09 0	0.06 0	0.06 0	0.11 0	0.12 0	0.16 0	0.01 0	0.14 0	0.08 0	0.08 0	0.16 0	0.11 0	0.13 0	0.13 0	0.11 0
40c Other transport	0.13 0.02	0.12 0.01	0.12 0.01	0.11 *	0.12 0.01	0.12 0.01	0.12 0.01	0.11 0.01	0.12 0.01	0.12 0.01	0.06 *	0.06 0.02	0.08 0.04	0.12 0.05	0.09 0.01	0.16 0.05	0.01 *	0.12 0.02	0.07 0.02	0.08 0.03	0.19 0.08	0.11 0.03	0.14 0.05	0.13 0.05	0.11 0.04
41a Communication	0.02 0.01	0.02 *	0.02 *	0.02 *	0.01 *	0.02 *	0.02 *	0.01 *	0.01 *	0.02 *	0.01 *	0.01 *	0.01 *	0.01 *	0.01 *	0.02 *	* *	0.01 *	0.01 *	0.01 *	0.02 *	0.01 *	0.01 *	0.01 *	0.01 *
41b Hotels and restaurants	0.03 0	0.04 0	0.04 0	0.04 0	0.04 0	0.04 0	0.04 0	0.04 0	0.04 0	0.04 0	0.02 0	0.02 0	0.02 0	0.03 0	0.03 0	0.04 0	* 0	0.04 0	0.02 0	0.02 0	0.04 0	0.03 0	0.03 0	0.03 0	0.03 0
41c Professional services	0.04 *	0.04 *	0.05 *	0.04 *	0.04 0	0.05 *	0.05 0	0.04 0	0.04 0	0.04 *	0.03 0	0.02 *	0.02 *	0.03 *	0.03 *	0.04 *	* *	0.04 *	0.02 0	0.02 *	0.05 *	0.03 *	0.04 *	0.04 *	0.03 *
41d Dwellings	0.12 0	0.14 0	0.14 0	0.14 0	0.13 0	0.15 0	0.15 0	0.14 0	0.13 0	0.13 0	0.08 0	0.06 0	0.06 0	0.10 0	0.11 0	0.14 0	0.01 0	0.13 0	0.07 0	0.07 0	0.15 0	0.11 0	0.12 0	0.12 0	0.10 0
41e Other services	0.05 0.01	0.05 0.01	0.06 0.01	0.06 0.01	0.05 *	0.05 *	0.05 *	0.05 *	0.05 *	0.06 0.01	0.03 *	0.02 *	0.02 *	0.03 *	0.04 *	0.06 0.01	* *	0.04 *	0.02 *	0.02 *	0.05 *	0.04 *	0.04 *	0.04 *	0.03 *
Domestic services	0.02 0	0.02 0	0.02 0	0.02 0	0.02 0	0.02 0	0.02 0	0.02 0	0.02 0	0.02 0	0.01 0	0.01 0	0.01 0	0.01 0	0.02 0	0.02 0	* 0	0.02 0	0.01 0	0.01 0	0.02 0	0.02 0	0.02 0	0.02 0	0.01 0
Public administration	0.07 0	0.08 0	0.09 0	0.10 0	0.09 0	0.10 0	0.10 0	0.10 0	0.09 0	0.10 0	0.06 0	0.04 0	0.04 0	0.06 0	0.08 0	0.09 0	0.01 0	0.10 0	0.05 0	0.05 0	0.10 0	0.07 0	0.08 0	0.09 0	0.07 0

The elements of **M**(3,3) are the upper entries in each cell, while the elements of $\mathbf{M}_1$ (3,3) are the lower entries.

Table 4.6 *Frequency distributions for the size of off-diagonal elements of the matrices* $\mathbf{M}_1$*(3,3) and* **M***(3,3)*

Element size	$\mathbf{M}_1$(3,3) (Leontief inverse)	**M**(3,3)
0	1324	49
* ⩽0.005	781	440
0.01 to 0.03	228	981
0.04 to 0.06	63	400
0.07 to 0.09	32	216
0.10 to 0.12	11	103
0.13 to 0.15	4	92
0.16 to 0.18	2	50
0.19 to 0.21	–	51
0.22 to 0.24	1	52
0.25 to 0.27	–	11
0.28 +	4	5
Total	2450	2450

25 Oils and fats	26 Coconut fibre and yarn	27 Petroleum and coal	28 Structural clay products	29 Ceramics	30 Cement	31 Basic metals	32 Light engineering	33 Transport equipment	34 Machinery, other equipment	35 Other manufactur-ing	36 Construction	37 Electricity	38 Road passenger transport	39 Rail transport	40a Wholesale trade	40b Retail trade	40c Other transport	41a Communication	41b Hotels and restaurants	41c Professional services	41d Dwellings	41e Other services	Domestic services	Public administration	
* 0	* 0	* 0	* 0	* 0	* 0	* 0	* 0	* 0	1.00 1.00	* 0	* 0	* 0	* 0	* 0	* 0	* 0	* 0	* 0	* 0	* 0	* 0	* 0	* 0	* 0	34 Machinery, other equipment
0.01 *	0.01 0	0.01 *	0.01 *	0.01 *	* *	* 0	* *	* *	0.01 *	1.01 1.00	0.01 *	0.01 *	0.01 *	0.01 *	0.01 *	0.01 *	0.01 *	0.01 *	0.01 *	0.03 0.02	0.01 0	0.01 *	0.01 0	0.01 0	35 Other manufactur-ing
0.02 *	0.02 *	0.02 *	0.02 *	0.01 0	0.01 *	0.01 *	0.01 *	0.01 *	0.01 *	0.02 *	1.02 1.00	0.02 *	0.02 *	0.07 0.05	0.02 *	0.02 *	0.02 *	0.04 0.03	0.02 *	0.02 *	0.08 0.06	0.02 0.01	0.02 0	0.02 0	36 Construction
0.03 0.01	0.02 *	0.04 0.03	0.02 *	0.05 0.04	0.06 0.06	0.01 *	0.02 0.01	0.01 *	0.01 *	0.02 *	0.02 0.01	1.01 1.00	0.02 0.01	0.02 0.01	0.02 0.01	0.02 0.01	0.02 *	0.08 0.02	0.02 *	0.02 *	0.01 *	0.01 *	0.02 0	0.02 0	37 Electricity
0.07 *	0.07 0	0.05 *	0.08 0	0.05 0	0.04 0	0.03 0	0.05 *	0.03 0	0.05 0	0.06 0	0.07 0	0.06 0	1.07 1.00	0.07 *	0.07 *	0.07 *	0.07 *	0.08 0.01	0.07 0	0.07 *	0.07 0	0.05 0.01	0.08 0	0.08 0	38 Road passenger transport
0.03 *	0.03 *	0.04 0.02	0.03 *	0.02 *	0.02 *	0.01 *	0.02 *	0.01 *	0.02 *	0.02 *	0.03 0.01	0.02 *	0.03 *	1.03 1.00	0.02 *	0.02 *	0.03 *	0.03 0.01	0.02 *	0.03 *	0.03 *	0.01 *	0.03 0	0.03 0	39 Rail transport
0.19 0.14	0.08 0.02	0.12 0.03	0.13 0.08	0.08 0.04	0.10 0.07	0.05 0.03	0.13 0.09	0.14 0.12	0.14 0.10	0.14 0.10	0.15 0.10	0.09 0.05	0.13 0.08	0.16 0.11	1.06 1.01	0.06 0.01	0.09 0.03	0.10 0.05	0.10 0.06	0.09 0.04	0.06 0.01	0.04 0.01	0.06 0	0.06 0	40a Wholesale trade
0.16 0	0.17 0	0.11 0	0.17 0	0.11 0	0.08 0	0.06 0	0.10 0	0.07 0	0.11 0	0.13 0	0.15 0	0.12 0	0.15 0	0.15 0	0.15 0	1.15 1.00	0.15 0	0.16 0	0.14 0	0.15 0	0.16 0	0.09 0	0.18 0	0.17 0	40b Retail trade
0.18 0.07	0.13 0.02	0.11 0.03	0.16 0.05	0.11 0.04	0.08 0.03	0.06 0.02	0.12 0.05	0.10 0.05	0.12 0.04	0.15 0.06	0.15 0.05	0.10 0.02	0.14 0.04	0.16 0.06	0.10 0.01	0.10 *	1.12 1.02	0.14 0.03	0.12 0.03	0.12 0.02	0.11 *	0.07 0.01	0.12 0	0.12 0	40c Other transport
0.02 *	0.02 *	0.02 0.01	0.02 *	0.01 *	0.01 *	0.01 *	0.02 0.01	0.01 *	0.01 *	0.01 *	0.02 *	0.01 *	0.02 *	0.02 0.01	0.03 0.01	0.03 0.01	0.02 0.01	1.08 1.07	0.01 *	0.06 0.05	0.02 *	0.05 0.04	0.02 0	0.02 0	41a Communication
0.04 0	0.04 0	0.03 0	0.04 0	0.03 0	0.02 0	0.02 0	0.03 0	0.02 0	0.03 0	0.04 0	0.04 0	0.03 0	0.04 0	0.04 0	0.04 0	0.04 0	0.04 0	0.04 0	1.04 1.00	0.04 0	0.04 0	0.02 0	0.05 0	0.05 0	41b Hotels and restaurants
0.04 *	0.05 *	0.03 *	0.05 *	0.03 *	0.02 *	0.02 0	0.03 *	0.02 *	0.03 *	0.04 *	0.04 *	0.03 *	0.04 *	0.04 *	0.04 *	0.04 *	0.04 *	0.05 *	0.04 *	1.05 1.00	0.04 *	0.05 0.02	0.05 0	0.05 0	41c Professional services
0.14 0	0.15 0	0.11 0	0.15 0	0.10 0	0.07 0	0.06 0	0.10 0	0.07 0	0.11 0	0.12 0	0.13 0	0.11 0	0.14 0	0.14 0	0.14 0	0.14 0	0.14 0	0.15 0	0.13 0	0.14 0	1.14 1.00	0.08 0	0.16 0	0.17 0	41d Dwellings
0.06 0.01	0.05 *	0.04 0.01	0.05 *	0.03 *	0.03 *	0.02 *	0.03 *	0.02 *	0.04 *	0.04 *	0.05 *	0.04 *	0.06 0.01	0.05 0.01	0.05 0.01	0.05 *	0.05 *	0.07 0.03	0.05 *	0.05 0.01	0.05 *	1.03 1.00	0.05 0	0.05 0	41e Other services
0.02 0	0.02 0	0.02 0	0.02 0	0.01 0	0.01 0	0.01 0	0.01 0	0.01 0	0.02 0	0.02 0	0.02 0	0.02 0	0.02 0	0.02 0	0.02 0	0.02 0	0.02 0	0.02 0	0.02 0	0.02 0	0.02 0	0.01 0	1.02 1.00	0.02 0	Domestic services
0.09 0	0.09 0	0.11 0	0.10 0	0.07 0	0.08 0	0.04 0	0.06 0	0.04 0	0.07 0	0.08 0	0.08 0	0.10 0	0.08 0	0.09 0	0.10 0	0.10 0	0.09 0	0.09 0	0.09 0	0.10 0	0.10 0	0.07 0	0.09 0	1.10 1.00	Public administration

Table 4.7 contains perhaps the most interesting results of all since it shows how factor demands and incomes might be influenced by exogenous increases in the demand for products. Thus, for example, column 19 shows that an increase in exogenous demand for Textiles would primarily increase the income of private capital, and of both urban and rural labour. Moreover, the table shows that while the effects on capital are larger than those on labour, it is nevertheless households which stand to benefit most (as opposed to companies), once we allow for the distribution of profits.

The table shows that Estate households stand to gain relatively little from any increased exogenous demands except for Tea (column 1); Rubber (column 3); and the products of the three linked-process coconut industries (columns 3, 15 and 25). With these exceptions the rows for households show remarkable homogeneity: almost any exogenous increase in demand for goods will generate extra incomes for urban, rural and estate households in roughly constant ratios. Thus alternative patterns of expansion of the economy are likely to have similar effects on income distribution among households according to these calculations: the main issue for income distribution from the point of view of the structure of production is whether demand increases for traditional exports or for other goods.

4 Some further comments

The results discussed briefly in the preceding section serve first and fore-

Table 4.7 *Components of the multiplier matrices* **M**(1,3) *and* **M**(2,3)

PRODUCTION ACTIVITY

			1 Tea	2 Rubber	3 Coconuts	4 Paddy	5 Livestock	6 Fishing	7 Logging and firewood	8 Other agriculture	9 Mining and quarrying	10a Rice milling	10b Flour milling	11 Dairy products	12 Bread	13 Other bakery products	14 Carbonated beverages	15 Desiccated coconut	16 Other processed food	17 Distilling	18 Tobacco	19 Textiles	20 Wood products	21 Paper	22 Leather	23 Rubber	24 Chemicals
Factors of production	Labour	Urban	0.20	0.19	0.19	0.19	0.19	0.26	0.23	0.19	0.22	0.20	0.18	0.10	0.13	0.21	0.32	0.22	0.01	0.35	0.13	0.16	0.34	0.35	0.34	0.47	0.30
		Rural	0.42	0.59	0.68	0.47	0.48	0.47	0.53	0.51	0.63	0.48	0.36	0.23	0.23	0.42	0.30	0.66	0.03	0.39	0.28	0.31	0.67	0.49	0.50	0.50	0.42
		Estate	0.57	0.29	0.12	0.03	0.07	0.04	0.03	0.04	0.03	0.03	0.05	0.02	0.02	0.04	0.02	0.10	*	0.03	0.01	0.02	0.03	0.02	0.03	0.06	0.02
	Capital	Housing	0.11	0.13	0.13	0.13	0.12	0.14	0.13	0.13	0.12	0.13	0.08	0.05	0.05	0.09	0.10	0.13	0.01	0.12	0.06	0.07	0.13	0.10	0.11	0.11	0.09
		Other private	0.88	1.18	1.28	1.55	1.42	1.61	1.55	1.46	1.26	1.50	0.72	0.56	0.50	0.82	1.07	1.26	0.05	1.30	0.65	0.62	1.23	0.74	0.96	0.75	0.78
		Public	0.02	0.02	0.02	0.02	0.02	–0.02	0.02	0.02	0.06	0.02	0.04	0.01	0.01	0.02	0.03	0.02	0.01	0.02	0.01	0.03	0.03	0.05	0.03	0.12	0.02
Institutions	Households	Urban	0.42	0.48	0.51	0.56	0.53	0.64	0.60	0.54	0.52	0.56	0.35	0.24	0.25	0.41	0.58	0.53	0.03	0.66	0.29	0.31	0.64	0.54	0.58	0.66	0.50
		Rural	1.05	1.43	1.58	1.55	1.47	1.59	1.61	1.53	1.51	1.53	0.88	0.62	0.59	1.00	1.06	1.56	0.06	1.30	0.74	0.75	1.55	1.03	1.19	1.06	0.98
		Estate	0.58	0.31	0.13	0.05	0.09	0.06	0.05	0.06	0.04	0.05	0.06	0.03	0.03	0.05	0.04	0.12	*	0.04	0.02	0.03	0.05	0.03	0.05	0.07	0.03
	Com-panies	Private	0.25	0.33	0.36	0.42	0.39	0.44	0.43	0.40	0.35	0.41	0.20	0.15	0.14	0.23	0.30	0.35	0.02	0.36	0.18	0.17	0.34	0.21	0.27	0.22	0.22
		Public	0.04	0.04	0.04	0.04	0.03	–0.01	0.04	0.03	0.07	0.04	0.05	0.02	0.02	0.03	0.05	0.04	0.01	0.03	0.02	0.04	0.05	0.06	0.04	0.14	0.03
	Government		0.12	0.15	0.16	0.17	0.16	0.18	0.18	0.17	0.16	0.17	0.10	0.07	0.07	0.11	0.14	0.16	0.01	0.17	0.08	0.09	0.17	0.13	0.14	0.15	0.12

most to illustrate the interdependence of social accounts and the structure of the particular set of accounts which we have implemented. This emerges most clearly from the decomposition of the general multiplier, **M**, and in particular, its component, $\mathbf{M}_2$. This last shows how an exogenous injection into the system will circulate within it, thus amplifying the initial impact. More generally, the full matrix **M** captures the repercussions of any impact on all the different accounts, thus extending multiplier analysis beyond the simple Leontief inverse in the same way that SAM extends the basic Leontief information system discussed in Chapter 3. The empirical results show that the difference between **M** and $\mathbf{M}_1$ is quite marked, so the extension is important.

As well as showing the structure of interdependencies among the accounts, the results in the previous section confirm and extend the discussion of structure and linkages in the economy presented previously in Chapter 2 and, in an abbreviated SAM, in the final section of Chapter 3. In particular, they show the importance of the estate sector and of food, especially rice, to the economy. In one sense the detail serves only to show that our extensive disaggregation of production is unnecessary to identify these basic structural issues – six production activities might provide a sufficient complement to six factors and six institutions from this point of view. Indeed, this is one of the lessons we draw from our work for future reference.

This said, there is merit in the detail which applications in subsequent chapters serve to bring out. This derives from the fact that policy has to be designed at a finer level with respect to government revenue and expenditure, for example, than the single account we have considered here. Chapter 6, in particular, demonstrates this point. Meanwhile, it should be noted that, against this, the accuracy of the data diminishes rapidly beyond some level of disaggregation: with respect to factor accounts this point is almost certainly reached, if not exceeded in our work.

A further comment on the preceding exercise is that the empirical results and their interpretation depend crucially on assuming a constant **A** matrix. This is a more substantial assumption than is common in input–output analysis because as equation (4.2) indicates, our **A** matrix includes not only the standard input–

			25	26	27	28	29	30	31	32	33	34	35	36	37	38	39	40a	40b	40c	41a	41b	41c	41d	41e		
			Oils and fats	Coconut fibre and yarn	Petroleum and coal	Structural clay products	Ceramics	Cement	Basic metals	Light engineering	Transport equipment	Machinery, other equipment	Other manufacturing	Construction	Electricity	Road passenger transport	Rail transport	Wholesale trade	Retail trade	Other transport	Communication	Hotels and restaurants	Professional services	Dwellings	Other services	Domestic services	Public administration
Factors of production	Labour	Urban	0.24	0.22	0.42	0.32	0.20	0.17	0.20	0.21	0.22	0.41	0.26	0.32	0.38	0.44	0.41	0.37	0.23	0.43	0.44	0.24	0.35	0.19	0.22	0.57	0.62
		Rural	0.66	0.73	0.48	0.79	0.53	0.35	0.23	0.38	0.24	0.37	0.41	0.68	0.56	0.69	0.67	0.49	0.41	0.70	0.82	0.44	0.48	0.36	0.30	0.93	0.94
		Estate	0.10	0.13	0.02	0.03	0.02	0.02	0.01	0.02	0.01	0.02	0.02	0.04	0.03	0.04	0.04	0.03	0.03	0.04	0.03	0.04	0.04	0.03	0.02	0.09	0.04
	Capital	Housing	0.13	0.13	0.10	0.14	0.09	0.07	0.05	0.09	0.06	0.10	0.11	0.12	0.11	0.13	0.13	0.13	0.13	0.13	0.13	0.12	0.13	1.05	0.07	0.15	0.15
		Other private	1.25	1.26	0.60	1.20	0.77	0.61	0.44	0.86	0.51	0.81	1.19	1.00	0.74	1.01	0.98	1.22	1.49	0.99	0.93	1.34	1.29	0.78	0.69	0.84	0.84
		Public	0.01	0.03	0.41	0.03	0.14	0.30	0.50	0.01	0.01	0.02	–0.01	0.03	0.26	–0.06	0.03	0.04	0.04	0.03	0.03	0.02	0.02	0.02	0.15	0.02	0.02
Institutions	Households	Urban	0.55	0.53	0.58	0.61	0.39	0.33	0.30	0.42	0.34	0.61	0.54	0.57	0.58	0.69	0.66	0.66	0.59	0.68	0.68	0.55	0.66	0.65	0.39	0.80	0.84
		Rural	1.54	1.62	0.92	1.65	1.09	0.79	0.55	0.99	0.61	0.96	1.24	1.40	1.10	1.43	1.38	1.35	1.45	1.42	1.50	1.38	1.39	1.45	0.79	1.56	1.57
		Estate	0.11	0.14	0.03	0.05	0.03	0.02	0.02	0.03	0.02	0.03	0.04	0.05	0.04	0.05	0.05	0.04	0.05	0.05	0.04	0.05	0.06	0.09	0.03	0.11	0.05
	Companies	Private	0.35	0.35	0.18	0.34	0.22	0.17	0.12	0.24	0.14	0.23	0.33	0.28	0.22	0.29	0.28	0.34	0.41	0.28	0.27	0.37	0.36	0.43	0.19	0.25	0.25
		Public	0.03	0.05	0.43	0.05	0.16	0.32	0.06	0.02	0.02	0.04	0.01	0.05	0.28	–0.04	0.04	0.06	0.06	0.04	0.05	0.04	0.04	0.04	0.17	0.04	0.04
		Government	0.16	0.16	0.19	0.17	0.13	0.14	0.08	0.11	0.08	0.13	0.14	0.15	0.17	0.15	0.16	0.17	0.18	0.16	0.16	0.16	0.17	0.18	0.12	0.17	0.17

output system ($\mathbf{A}_{3.3}$ in our notation), but six other coefficient matrices as well. At the present moment, we are agnostic on the question of whether these six matrices are close enough to constant over time to give our modelling approach any real operational significance. But we would stress again the link between appropriate classification and modelling. Provided that classification has been carried out so that the differences between the coefficients relating to different factors, institutions and activities is sufficiently great, then the models just discussed can be of analytical value even though the absolute constancy of many individual coefficients is in doubt. This is because the size of the feasible changes in coefficients over a period of time will be insufficient to erode the differences between coefficients, which indicate the fundamental structure of the economy.

We should also add that the multiplier analysis based on a fixed **A** is probably a good guide to a number of issues in the context of Sri Lanka in 1970 because production was not limited by capacity in most sectors. However, in a different case this would not be so, and one or both of two modifications would then be needed. These would be to allow the **A** matrix to change, say, as a result of price changes or a change in import dependence.* Alternatively, some allowance would need to be made for increasing capacity in response to increased demand on a sector. Following this approach, investment becomes endogenous, thus increasing its interdependencies and increasing the multipliers attached to the remaining exogenous forces.† How best to pursue these alternative lines of development is a question we leave open. For now the point is simply that one can go only so far with simple models as a guide to either policy or prognosis.

Finally we should mention that although the models discussed in this chapter have said nothing explicitly about employment, this weakness is easily remedied by making some simple (perhaps fixed coefficient) assumption about the links between gross output and employment in each production activity. The models can then generate the employment implications of any of the exogenous changes which the analysis identifies.

*This is the development explored tentatively in Pyatt *et al.* (1972).

†This line has been pursued by our collaborator in the present study, Neil Karunaratne. See Karunaratne (1973).

5

An analysis of household consumption and expenditure patterns

1 Introduction

An important respect in which our particular SAM approach deviates from the UN standard is in disaggregation of the household sector. Our view is that concern for income distribution requires such disaggregation, in the same way that to go beyond national product into questions of output structure requires a disaggregation of production into separate, but interrelated, activities. In terms of incomes received the disaggregation of households implies that income inequalities between household types can be traced to differences in their endowments of factors and to the demand for them which derive from the structure of production, as well as to the system of current transfers. This then is a first step in explaining how income inequalities arise. On the expenditure side, differences in tastes and/or income levels between households imply that consumer demand for commodities will be sensitive to the distribution of income and hence output structure will depend on income distribution. There is therefore a two-way relationship between output structure and income distribution which is captured in its essential form by the pair of equations (4.6) and (4.8) which together define the model discussed in Section 2 of the previous chapter.

As discussed in the previous chapter, the way in which income distribution contributes to production structure is via the matrix of propensities to consume particular products by households of different types. This matrix has been denoted as part of $\mathbf{A}_{3.2}$ in Chapter 4, and the point has been made there that columns of $\mathbf{A}_{3.2}$ must be different, that is, household types must have different propensities to consume, if a redistribution of income between households is to have any influence on the structure of production. The question asked in this chapter is whether columns of $\mathbf{A}_{3.2}$ do in fact differ. In addition to providing a further illustration of the use of a SAM, some particular features are usefully exposed by the answer to this question.

2 Consumption patterns – all-island analysis

Tables 5.1 and 5.2 set out some basic data on household expenditure. The first of these shows a two-dimensional disaggregation of households by sector of location and by income group. The table records the levels of total expenditure according to these criteria. As noted in Appendix 1, these estimates have been derived after taking account of certain well-known underrecordings.* They include imputed expenditures of own-produced goods (e.g. food) but exclude consumption of rationed rice. Unrationed rice, consumption of which is

*See Appendix 1, p. 118.

Table 5.1 *Total expenditure by income group and sector of location, 1969/70 (Rs million)*

Income group (Rs household/month)	Urban	Rural	Estate	Total
0–199	181.7	1494.6	359.4	2035.7
200–399	593.4	2303.7	317.3	3214.4
400–599	414.5	1168.6	60.2	1643.3
600–799	254.2	494.6	14.7	763.5
800–999	193.5	200.7	3.1	397.3
1000 +	538.7	235.6	8.5	782.8
Total	2176.0	5897.8	763.2	8837.0

included in the estimates, is referred to as 'outside ration rice' in the following discussion. Table 5.2 shows the expenditure vectors for each household income group, for Sri Lanka taken as a whole. The classification of these expenditures is by consumer goods with 28 separate commodities being recorded.*

As an illustration of the data in Table 5.2, that part of it which relates to outside rationed rice is extracted in Table 5.3 and presented graphically in Figure 5.1. The table shows that the lowest income group spends 12.3 per cent of its total expenditure on outside ration rice, and that this percentage falls as incomes rise, so that for the highest income group it is down to 3.5 per cent. Graphically, this behaviour is represented by a continuously falling curve, implying that the income elasticity of demand for outside ration rice is less than one.†

This approach to the data could be repeated separately for each of the consumer commodity groups distinguished in Table 5.2, but it proves rather more interesting to consider sets of such commodities in order to extract some general features. As an initial step in this analysis, Table 5.4 shows the distribution of aggregate expenditures across all 28 consumer commodities for each income group in each sector as well as for all-island. Some comments on the inter-sectoral comparison will be made later, but first the analysis will centre upon the all-island results.

*Table A.20(b) of Appendix 1 shows the same detail but with the further disaggregation of households by sector of location. Thus corresponding elements in the expenditures of Urban, Rural and Estate households as shown in Table A.20(b) sum to the elements shown in Table 5.2.

†A horizontal curve would show a unitary income elasticity of demand and an upward sloping curve implies an elasticity greater than one.

Commodity groups 1 to 14 disaggregate total foodstuffs, and it is clear from the table that the percentage of total expenditure attributable to the sum of these items declines as income rises. In other words, the income elasticity of demand for food is less than one. This result also holds for 11 out of the 14 individual items classified as foodstuffs. Data for four of these commodities, which may be thought of as 'essential' foodstuffs (rice, condiments, sugar and wheat flour), are shown graphically in Figure 5.2 along with the three exceptions to the generally declining relationship with income, fish, dairy products and meat. None of these last items has a constant elasticity (which would imply a monotonic graph) but instead they exhibit changing gradients over the income range. A fairly immediate explanation for this phenomenon is that since the majority of households live at or around subsistence levels, a large proportion of the population can only afford to eat basic foodstuffs such as rice, flour and sugar. Meat and dairy products are therefore luxuries over the initial income range; or perhaps more correctly they can be described as 'semi-essential' foodstuffs. As income rises these items command increasing shares of the household budget. Fish is not quite in this category. It is a reasonably plentiful commodity in and around Sri Lanka and consumption generally declines as income rises. But it is

Table 5.2 *All-island household expenditure by income group, 1969/70 (Rs million)*

Consumer commodity	0–199	200–399	400–599	600–799	800–999	1000+	Total
1 Outside ration rice	249.8	341.4	146.1	52.8	21.3	27.5	838.8
2 Wheat flour	75.9	68.7	20.0	6.9	1.7	2.7	175.8
3 Other grains and cereals	84.1	114.5	50.2	22.9	9.5	14.5	295.8
4 Condiments	150.0	198.2	83.1	32.2	14.1	20.6	498.1
5 Pulses	33.7	42.4	16.7	5.9	2.4	3.6	104.7
6 Coconuts	94.1	114.8	46.8	18.3	8.0	10.3	292.2
7 Vegetables and fruits	147.1	205.2	97.4	41.1	21.6	32.1	544.6
8 Meat	21.5	44.7	31.6	15.7	7.3	18.2	139.0
9 Fish	124.3	214.6	97.7	39.8	16.6	29.4	522.4
10 Milk and milk products	36.9	88.7	51.7	27.7	14.2	27.0	246.3
11 Oils, fats, including butter	33.4	45.2	26.1	9.0	4.6	8.3	126.6
12 Tea	24.1	34.1	10.8	4.8	3.0	3.3	80.2
13 Sugar	112.7	158.8	68.9	25.1	10.7	13.9	390.2
14 Other food and beverages	52.4	68.7	28.6	11.8	7.2	12.0	180.7
15 Meals away from home	34.5	77.9	45.1	18.8	8.9	14.4	199.6
16 Toddy	16.5	20.2	9.0	3.5	0.4	0.0	49.6
17 Other alcoholic beverages	44.3	90.6	48.4	17.9	8.4	23.3	232.8
18 Traditional tobacco	54.2	51.8	13.9	4.6	1.2	0.9	126.7
19 Modern tobacco	49.9	139.9	92.4	36.5	17.2	28.9	364.8
20 Clothing and footwear	129.3	249.0	132.5	71.3	34.1	50.9	667.1
21 Rent, rates and water charges	126.1	209.7	142.9	72.0	48.5	107.9	707.2
22 Fuel and light	86.7	116.3	50.4	20.5	9.7	17.1	300.7
23 Consumer durables	20.4	58.3	47.4	28.4	12.4	52.4	219.2
24 Household operations	57.0	103.2	61.7	32.3	20.4	50.3	324.9
25 Personal care and health	54.7	91.0	46.3	21.5	10.8	18.6	242.9
26 Transport and communications	85.4	163.5	103.5	77.2	54.6	144.2	628.5
27 Recreation	28.5	80.6	60.4	37.2	20.4	43.8	271.0
28 Miscellaneous	8.3	22.2	13.4	7.8	8.2	6.8	66.7
Total	2035.7	3214.2	1643.3	763.5	397.5	782.8	8837.0

Table 5.3 *Percentage of total expenditure on outside-ration rice (all island)*

Income group	0–199 (1)	200–399 (2)	400–599 (3)	600–799 (4)	800–999 (5)	1000+ (6)
1 Expenditure on commodity (Rs million)	249.8	341.4	146.1	52.8	21.3	27.5
2 Total expenditure (Rs million)	2035.7	3214.4	1643.3	763.5	397.5	782.8
1 ÷ 2 (%)	12.3	10.6	8.9	6.9	5.4	3.5

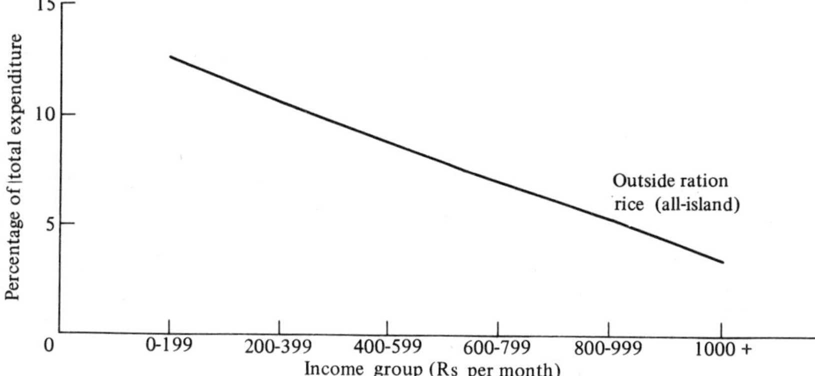

Figure 5.1 Expenditure on outside ration rice by income group. Source: Table 5.4.

still a luxury good for the lowest income groups. The curve in Figure 5.2 therefore rises at first, and then falls for higher income groups.

Figure 5.3 extends this analysis to some of the remaining commodities in Table 5.4. Certain of these command luxury status on the basis of their income elasticity of demand being greater than unity. Examples are transport and communications, furniture and furnishings, housing and consumer durables. These are shown in Figure 5.3 to be more or less continuously increasing in importance throughout the income range. It can be noted that if similar data for a developed country were being examined, then housing and furniture, for example, would not be expected to manifest the characteristics of luxury goods. But in Sri Lanka they do.

Also shown in Figure 5.3 are two commodities where the percentage expenditure curves first rise and then fall. These are clothing and footwear, and modern tobacco. As with the semi-essential foodstuffs, these are commodities which, for the poorest households, are luxury goods, but for which satiation of the luxury aspect is reached within the income range observed, so that the income elasticity of demand becomes less than unity after a certain point.

While the data largely bear out prior expectations, it is perhaps appropriate to sound a cautionary note on some of the *Socio-Economic Survey* (SES) data which underlie the comparisons. In Table A.18 of Appendix 1, the sampling distribution of households in the SES, classified by sector and income group, is shown. For some categories only a very small number of households were sampled, and while we have no independent evidence as to the population size,

Table 5.4 *Percentage of total expenditure on consumer commodities, by sector*

Consumer commodity	Urban 0–199	200–399	400–599	600–799	800–999	1000+	Rural 0–199	200–399	400–599	600–799	800–999	1000+	Estate 0–199	200–399	400–599	600–799	800–999	1000+	All-island 0–199	200–399	400–599	600–799	800–999	1000+
1 Outside ration rice	8.9	8.0	6.2	5.4	4.4	2.7	13.2	11.3	9.8	7.7	6.3	5.4	10.1	10.6	9.8	6.8	3.2	2.4	12.3	10.6	8.9	6.9	5.3	3.5
2 Wheat flour	1.4	1.1	0.7	0.6	0.4	0.3	2.6	1.5	1.1	1.0	0.4	0.4	9.6	8.7	7.1	2.7	3.2	1.2	3.7	2.1	1.2	0.9	0.4	0.3
3 Other grains and cereals	5.7	4.9	4.0	3.3	2.8	1.9	4.5	3.5	2.8	2.9	2.0	1.7	1.8	1.5	1.5	1.4	3.2	3.5	4.1	3.6	3.1	3.0	2.4	1.9
4 Condiments	7.2	6.2	5.0	4.2	3.7	2.5	7.6	6.0	5.0	4.2	3.4	2.9	6.5	7.3	6.5	4.8	3.2	3.5	7.4	6.2	5.1	4.2	3.5	2.6
5 Pulses	1.3	1.1	0.9	0.7	0.6	0.4	1.4	1.2	1.0	0.8	0.6	0.6	2.9	2.6	2.2	1.4	0.0	0.0	1.7	1.3	1.0	0.8	0.6	0.5
6 Coconuts	4.2	3.5	2.7	2.2	1.9	1.1	4.8	3.6	2.9	2.5	2.1	1.8	4.1	3.5	2.8	2.0	3.2	1.2	4.6	3.6	2.8	2.4	2.0	1.3
7 Vegetables and fruits	6.4	6.3	6.0	5.4	5.2	3.8	7.6	6.5	5.9	5.4	5.7	4.8	6.1	5.7	6.0	4.8	3.2	3.5	7.2	6.4	5.9	5.4	5.4	4.1
8 Meat	1.9	2.2	2.5	2.5	2.6	2.6	0.8	1.1	1.7	1.8	1.1	1.6	1.7	2.0	2.3	2.7	3.2	4.7	1.1	1.4	1.9	2.1	1.8	2.3
9 Fish	8.1	7.7	6.6	5.5	4.8	3.4	6.2	6.7	5.8	5.1	3.6	4.6	4.7	4.6	4.3	4.1	3.2	2.4	6.1	6.7	5.9	5.2	4.2	3.8
10 Milk and milk products	2.4	3.3	3.8	3.7	4.3	3.6	1.6	2.6	2.9	3.6	2.9	3.1	2.4	2.9	3.5	3.4	3.2	3.5	1.8	2.8	3.1	3.6	3.6	3.4
11 Oils, fats including butter	1.5	1.5	1.5	1.5	1.5	1.2	1.5	1.3	1.6	1.0	0.8	0.7	2.3	2.0	2.0	1.4	3.2	2.4	1.6	1.4	1.6	1.2	1.2	1.1
12 Tea	1.4	1.0	0.8	0.7	0.6	0.4	1.2	1.1	0.6	0.6	0.9	0.5	1.0	0.9	0.8	0.7	0.0	0.0	1.2	1.1	0.7	0.6	0.7	0.4
13 Sugar	5.6	5.0	3.9	3.1	2.6	1.5	5.8	5.0	4.3	3.4	2.8	2.4	4.4	4.4	4.2	2.7	3.2	2.4	5.5	4.9	4.2	3.3	2.7	1.8
14 Other food and beverages	1.7	1.6	1.5	1.6	1.7	1.5	2.6	2.2	1.8	1.5	1.9	1.6	2.9	2.7	2.3	2.0	3.2	1.2	2.6	2.1	1.7	1.5	1.8	1.5
Σ 1–14	57.7	53.4	46.1	40.4	37.1	26.9	61.4	53.6	47.2	41.5	34.5	32.1	60.5	59.4	55.3	40.9	38.4	31.9	60.9	54.2	47.1	41.1	35.6	28.5
15 Meals away from home	3.0	3.0	2.6	2.5	2.4	1.6	1.8	2.5	2.9	2.5	2.1	2.4	0.6	0.8	0.7	0.7	0.0	1.2	1.7	2.4	2.7	2.5	2.2	1.8
16 Toddy	0.7	0.7	0.4	0.2	0.2	0.0	0.8	0.6	0.6	0.6	0.0	0.0	0.9	0.7	0.5	0.5	0.1	0.0	0.8	0.6	0.5	0.5	0.1	0.0
17 Other alcoholic beverages	1.0	2.3	2.2	2.6	1.9	3.4	2.1	2.9	3.2	2.2	2.3	2.0	3.1	3.2	3.1	2.6	2.3	2.9	2.2	2.8	2.9	2.3	2.1	3.0
18 Traditional tobacco	1.7	0.9	0.4	0.2	0.1	0.0	2.7	1.7	1.0	0.8	0.5	0.4	3.0	2.3	1.0	0.7	0.0	0.0	2.7	1.6	0.8	0.6	0.3	0.1
19 Modern tobacco	4.0	5.7	6.6	5.9	5.2	4.0	2.3	4.3	5.4	4.2	3.5	3.0	2.3	2.2	3.3	4.7	4.3	3.6	2.5	4.4	5.6	4.8	4.3	3.7
20 Clothing and footwear	4.7	6.3	7.0	8.3	8.2	6.0	5.6	7.7	8.3	9.8	8.8	7.5	10.3	10.8	10.8	11.6	19.4	10.6	6.3	7.7	8.1	9.3	8.6	6.5
21 Rent, rates and water charges	8.5	8.3	11.3	13.4	14.3	16.8	6.3	6.4	8.0	7.4	10.2	6.9	4.6	4.1	4.2	9.4	12.2	13.8	6.2	6.5	8.7	9.4	12.2	13.8
22 Fuel and light	5.2	3.8	3.3	3.1	2.9	2.4	4.3	3.6	3.0	2.5	2.0	1.7	3.6	3.4	2.8	2.0	3.2	2.4	4.3	3.6	3.1	2.7	2.4	2.2
23 Consumer durables	0 8	1.7	2.4	2.4	3.4	5.6	1.1	1.9	3.1	4.4	2.9	9.3	0.7	1.4	2.0	3.4	0.0	3.5	1.0	1.8	2.9	3.7	3.1	6.7
24 Household operations	3.6	3.7	4.2	4.7	5.4	6.3	2.7	3.1	3.6	4.0	4.9	6.7	2.8	3.1	3.7	4.2	5.2	6.5	2.8	3.2	3.8	4.2	5.1	6.4
25 Personal care and health	2.9	2.9	2.8	3.0	3.0	2.5	2.8	2.9	2.8	2.7	2.5	2.1	2.1	2.2	3.3	3.4	0.0	2.4	2.7	2.8	2.8	2.8	2.7	2.4
26 Transport and communications	4.3	4.4	5.6	7.6	9.3	18.3	4.3	5.4	6.6	11.4	18.1	18.8	3.7	4.1	5.3	10.2	9.7	15.6	4.2	5.1	6.3	10.1	13.7	18.4
27 Recreation	1.6	2.2	4.2	5.0	6.1	5.2	1.4	2.7	3.5	4.8	4.2	6.5	1.3	1.7	3.5	5.0	5.2	5.6	1.4	2.5	3.7	4.9	5.1	5.6
28 Miscellaneous	0.3	0.7	0.9	0.7	0.6	1.0	0.4	0.7	0.8	1.2	3.5	0.6	0.5	0.6	0.5	0.7	0.0	0.0	0.4	0.7	0.8	1.0	2.1	0.9
Total	100.0	100.0	100.0	100.0	100.0	100.0	100.0	100.0	100.0	100.0	100.0	100.0	100.0	100.0	100.0	100.0	100.0	100.0	100.0	100.0	100.0	100.0	100.0	100.0

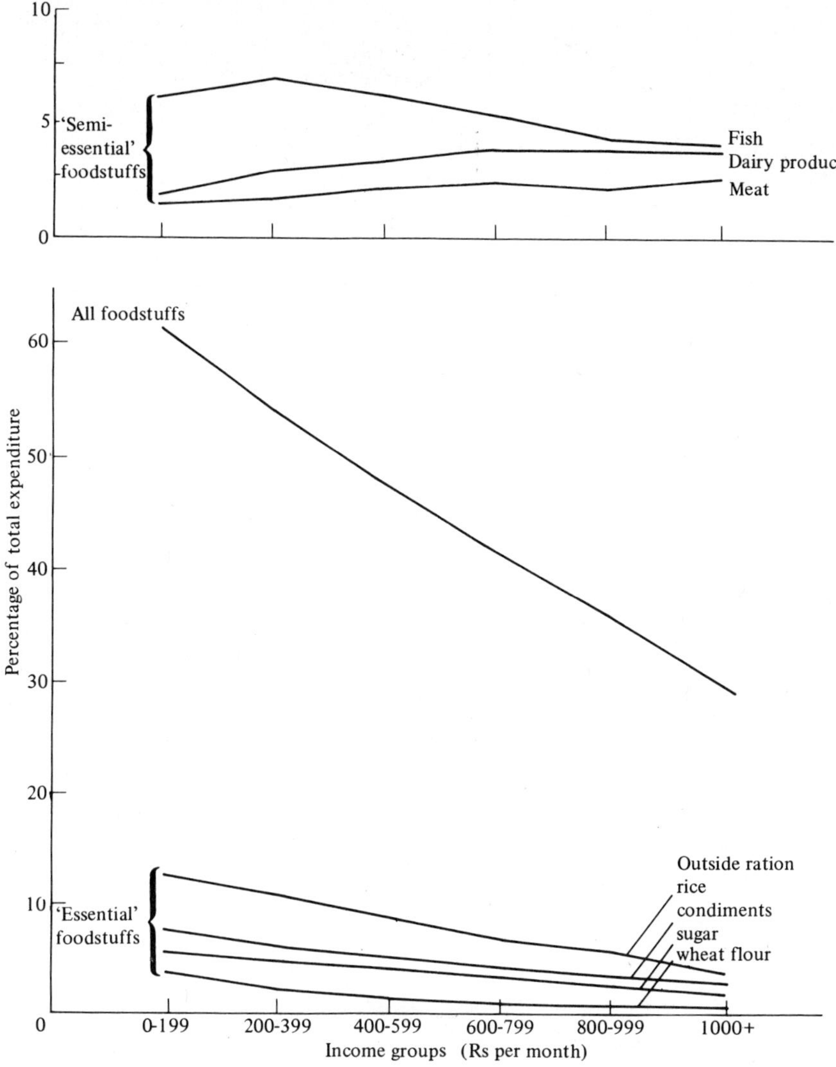

Figure 5.2 Expenditure on food by income group. Source: Table 5.4.

it is fair to remark that the sampling fraction which underlie these sample sizes may well be small also. Unless the variability of the observations is very small, large sampling errors are likely to result. It is primarily for this reason that the all-island analysis of data on expenditure patterns across income groups is much more reliable than the sectoral comparisons which could be carried out. Sampling errors may also account for some of the departures from monotonicity observed in some of these relations.

3 Balance of payments and government revenue implications

Interdependence between demand structure and the distribution of income is not the only mechanism whereby the latter can have an immediate influence on the capabilities of an economy. In particular the import content of household budgets may differ by household group so that an income redistribution would have repercussions on the balance of payments. Similarly, depending on the progressivity of indirect taxation, government revenue is not independent of the pattern of expenditure across households. Our social-accounting matrix provides a ready means of investigating these issues.

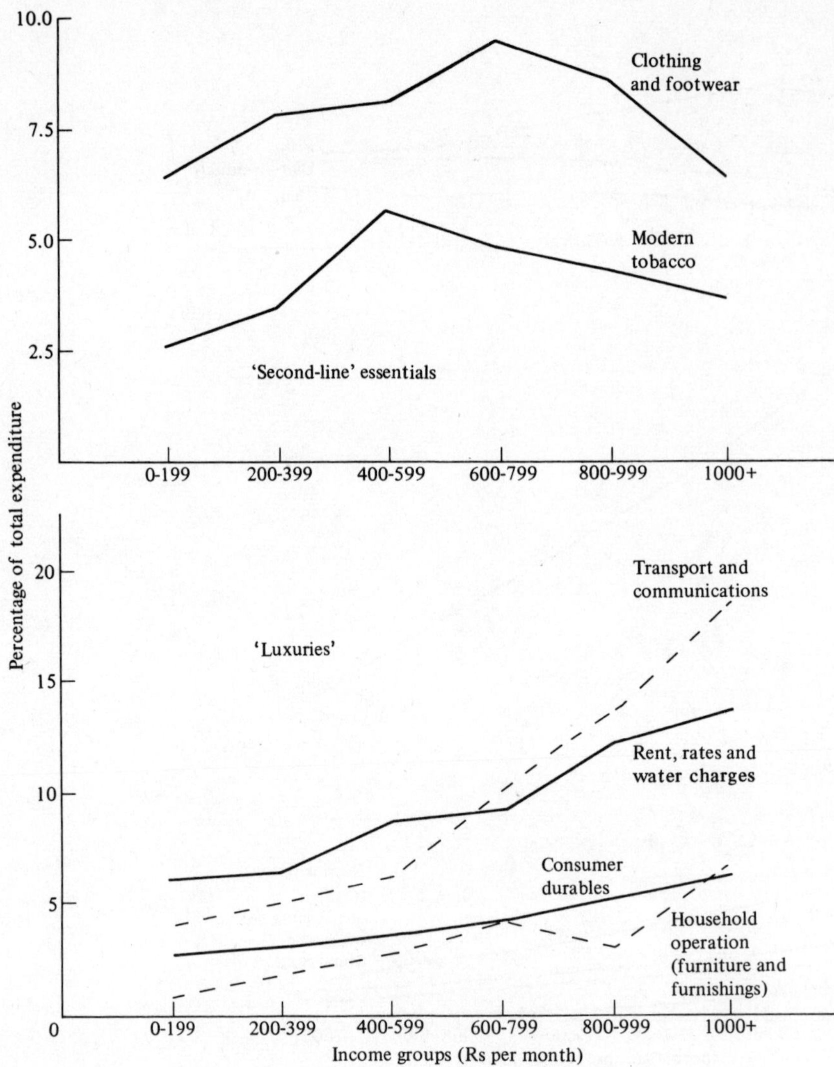

Figure 5.3 Expenditure on other items. Source: Table 5.4

To ascertain the import and indirect tax content of household budgets provides a particular example of a more general problem which our social accounting work has had to face. This arises from the fact that sources of information on household budgets naturally make use of a classification of commodities which is most convenient to the subject matter. However, in any economic model and *a fortiori* in our SAM, consumer demands need to be expressed as demands on production activities, expressed at basic values. Basic values are not, of course, the same as market prices; they exclude indirect taxes as well as trade and transport margins. The natural categories for analysis of domestic production activities differ from the natural consumer expenditure categories, not least because they exclude imports. Accordingly, we need a classification converter which translates expenditure on any one consumer commodity into demands (at basic values) on different domestic production activities, imports and indirect taxes. Such a converter is presented in Appendix 1 as Table A.2, while the supporting text explains how it was derived.

If the classification converter is denoted by a matrix then in our case its dimensions are 50 × 28 since we have 50 activities plus indirect tax categories and 28 commodity groups as in Table 5.2. If we now form

$$\bar{\mathbf{C}} = \Gamma \mathbf{C} \tag{5.1}$$

then Γ is the matrix that maps from the vector of household expenditures to demands on different activities and the leakages in domestic demand due to imports and indirect taxes. Equation (5.1) has two components. One is the matrix **C** which maps from household expenditures to consumer commodity groups. This matrix is derived from Table 5.2 by expressing the elements in each column as a fraction of the column total. The second contribution to $\bar{\mathbf{C}}$ is the classification converter, Γ, which shows how one unit of expenditure on each consumers' good can be accounted for by outputs of domestically produced (input–output) commodities at basic prices, together with trade and transport margins, plus the components accounted for by indirect taxes on consumption, imports, customs duties and FEECs.

If different households (e.g. in different income groups or sectors) purchase differing kinds of commodities even though these commodities may be classified under the same consumers' good category, then the converter matrix appropriate to each household type would differ. In spite of this possibility, we make the assumption that the converter can be applied to all vectors of household expenditure to convert them to the input–output classification, and hence reach some conclusions about the import content together with local indirect tax components. Table 5.5 sets out some results on this basis. It can be noted that in the table expenditure on imported goods is shown net of all duties, and so directly indicate loss of foreign exchange earnings.

Figure 5.4 graphs some of the data from Table 5.5 and invites some fairly obvious conclusions. The uppermost graph shows that a continuously declining proportion of total expenditure is incurred on imports as income rises. Thus the income elasticity of demand for imported goods in Sri Lanka would appear to be less than unity. This is an unusual result in the context of a developing economy, since one would expect the high income groups, which consume proportionately more of the luxury goods, to have a relatively higher import content in their expenditures. There are two main reasons for this opposite finding in Sri Lanka. One is simply that foodstuffs have an unusually high import content as shown in Table 5.6. Thus since low income households have proportionally higher expenditures on foodstuffs, then they also have higher percentage expenditures on imports. The second factor in the explanation is that stringent controls largely preclude imports of consumer luxury items in Sri Lanka so that the effect of the import content of food items can dominate the graph.

On the basis of these results it is tempting to conclude that a general policy of redistribution of income from high to low income households would raise the total import content of expenditures in Sri Lanka and will consequently adversely affect the balance of payments. This tentative result needs to be heavily qualified in a number of respects, however. First, it assumes that product mix and technology would both remain unchanged. This would not be the case if, for example, redistributional policies were accompanied by, or took the form of, particular policies to speed import substitution with respect to foodstuffs. Second, we are referring here only to imports for household consumption; hence we are implicitly assuming that imports for all other uses remain constant, which may not be the case. Third, import content has been represented as a proportion of total *expenditure*. If, therefore, the marginal propensity to save increases with income, then a redistribution of household income will not necessarily produce

Table 5.5 *Percentage of total expenditure on imports and consumption taxes by income group and sector, 1969/70*

	Urban						Rural					
	1	2	3	4	5	6	1	2	3	4	5	6
1 Imports (excluding ration rice and net of duties)	9.4	8.9	7.8	7.4	7.0	6.3	10.9	9.8	9.0	8.6	7.8	7.8
2 Customs duties	1.1	1.2	1.2	1.3	1.3	1.6	1.1	1.3	1.4	1.5	1.5	1.9
3 Indirect taxes	1.9	2.8	2.9	3.1	2.8	3.7	2.4	3.1	3.4	2.9	2.7	2.8
4 Government food profits	2.8	2.5	2.0	1.6	1.3	0.8	3.0	2.5	2.2	1.7	1.4	1.2
5 FEECS	0.9	1.0	1.1	1.3	1.4	1.6	1.0	1.2	1.3	1.6	1.7	1.8
6 Taxes on consumption (Σ 2 to 5)	6.7	7.5	7.2	7.3	6.8	7.7	7.5	8.1	8.3	7.7	7.3	7.7

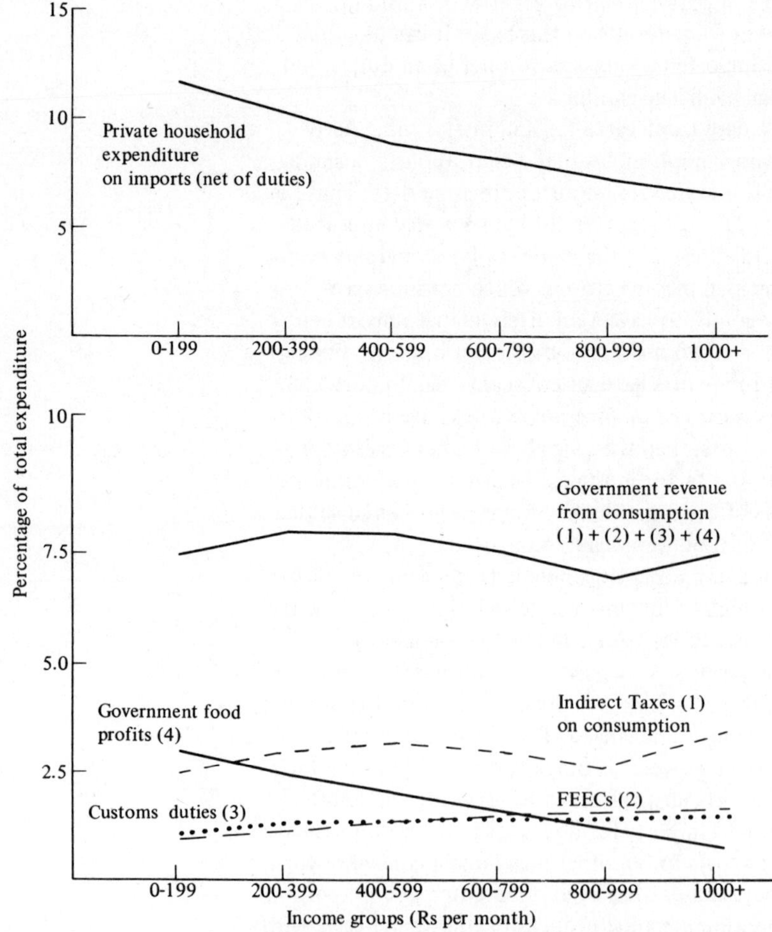

Figure 5.4 Percentages of total expenditure – all island. Source: Table 5.5.

Estate 1	2	3	4	5	6	All-island 1	2	3	4	5	6	
15.7	15.1	13.7	10.0	9.5	7.6	11.6	10.2	8.9	8.2	7.4	6.7	1 Imports (excluding ration rice and net of duties)
1.1	1.2	1.3	1.6	1.2	1.5	1.1	1.3	1.3	1.4	1.4	1.7	2 Customs duties
2.8	3.3	3.4	4.4	1.8	2.2	2.5	3.0	3.2	3.0	2.7	3.4	3 Indirect taxes
2.7	2.7	2.4	1.5	1.8	1.2	2.9	2.5	2.1	1.7	1.3	0.9	4 Government food profits
1.3	1.4	1.5	1.8	2.3	1.9	1.0	1.2	1.4	1.5	1.6	1.6	5 FEECS
8.1	8.6	8.6	9.3	7.1	6.8	7.5	8.0	8.0	7.6	7.0	7.6	6 Taxes on consumption (Σ 2 to 5)

the suggested effect on the balance of payments. These three qualifications will not necessarily eliminate or even mitigate the redistributional effects on the import bill, but one must be cautious in making too firm a conclusion along the stated lines. Nothing short of a fully operational model which can take into account variations in all of these endogenous variables can give an explicit answer on the effects of a redistributive policy. One can only make tentative suggestions about its outcome. Meanwhile the importance of this analysis cannot be overemphasised: there is evidence presented by the Central Bank that there has been a significant redistribution of income between 1963 and 1973.* It would be interesting to examine the extent to which this has in fact contributed to the contemporary seriousness of the balance of payments.

Figure 5.4 also shows the incidence of taxes on consumption. The total effect from individual taxes does not produce a smooth Engel curve. Some clarification as to why this is can be obtained by splitting total taxes on consumption into their four components as illustrated in the figure. This shows that revenue from government food profits is income inelastic, which is consistent with the income inelasticity of demand for food. Customs duties and FEECs both show an income elasticity that is discernibly greater than unity. Table 5.6 indicates that this also corresponds to expectations since the incidence of customs duties and FEECs tends to be higher on goods with income elasticities greater than one. The income elasticity of indirect taxes as such is less clear, but the overall tendency is for it to be greater than unity; which again is consistent with the evidence of Table 5.6. Thus, although the overall picture for taxes on consumption shows no obvious pattern, the components do show some tendencies which would accord with expectation.

This cursory inspection of the effects of a redistribution of income on government revenue yields no particularly strong conclusions. However, once again, one must note the proviso that the data refer only to revenue from taxes on household consumption and therefore exclude taxes upon income, production, etc. In addition, taxes on household consumption only account for 5 per cent of total

*See *Survey of Sri Lanka's Consumer Finances, 1973*, Central Bank of Ceylon, 1975, page 61, which indicates that the Gini coefficient for income receivers declined from 0.49 to 0.41, and likewise the comparable figures for spending units showed a decline from 0.45 to 0.35.

Table 5.6 *Import and revenue content of consumers' expenditure*

Consumer commodity	Percentage of total consumers' expenditure	Percentage content of total expenditure on each consumer commodity			
		Imports	Customs duties	Indirect taxes	FEECs
1 Outside ration rice	9.5	13.8	0.2		
2 Wheat flour	2.0	63.1			
3 Other grains and cereals	3.4	0.3		3.7	
4 Condiments	5.7	14.9		0.4	1.6
5 Pulses	1.2	60.0		−11.4	
6 Coconuts	3.3				
7 Vegetables and fruits	6.2			−0.7	
8 Meat	1.6	0.7			
9 Fish	5.9	16.1		0.4	
10 Milk and milk products	2.8	3.7	1.6	2.0	0.4
11 Oils, fats, including butter	1.4	4.0	0.8	4.0	2.4
12 Tea	1.0			5.6	
13 Sugar	4.4	37.1	8.7		
14 Other food and beverages	2.0	17.2	0.6	2.2	3.3
15 Meals away from home	2.2				
16 Toddy	0.6			23.1	
17 Other alcoholic beverages	2.6	0.9	3.9	62.2	0.4
18 Traditional tobacco	1.4				
19 Modern tobacco	4.1	0.3	0.3	2.2	
20 Clothing and footwear	7.6	14.1	2.5	3.3	7.6
21 Rent, rates and water charges	8.0			2.1	
22 Fuel and light	3.4	2.0	0.7	3.0	1.0
23 Consumer durables	2.5	6.0	7.8	5.1	2.8
24 Household operations	3.6	1.6	1.6	0.4	0.8
25 Personal care and health	2.7	9.9	2.1	3.3	
26 Transport and communications	7.1	9.5	2.2	0.3	3.6
27 Recreation	3.0	3.4	1.5	3.7	1.9
28 Miscellaneous	0.7				
Total	100.0	12.2	1.4	−1.2	1.2

government revenue. Thus the revenue effects of redistribution would be unlikely to be very great even if some clear pattern did exist.

4 Contrasts between urban, rural and estate households

So far the analysis has concentrated on comparisons between households grouped according to income. It is also of considerable interest to view expenditure patterns across sectors of location. For example, one may have prior expectations that there is a difference in expenditure patterns between the South Indian estate workers and other groups in the Rural or Urban sectors. Figures 5.5 and 5.6 illustrate such differences for selected items and are derived from the detailed figures given in Tables 5.4 and 5.5. They show that the Urban and Rural sectors are more alike than the Estate sector which, for example, shows a much lower level of demand for fish.

The pattern for imports shown in Figure 5.6 indicates that consumption in the Estates sector has the highest import content followed by the Rural and the Urban sectors. This is entirely consistent with the previous analysis in terms of income levels.

It is again tempting to conclude from this last result that redistribution away from the Estate sector would reduce import dependence. However the facts are not all as they seem. Our data exclude outside rationed rice which has a sub-

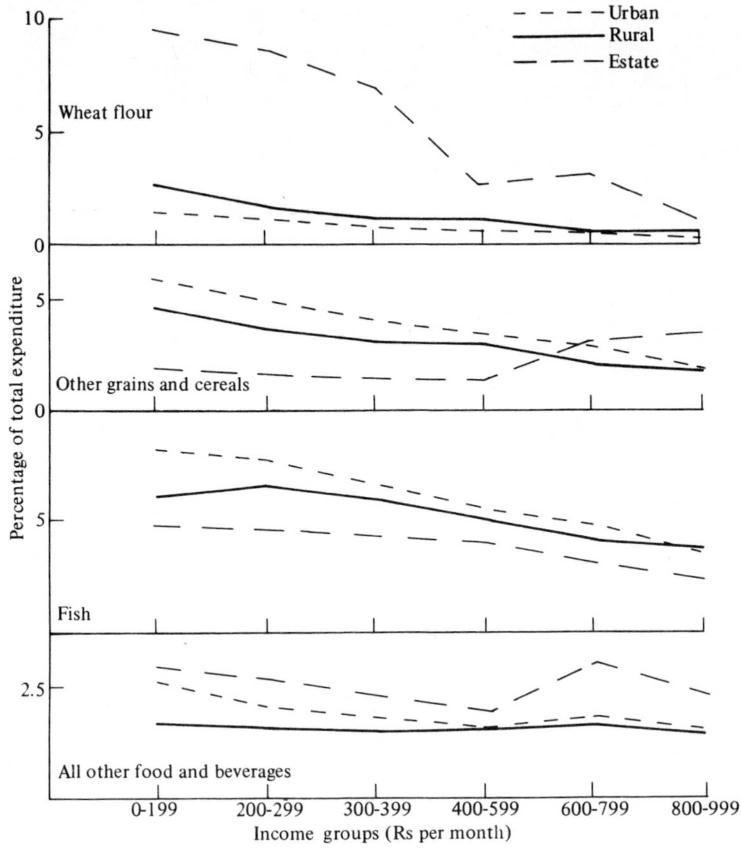

Figure 5.5 Inter-sectoral variations in expenditure patterns – selected food commodities. Source: Table 5.4.

stantial import content and is consumed predominantly by the non-Estate households. If this was taken into account the apparently larger propensity to consume imported goods of the Estate sector might well disappear. It can also be noted that the graphs shown in Figures 5.5 and 5.6 for the Estate households are not as smooth as one might expect. This may be due to sampling errors since small numbers of households are covered in the relevant cells of the basic source. However, it can also be noted that senior managers on the states are typically Singhalese. Accordingly their consumption patterns are likely to be more like those of other similarly well paid individuals in other sectors. Figure 5.6 especially gives some support to this view.

5 Conclusions

The simple descriptive comparisons of this chapter reveal several important features of the consumption structure of the Sri Lankan economy and its interaction with the major macroeconomic constraints. Not surprisingly food, in the aggregate, is revealed as an essential item of consumption having an income elasticity of less than one, while a few individual food items, such as meat, reveal the characteristics of luxury goods. Several non-food items which, in a developed country, would almost certainly be classified as essentials appear, in Sri Lanka, to have characteristics of luxury goods. Again, this is not particularly surprising. What is surprising, and rather worrisome, is the conclusion that income redistribution to the poor would exacerbate the balance of payments problem because

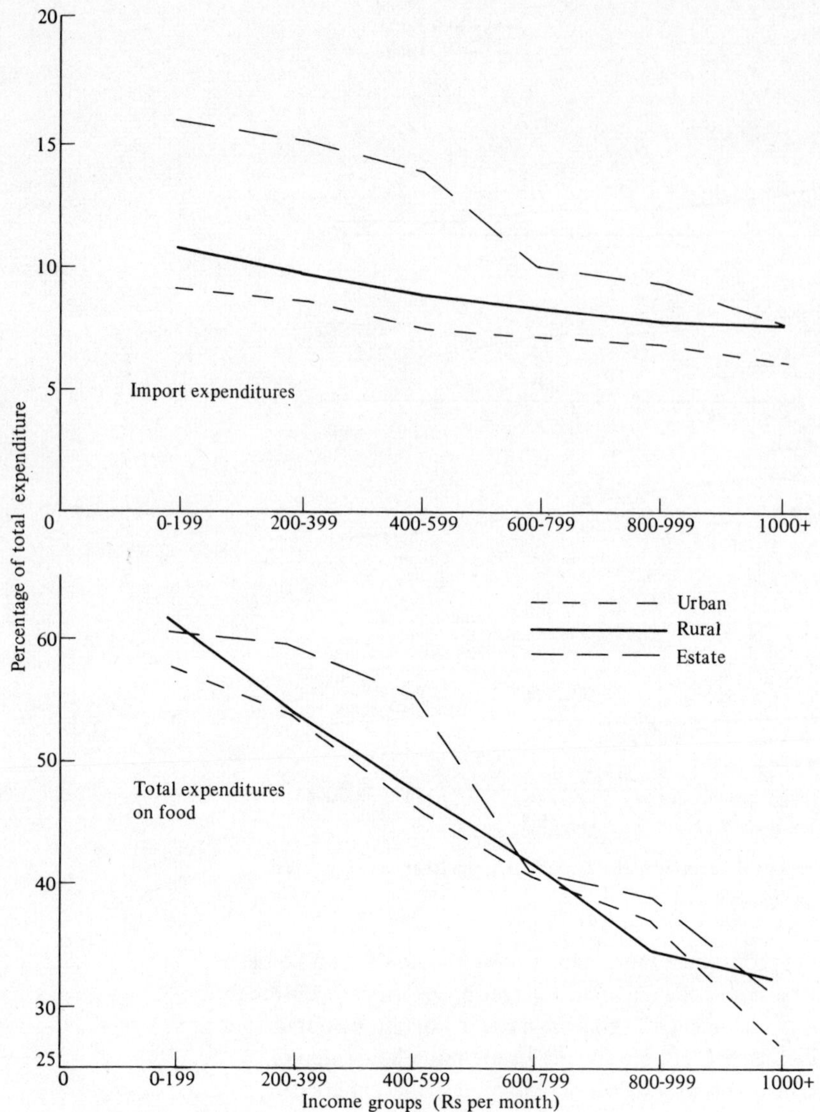

Figure 5.6 Inter-sectoral variations in expenditure patterns. Source: Table 5.4

of the high import content of food expenditures. This is in contrast to what is often argued about the external consequences of redistribution in developing countries.

To go further with the exploration of such conclusions requires a use of model techniques and cannot be sustained by the simple arithmetic deployed in this chapter. Meanwhile, however, the approach adopted here has produced an interesting and controversial question, directly from analysis of SAM. It has also produced an agenda of items which would need to be considered in any attempt to explore these questions. One of these concerns whether or not it is adequate to assume that the classification converter, Γ, is independent of household types, incomes or prices. This is an empirical matter to be answered in a specific context. However, in general our view is that fixed Γs cannot be assumed in model work.*

*See Pyatt and Thorbecke (forthcoming) for discussion as to how Γ might be modelled.

One final point can usefully be made about the role of a consumer classification converter. It is that such a converter is the unavoidable minimum requirement in a data system which tries to avoid having explicit commodity accounts. It has already been noted that we regard the absence of such accounts as a weakness in the present schema, and that a subsequent study in Swaziland has adopted a treatment more in line with the pioneering work of the Cambridge Growth Project* and the new UN SNA. Either of these sources can be consulted for discussion of the links between consumer classification converters and more general treatment in terms of commodity accounts. Meanwhile, with respect of the analysis of the household sector, our present approach involves no loss of generality. Furthermore, the comparisons set down above lead on to a number of additional pieces of analysis. In particular, they can be used in conjunction with the results of the next chapter, to reveal something about the burden on individual household categories of the taxation of particular categories of consumption.

*See Cambridge, Department of Applied Economics (1962–).

6

Fiscal policy, resource allocation and effective protection

1 The incentive to export

As final illustrations of the analytical uses to which our data system might be put we turn, in this chapter, to some issues in the general area of fiscal policy and resource allocation. The analysis here is essentially descriptive though it involves a good deal more manipulation of the basic data than was the case in the previous chapter. Our starting point is an issue raised in Chapter 2; the potential importance to balance of payments equilibrium of non-traditional exports and the incentives directed towards them.

For several years Sri Lanka has faced severe balance of payments difficulties in spite of stringent import controls on many items. A major factor in this situation has been the continued heavy reliance on three traditional export commodities, tea, rubber and coconut, which accounted for ninety per cent of visible exports in 1970; and the poor price and quantity performance of these commodities over long periods of the recent past. With relatively poor prospects for these main export commodities in the future, it is clear that the improvement in overall export performance which is required to achieve external balance must rely heavily on a large expansion of non-traditional exports. Consequently, it is of clear interest to examine whether the existing pattern of export incentives is consistent with the required expansion.

We begin with an extremely simple calculation of variations between sectors of the fiscal impact on the incentive to export. This relies entirely on data derived directly from Appendix 1 and details are set out in Table 6.1. Column 1 of the table assumes that exporters of all types are affected equally by profits taxation. This is not strictly correct for several reasons including the differential rates of company taxation applied, for example, to non-resident companies. However, subject to this caveat the data in column 1 show the amount of foreign exchange earned by each of the productive sectors, while column 4 shows the part of these proceeds actually received by the producers. Column 5 compares these two figures and shows, in effect, the number of rupees (equivalent) that have to be earned in foreign exchange in order to yield 1 rupee of income in the hands of producers. It can be seen that producers operating in traditional products such as rubber, tea and coconut need to earn approximately 1.25 rupees equivalent of foreign currency in order to earn 1.0 rupees of local income, while producers of non-traditional commodities need to earn as little as 0.50 rupees (equivalent) to receive a local income of 1 rupee.

The restructuring of incentives through the tax system, as implied by these calculations, is clearly desirable, at least insofar as the direction of change is con-

Table 6.1 *Export receipts by industry – before and after tax (Rs million)*

Production activity	Exports foreign currency receipts (1)	Export duties (2)	FEEC rebates (3)	(1)–(2)+(3) exporters receipts (4)	(1) ÷ (4) (5)
1 Tea	1036	197		839	1.23
2 Rubber	411	70		341	1.21
3 Coconuts	3	1		2	1.35
4 Paddy					
5 Livestock					
6 Fishing					
7 Logging and firewood					
8 Other agriculture	66	5	46	106	0.62
9 Mining and quarrying	12	2	10	19	0.63
10 Milling	2		1	3	0.60
11 Dairy products					
12 Bread					
13 Other bakery products	1		–	1	0.80
14 Carbonated beverages					
15 Desiccated coconut	109	26		83	1.31
16 Other processed food	4		3	7	0.61
17 Distilling	1		1	2	0.50
18 Tobacco	1		–	1	0.70
19 Textiles	6		5	11	0.57
20 Wood products	–		–		0.75
21 Paper					
22 Leather	4		2	6	0.65
23 Rubber	1		–	1	0.60
24 Chemicals	7		5	12	0.59
25 Oils and fats	101	27		74	1.36
26 Coconut fibre and yarn	33		26	58	0.56
27 Petroleum and coal	34		23	57	0.60
28 Structural clay products					
29 Ceramics					
30 Cement					
31 Basic metals					
32 Light engineering	1		1	2	0.55
33 Transport equipment					
34 Machinery, other equipment					
35 Other manufacturing	1		1	1	0.50
36 Construction					
37 Electricity					
38 Road passenger transport					
39 Rail transport	1			1	1.00
40 Trade, and other transport	190		12	202	0.94
41 Services	223		64	287	0.78
Total	2243	327	197	2113	1.06

cerned. And it obviously reflects, quite logically, some of the differences in the elasticities of foreign demand between commodities. However, the comparison of Table 6.1 is a comparison between sectors. As we shall see later, the strength of the incentive to export in the non-traditional sectors is a good deal less, or even negative, when one compares the fiscal incentives for exporting with the fiscal incentives for domestic uses of output within certain of these sectors.

2 Protection levels: nominal and effective

The above conclusion is one of several which emerges from the next set of calculations which concern the impact of fiscal arrangements on resource allocation. These calculations focus on the effect of Sri Lanka's structure of protection and involve an attempt to use our data to calculate the 'effective protection' accorded to each sector. Corden (1966) defines the effective rate of protection as the percentage increase in value added per unit in an economic activity made possible by the tariff structure relative to the situation in the absence of tariffs. The concept is of obvious interest to economists since it is the effective tariff which will bear on resource allocation, as opposed to the nominal tariff which mostly affects prices and government revenues.

Numerous empirical studies of effective projection have been undertaken both in respect of developed and underdeveloped countries.* But these have invariably encountered the problem of the non-availability or inconsistency of some part of the necessary data, and have involved the extremely difficult task of making international price comparisons at what is often a relatively high level of aggregation. Our own calculations for Sri Lanka are based almost entirely upon the SAM data for 1970 and thereby avoid this difficulty. However, this approach introduces problems of its own, notably the inability to correctly reflect the protection arising from quantitative as opposed to tariff barriers. The implications of this are returned to later. Meanwhile, we acknowledge that our procedures would apply more easily in economies having lower reliance on quantitative restrictions than is the case in Sri Lanka. These procedures are based essentially on Corden (1966), but with a few additional assumptions which are described as and when they appear.

*See for example, Basevi (1966), Little *et al.* (1970) and Balassa *et al.* (1971).

Formalising the definition of effective protection given above we have

$$G_j \equiv \frac{V_j' - V_j}{V_j} \tag{6.1}$$

where G_j = effective protection rate for j

V_j = value added per unit of gross output of j in absence of tariffs, i.e. at 'world prices'

V_j' = value added per unit of gross output made possible by the tariff structure.

Our task is therefore to estimate both V_j' and V_j. The former presents no problem and can be taken directly from the inter-industry transactions matrix shown as Appendix 1, Table A.16. However, V_j needs to be calculated from estimates of world prices and nominal tariffs. To do this requires estimates of the value of total output in each activity and its inputs at world (i.e. non-tariff) prices so that the difference, V_j, can be obtained.

A first step in the calculation of the V_js is to allocate each industry to one of four categories, namely:

(i) importables (*M*)
(ii) exportables (*X*)
(iii) non-traded goods (*NT*)
(iv) dually-traded goods (*DT*)

Here an importable is defined as a good or service which is imported into Sri Lanka but which is not also exported. An exportable similarly is one which is exported but not imported. A non-traded good is a good or service which is neither imported nor exported. And a dually-traded good is both imported and exported.* Table 6.2 shows how each of the sectors is classified according to this schema.

*The only exception to this classification was railways which were classified intuitively as 'non-traded' despite the fact that the trade figures showed an export of Rs 1m.

The next step is to note that by definition, for each commodity, j

$$P_j' = P_j\,(l + t_i) \tag{6.2}$$

Table 6.2 *Value added before and after tariffs*

	(1) Classification of items	(2) Nominal tariff	(3) Price raising effects of tariffs (%)	(4) Value added after tariffs V'_j (Corden) Rs m.	(5) Value added after tariffs V'_j (Balassa) Rs m.	(6) Value added before tariffs V_j (Corden) Rs m.	(7) Value added before tariffs V_j (Balassa) Rs m.
1 Tea	X	−0.23	0	614	587	884	851
2 Rubber	X	−0.21	0	322	320	405	403
3 Coconuts	X	−0.35	0	529	529	549	549
4 Paddy	NT	0	0	1047	977	1062	992
5 Livestock	M	0.09	9.09	219	219	214	214
6 Fishing	NT	0	0	246	246	249	249
7 Logging and firewood	NT	0	0	126	126	127	127
8 Other agriculture	DT	0.14	11.19	1030	1030	898	898
9 Mining and quarrying	DT	0.10	4.44	103	95	94	86
10 Milling	DT	0.02	1.52	1081	54	1075	47
11 Dairy products	M	0.24	23.54	10	9	3	2
12 Bread	NT	0	0	51	48	68	65
13 Other bakery products	DT	0	0	29	28	43	42
14 Carbonated beverages	NT	0	0	9	8	10	9
15 Desiccated coconuts	X	−0.31	0	2	2	34	34
16 Other processed food	DT	0.24	22.96	33	28	65	60
17 Distilling	DT	2.91	297.34	42	42	5	5
18 Tobacco	DT	1.00	100.00	135	135	46	46
19 Textiles	DT	0.51	51.43	131	127	63	59
20 Wood products	DT	0.68	68.18	130	113	67	50
21 Paper	M	0.43	42.61	86	82	64	60
22 Leather	DT	0.45	46.67	21	20	11	10
23 Rubber	DT	0.88	88.83	28	27	9	8
24 Chemicals	DT	0.27	26.75	128	126	125	123
25 Oils and fats	DT	0.41	74.74	7	5	−81	−83
26 Coconut fibre and yarn	X	0.44	0	71	70	58	58
27 Petroleum and coal	DT	0.74	82.60	108	105	45	40
28 Structural clay products	M	0.54	54.17	34	32	21	19
29 Ceramics	M	0.87	86.96	17	16	8	7
30 Cement	M	0.69	69.27	45	40	23	18
31 Basic metals	M	0.56	55.77	17	17	12	12
32 Light engineering	DT	0.72	72.43	195	192	94	91
33 Transport equipment	M	0.89	88.88	8	8	−0.3	−0.3
34 Machinery, other equipment	M	0.83	82.56	38	38	14	14
35 Other manufacturing	DT	0.85	86.25	20	20	6	6
36 Construction	NT	0	0	986	979	1237	1237
37 Electricity	NT	0	0	97	94	101	101
38 Road passenger transport	NT	0	0	220	219	267	266
39 Rail transport	NT	0	0	101	93	102	94
40 Trade, and other transport	DT	0.20	21.65	2045	2032	1784	1771
41 Services	DT	0.11	9.17	1470	1357	1328	1248

where P_j = world price
P'_j = domestic price after tariffs
and t_j = import tariff rate

It is now assumed that t_j is zero for all non-traded goods and all exportables. Thus, world prices for such goods can be taken as equal to their domestic prices. More precisely, these assumptions imply that the internal price of an importable is the world price plus the tariff. The internal price of an exportable, when sold internally, is assumed to be the same as the world price and is unaffected by any export taxes and/or subsidies. (The revenue received from exportables when exported is, of course, equal to the world price *minus* export taxes). The price of a non-traded good is assumed to be determined exogenously and is specific to the economy. It is unaffected by the removal of any tariffs. The internal price of a dually traded good is assumed to be equal to the internal price of imports, i.e. to world price plus tariff, with export taxes/subsidies affecting the value added in exporting but not the internal price.

The final step in our procedure is to estimate the nominal tariff rates, t_j. In doing this we have followed conventional practice and treat export subsidies as equivalent to tariffs, and export taxes as equivalent to import subsidies in terms of nominal rates. The only exceptions to these rules arise in the case of dually-traded goods where we took an average of import and export duties weighted by proportions of production for the domestic market and exports.* It is to be noted that in calculating the nominal tariff for each good we did not take the usual step of going to the tariff book and extracting the relevant data in *ad valorem* terms. Instead we used the data from the social-accounting matrix and thus, in the case of an importable, expressed the nominal tariff for good j as:

$$t_j = \frac{D_j + F_j}{M_j} \tag{6.3}$$

where D_j is the value of import duties paid on imports of good j; F_j is the value of FEECs paid on imports of good j; and M_j is the value of imports of good j exclusive of duties. For exportables the rate of duty was calculated as the difference between FEEC rebates and export taxes as a proportion of the value of exports (including export taxes). For dually-traded goods the weighted average described above was utilised; and for non-traded goods the rate was taken as zero despite the fact that the tariff book may show a nominal duty.

*In the case of a dually-traded good

$$t_j = \frac{m_j Q_j + x_j X_j}{Q_j + X_j}$$

where t_j = nominal tariff on dually-traded good j, m = import duties on j, x = net export subsidies on j, Q_j = production of j sold on domestic market, X_j = exports of j.

The results of these exercises are presented in Table 6.2. This shows (column 2), nominal tariff rates varying from 291 per cent for the distilling sector, to –35 per cent on coconuts. Traditional exports tend to have high negative tariffs as a result of high export taxes, while the manufacturing sector as a whole tends to have high positive tariffs resulting from a mixture of import duties and FEECs – with FEECs on average being twice the value of import duties. The two service sectors (trade and services), both have positive rates of duty as a result of FEECs on payments abroad. And at this point we should recall that as a result of our failure to reflect the effect of quantitative restrictions, our results tend, if anything, to understate levels of protection.

Table 6.2 also shows various components of the calculation of effective tariff rates. In order to calculate the value added at world prices of each sector it was necessary to deflate all the items to world prices using the assumptions set out earlier. Column 3 shows the result of applying these assumptions and provides the basis for deflation to world prices. It can be seen that for non-traded goods and exportables there are no price-raising effects since our assumption sets internal prices equal to world prices for this category of goods. It must be stressed that for exportables, the price raising effects in column 3 relate only to that part of the output sold in domestic markets. For importables and dually-traded goods, the deflation is the nominal import tariff rate including FEECs, since the internal price is assumed to be the world price plus tariffs.

As a next step, the gross output of each sector was reduced to world prices using the deflation shown in Column 3 with export taxes being added back in the case of exportables since our inter-industry transactions matrix is net of export taxes. Domestically produced intermediate goods were similarly deflated by multiplying each element of the inter-industry transactions matrix by the reciprocal of one *plus* the vector of price-raising effects, and aggregating so as to obtain the value of domestically produced intermediate inputs adjusted for tariffs for each commodity. Finally, costs of imported inputs into production were put into world price terms by simply reducing our vector of imports by the import duties and FEECs applying to them.

Given this information it is a matter of simple arithmetic to determine value added at world prices and to compare this with value added after tariffs from SAM and so calculate the rate of effective protection using equation (6.1). We have done this using two slightly different methods. The 'Corden' method treats non-traded inputs as part of value added which means that they also appear in the denominator of the expression for effective protection. The alternative 'Balassa' method treats non-traded inputs as ordinary inputs but with zero duties. In general, the Balassa method will result in slightly lower rates of effective protection than the Corden method. The vectors of value added on both of these bases, and both before and after allowing for tariffs, are shown in columns 4 to 7 of Table 6.2.

Table 6.3 continues the story and shows, in columns 2 and 3, the rates of effective protection on both the Corden and Balassa bases. The effective rates of protection come out higher or lower than the nominal rates depending on the size of the weighted average of the nominal tariff on inputs. The results show, as one would expect, that those items with zero nominal tariffs in fact carry negative effective rates as a result of tariffs on inputs. Similarly, those items having negative nominal protection as a result of export duties, normally have the extent of this negative protection increased as a result of tariffs on inputs. In only one industry, namely 'other processed food', is the effective rate negative and the nominal rate positive (i.e. there is a positive import duty but this is less than the weighted average of duties on inputs into the sector). In the cases of the two industries, oils and fuels and transport equipment, the free trade value added would actually be *negative*. In other words, inputs valued at world prices exceed outputs similarly valued.

The results in columns 2 and 3 of Table 6.3 clearly show that the levels of protection accorded to several of the manufacturing sectors is extremely high. The consequent distortion in resource allocation is potentially considerable and deserves to be explored much more fully to ascertain its consequences for employment and in other respects. Meanwhile it can be noted that although the rank correlation coefficient between the nominal and effective rates shown in columns 1 and 2 was 0.88 (as was the corresponding coefficient relating columns 1 and 3), this fails to indicate the extremely large differences between effective and nominal rates in individual cases. Certainly, there is little justification for using nominal rates of protection as proxies for the more meaningful effective rates on the basis of the results in the table.

Columns 4 and 5 of Table 6.3 take account of certain general equilibrium effects of a tariff. If tariffs are imposed (or alternatively removed or altered)

Table 6.3 *Nominal and effective tariffs and the bias against exporting*

	(1) Nominal protection	(2) Effective protection (Balassa)	(3) Effective protection (Corden)	(4) Net effective protection (Balassa)	(5) Net effective protection (Corden)	(6) Bias against exporting	(7) Foreign currency receipts ÷ local currency receipts of exporters (from Table 6.1)
1 Tea	−0.23	−0.31	−0.31	−0.41	−0.40	+0.31	1.23
2 Rubber	−0.21	−0.21	−0.21	−0.31	−0.31	+0.06	1.21
3 Coconuts	−0.35	−0.04	−0.04	−0.16	−0.16	+0.54	1.35
4 Paddy	0	−0.02	−0.01	0	0	–	–
5 Livestock	0.09	0.02	0.02	−0.11	−0.11	−0.34	–
6 Fishing	0	−0.01	−0.01	−0.01	−0.01	–	–
7 Logging and firewood	0	−0.01	−0.01	0.01	0.01	–	–
8 Other agriculture	0.14	0.15	0.15	0	0	−0.29	0.52
9 Mining and quarrying	0.10	0.10	0.09	−0.05	−0.05	+0.31	0.63
10 Milling	0.02	0.15	0.01	−0.74	−0.12	−0.92	0.60
11 Dairy products	0.24	4.00	2.57	2.91	2.03	−0.69	–
12 Bread	0	−0.26	−0.25	0.06	0.05	–	–
13 Other bakery products	0	−0.33	−0.32	−0.42	−0.41	−0.59	0.80
14 Carbonated beverages	0	−0.07	−0.06	0.01	0.01	–	–
15 Desiccated coconut	−0.31	−0.94	−0.94	−0.95	−0.95	*	1.31
16 Other processed food	0.24	−0.53	−0.50	−0.75	−0.72	−0.57	0.61
17 Distilling	2.91	7.57	7.57	6.37	6.37	*	0.50
18 Tobacco	1.00	1.93	1.93	1.55	1.55	+0.50	0.70
19 Textiles	0.51	1.15	1.07	0.85	0.80	−0.06	0.57
20 Wood products	0.68	1.28	0.95	0.90	0.70	+0.20	0.75
21 Paper	0.43	0.36	0.34	0.17	0.16	−0.14	–
22 Leather	0.45	0.92	0.85	0.66	0.61	−0.18	0.65
23 Rubber	0.88	2.46	2.23	2.01	1.81	+0.64	0.60
24 Chemicals	0.27	0.02	0.02	−0.11	−0.11	−0.35	0.59
25 Oils and fats	0.41	*	*	*	*	*	1.36
26 Coconut fibre and yarn	0.44	0.20	0.21	0.05	0.05	−0.53	0.56
27 Petroleum and coal	0.74	1.63	1.40	1.24	1.12	+0.60	0.60
28 Structural clay products	0.54	0.71	0.64	0.47	0.43	−0.01	–
29 Ceramics	0.87	1.46	1.27	1.11	0.98	+0.45	–
30 Cement	0.67	1.22	0.96	0.86	0.70	+0.33	–
31 Basic metals	0.56	0.43	0.43	0.24	0.24	+0.02	–
32 Light engineering	0.72	1.12	1.08	0.83	0.81	+0.32	0.55
33 Transport equipment	0.89	*	*	*	*	*	–
34 Machinery, other equipment	0.83	1.64	1.64	1.79	1.79	+0.59	–
35 Other manufacturing	0.85	2.39	2.39	3.00	3.00	+0.49	0.50
36 Construction	0	−0.21	−0.20	−0.15	−0.15	–	–
37 Electricity	0	−0.07	−0.04	−0.02	−0.02	–	–
38 Road passenger transport	0	−0.18	−0.18	−0.14	−0.14	–	–
39 Rail transport	0	−0.01	−0.01	−0.06	−0.05	–	1.00
40 Trade, and other transport	0.20	0.15	0.15	0	0	−0.24	0.94
41 Services	0.11	0.06	0.05	−0.06	−0.06	−0.35	0.78

then there will be a tendency for resources to shift into those industries which offer a potentially higher value added. These shifts will have a macroeconomic effect which, among other things, will raise the equilibrium exchange rate provided we assume no significant change in the unemployment rate. In general, an economy will be able to maintain its balance of payments in equilibrium at a higher exchange rate if it imposes a tariff than if it does not. If we are to present a meaningful set of tariffs, then allowance must be made for this change in the equilibrium exchange rate, and this is the purpose of the calculations leading to columns 4 and 5 of the table.

Balassa and Associates (1971) produce a formula which defines the change in the exchange rate necessary to maintain external balance if tariffs are removed.[1] An estimate for Sri Lanka for 1970 using this formula suggested an over-evaluation of 15 per cent of the official value of the rupee.[2] In order, therefore, to make a valid comparison between the tariff position and the free trade position all world prices (i.e. world price of output and thus all internal prices, and also the value of imports) were increased by 15 per cent. The new figures were then reworked as in the earlier calculation of effective protection rates using both the Balassa and Corden methods. The results are presented in columns 4 and 5 of Table 6.3.

Once again the results obtained show significantly different values for levels of effective, as compared with nominal protection. However, there appears to be no general pattern to the way in which the protection of individual sectors changes. Corden's method, for example, leads to 18 items registering higher net effective rates than nominal rates, 20 items registering lower, 1 remaining unchanged and two unquantifiable due to negative value added at non-tariff prices. Also there seems to be no pattern within sets of goods, such as manufacturing, traditional exports etc., both showing some higher and some lower rates. Each case has to be examined separately, taking into account all the variables that affect the level of net effective protection in both directions. (The height of some rates of effective protection in both directions is worth note however.) Once again, while magnitudes did change, the ranking of sectors by levels of protection did not change so significantly. A rank correlation of the nominal rates with Balassa's net effective rates was calculated to be 0.81 (and with Corden's rate as 0.83).[3]

Six sectors change rank significantly when net effective rates of protection (Corden's) are compared with the nominal rates. Four of these rank higher with respect to effective rates. Dairy products have a nominal rate of 0.24 with a ranking of 20 but the effective rate is 2.03 with a ranking of 5. Both Rail Transport and Bread have zero nominal rates with rankings of 32 but effective rates of 0.05 and a ranking of 20. Oils and fats nominally rank 18 at 0.41 but its effective rate is incalculably higher due to negative value added and is therefore ranked 1.[4] However, this sector may be a special case statistically.[5] Two sectors showed the reverse tendency. 'Other processed food' nominally ranks 20 at 0.24 but its effective rate is –0.72 with a ranking of 40 out of 41. Similarly chemicals rank 19 with a nominal rate of 0.27 but rank 31 with respect to their effective rate of –0.11.

3 A further look at the incentive to export

A major example of the way in which the structure of protection can distort the allocation of resources is by altering the relative returns attached to producing a product for domestic use as opposed to export. We conclude our discussion of the impact of protection by examining whether there is any bias in

1 The formula is

$$R'/R = \frac{\epsilon_f X + \eta_m M + D}{\dfrac{\epsilon_f X}{1+S} + \dfrac{\eta_m M}{1+T}}$$

where

R'/R = change in exchange rate
ϵ_f = elasticity of demand for foreign exchange
η_m = elasticity of demand for imports
X = exports
M = imports
D = balance of payments deficit
S = export duties
T = import duties.

2 This assumed $X = 2113$, $M = 2522$, $D = 170$, $S = -0.06$, $T = 0.36$ and in addition $\eta_m = 0.62$, $\epsilon_x = 1$, $\eta_x = 15$ and hence $\epsilon_f = 0.88$ since

$$\epsilon_f = \frac{\epsilon_x(\eta_x - 1)}{\epsilon_x + \eta}$$

where

ϵ_x = elasticity of supply of exports
η_x = elasticity of demand for exports.

This seemed a reasonable figure in terms of assumptions and of results obtained compared to those countries examined by Balassa. Comments received since carrying out the calculations suggest that a 15 per cent overvaluation is probably too low.

3 It should be noted that this implies a change of ranking for Corden's rates as a result of the exchange rate changes, contrary to the suggestion in Balassa and associates (1971) that 'the adjustment for overvaluation does not affect the ranking of industries by effective rates. Nor does the introduction of non-traded inputs modify either the method of adjustment or the ranking of industries by effective rates as long as the Corden method is applied.' (p. 325). However, this statement is somewhat misleading since it only applies in the special case

4, 5 overleaf

favour of, or against, exporting inherent in the tariff structure operating in Sri Lanka. Balassa[6] defines the bias against exporting as the 'percentage excess of domestic value added in import substitution over that obtainable in exporting'. When value added domestically is higher than value added in exporting, then there is said to be a bias against exporting.

The following definitions, all of which are consistent with our earlier calculations of effective protection rates, can be employed to calculate the extent of this bias:

Value added in domestic market = internal value of gross output – intermediate inputs – imported inputs – taxes on inputs and production

where internal value of gross output = output valued at world price + import duties

and value added for exporting = world value of gross output – intermediate inputs – imported inputs – taxes upon imports + subsidies upon exports (net).

The bias against exporting, B, is then calculated using the formula

$$B = \frac{V_j^{DM} - V_j^*}{V_j^*} \tag{6.4}$$

where V_j^{DM} is value added in production for domestic market, and V_j^* is value added in exporting.

One small adjustment was made in the calculation. Export subsidies in the form of FEEC rebates were not taken as actual rebates but rather as the nominal 55 per cent applying in 1970. This was felt to be more meaningful when considering the decision whether or not to export and does not in any way affect the calculations of world prices. However, it is sensitive to the composition of output within a sector. The only effect it has is to bias the calculation slightly in favour of exporting in those industries entitled to FEEC rebates, since FEEC rebates are not usually given on every item of output within a sector.

The results of these calculations are presented in column 6 of Table 6.3. The results are of interest because 14 of the 28 sectors which export and for which calculations are possible show a bias against exporting (column 6) despite the 55 per cent subsidy. A comparison with column 7, which reproduces data from the last column of Table 6.1 above, shows that there is even a bias against exporting in several of the sectors in which the foreign exchange receipts needed to produce one unit of local currency is extremely low. One can also note that there is a bias against exporting, or only a small bias in favour, in several sectors where a country of Sri Lanka's level of development might have some hope of achieving exporting successes, such as textiles, rubber products, ceramics, and other manufacturing. Overall, the structure of the bias does not appear entirely rational, given the severe balance of payments difficulties of the country and the high levels of excess capacity and unemployment.

Turning to the industries marked with an asterisk, the results for Oils and fats and desiccated coconus and copra should be treated with reservation as aggregation has distorted the figures to such an extent as to imply a negative value added in exporting although exporting does in fact take place. The other two, namely Distilling and Transport equipment are in effect so highly protected, with a resultingly high internal price, that exporting would result in a negative value added. This is taken to imply an infinite bias against exporting.

where non-traded industries are excluded from the rankings. If they are included then the results will be different, as the value of output on non-traded goods is assumed to be held constant while the cost of traded inputs into them would increase by the extent of the overvaluation. Traded goods, however, see their output and inputs both increase by the same proportion. Thus while traded goods are ranked invariantly among themselves, non-traded goods will alter the overall rankings.

4 With negative value added the conventional arithmetical calculation of effective protection breaks down. It was assumed that the change from negative to positive value added implied a very large percentage increase and thus a very high effective rate. While placing no numerical value on this amount the two commodities in question were ranked as joint first.

5 'Oils and fats' primarily involves the production of coconut oil and at internal prices has an output of 217, intermediate inputs of 211 (of which coconuts are 187) and a value added of only 5, that is 2½ per cent of turnover. We have made rigid assumptions about the relationship between internal and world prices and a slight change to these, or even perhaps allowances for transport costs, may radically change the estimation of value added at world prices in this case. It is likely that the operation is a cost plus exercise in accounting terms and if the price of inputs changed so would output. On the other hand however the estimate for value added at world prices (Corden) is significantly negative at –93.1.

6 Balassa and associates (1971).

In examining the results further it becomes apparent that there is a positive bias against exporting in the cases of the traditional exports. This is as one would expect because of the export taxes on these products and their relative inelasticity of supply. Equally, the alternative of selling output on the home market is clearly only available in respect of a very small proportion of the output of these sectors and the true bias against exporting is therefore rather less than our figures suggest.

Another interesting pattern is found in most processing industries where the potential export subsidy normally outweighs the price raising effect of import duties, giving a positive incentive to export. In other manufacturing sectors the picture is less clear cut, although on balance there is a distinct bias against exporting, due again to the price raising effect of high duties.

The main conclusion which emerges is that the 55 per cent FEEC rebate prevailing in 1970 was not high enough to give a genuine incentive to export in many sectors, contrary to the situation that policy makers had envisaged. This hopefully indicates yet again the role of a data schema such as ours in assisting the formulation of policies capable of achieving their stated objectives.

4 The price-raising effects of indirect taxation

Almost all governments have the ability to rearrange their taxation and expenditure policies in such a way as to change the existing distribution of real income. Whether or not they choose to make use of this ability will depend on priorities, since the establishment of a 'better' income distribution, however that may be defined, is not the only objective of fiscal policy; for one thing this objective will often conflict with other goals, notably that of economic growth. The purpose of a macroeconomic information system is not to reflect judgements about how a government should resolve this and other similar conflicts between objectives. Rather, its purpose is to show statistically the implications of different policies on different objectives and thereby aid a rational weighting of these objectives. In the last part of this chapter we provide a contribution to income distribution analysis in Sri Lanka by attempting to calculate the extent to which the price of each commodity is altered by existing subsidies and taxation. In conjunction with the analysis of the consumption patterns of different income groups in Chapter 5, this provides a basis for reaching some conclusions about the distributional consequences of indirect taxation.*

In its own study of tax incidence,† the 1968 Taxation Commission made two simplifying assumptions which potentially weaken its results. These were:

(i) that all indirect taxes are 'shifted' fully on to consumers;

(ii) that the indirect price effects of taxes levied on production are zero.

The first of these assumptions is equivalent to saying that the elasticity of demand for all taxed commodities is zero, and is evidently incorrect for the vast majority of commodities. Its effect is to overstate the price effects of taxation. The second leads to results which ignore the diffusion of price changes that will occur in the production sector if those industries subjected to a tax pass it on in higher prices to other industries. While our data system readily permits us to overcome the second of these objections it helps relatively little with the first. However, in what follows we attempt to allow for both difficulties.

In an earlier section of this chapter we utilised a theory of pricing for traded goods which said that the internal price of any commodity, before consumption taxes are levied, is equal to the world price plus any import duties and FEECs upon the commodity. We use the same assumption here, but proceed to consider

*It can be noted that direct taxation in Sri Lanka is sharply progressive. See Rasaputram (1972).

†See Ceylon, Sessional Papers (1968).

also the effect on price of consumption taxes. In addition, we explore the price-raising effect of taxes on non-traded goods.

The price-raising effect of import duties including FEECs was calculated in the previous section as the total value of these duties as a proportion of the import bill of the relevant commodity. The results of this calculation are reproduced as column 5 of Table 6.4. It is important to note that, given our pricing assumption, it is only import duties and FEECs which affect the producer price of a commodity. Production taxes, whether levied indirectly on the product in question or indirectly on its inputs, will affect the cost structure of the producer but will not force a price increase above world price *plus* import duties, i.e. above the price at which competing imports can be sold.

The effect of taxes on producer prices may be of interest in itself but here we are also concerned with the effect on retail prices. In order to calculate this we need to examine consumption taxes which are separately identified in our SAM and are defined as taxes which are paid only when a good is consumed. Accordingly, they do not discriminate between domestic and imported supplies. The vector of consumption taxes is shown as column 7 of Table 6.4 and is taken directly from Table A.13 of Appendix 1. In order to make these taxes consistent with the price-raising effects of import duties shown in column 5, we must

Table 6.4 *Calculation of the price-raising effect of indirect taxation*

	World price of output (1)	Value of imports (world price) (2)	Exports (net of export taxes) (3)	Gross output (4)	Price raising effect of import taxes (5) %	Value of domestic consumption at world prices (6)
1 Tea	1060.7		839	864	0	25.0
2 Rubber	444.0		341	376	0	33.0
3 Coconuts	577.7		2	577	0	575.0
4 Paddy				1133	0	1133.0
5 Livestock	243.8	2.2		266	9.09	246.0
6 Fishing				260	0	260.0
7 Logging and firewood				130	0	130.0
8 Other agriculture	1070.3	177.9	106	1190	11.19	1152.8
9 Mining and quarrying	103.4	4.5	19	108	4.44	89.7
10 Milling	1122.9	590.6	3	1140	1.52	1710.6
11 Dairy products	62.3	54.8		77	23.54	117.1
12 Bread				200	0	200.0
13 Other bakery products	73.0	0.6	1	73	0	72.6
14 Carbonated beverages				14	0	14.0
15 Desiccated coconut	296.6		83	271	0	188.0
16 Other processed food	101.7	274.0	7	125	22.96	370.0
17 Distilling	18.6	3.8	2	74	297.37	21.9
18 Tobacco	100.5	0.5	1	201	100.00	100.5
19 Textiles	229.1	198.7	11	347	51.43	420.6
20 Wood products	140.9	11.0	0.4	237	68.18	151.7
21 Paper	110.1	52.8		157	42.61	162.9
22 Leather	35.5	1.5	6	52	46.67	32.9
23 Rubber	28.1	17.9	1	53	88.83	45.4
24 Chemicals	229.6	210.5	12	291	36.75	430.6
25 Oils and fats	124.2	9.9	74	217	74.74	91.7
26 Coconut fibre and yarn	70.5		58	59	0	1.0
27 Petroleum and coal	147.9	74.7	57	270	82.60	191.3
28 Structural clay products	27.2	2.4		42	54.17	29.6
29 Ceramics	15.5	13.8		29	86.96	29.3
30 Cement	69.7	20.5		118	69.27	90.2
31 Basic metals	37.9	104.9		59	55.77	142.8
32 Light engineering	263.3	202.4	2	454	72.43	464.5
33 Transport equipment	27.0	120.6		51	88.88	147.6
34 Machinery, other equipment	50.9	168.0		93	82.56	218.9
35 Other manufacturing	20.9	16.0	1	39	86.25	36.4
36 Construction				1745	0	1745.0
37 Electricity				114	0	114.0
38 Road passenger transport				348	0	348.0
39 Rail transport			1	144	0	143.0
40 Trade, and other transport	1934.3			2353	21.65	1934.3
41 Services	1627.8			1777	9.17	1627.8

Source: Table A.13

express them as percentages of the world price of consumption of the relevant commodities. The import element of this consumption vector as shown in Table A.9 of Appendix 1 is already available in world price terms. This is reproduced as column 2 of Table 6.4. The domestic element of this consumption vector is derived as follows. From the gross output of each sector, column 4, we subtracted exports, column 3, to arrive at domestic uses of domestic production at internal prices. This was then deflated to world price terms using the deflation implied by column 5.

In column 6, we show the sum of the imported element of domestic consumption and the domestically produced element, both at world prices. The price-raising effect of consumption taxes is then calculated by expressing column 7 as a percentage of column 6; and the result of this is shown in column 8. The price-raising effects of consumption taxes and import duties combined is calculated as the sum of column 5 and column 8 and is shown in column 9.

These calculations indicate the price effects of taxation when the demand curve for the commodity is completely inelastic so that taxes can be fully shifted forward on to consumers. In an attempt to modify this and estimate the degree of shift we have made use of a method recently suggested by Karageorgas (1973) which involves estimating a regression equation of the form

Taxes on consumption (7)	Taxes on consumption (7) ÷ (6) (8) %	Total tax (5) + (8) (9) %	Taxes on inputs into non-traded goods (10)	Taxes on on non-traded goods (10) ÷ (4) (11) %	Shift coefficient (12)	Total price raising effect [(9) + 11)] × (12) (13) %	
4.7	18.80	18.80			0.83	15.6	1 Tea
					0.83	0	2 Rubber
12.2	2.12	2.12			0.83	1.7	3 Coconuts
			14.0	1.24	1.00	1.2	4 Paddy
		9.09			0.83	7.6	5 Livestock
			3.0	1.15	0.83	1.0	6 Fishing
			1.0	0.77	0.83	0.6	7 Logging and firewood
4.1	0.36	11.55			0.83	9.6	8 Other agriculture
		4.44			0.83	3.7	9 Mining and quarrying
−559.0	−32.68	−31.16			1.00	−31.2	10 Milling
3.3	2.82	26.36			0.83	21.9	11 Dairy products
			16.7	8.35	0.83	6.9	12 Bread
11.0	15.2	15.20			0.83	12.6	13 Other bakery products
1.0	7.14	7.14	0.4	2.86	0.83	8.3	14 Carbonated beverages
					0.83	0	15 Desiccated coconut
205.0	55.41	78.37			1.00	78.4	16 Other processed food
140.2	640.18	937.55			1.00	937.6	17 Distilling
7.6	7.56	107.56			1.00	107.6	18 Tobacco
11.5	2.73	54.16			0.83	45.0	19 Textiles
4.6	3.03	71.21			0.83	59.1	20 Wood products
6.7	4.11	46.72			0.83	38.8	21 Paper
2.7	8.21	54.88			0.83	45.6	22 Leather
0.3	0.66	89.49			0.83	74.3	23 Rubber
7.7	1.79	28.54			0.83	23.7	24 Chemicals
		74.74			0.83	62.0	25 Oils and fats
					0.83	0	26 Coconut fibre and yarn
11.5	6.01	88.61			1.00	88.6	27 Petroleum and coal
		54.17			0.83	45.0	28 Structural clay products
0.2	0.68	87.64			0.83	72.8	29 Ceramics
		69.27			0.83	57.5	30 Cement
		55.77			0.83	46.3	31 Basic metals
6.2	1.33	73.76			0.83	61.2	32 Light engineering
1.5	1.02	89.90			0.83	74.6	33 Transport equipment
		82.56			0.83	68.5	34 Machinery, other equipment
2.1	5.77	92.02			0.83	76.4	35 Other manufacturing
			217.1	12.44	0.83	10.3	36 Construction
			5.9	5.18	1.00	5.2	37 Electricity
			42.0	12.07	1.00	12.1	38 Road passenger transport
			0.7	0.46	1.00	0.5	39 Rail transport
		21.65			0.83	18.0	40 Trade, and other transport
		9.17			0.83	7.6	41 Services

$$\frac{Y_c}{Y_d} = a + b_1 W + b_2 M + b_3 T + \mu \qquad (6.5)$$

where Y_c and Y_d are respectively gross domestic product at current and at constant prices (implying that their ratio is an implicit price index); W is an index of wage rates; M is a price index of imported raw materials inputs; T is a weighted index of indirect tax rates; and a_1, b_1, b_2 and b_3 are constants.

In his own study for Greece, Karageorgas estimated b_3 to be equal to 0.862 and thereby concluded that for indirect taxes taken as a whole, 86 per cent of the burden is shifted forward on to the consumer while 14 per cent is borne by producers. However, he argued that for some indirect taxes, notably those on tobacco, sugar and the products of state monopolies, the shift coefficients were surely close to unity, implying that the coefficients on other commodities must be less than 0.86.

Despite the objections which might be raised against the method used to calculate the overall shift coefficient of indirect taxation, results of this type are extremely useful in the study of incidence since they provide a reference point to which one can relate detailed knowledge of the shift characteristics of individual taxes. Accordingly, for purposes of illustration, we have adopted the Karageorgas estimate of the overall shift factor of 0.86. Clearly it would have been better to estimate this figure directly for the Sri Lanka data but we have not yet done this. We have also assumed that the shift factor in respect of alcohol, tobacco, all government food profits/subsidies and several public utilities is unity. Since these account for about 20 per cent of all indirect tax revenues, the shift coefficient for all other indirect taxes must be 0.83 to give an overall average of 0.86. The vector of shift coefficients is shown as column 12 in Table 6.4.

At first sight, this exercise might appear inconsistent with our earlier calculation of rates of effective protection. However this turns out not to be the case since the adjustment made there, to allow for exchange rate overvaluation, happens to be almost identical in magnitude with the one made here for tax shifting. More specifically, an overvaluation of 12 per cent implies an exchange rate adjustment of $\frac{1}{1.15}$ or 0.87. This is pure coincidence but it does mean that our numerical results on effective protection are fully consistent with those on the price-raising effects of taxation.

Finally in this section we turn our attention to non-traded goods, which have so far been ignored. The approach here had to be different since the internal price need bear no relation to the world price even when there are no taxes. So, in this case, the effect of indirect taxes was calculated by examining the inputs into the non-trading sectors and calculating the weighted average price increase on these using the figures in column 5 of Table 6.4. This procedure was complicated in the case of sectors 36 and 39 as each utilised the outputs of the other. This complication was handled by setting up two simultaneous equations and solving them. Attention was directed only at the inputs into non-traded goods and not to inputs into inputs, etc. Again this is legitimate procedure given the pricing assumptions underlying column 5.

The results of our calculations for non-traded goods are shown in column 11 of Table 6.4 and the full summary of the price-raising effect of indirect taxes is given in column 13. Not surprisingly the prices of distilling and tobacco (Sectors 17 and 18) are massively and positively influenced by indirect taxation, while

Rice and Flour Milling (Sector 10) is generously subsidised. In general, agricultural product prices are relatively little affected by taxation, while most manufactured goods are heavily affected. Thus, not surprisingly, the accompaniment to the high levels of protection noted earlier is a large increase in many key components of the cost of living index.

We have not taken the obvious next step of comparing the price-raising effects of indirect taxation shown in the last column of Table 6.4 with the data on consumption patterns identified and discussed in Chapter 5. However, this would clearly be a relatively easy step to take and would provide valuable insights into some of the distributional consequences of the present fiscal system.

5 Conclusions

The analysis of this chapter has demonstrated the manner in which the tax and other data of our system can be manipulated to generate conclusions about various implications of the fiscal system. We have conceded that the results on levels of protection must be heavily qualified because they fail to take account of quantitative restrictions. Such restrictions are, in effect, additional import duties with the difference that the proceeds from them accrue to the importer. However, the general point remains that the data system can serve as a valuable basis for fiscal analysis while further work needs to relax some of the fixed coefficient assumptions which underlie the present calculations.

The analysis has shown that levels of effective protection are extremely high in certain sectors and are not adequately indicated by levels of nominal protection. It has shown that while the tax structure appears to provide a valuable incentive to non-traditional exports if one makes comparisons as between sectors, this incentive is sharply moderated when one compares the returns to domestic sales with the returns to export sales within individual sectors. Indeed, one could argue that the pattern of export incentives as calculated in this way is irrational given the export possibilities of certain sectors. Finally, the analysis has revealed the extent to which the structure of indirect taxes raises the domestic prices of certain goods and thereby introduces potential distributional consequences additional to those arising from direct taxation.

7

Some thoughts on future work

As explained in the preface, this volume has its origins in the International Labour Office, World Employment Programme mission to Sri Lanka. However, our first attempt to complete a data framework incorporating questions of distribution alongside more conventional national accounts and input–output was made in relation to a subsequent WEP mission to Iran. That work, which was the basis for a macroeconomic projection model, has been published as Technical Appendix 12 to the mission report.*

*See Pyatt *et al.* (1973). The model is also discussed in Chapter 5 of Blitzer, Clarke and Taylor (1975).

The data work on Iran was rudimentary by comparison with the subsequent research in Sri Lanka reported here. However, it did show that something useful could be achieved, notwithstanding a weak data base, in organising facts and associated modelling, to recognise not only that income distribution conditions final demand and hence, through input–output, the structure of production, employment and the balance of payments, but also that there is an important feedback: specifically, that the structure of production generates a pattern of factor demands and hence, through the ownership of factors, a pattern of income distribution. Thus the modelling work for Iran involved simultaneous and consistent solutions for output, employment and incomes, with each being disaggregated to some extent.

The demonstration of possibilities achieved by the Iran work was the justification for research in Sri Lanka as reported here. The emphasis in this case was on the data base itself, since it was felt that the most useful next step was to clarify ideas both about what information was needed to design an employment cum distribution orientated development strategy and, through a test case, to see how far one could go with implementation. This book is the result, with its findings and conclusions also providing a major input into a forthcoming volume by Pyatt and Thorbecke.†

†An overview of the Pyatt and Thorbecke volume has been published by the ILO. See Pyatt and Thorbecke (1976).

This forthcoming volume is an attempt to bring together the issues that emerge when development planning is directed to the multiple objectives of growth, redistribution and employment, with emphasis on reducing poverty. The Iran work previously referred to is drawn on, as are other studies, as an example of how insights can be obtained within a general conception that sees inequalities and growth as inextricably interwoven in the development process. Thus the conception of distributional and other similar problems as a crucial byproduct of the process of 'development' is the main theme. At the same time, no attempt is made to produce a general model which will explain all these issues, not least because there is too little known about some of the key relationships to justify commitment to any particular formulation. Ultimately, however, all this work is leading to models which are more general than those considered, for example, in Chapter 4, both in the sense that more aspects of development are embraced by them and in the sense that, for a given set of variables, more feedbacks are specified.

These aspects of contemporary research are well illustrated by The Bacchue series of models being developed as part of the ILO World Employment Programme research programme.* In these models education and demographic submodels act on, and are influenced by, an economic sub-model, so that the three submodels together simulate the likely future evolution of a society and its response to a wide range of possible policy intervention in the areas of land reform, population policy, fiscal policy and so on. The models have much in common with our own work in so far as their data requirements are concerned but go much further in that they incorporate a menu of behavioural elements far richer than anything which we have attempted. The obverse is a rather more cavalier approach to the data problems which their work encountered. A second example is the work of Adelman and Robinson on a model of Korea in which the detailed treatment of economic relationships recognises a variety of price feedbacks as well as quantity balances, and in which expectations play an important role in determining investment behaviour and other variables.

*For example see Wery *et al.* (1974).

While the servicing of models of this type may be an ultimate objective, there are a great many other reasons for getting together a body of data in a SAM format. The arguments in terms of improving the usefulness of otherwise independent and possibly conflicting statistical series have been emphasised. Beyond this, a simple but major reason for such an exercise is to provide a readily intelligible picture of what is going on in the economy. The logic here is that the first step to forming perceptions about what is happening in the development process is to show how the issues of distribution, employment, production, etc. are interlinked at some point, or series of points, in time. Thus the psychological novelty of data presentation provides a justification for the work even where there is scepticism about using this, in conjunction with specific modelling assumptions, to try to anticipate future developments.

Having built up a SAM for one or more years, there is much that can be done by relatively simple manipulation to throw light on particular aspects of economic concern. For example, the whole pattern of wage rates by skill and labour market, and of labour productivity, can be spelled out readily enough from our SAM tables and the associated manpower matrix in Appendix 2. Similarly, making the assumptions set out in Chapter 6, it would be straightforward to reproduce the accounts at something near to world prices as opposed to domestic prices, or to show transactions in pre- or post-tax terms, and other exercises are already underway as part of current research.†

†Financed by SSRC and under the direction of Alan Roe.

Our contention is that even before modelling begins the SAM approach to a macro-consistency analysis of development affords a panoramic view (yet one containing considerable detail), of economic structure. Inevitably this view is conditioned by the classifications used, and an exercise of attempting to classify production activities by location is but one example of the enormous range of possibilities. As explained in Chapter 3, practical work with secondary sources is circumscribed by the classifications which they adopt. But it is by no means obvious that the classifications which were thought to be most useful twenty years ago remain the best to serve our evolving perceptions. Thus there is much to be done at the research level in exploring new classification criteria. Chapter 3 sets out some initial ideas and these are taken further elsewhere.* Again as the Iran work initially suggested, it would seem to be important as a prior step to

*See Pyatt and Thorbecke (forthcoming).

complex modelling to sort out ideas on what the appropriate variables and classifications for such models might be.

Pending the results of current research on classifications we are inevitably obliged to work with the tools to hand. Chapters 4 to 6 provide a number of examples as to how established techniques of analysis are facilitated by the availability of a SAM, and much more remains to be done in these directions. But meanwhile there are other areas of policy and decision making to those considered in Chapters 4 to 6 and work subsequent to that in Sri Lanka has taken a complementary path, starting from the same basic SAM origin.

This subsequent work has involved many of the same individuals as the Sri Lanka study working, in association with colleagues in the UK Overseas Development Ministry, on a social-accounting matrix for Swaziland. This Swaziland study was undertaken, in the first instance, to check the extent to which Sri Lanka was a fortunate test case. By and large this proved to be not so, and the Swaziland study therefore provides a basis for maintaining that the SAM approach as presented here is of wide general applicability. However, our concern in Swaziland was to go further by attempting to advise policy on a number of key issues beyond those mentioned in this present volume. In this case the SAM provided a statistical basis for more specialised work in particular areas which was coordinated through the discipline of the social accounts. Accordingly any differences in view were restricted to differences in interpretation, and had to be sustainable in terms of their repercussions on other facets of the economy and not simply in their own partial context.

Beyond this, subsequent work on Swaziland has focused on the application of SAM to project analysis.* Since Swaziland is a small country, it is typically the case that what would be a more substantial project in most countries is very definitely not marginal there. Accordingly conventional techniques of project appraisal which build heavily on the assumption of marginality cannot be sustained. At this point it would seem that the SAM data frame has a great deal to offer, although a final judgement on this must clearly await further progress in the work.

*Carried out under the direction of Jeffrey Round through technical assistance to the Swaziland Government.

Beyond these efforts there are other studies in hand which are directed towards the analysis of development using an initial SAM standpoint. These include an intensive study of the development of the Muda river area in Malaysia,† a macro-planning study of the same country,* and a study of the statistical needs of integration in the Caribbean.†

†Being undertaken by Clive Bell and Peter Hazell at the Development Research Centre of the World Bank. See Bell and Hazell (1976).

*By Ahuwalia and Pyatt, also at the Development Research Centre.

†By Alan Roe and others under the auspices of UNDP and the Caribbean Community Secretariat. See Roe and associates (1975).

It is too early yet to judge where all this might finally lead but two points are worth emphasising. The first is that although the creation of an initial SAM requires a good deal of painstaking (one might say, tedious) work, it is something which, given the correct input of skills, can be done quite quickly. The production of the Sri Lanka system, for example, occupied some five months of the time of a group, on average, of five people. Thus it was very cheap compared with the many types of technical assistance which are given to developing countries for the production of partial data. This partial data is often important but would surely be enhanced more often than not by the existence of a SAM, not least because the latter can provide a guide to priorities in further partial statistical enquiry. It seems likely that maintenance of a SAM should be much less of a problem than its initial creation, and future work will include investigation of procedures for updating which hopefully will avoid retabulation *de nouveau.* As with national accounts, however, the effort involved will not prove to be worthwhile unless at some point the SAM approach comes to play an important part in planning and is used in practical decision making.

The second main conclusion to be drawn is that the integration of income distribution into the overall macro-data schema fulfills a need which is perceived in many quarters. Input–output and national accounts as such are quite inadequate for coming to grips with many of the questions which arise from the contemporary perception of development issues as discussed in Chapter 1. Thus the approach to data which we have illustrated here is a response and, as far as we know, the only response* to a need which must be met if concern for distributional issues is to be translated into action derived from a quantitative macroeconomic approach. Of course much remains to be done. There is a wide range of issues concerning disaggregation, classification, asset and wealth accounts, etc. which we have hardly touched on, if at all. Equally other aspects of social statistics, such as education, demography, etc. must be linked with the main economic framework if the latter is to grow in response to our needs. We have only made a start here by bringing income distribution into the central synoptic framework. In other places we have considered the integration into the framework of other aspects of economic and social change which are more commonly analysed in isolation.†

Meanwhile, without going further and joining in the all too familiar laments about what could be done with better data, there is much that remains to be achieved in the analysis of our results for Sri Lanka going beyond the presentation in Chapters 4 to 6. The intention is that this area of our work should proceed in two stages. In the first, we propose to continue with our experiments on the rather mechanical models discussed in Chapter 4. This will include an examination of the sensitivity of the results to different assumptions about the major inconsistencies in our raw data,* examining the consequences of moderating the fixed-coefficient assumptions, introducing certain policy instruments such as input-substitution policy, and so on. In the second stage, we will try to move to a broadening of our range of behavioural assumptions and, by implication, the data framework which is needed to implement the models which are used. In particular, it seems important to do much more to specify the manner in which the income distribution arises from the pre-existing distribution of wealth and from the operation of the labour market. Also there is a need to recognise more elements of the urban–rural duality than the structural one upon which we have so far concentrated, and to say more about, for example, price formation and price responses.

However, in all this, a serious attempt will be made to ensure that analytical techniques are developed in parallel with consideration of the possibilities of implementing the necessary change in the data base for Sri Lanka (and any other country which we may study). Our main purpose is to demonstrate the uses of quantitative techniques in distribution- and employment-orientated planning, and we fail in this purpose if we evolve techniques which are not operationally relevant, and statistically viable in the circumstances of the 'typical' developing country.

*Of course others have made substantial contributions of which the most outstanding is the work of Seers (see Seers (1961)). However, this work is not in the mainstream of UN-type thinking on statistics, although it is understood that Seers is currently working on substantial developments of his highly original, and important, earlier contributions and their relationship with UN systems. Meanwhile the UN itself has produced a system of social statistics which covers distributional questions and which is consistent with, but not built into, the main economic data system: the SNA set out in UNSO (1968), and referred to both in Stone's Foreword to this volume and in Chapter 3.

†See Pyatt and Thorbecke (1976) and (forthcoming) for a discussion of some aspects of extended SAM frameworks. The unpublished report on Swaziland contains empirical results on some relatively simple aspects.

*Notably the under-recording of income in the household budget survey which is a problem which applies not only in the Sri Lankan survey but also in virtually every other household survey ever conducted in the developing world.

APPENDIX 1

The compilation of the social-accounting matrix*

Outline

This appendix describes the methods used to construct the social-accounting matrix set out in aggregated form in Table 3.7 of the main text. It therefore contains the primary substance of our research to date. It is presented as an appendix only because the content is rather detailed and technical, and hence less easily digested than most other parts of the text.

*Unless otherwise stated, all money values are Rs millions but the prefix Rs has been omitted, and 'million' has been abbreviated to 'm.'

There are two preliminary points about our methodology which need to be made clear at the outset. First, faced with data inconsistencies of the type detailed in Chapter 2, it was necessary in order to get started, to accept some data as being relatively more accurate than the rest. We decided to place our faith initially in the National Income estimates produced by the Central Bank and published in the *Central Bank Report* for 1972. As work proceeded we detected a few cases where the Central Bank figures seemed less reliable than certain alternatives, but the incidence of such cases was fortunately rather low. Secondly, we built up the matrix in a sequence which began with those areas where the data was judged to be relatively most reliable and moved progressively to those areas where the data was judged to be least reliable. Whenever there were inconsistencies between data sets as revealed by the accounting identities linking them together, or simply discrepancies which violated economic common sense, we preferred to remove these inconsistencies by amending the later data rather than the earlier. In practice a good deal of iteration was also involved at a number of stages. In broad terms, data relating to consumption expenditure, government expenditure, exports and tax payments were adjudged relatively reliable, while data on certain types of production and most factor payments were adjudged relatively unreliable. However, there are several exceptions to this general predisposition which are to be discussed in detail later.

The sequence of filling in the matrix is in eight stages, and we have reserved a separate section of this appendix for each of the stages identified. We have also reprinted the summary matrix Table 3.7 from Chapter 3 (here labelled Table A.1) to facilitate cross-reference and all row and column references in this appendix relate to that table.

Stage 1 Disaggregation of final demands (i.e. household consumption, government consumption, capital formation and exports) into source of supply at factor cost (i.e. the disaggregation of most of row 6 of Table A.1).

Stage 2 Identification of the import content of each of the final demand categories, together with the various indirect taxes and subsidies applying

Table A.1 *Social-accounting matrix for Sri Lanka, 1970 (full aggregation)*

Receipts \ Payments	(1) Factors of production	(2) Institutions current accounts: Firms	(3) Institutions current accounts: Household	(4) Institutions current accounts: Government	(5) Combined capital account §	(6) Production activities	(7) Rest of world (current)	Total
(1) Factors of production			100	1275		10 098	–113	11 360
(2) Institutions current accounts: Firms	1575			294				1869
(3) Institutions current accounts: Households	9785	644		248			18	10 698
(4) Institutions current accounts: Government	–	376	567*	104	313	856	130	2346
(5) Combined capital account §		833	1339	42‡			425	2640
(6) Production activities			7601	302	1962	4358	2113	16 336
(7) Rest of world (current)		16	1091	79†	364	1024		2473
Total	11 360	1869	10 698	2346	2640	16 336	2573	

* includes indirect taxes on consumption expenditure
† includes imports and current transfers to rest of world
‡ not exactly accurate because of rounding errors
§ includes rest of world capital account

to these categories (i.e. the disaggregation of row 7 and part of row 4 of Table A.1).

Stage 3 Estimation of inter-industry transactions (i.e. the disaggregation of the intersection of row 6 and column 6 by both row and column); the total value-added payments by each production activity (i.e. the disaggregation of the intersection of row 1 and column 6, but only by column); the imports into each production activity (i.e. the intersection of row 7 and column 6, but only by column); and the duties on the inputs into each production activity (i.e. partial disaggregation of the intersection between row 4 and column 6 by both row and column).

Stage 4 Disaggregation of consumers expenditure by type of household (i.e. the disaggregation of column 3 by component columns).

Stage 5 Disaggregation of government current expenditure by type of expenditure (i.e. the disaggregation of column 4 by component columns).

Stage 6 Summary of all balance of payments entries (i.e. a summary of entries in row and column 7).

Stage 7 Summary of all government account entries (i.e. a summary of entries in row and column 7).

Stage 8 Reconciliation of household and firms institution accounts. This involves the disaggregation of value-added payments according to the type of factor receiving them (i.e. disaggregation of the intersection of columns 3, 4, 6 and 7, with row 1), as well as the disaggregation of each category of factor payment by receiving institution (i.e. the disaggregation of the intersection of column 1 with rows 2 and 3).

The stages of this procedure which are potentially most contentious are Stages 3 and 8 since the incidence of 'guestimation' here was relatively high.

Stage 1 Final demands

Private consumption expenditure

Our estimates of consumers' expenditure involved a methodology broadly similar to that employed by the Central Bank, namely the scaling up of survey data. However, because of a number of differences in assumptions about scaling, and other factors, our figure for total consumers' expenditure at market prices differs from that shown by the Central Bank (e.g. Table 10 of the 1972 Report) by about 1 per cent.

Our approach involved two phases, namely:

(a) the estimation of the expenditure by households on various categories of goods and services such as food, clothing, fuel and light, etc.;

(b) the decomposition of each of these expenditures into imports, expenditure on domestic products and indirect taxes.

On the first of these, the *Socio-Economic Survey* (SES) of 1969/70 is almost the sole source of information which has been used. Chapter 3 has already referred to the high degree of detail provided by this source and our approach to its aggregation. We now need to discuss the various problems of using the SES as a basis for estimates of consumers' expenditure and, in particular, problems of sampling error, coverage and reporting bias.

(i) Sampling error

The survey was carefully stratified with a low rate of non-response and covered nearly 10 000 households. The formal sampling errors should therefore in most cases be acceptably low (though these have not been calculated), especially for estimates of total and sub-totals of expenditure. Nevertheless for individual items, purchased infrequently, sampling errors could be as high as 100 per cent of the estimates. This would be even truer of estimates which apply to small sub-groups of the sample, e.g. to particular income groups within the estate sector. Unfortunately there are few independent checks on the survey estimates.

(ii) Coverage

Households containing only one person, lodgers and the whole of the non-household population (nomads, persons without fixed residences, the population living in institutions, and non-profit making organisations whose expenditure) were excluded from the survey. The total population estimated to be covered by the survey was 11.875 m. persons, compared with a provisional intercensal estimate of the population of 12.514 m. persons made by the Department of Census.

To provide the estimates of the social accounts, the survey figures were grossed up to the larger of the two population estimates, which is equivalent to assuming that the pattern of expenditure by the population not covered by the survey was the same as that covered. This assumption is clearly not true, especially as concerns such expenditures as those on Household operation, but it should not amount to a major source of error.

A further possible source of error is the time coverage of the survey, which differs from the calendar year 1970 by two months at either end. This raised some specific problems. For example, the issue of the second measure of rice at 75 cents per measure (= 2 lbs) under the rationing scheme was reintroduced with effect from 26 September 1970. The increase in the consumption of rationed rice during the last three months of 1970 is obviously not reflected in the survey data. However, in this particular case, we have made the necessary adjustments to the 'blown-up' estimates of the consumers' expenditure on rationed and unrationed rice, derived from the survey data. Seasonal variations were, however, eliminated for the sample as a whole by using the 4-round information instead of the 2-round data published in the *Preliminary Report*. There is no guarantee, however, that the sample is fully seasonally balanced for all sub-groups tabulated.

(iii) Reporting biases

For the most important elements of the private consumers' expenditure estimates, experience in other countries suggests that, as far as sampling errors and coverage are concerned, the survey provides a first-class source. It would only be in cases where very reliable records were available of total production, exports, imports, stock changes and purchases by non-household users that it would be possible to reject the survey estimates in favour of supply-based estimates. The more serious source of possible error, and indeed bias, derives from the method of recording, and here experience suggests that certain survey estimates could be seriously wrong.

As regards *food expenditure*, where records were kept for one week (including, in most cases, records of quantities) one could expect relatively small errors and little bias. Where food supplies were bought for more than one week, investigators checked these and reduced them to an equivalent one week's purchases. Although this is not as rigorous as a full check of beginning-of-week and week-end stocks, it was probably satisfactory. Within the computer, these weekly figures were grossed up to monthly figures. Unfortunately, the magnitude of the multiplier used to gross up the weekly figures to monthly figures is not explicitly stated in the preliminary report on the survey (October 1971), though one is able to deduce from the annual estimates given in that report (page xv) that the monthly figures require multiplication by 12 and not 13 to gross to annual data. We have, therefore, assumed that the monthly figures need to be grossed up 12 times to obtain the annual figures.

Expenditure on *drink and tobacco* were also recorded for one week. It is common experience that such data are usually greatly underrecorded, partly because most of such purchases are made by individuals outside the normal routine of housekeeping. Sri Lanka is no exception and it was found, by an examination of tobacco production, distillation, imports and duties, that private expenditure must be considerably underestimated in the survey. The tobacco expenditure figure was therefore raised from 257 m. to 489 m. and the expenditure on alcoholic beverages from 191 m. to 285 m. The latter excludes consumers' expenditure on illicitly distilled liquor and there was no way of estimating this in the present exercise. Hence, the estimates given by us are the *minimum* plausible amounts necessary to match domestic production *plus* imports.

The item of *miscellaneous expenditures* recorded in the SES includes transfer payments within the household sector such as gifts and donations. We have excluded such transfers on the grounds that there are no purchases of goods and services by households corresponding to these expenditures.

There is much more scope for error and bias in the reporting of *non-durable goods and services*, on which the survey relied on memory of expenditure over the previous month, and for *durables*, where the memory period was the previous twelve months. It has to be admitted that estimates obtained in this way are subject to grave doubts. Even the direction of possible bias is unknown and liable to be different for individual commodities. In only one case, however, was the evidence from the supply side sufficient to justify an actual alteration of the estimates provided by the survey, namely that of expenditure on transport and communications which was raised from 381 m. to 629 m. This was due, it appears, to a survey underestimate of expenditures on road transport.

An interesting conceptual point worth mentioning here concerns the consumers' expenditure on domestic servants. The blown up figure according to SES is only 40 m., representing the cash payments made by households to domestic servants. But, for the purpose of computing the national income, the value added by domestic servants includes payments received both in cash and kind. On the basis of the estimated number of domestic servants, which we calculate (see Appendix 2) as 65 000 in 1970, and an average monthly income, including monetary and non-monetary income of Rs 130, the total income received by domestic servants comes to 100 m. Accordingly, we have increased the consumers' expenditure on domestic servants from 40 m. to 100 m. Since domestic servants formed part of the household sector in the SES, it is justifiable to assume that their spendings are included in the total recorded expenditure.

It is useful to note that the preliminary report on the SES makes a clear distinction between monetary and non-monetary income, while in the case of expenditures one is only able to infer that the consumers' expenditures given in the main tabulations include the imputed values of home grown produce, free goods and services and rents of owner-occupied houses. This is clearly borne out in the discussion appearing in pages xv–xix of the preliminary report.

Broadly, there are two areas in which the estimates derived from the SES data differ seriously from those published by the Central Bank in its annual report. First, the net rental of residential buildings as estimated from the SES is 648 m. as against 400 m. given in the Central Bank report for value added by the sector

– ownership of dwellings. Second, the expenditure on domestic servants derived from the SES is 100 m. as against 337 m. given in the Central Bank report for expenditure on domestic services. These estimates should be further checked when the results of the survey on Consumer Finances for 1973 conducted by the Central Bank become available. In the present exercise, we have used the SES estimates, as all the evidence we have indicates that the SES figures are closer to reality.

The above deals with the first phase of our estimation of consumers expenditure, and produces the vector of expenditures shown as the 'All-island' column of Table A.19 on page 146. We now turn to the second stage, namely, the identification of the source of supply of each commodity in the classification. The procedure here was to identify the c.i.f. import component of the supply of each commodity from the detailed listing of consumption goods imports produced by the Customs Department, and the indirect tax element. The residual part of the supply of each commodity after removing these elements was then disaggregated by production activity – a relatively straightforward matter, given the 1 to 1 correspondence of commodities and production activities in many cases and the considerable commodity detail available from the SES. The major difficulty related to the estimation of each commodity, and this was dealt with by drawing heavily on the work already documented in PMC.

The result of this exercise is shown in coefficient form in what we have termed the 'classification converter' of Table A.2. Further detail on the estimation of the import and indirect tax element of each column is provided in subsequent sections. The vector of consumer expenditure by production activities is shown as the first column of Table A.6.

Government consumption

The accounts of the Ceylon government, as with the accounts of most governments, contain a wealth of detail about the nature of government expenditures and the sources of its revenues. However, and this is again true of government accounts in most countries, the classifications adopted are designed for the purposes of accounting for, and controlling, the administrative functions of government, and are not directly usable for the purposes of economic planning and economic decision making generally.

From the point of view of constructing a social-accounting matrix geared to the needs of planning this means two things. First, it means that a considerable rearrangement and reclassification of the various detailed statistics on government activities is necessary. Second, and more seriously, it means that some of the detail that one would like to have in order to build a useful and usable matrix does not exist and has to be generated by guesswork – normally by guesses about the size of the components of known totals.

Central government expenditures in the official accounts are listed under some 125 'heads', each of which corresponds to an administrative department of government. Within each of these headings, expenditure is subdivided into seven 'votes' which are numbered sequentially from 1 to 7. The labels attaching to these votes are as follows:

Vote 1 Personal emoluments and other allowances of staff
Vote 2 Administration charges – recurrent expenditure
Vote 3 Administration charges – capital expenditure
Vote 4 Services provided by the department – recurrent expenditure
Vote 5 Services provided by the department – capital expenditure

Table A.2 *Classification converter for consumers' expenditure*

	Rationed rice	Outside ration rice	Wheat flour	Other grains & cereals	Condiments	Pulses	Coconuts	Vegetables fruits and other nuts	Meat	Fish	Milk and milk products	Oils and fats including butter	Tea	Sugar	All other foods and beverages
1 Tea													0.8539		
2 Rubber															
3 Coconuts							0.8733								
4 Paddy															
5 Livestock									0.8571		0.4490				
6 Fishing										0.4742					
7 Logging and firewood															
8 Other agriculture				0.0606	0.6151	0.3810		0.8585							0.450
9 Mining and quarrying					0.0179										
10a Rice milling	5.1944	0.7700													
10b Flour milling			0.0852												
11 Dairy products											0.2857	0.0160			
12 Bread				0.6532											
13 Other bakery products				0.1818											0.088
14 Carbonated beverages															0.038
15 Desiccated coconut															
16 Other processed food					0.0595					0.0191				0.0128	0.061
17 Distilling															
18 Tobacco															
19 Textiles															
20 Wood products															
21 Paper															
22 Leather															
23 Rubber															
24 Chemicals															
25 Oils and fats												0.6880			
26 Coconut fibre and yarn															
27 Petroleum and coal															
28 Structural clay products															
29 Ceramics															
30 Cement															
31 Basic metals															
32 Light engineering															
33 Transport equipment															
34 Machinery, other equipment															
35 Other manufacturing															
36 Construction															
37 Electricity															
38 Road passenger transport															
39 Rail transport															
40a Wholesale trade															
40b Retail trade	0.2500	0.0596	0.1477	0.0438	0.0873	0.0857	0.0856	0.0993	0.0929	0.2275	0.1265	0.1200	0.0562	0.0332	0.08
40c Other transport	0.1389	0.0297	0.0796	0.0202	0.0436	0.0476	0.0411	0.0496	0.0429	0.1148	0.0613	0.0640	0.0337	0.0179	0.04
41a Communication															
41b Hotels and restaurants															
41c Professional services															
41d Dwellings															
41e Other services															
Domestic servants															
Customs duties	0.0694	0.0024									0.0163	0.0080		0.0870	0.0
Indirect taxes (local)	−7.9444			0.0370	0.0040	−0.1143		−0.0074		0.0038	0.0204	0.0400	0.0562		0.02
Imports	3.2917	0.1383	0.6307	0.0034	0.1488	0.6000			0.0071	0.1606	0.0367	0.0400		0.3708	0.1
Government food profits			0.0568		0.0079									0.4783	
FEECs					0.0159						0.0041	0.0240			0.0
Total expenditure	1.0000	1.0000	1.0000	1.0000	1.0000	1.0000	1.0000	1.0000	1.0000	1.0000	1.0000	1.0000	1.0000	1.0000	1.0

Vote 6 Economic development – current expenditure
Vote 7 Economic development – capital expenditure

Taking account of both these classifications (heads and votes), government expenditure subdivides into over 800 categories and then further subdivides since each vote is typically specified in some detail.

There is little apparent use from the viewpoint of economic analysis in the distinction between the pairs of votes 2/3, 4/5 and 6/7 and the organisational usefulness of the distinction is also somewhat obscure. However, the distinction between votes 1, 2, 4 and 6 on the one hand and 3, 5 and 7 on the other does correspond, nominally at any rate, with the standard national income and social-accounting distinction between current and capital expenditures. This nominal

	Toddy	Other alcoholic beverages	Traditional tobacco	Modern tobacco	Clothing & footwear	Rent rates & repairs	Fuel & light	Consumer durables	Household operations (services)	Household operations (goods)	Personal care & health	Transport and communications	Recreation	Miscellaneous
1 Tea														
2 Rubber														
3 Coconuts	0.6538													
4 Paddy														
5 Livestock														
6 Fishing														
7 Logging and firewood							0.2725							
8 Other agriculture														
9 Mining and quarrying														
10a Rice milling														
10b Flour milling														
11 Dairy products														
12 Bread														
13 Other bakery products														
14 Carbonated beverages														
15 Desiccated coconut														
16 Other processed food														
17 Distilling		0.2189												
18 Tobacco			0.8268	0.8453										
19 Textiles					0.3847									
20 Wood products								0.2477						
21 Paper													0.2799	
22 Leather					0.0524									
23 Rubber												0.0111		
24 Chemicals							0.0332			0.4516	0.2510			
25 Oils and fats														
26 Coconut fibre and yarn														
27 Petroleum and coal							0.1528					0.0143		
28 Structural clay products														
29 Ceramics										0.0565				
30 Cement														
31 Basic metals								0.3211		0.2419	0.0412	0.0445	0.0746	
32 Light engineering								0.0963						
33 Transport equipment														
34 Machinery, other equipment					0.0150		0.0631	0.0046						
35 Other manufacturing														
36 Construction							0.0897							
37 Electricity												0.5469		
38 Road passenger transport												0.1717		
39 Rail transport														
40a Wholesale trade														
40b Retail trade	0.0769	0.0730	0.1181	0.0856	0.1662		0.2159	0.0780		0.1048	0.0864	0.0191	0.0485	
40c Other transport	0.0385	0.0343	0.0551	0.0414	0.0824		0.1064	0.0367		0.0564	0.0411	0.0095	0.0261	
41a Communication												0.0254		
41b Hotels and restaurants														
41c Professional services					0.0240				0.4490		0.4280			
41d Dwellings						0.9787								
41e Other services									0.0408				0.4664	1.0000
Domestic servants									0.5102					
Customs duties		0.0386		0.0028	0.0254		0.0066	0.0780		0.0323	0.0206	0.0223	0.0149	
Indirect taxes (local)	0.2308	0.6223		0.0221	0.0329	0.0213	0.0299	0.0505		0.0081	0.0329	0.0032	0.0373	
Imports		0.0086		0.0028	0.1407		0.0199	0.0596		0.0323	0.0988	0.0954	0.0336	
Government food profits														
FEECs		0.0043			0.0763		0.0100	0.0275		0.0161		0.0366	0.0187	
Total expenditure	1.000	1.000	1.000	1.000	1.000	1.000	1.000	1.000	1.000	1.000	1.000	1.000	1.000	1.000

correspondence is slightly misleading because, in practice, there are a large number of items of a capital nature which are included in votes 2, 4 and 6. These are mainly small items of equipment and maintenance expenditures: it is established national accounting practice in Sri Lanka to adjust for these in calculating the current expenditure breakdown. We have followed this practice; the amount involved in 1970 being 57 m. or approximately 4 per cent of our figure for current expenditures. As a consequence of our definition of the government sector (see Chapter 3), it is also necessary to remove the gross expenditures of the main enterprise departments of government which are included in the totals for each of the votes.

Having made these various adjustments one is left with appropriate totals for government current expenditures and government capital expenditures. The next problem is to subdivide both the current and the capital expenditures into those which involve the purchase of goods and services and transfer payments. The government accounts, as they stand, do not readily show this distinction. Thus the Sri Lanka national income statisticians are required to examine each subdivision of each expenditure vote and allocate it according to whether it is a transfer item or an expenditure on goods and services. For 1970 this procedure yields a total of 862.2 m. for current transfer payments, of which interest on the national debt accounts for about a third. Our only objection to the approach currently adopted concerns the treatment of government payments of *pensions*. This is discussed more fully below.

The results of the calculations thus far are summarised in Table A.3 below.

The last figure in this table follows the recommendation of the United Nations, *A System of National Accounts* (SNA) (1968) in including imputed pension contributions of participants in the government's non-contributory pension scheme (see SNA paragraph 7.17). Unfortunately in the social accounts of Sri Lanka the amount chosen for imputation is made exactly equal to the amount of pensions actually paid out (183 m. in 1970). This has caused considerable confusion in the past, not least to ourselves, and in particular, has encouraged the view that government pension *payments* are being treated as expenditure on goods and services rather than in the correct manner, as transfer payments. The correct accounting requires three entries:

(i) an increase in the first entry in Table A.3 to take account of the imputed contributions;
(ii) inclusion of pension payments in transfers;
(iii) the recording of a government receipt of imputed pension contributions

Table A.3 *The calculation of government current expenditures and transfers (1970) (Rs million)*

Totals of votes 1, 2 4 and 6	2701.6
Less expenditure of main enterprise departments (Posts and Telecommunications, Port Commission, Railways) – Votes 1, 2, 4 and 6.	270.4
	2431.2
Less capital expenditure included in current votes Total central government	57.1
	2374.1
Plus local government current expenditures (CBR, Table 8)	125.0
Total government current expenditures and transfers	2499.1
of which transfers (Central Bank's social accounts division)	862.2
	1636.9
Plus imputed rent on government buildings	25.5
Less statistical discrepancy	13.7
Total expenditure on goods and services (CBR, Table 8)	1648.7

from households. In conjunction with item (i), this ensures that the imputation procedure has no effect on the size of the government's deficit/surplus.

Relating these procedures to Table A.3, they mean that the last entry stays the same but that the transfers total increases by 183 m. to 1045.1 m.

Having estimated the total of government current expenditure on goods and services (1649 m.), the next step was to remove from this the wage and salary payments of public servants and local government employees (1275 m.), imputed rent on government buildings which we have treated as an indirect tax (26 m.), the import component of Government spending (43 m.) and the duty components (3 m.). All of these items could be estimated from Central Bank or Customs Department sources. The residual of 302 m. is government expenditure on locally produced goods and services. This was then disaggregated by production sector using the work already documented, in PMC, and the results are shown as the second column of Table A.6.

Capital formation

The capital formation figures shown in Table A.6 include both fixed capital formation and investment in stocks, and we will need to discuss these two components separately. The starting point for the fixed capital formation figures is the Central Bank's estimate for gross fixed capital formation in market prices of 2441.7 m. (CBR, Table 8). The disaggregation of this total by productive sectors supplying the inputs, and by imports and indirect taxes is as shown in Table A.4 below, and was based almost entirely on the work already carried out by the social accounts division of the Central Bank.

Available information on *stock* changes in Sri Lanka is very scanty. Only in two cases, tea and rubber, are firm estimates available for changes in stocks. Changes in stocks of rice, wheat flour and sugar are confined to imports only and that on paddy to purchases under the guaranteed price scheme (GPS). The estimates that we have used for tea, rubber and paddy are identical to those appearing in Table 7 of the CBR for 1972, and in other cases we have made independent estimates whenever possible. These are certain to be subject to large errors.

Table A.4 *Components of gross fixed capital formation, 1970 (Rs million)*

Production activity	Market price	Distribution cost	Imports c.i.f.	Customs duties	FEECs	Domestic inputs at producer prices
1 Tea	30.9	–	–	–	–	30.9
2 Rubber	21.7	–	–	–	–	21.7
3 Coconuts	29.3	–	–	–	–	29.3
20 Wood products	10.5	2.7	–	–	–	7.8
32 Light engineering	125.6	24.3	55.5	15.7	30.1	–
33 Transport equipment	268.6	48.4	105.6	43.5	57.8	13.3
34 Machinery, other equipment	360.4	78.4	167.0	11.9	90.3	12.8
36 Construction	1594.7	–	–	–	–	1594.7
40 Trade, and other transport	–	–	–	–	–	153.8
Total	2441.7	153.8	328.1	71.1	178.2	1864.3

Finally, we can relate the 'total' entry from Table A.4 to similar figures for stocks and thereby show the relative contributions of fixed investment and stocks to the entries in the relevant column of Table A.6. This is done in Table A.5 below.

Exports

Exports subdivide into exports of merchandise and exports of services. For merchandise exports the figures we used are essentially those shown in Tables II(K)3 and 14 of the CBR for 1972. Minor adjustments were made to these to ensure consistency with the overall balance of payments figures shown in Table 44 of the CBR and discussed more fully in Stage 6 below. Finally, the trade and transport margins associated with each export were subtracted on the basis of ratios set down in PMC. These margins total to 90.2 m. which is credited to the transport and services sectors, namely sectors 40 and 41.

Information on the total exports of *services* of 226.9 m. was derived from Table 44 of the CBR and allocated directly to sector 41, except for 2.7 due to transport earnings other than ports which was allocated directly to sector 40c.

Summary

The results of applying these various procedures are the vectors of final demands set down in Table A.6, in which the major aggregates are cross-referenced to Table A.1. Table A.6 also summarises a number of entries which are discussed more fully in subsequent sections.

Stage 2 Imports, import duties, FEECs and other indirect taxes

Table A.6 in the previous section summarised our estimates of the imports and duties thereon in each of our four final demand categories, namely consumption, government, capital formation and change in stocks. However, we have not discussed the source of these estimates in any detail and this is something which we need to do before discussing inter-industry transactions. The reason for this is that in each of the three cases (i.e. imports, import duties and FEECs), the estimates of the components applicable to inter-industry transactions make at least some use of the estimates of the components applicable to final demands. For example, in the case of imports, the inter-industry component was derived as a residual. The procedures used are set out below. In all cases they can be viewed as a disaggregation of some part of Table A.6 above.

Table A.5 *Relative contributions of fixed capital formation and stocks to total investment (Rs million)*

	Market price	Imports c.i.f.	Customs duties	FEECs	Domestic inputs at producer prices
Fixed capital formation (Table A.4)	2442	328	71	178	1865
Stocks	153	35	2	19	97
Total as in Table A.6		364	73	197	1962

Table A.6 *Disaggregation of final demand entries by source of supply (i.e. by rows) (Rs million)*

Production activity	Household consumption – intersection of row 6 col. 3	Government consumption –intersection of row 6 col. 4	Capital formation – intersection of row 6 and col. 5	Exports – intersection of row 6 and col. 7
1 Tea	76	2	–55	839
2 Rubber	–	–	25	341
3 Coconuts	289	4	29	2
4 Paddy	–	–	49	–
5 Livestock	230	4	–	–
6 Fishing	248	3	–	–
7 Logging and firewood	82	–	–	–
8 Other agriculture	916	9	–	106
9 Mining and quarrying	9	–	–	19
10a Rice milling	1020	18	56	–
10b Flour milling	15	–	–	3
11 Dairy products	72	3	–	–
12 Bread	194	2	–	–
13 Other bakery products	70	–	–	1
14 Carbonated beverages	7	–	3	–
15 Desiccated coconut	–	–	–	83
16 Other processed food	56	3	34	7
17 Distilling	51	–	–	–
18 Tobacco	411	–	–	–
19 Textiles	257	5	50	11
20 Wood products	54	2	8	–
21 Paper	75	7	–	–
22 Leather	35	–	–	6
23 Rubber	7	–	–	1
24 Chemicals	127	–	–	12
25 Oils and fats	86	–	–	74
26 Coconut fibre and yarn	–	–	–	58
27 Petroleum and coal	55	1	–69	57
28 Structural clay products	–	–	–	–
29 Ceramics	7	–	–	–
30 Cement	–	–	–	–
31 Basic metals	–	–	–	–
32 Light engineering	158	23	–35	2
33 Transport equipment	21	–	25	–
34 Machinery, other equipment	–	–	93	–
35 Other manufacturing	30	–	–	1
36 Construction	–	92	1595	–
37 Electricity	27	28	–	–
38 Road passenger transport	344	–	–	–
39 Rail transport	108	–	–	1
40a Wholesale trade	–	–	108	172
40b Retail trade	769	39	–	–
40c Other transport	385	20	46	30
41a Communication	16	30	–	7
41b Hotels and restaurants	198	–	–	14
41c Professional services	208	1	–	10
41d Dwellings	690	–	–	–
41e Other services	198	6	–	256
Total as in Table A.1, row 6	7601	302	1962	2113
Imports as in Table A.1, row 7†	1091	43*	364	–
Indirect taxes/subsidies	–311	26	–	327
Customs duties†	120	3	73	–
Government food profits	201	–	–	–
FEECs on imports (+)/ exports (–)†	109	–	197	–197
Total government receipts included in Table A.1, row 4	119	29	270	130
Domestic services as in Table A.1, row 1	100	–	–	–

* The difference between this figure and the 79 shown in Table A.1, row 9 is 36 of Government transfer payments to the rest of the world and mainly debt interest.

† For full details on these entries see Tables A.10, A.11 and A.12 below.

Imports

The total c.i.f. value of imports in 1970 was 2521 m. (comprising 2332 of merchandise imports and 189 of service imports (CBR, Table 44)).

For the purpose of incorporating entries in the social-accounting framework this estimate has to be disaggregated in two directions. In the first instance a disaggregation is required to show imports by type of commodity, and for this the 41 sector classification is adopted. A second dimension to disaggregation is the breakdown into imports for current use by consumers ($\mathbf{m}_c$) and government ($\mathbf{m}_g$), imports of capital goods ($\mathbf{m}_K$ and $\mathbf{m}_{\Delta s}$); and imports for intermediate use ($\mathbf{m}_R$).

Thus if **m** is the 41 element vector of merchandise imports *plus* imports of services, then

$$\mathbf{m} = \mathbf{m}_c + \mathbf{m}_g + \mathbf{m}_K + \mathbf{m}_{\Delta s} + \mathbf{m}_R$$

where all of these entries are recorded at c.i.f. values.

The total c.i.f. value of merchandise imports is given in the balance of payments as 2332 (CBR, Table 44). Customs department data was available showing the breakdown of imports by BTN code heading and this detailed information was aggregated into our 41 sector classification. In the case of those imports handled by the Food Commissioner we replaced customs department data by those available from the Food Commissioner since these seemed likely to be the more accurate (an indication of the size of the discrepancy between these two estimates was given in Chapter 2). The total merchandise imports after adjusting for Food Commissioner's imports amount to 2318 and the discrepancy between this and the balance of payments figure of 2332 was taken to be due to the non-inclusion of certain imports. However, two items not correctly included were readily identified from an independent source used in estimating $\mathbf{m}_c$. The remaining small residual between the balance of payments figures for merchandise imports and the amended Central Bank figures was added to production sector 27. This sector was chosen because it was known that discrepancies existed in the recording of imports by the Ceylon Petroleum Corporation on the one hand and the Customs Department on the other (CBR, 1971, p. 214).

At this stage imports were not classified by *using* industries but only by *type* of import; it was only at a later stage (described fully in Stage 3 below) that this second dimension of disaggregation was introduced.

In addition to merchandise imports there are other expenditures, mainly services detailed in the balance of payments figures for 1970 (CBR Table 44) which must be included in the vector **m**. These are shown in Table A.7 below, together with their classification by type of input and also by user sector, whether of intermediate or final variety.

The total import of services of 189 m. together with the total merchandise imports of 2332 m. make up our import total of 2521 m. as shown in Table A.9.

In order to obtain a disaggregation of the total into the four categories of final use (namely $\mathbf{m}_c$, $\mathbf{m}_g$, $\mathbf{m}_K$ and $\mathbf{m}_{\Delta s}$), a certain amount of independent information was used. For vector $\mathbf{m}_c$, in addition to the Central Bank estimates of merchandise imports, Food Commissioner's data for rice, flour and sugar were incorporated: and this necesistated a method for dividing total imports of these items as between consumption and intermediate use.

The sub-division in the case of rice and flour imports is shown in Table A.8 below. The division between consumption and intermediate use of flour was made on the basis of consumption of bread and flour as reported in the SES and it is use-

Table A.7 *Imports of services, 1970 (Rs million)*

Item	Classification			Amount (Rs million)
	Type of import	User		
Non-monetary gold	(31)	Production sector	(35)	2.1
Freight and merchandise insurance	(41)	Production sector	(40)	3.3
Passenger fares	(40)	Consumers' expenditure		10.9
Port expenditures	(40)	Production sector	(40)	3.8
Other	(40)	Production sector	(40)	7.4
Travel	(40)	Government current expenditure		1.0
		Consumers' expenditure		19.3
Government expenditure not included elsewhere	(41)	Government current expenditure		23.6
Other services	(41)	Production sector	(41)	117.5
				188.8

Source: CBR (1972), Table 44.

Table A.8 *Imports of rice and flour, 1970 (Rs million)*

Commodity	Total value of imports	Consumers' expenditure	Intermediate use
Rice	353	353	–
Flour†	225	110	115

Source: CBR (1972), Table II(K)17 and SES data on bread and flour consumption.
†Production sector 10b includes whole wheat imported by the Flour Mill Corporation and this amounted to 12 m. in 1970. This amount is not included here.

ful to note that the Central Bank's estimate of flour for intermediate use is grossly understated. In the case of sugar, the final use element was estimated as 144 m. on the basis of data provided by the social accounts division of the Central Bank.

For most other imports, we accepted the identification of the consumption goods element which had already been carried out by the social accounts division of the Central Bank. One of the few exceptions to this was a small import of raw cotton which had been erroneously identified as a consumption good.

Information regarding imports of goods and services for government current purposes was also supplied by the Central Bank, social accounts division. When this was supplemented by information about imports of services by government the total c.i.f. value of government imports amounted to 42.8 m. This was classified by type of import (i.e. by sector) on the basis of the pattern given in PMC.

Imports of capital goods both in total and disaggregated into the three types (i.e. production sectors 32, 33 and 34), were also a direct estimate from the

Central Bank, as was the margin of FEECs and duties associated with them. The total c.i.f. value of imports of capital goods was 328.1.

The final import vector $\mathbf{m}_R$ – imports of intermediate goods – was obtained as a residual. This was so for all elements except for production sectors 32 and 34 where separate allowances had to be made for delivery to and draining from stocks. This proved necessary to achieve an overall balance for the social-accounting matrix, and did not seem inconsistent with economic trends for these sectors.

The following table, A.9, shows the breakdown, at c.i.f. values, of all imports according to both category of use and type of import.

Table A.9 *Imports, 1970 (Rs million at c.i.f. value)*

Sector (type of import)	(i) Imports of consumption goods ($\mathbf{m}_c$)	(ii) Imports by government ($\mathbf{m}_g$)	(iii) Imports of capital goods ($\mathbf{m}_K$)	(iv) Imports to stocks ($\mathbf{m}_{\Delta s}$)	(v) Imports of intermediate goods ($\mathbf{m}_R$)	(vi) Total imports
1 Tea						
2 Rubber						
3 Coconuts						
4 Paddy						
5 Livestock	0.8	0.4			1.0	2.2
6 Fishing						
7 Logging and firewood						
8 Other agriculture	138.1				39.8	177.9
9 Mining and quarrying					4.5	4.5
10 Milling	464.0				126.6	590.6
11 Dairy products	14.3				40.5	54.8
12 Bread						
13 Other bakery products	0.6					0.6
14 Carbonated beverages						
15 Desiccated coconut						
16 Other processed food	259.7				14.3	274.0
17 Distilling	1.9				1.9	3.8
18 Tobacco	0.5					0.5
19 Textiles	93.5	1.5			103.7	198.7
20 Wood products					11.0	11.0
21 Paper	1.9	0.7			50.2	52.8
22 Leather	0.1	0.1			1.3	1.5
23 Rubber	4.9	0.7			12.3	17.9
24 Chemicals	24.3	6.1			180.1	210.5
25 Oils and fats	0.1				9.8	9.9
26 Coconut fibre and yarn						
27 Petroleum and coal	19.0	0.7			55.0	74.7
28 Structural clay products					2.4	2.4
29 Ceramics	3.8	0.5			9.5	13.8
30 Cement					20.5	20.5
31 Basic metals					104.9	104.9
32 Light engineering	21.1	4.4	55.5	63.0	58.4	202.4
33 Transport equipment	5.6	2.4	105.6		7.0	120.6
34 Machinery, other equipment			167.0	–27.6	28.6	168.0
35 Other manufacturing	6.6	0.6			8.8	16.0
36 Construction						
37 Electricity						
38 Road passenger transport						
39 Rail transport						
40 Trade, and other transport	10.9	1.0			11.2	23.1
41 Services	19.3	23.6			120.7	163.6
Total as in Table A.1*	1091.0	42.8	328.1	35.4	1023.9	2521.2

* To be strictly correct, it is only the totals of columns (i) to (iv) inclusive which appear in Table A.1 and (iii) to (iv) appear aggregated together.

FEEC payments on imports

Goods and services imported at the least favourable of the two exchange rates are recorded in the SAM at the local currency value implied by the 'official' exchange rate, with the extra cost associated with the use of the less favourable exchange rate (i.e. the FEEC payment) being recorded separately (see Chapter 2 for details of the dual exchange rate system). This procedure means that, as with imports, we need to disaggregate FEEC payments in two directions; by *type* of import (i.e. the 41 sector classifications) with which they are associated and by *user*.

The total FEEC receipts for 1970 recorded in government accounts amount to 643 m. The breakdown of this total is as shown in Table A.10.

The FEEC scheme applies to both visible and invisible accounts of the balance of payments, though not all items in these accounts are subject to FEECs. FEECs on merchandise imports have been estimated on the basis of updated information shown in PMC. It should be noted that we have not attributed any FEECs to sugar although one of our major sources of information on this matter has erroneously done so (see Ministry of Planning, *The Projection of Government Revenue*, 1971, mimeo). A listing of imports of services subject to FEECs was supplied by the Central Bank. The FEEC purchases by Government for servicing the foreign debt are given in the ERE and it should be noted that these transactions appear on both sides of the Government accounts. Combining all these factors, the total value of FEECs assigned to imports of merchandise goods and services came to 586 m. (i.e. the total of the non-negative asterisked items in the table). The FEEC payments for each commodity imported will either be equal to or less than the standard FEEC rate on imports: that is 55 per cent in 1970. This is simply because in any sector, some commodities are imported at the official exchange rate while others are subjected to an additional FEEC payment.

For fixed capital formation, a combined debit for both FEECs and duties was supplied by the Central Bank and the FEEC figure alone had to be chosen to fit in with this. In fact, import duties were debited first and the FEEC figures were taken to be the residual.

As noted in Chapter 2, the FEEC scheme also applies to exports in the sense that foreign earnings from certain categories of non-traditional exports are converted into local currency at the more favourable FEEC rate rather than the

Table A.10 *Summary of FEEC revenues, 1970 (Rs million)*

*Consumer goods and services	109
*Investment goods	178
Private transfer	5
Private interest payments	2
Public interest payments	14
Capital repayments (public)	25
*Stocks	19
Private capital repayments	11
*Intermediate goods and services	280
	643
*FEEC rebates on exports	–197
Total FEEC revenues	446

* Indicates an item appearing in the final demand and inter-industry part of our matrix.

official rate. The total of extra revenues to exporters arising from this scheme in 1970 was 197 m. of which 121 m. was for payments in respect of non-traditional merchandise exports and 76 m. was in respect of exports of services. The FEEC rebate operates on the f.o.b. value of exports and accordingly the entire premium values received by exporters of non-traditional products are assigned to the respective sectors. This implies that though the trade and transport margins on exports have been allocated to sector 40, the FEEC rebates are fully allocated to the respective industries engaged in production for export. Strictly, if the commodities are exported through the trade sector then it is the latter that benefits directly from the FEEC rebate scheme, though at least a part of this may be passed on to the industries concerned. The assumption made here is, then, that the full benefit of the FEEC rebate scheme is enjoyed by the respective industries and that the trade sector does not receive any share of the FEEC rebate.

The full detail on FEEC receipts and repayments is as shown in Table A.11 below.

Import duties

The total import duties paid during 1970 amounted to 297.8 m. As with FEEC revenue it is necessary to obtain a disaggregation of this figure both by commodity classification and by category of use of the dutiable imports. Basic information available to make this allocation was obtained from the Ceylon Government Gazette (No. 14813/2), which details the rates of duty levied on each commodity. Using this, the social accounts division of the Central Bank made estimates of the duty payable by each commodity grouped by BTN code number, after taking account of the revisions to the duty rates applicable for 1970. This method gave rise to a figure of total duty payable of 428.2 m. However, the actual duty paid in 1970 as recorded in the published Government accounts was 298 m.; a discrepancy of 130 m.

For two of the final demand categories, namely consumers expenditure and investment, some controls on duty paid are already available from the social accounts division of the Central Bank. These figures were 120.2 m. and 71.1 m. for consumption and investment respectively. The remaining broad totals for duty paid, as well as the allocation by production sector were calculated by using the detail available on duties *payable* and scaling these up *pro rata* to match the total of duties actually *paid* from the Government accounts. This yielded the distribution of duty payments shown in Table A.12 below.

Indirect taxes/subsidies (including government food profits)

As already noted in Chapter 3, our definition of indirect taxes includes profits on government food transactions as a positive item and food subsidies as a negative item. Our totals for these two items were 243 m. and 588 m. respectively and are the official figures from the Food Commissioner. They differ slightly from the figures shown in CBR (Table II(G)5) which relate to the financial year. The Food Commissioner's information indicates that 16 m. of the total subsidy relates to the consumption of rice. This information also indicates that 201 m. of total food profits relates to consumption items and mainly sugar, while the balance relates to further processing of the items affected.

Detailed information on all other items of indirect tax was available from the ERE and this information together with supplementary information from the Ministry of Planning was used to allocate taxes between consumption on the one hand and production on the other, and also to allocate as between our 41 production sectors. In brief, other duties on *consumption* summed to 274 m. of

Table A.11 *FEEC revenues, 1970 (Rs million)*

Sector	(i) $FEEC_C$	(ii) $FEEC_g$	(iii) $FEEC_K$	(iv) $FEEC_{\Delta S}$	(v) $FEEC_R$	(vi) $FEEC_M$	(vii) FEEC rebates on exports
1 Tea							
2 Rubber							
3 Coconuts							
4 Paddy							
5 Livestock							
6 Fishing							
7 Logging and firewood							
8 Other agriculture	8.3				1.7	10.0	45.5
9 Mining and quarrying							9.5
10 Milling							1.2
11 Dairy products	4.3				3.9	8.2	
12 Bread							
13 Other bakery products							0.2
14 Carbonated beverages							–
15 Desiccated coconut							–
16 Other processed food	6.1				7.9	14.0	2.7
17 Distilling	1.1						1.1
18 Tobacco	0.3						0.3
19 Textiles	51.4				28.8	80.2	4.7
20 Wood products					6.0	6.0	0.1
21 Paper	1.0				14.6	15.6	
22 Leather							2.1
23 Rubber	2.7				6.8	9.5	0.4
24 Chemicals					40.0	40.0	4.9
25 Oils and fats					5.4	5.4	–
26 Coconut fibre and yarn							25.5
27 Petroleum and coal	2.2				30.2	32.4	22.8
28 Structural clay products					1.3	1.3	
29 Ceramics	2.1				5.2	7.3	
30 Cement					11.3	11.3	
31 Basic metals					52.7	52.7	
32 Light engineering	11.2		30.1	19.2	32.1	92.6	0.9
33 Transport equipment	3.1		57.8		3.9	64.8	
34 Machinery, other equipment			90.3		15.6	105.9	
35 Other manufacturing	3.6				4.8	8.4	0.5
36 Construction							
37 Electricity							
38 Road passenger transport							
39 Rail transport							
40 Trade, and other transport	5.0					5.0	12.0
41 Services	7.0				8.0	15.0	64.0
Total (As in Table A.1)	109.4	–	178.2	19.2	280.2	587.0	197.0

* columns (i), (ii), (iii), (iv) and (vii) only.

which 140 m. is the total of duties on liquor, including profits from the sale of arrak, and the balance is turnover tax. Other duties on *production* summed to 433 m. of which the tobacco tax accounts for 210 m., local government rates account for 51 m.; the turnover tax accounts for 144 m., and stamp duties and licences account for 48 m.

The figure for indirect taxes also includes a negative figure for the losses of

Table A.12 *Duties levied on imports, 1970 (Rs million)*

Sector	(i) Duty_C	(ii) Duty_g	(iii) Duty_K	(iv) $\text{Duty}_{\Delta S}$	(v) Duty_R	(vi) Duty_M
1 Tea						
2 Rubber						
3 Coconuts						
4 Paddy						
5 Livestock					0.2	0.2
6 Fishing						
7 Logging and firewood						
8 Other agriculture	0.4				9.5	9.9
9 Mining and quarrying					0.2	0.2
10 Milling	7.1				1.9	9.0
11 Dairy products	4.6				0.1	4.7
12 Bread						
13 Other bakery products						
14 Carbonated beverages						
15 Desiccated coconut						
16 Other processed food	34.3				14.6	48.9
17 Distilling	9.1				2.2	11.3
18 Tobacco	0.5					0.5
19 Textiles	16.7				5.3	22.0
20 Wood products					1.5	1.5
21 Paper	0.3				6.6	6.9
22 Leather	0.1				0.6	0.7
23 Rubber	2.4	0.2			3.8	6.4
24 Chemicals	5.1	0.6			10.6	16.3
25 Oils and fats					2.0	2.0
26 Coconut fibre and yarn						
27 Petroleum and coal	13.9	0.4			15.0	29.3
28 Structural clay products						
29 Ceramics	3.7	0.2			0.8	4.7
30 Cement					2.9	2.9
31 Basic metals					5.8	5.8
32 Light engineering	14.7	1.5	22.8	2.0	13.0	54.0
33 Transport equipment	3.8	0.7	26.5		1.4	32.4
34 Machinery, other equipment			21.8		1.0	22.8
35 Other manufacturing	3.4				2.0	5.4
36 Construction						
37 Electricity						
38 Road passenger transport						
39 Rail transport						
40 Trade, and other transport						
41 Services						
Total as included in row 4 of Table A.1*	120.2	3.6	71.1	2.0	101.0	297.8

* columns (1), (ii), (iii) and (iv) only.

government enterprises (Railways, Port Commission and Posts and Telecommunications). Since all of these services are government monopolies, it is argued that a pricing policy which results in a loss is equivalent to a subsidy directed at the productive sectors concerned. There is some ambiguity about the precise magnitudes involved, but using the detail contained in the ERE we have calculated figures of –18 m., 14 m. and –24 m. for Railways, Posts and Telecommunications, and the Port Commission respectively. The total subsidy element associated with these services is therefore 28 m.

In addition to these items the government is imputed as paying 26 m. on the buildings which it occupies (CBR, Table 8), and we have included this as an indirect tax. It is also added into the government expenditure and therefore has no net effect on the government surplus/deficit.

On export duties all that needs to be said is that both the total duty paid and the allocation among paying sectors is taken directly from the ERE.

The full detail of the allocation of indirect taxes among sectors and categories of demand is as shown in Table A.13 below.

Table A.13 *Other indirect taxes/subsidies (including government food profits), 1970 (Rs million)*

	(i) Taxes on consumption	(ii) Taxes on government purchases	(iii) Taxes on intermediate goods	(iv) Taxes on exports
1 Tea	4.7		13.0	196.7
2 Rubber			2.0	70.0
3 Coconuts	12.2		12.0	0.7
4 Paddy			3.0	
5 Livestock				
6 Fishing				
7 Logging and firewood				
8 Other agriculture	4.1		3.0	5.0
9 Mining and quarrying				2.4
10 Milling	–559.0			
11 Dairy products	3.3			
12 Bread			11.0	
13 Other bakery products	11.0			
14 Carbonated beverages	1.0			
15 Desiccated coconut				25.6
16 Other processed food	205.0		35.0	
17 Distilling	140.2			
18 Tobacco	7.6		210.0	
19 Textiles	11.5		1.0	
20 Wood products	4.6			
21 Paper	6.7		3.0	
22 Leather	2.7		1.0	
23 Rubber	0.3		1.0	
24 Chemicals	7.7		8.0	
25 Oils and fats				26.8
26 Coconut fibre and yarn				
27 Petroleum and coal	11.5			
28 Structural clay products				
29 Ceramics	0.2		1.0	
30 Cement			7.0	
31 Basic metals				
32 Light engineering	6.2		1.0	
33 Transport equipment	1.5			
34 Machinery, other equipment				
35 Other manufacturing	2.1			
36 Construction			23.0	
37 Electricity				
38 Road passenger transport			2.0	
39 Rail transport			–18.0	
40 Trade, and other transport			102.0	
41 Services		25.5	54.0	
Total as included in row 4 of Table A.1*	–110.0	25.5	475.0	327.2

* columns (i), (ii) and (iv) only.

n.b. This Table differs from those relating to FEECs and import duties (A.11 and A.12) in that duties on intermediate goods as shown in column (iii) are classified according to the *user* of the goods, subject to tax. Further calculations, described in the next section, are necessary to get us to this stage in the case of FEECs and import duties.

Summary of indirect tax entries

Finally, we can remind ourselves that Tables A.11, A.12, A.13, all represent partial disaggregation of row 4 of the aggregated Table A.1 shown at the beginning of this appendix. We conclude this section by summarising, in Table A.14 below, the items of row 4 which we have now discussed and indicating the magnitude of the items in that row which have not yet been discussed in detail. The residual is discussed in Stage 7 on the government balance.

Table A.14 *Summary of entries in row 4 of Table A.1 (Rs million)*

	Column (2) Firms	Column (3) Households	Column (4) Government	Column (5) Capital a/cs	Column (6) Production	Column (7) Rest of world
FEECs (Table A.11)		109	–	197	280	–197
Import duties (Table A.12)		120	4	73	101	–
Other indirect taxes (Table A.13)		–110	26		475	327
Balance to be discussed (see Table A.25 below)	376	448	74	43	–	–
Total at in row 4 of Table A.1	376	567	104	313	856	130

Stage 3 Inter-industry transactions and value added

The usual problem involved in estimating flow matrices for a given accounting year, subject to known consistent row and column sums and with knowledge of the same flow matrix for some earlier year, is readily met by several variants of the RAS technique of adjustment. See, for example, Bacharach (1970). In the present study however, the problems are compounded by the general scarcity of firm estimates for many of the vectors which are incorporated in the general framework of the RAS method. A procedure was adopted therefore which iteratively produced a consistent framework for the central elements using a few 1970 vectors which were taken as firm estimates, together with the 1965 input–output framework from PMC and some *ad hoc* knowledge of technical change during the period 1965–70.

The schema

As a preliminary to the discussion which follows it will prove useful to set out that part of the framework which is to be estimated in schematic form, together with some basic notation. This is shown in Table A.15 below.

The notation to be used is as follows:

Let $\mathbf{g} = \hat{\mathbf{p}}\mathbf{q}$ = value of gross output

$\mathbf{S} = \mathbf{A}\mathbf{g}$ = intermediate transactions between domestic production activities

$\mathbf{w}$ = vector of value added from production activities

$\mathbf{f}$ = vector of final outputs of domestic production activities

$\mathbf{t}_I$ = vector of indirect taxes levied on domestic production activities other than FEECs and import duties

$\mathbf{e}$ = vector of FEEC rebates on exports and therefore shown as negative elements, as though they are subsidies

The notation for imports carries over from before (e.g. as in Table A.9)

Recall that,

$\mathbf{m}_R$ = c.i.f. value of imports to intermediate account classified by *type* of product imported

Table A.15 *Schematic form of production accounts*

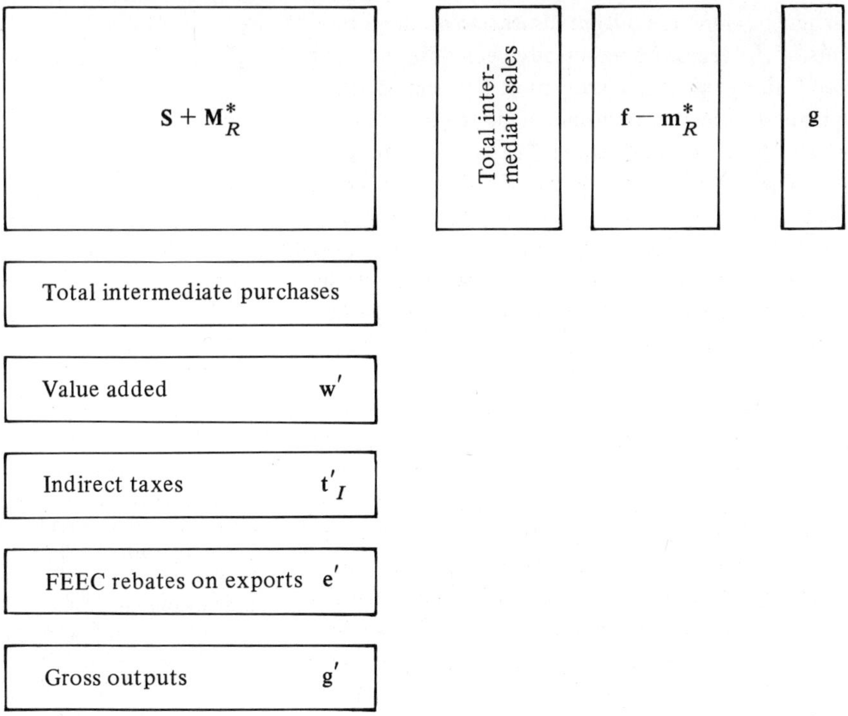

$\mathbf{S} + \mathbf{M}_R^*$	Total intermediate sales	$\mathbf{f} - \mathbf{m}_R^*$	$\mathbf{g}$
Total intermediate purchases			
Value added $\mathbf{w}'$			
Indirect taxes $\mathbf{t}'_I$			
FEEC rebates on exports $\mathbf{e}'$			
Gross outputs $\mathbf{g}'$			

Thus if

$\mathbf{M}_R$ = matrix of imports at c.i.f. value classified by type of product and by using domestic activity

then

$$\mathbf{m}_R = \mathbf{M}_R\ \mathbf{i}$$

Likewise, imports valued inclusive of FEECs and import duties may be expressed as

$$\mathbf{m}_R^* = \mathbf{m}_R + \mathbf{FEEC}_R + \mathbf{Duty}_R$$

and as before

$$\mathbf{m}_R^* = \mathbf{M}_R^*\ \mathbf{i}$$

where

$\mathbf{M}_R^*$ is similarly defined.

In a similar manner and notation, imports for each of the final account categories may be defined inclusive of FEECs and duties, so that $\mathbf{f}$ can be expressed as:

$$\mathbf{f} = (\mathbf{c} - \mathbf{m}_c^*) + (\mathbf{g} - \mathbf{m}_g^*) + (\mathbf{K} - \mathbf{m}_K^*) + (\Delta s - \mathbf{m}_{\Delta s}^*) + \mathbf{x}$$

From Table A.15 some accounting balances can now be confirmed.

Total intermediate sales $= (\mathbf{S} + \mathbf{M}_R^*)\ \mathbf{i}$

Total intermediate purchases $= (\mathbf{S} + \mathbf{M}_R^*)'\ \mathbf{i}$

and the balance equations are

$$\begin{aligned} \mathbf{g}' &= (\mathbf{S} + \mathbf{M}_R^*)\ \mathbf{i} + \mathbf{f} - \mathbf{m}_R^* \\ &= \mathbf{S}\ \mathbf{i} + \mathbf{f} \qquad (1) \end{aligned}$$

and

$$\mathbf{g}' = (\mathbf{S} + \mathbf{M}_R^*)'\ \mathbf{i} + \mathbf{w} + \mathbf{t}_I + \mathbf{e} \qquad (2)$$

The procedure for balancing the SAM

In the above schema, some vectors have firmer estimates associated with them than others. In particular, along the output dimension of the production accounts, the elements of the vector **f** have already been described and are presented in detail in Stage 1 above, and these are part of the firmest estimates. The remainder of the firmest estimates are found along the input dimension of the production accounts. These are the vectors $\mathbf{m}_R^*$, $\mathbf{t}_I$ and **e** and they have been described in Stage 2. These vectors, readily identifiable in our schema above, were taken as our firmest estimates. However, our confidence in them should be qualified in those cases where the figures relate to changes in stocks of commodities. Estimates of changes in stocks are not very reliable. Hence in the iterative balance which is used and which will shortly be described, this particular vector was allowed to be less firm than the other component vectors of final demand.

Estimates of some of the other vectors in the schema are available but were not considered to be reliable. For example, although some estimates of value added exist* these were not taken as firm estimates, at least not at the outset.

*Two alternative estimates of value added were recognised. First the Central Bank estimates (CBR (1972), Table 4 with further disaggregations provided by the social accounts division) were put on the 41 sector classification. Second, the working papers for the Medium Term Plan provided alternative estimates which were consistent with the estimates used in the 1965 input–output table. A third set could be obtained from the aggregate estimates of the Department of Census and Statistics.

The notable unknowns in the schema are the vector of gross outputs **g**, along with the elements of matrices **S** and $\mathbf{M}_R^*$. The problem which confronts us then is to derive consistent estimates for these unknowns together with firmed up estimates of value added. The schema illustrated in Table A.15 is the starting point of the procedure. If elements of the combined matrix $(\mathbf{S} + \mathbf{M}_R^*)$ can be obtained then a further stage is to extract the matrix $\mathbf{M}_R^*$. This is made possible in view of the fact that we have identified $\mathbf{m}_R^*$ as a firm vector. The final stage in obtaining estimates for this central element is to split $\mathbf{M}_R^*$ so as to extract FEECs and import duties on intermediate account as debits from the production activities.

As has already been intimated, the input–output table for 1970 has not been compiled exclusively from data collected for 1970 but has been derived from the 1965 input–output table given in PMC. In the cases of a few important industrial groups, tea, rubber and coconuts, direct cost data for 1970 have been used for the updating of the 1965 matrix. The most recent cost data in paddy applies to the Maha season 1966/67. The updating of the input–output table also took account of the industries that came into existence after 1965 and which were in commercial production in 1970. The cost structure of the subgroups falling within the services sector were obtained from the original worksheets used in the compilation of the 1965 input–output table. The treatment of new industries and the disaggregation of trade and services will be explained in more depth shortly, but it may prove useful to outline the way in which we moved through the matrix.

The strategy of working through the matrix emphasised four main stages. The first stage was to identify those sectors (e.g. tea) which made no commodity sales to the intermediate accounts and where therefore, all sales were sales of final goods. The second group of sectors to be investigated were those which formed distinct 'process loops'. For example, the growing of coconuts and manufacture of coconut products form one process loop. Consistency is very easy to check within a process loop where sales and purchases between sectors can be readily identified. The remaining sectors were approached at the third stage where, notably, many of the entries for sales and purchases of these sectors had already been estimated in the first two stages. The final stage was the repeat of the first three stages, which proved necessary because of the inevitable inconsistencies which became apparent during the operations of the third stage. We shall now describe with some illustrative detail the operation of this strategy.

It is clear from the 1965 matrix that there are four sectors which make no sales on intermediate account whatsoever.*

These sectors are:

Production sector number	*Activity*
1	Tea
12	Bread
13	Other bakery products
18	Tobacco manufacturing

*Throughout this section 'sales on intermediate accounts' should be taken to imply purchase by domestic production activities of a commodity whether it be imported or domestically produced. That is, we refer to elements in the rows of the matrix $\mathbf{S} + \mathbf{M}_R^*$.

These sectors were the first to be investigated since in these cases final sales, **f**, must also be equal to gross sales and gross output. On the input side, with gross outputs now ascertained, a set of coefficients applied to these column sums determine intermediate input flows, and value added emerges as the residual (see equation 2 above).

The coefficients used to determine input structure were in fact derived from updated versions of the 1965 input–output table as provided by the Ministry of Planning. Some estimates of change in technology were introduced here; thus for example, increases in chemical fertilizer inputs into many of the agricultural sectors per unit of output were accommodated.

A number of other sectors were known to have few intermediate sales and were therefore almost as easy to introduce as those which had no sales on intermediate account whatsoever. Examples of these are sectors 2 (Rubber), 6 (Fishing), 14 (Carbonated beverages) and 17 (Distilling).

The next groups of sectors to be investigated were those that fell into what we term 'process loops'. The coconut group, namely Coconut, Desiccated coconut, Coconut fibre and yarn is one example of such a loop. A second is the Paddy, Milling, Bread and Other bakery products group. For these sectors intermediate sales and purchases do exist but are largely confined *within* the process loop and so can easily be estimated from the final demand and other initial vectors available to us, given some knowledge of the nature of the interaction between the various sectors within a loop. So, for example, the gross output of sector 26, Coconut fibre and yarn, can be set equal to its final demand entry since it has almost no intermediate sales. This gross output in conjunction with some knowledge of its input structure determines the order of magnitude of its demand upon sector 3, Coconut. With similar reasoning in relation to the other sectors within the loop, it was clearly possible to iterate to feasible (though admittedly, not unique) solutions for the gross output, value added and intermediate transactions of each of the sectors involved.

The sectors which remain are those which lie outside of 'process loops' and those which have intermediate sales to a smaller or larger extent. The order in which sectors were considered was in general determined by the extent to which the entries on intermediate sales have already been made. These clearly arise because input requirements are determined for the sectors considered earliest, and these, in turn, are viewed as intermediate sales from other sectors.

This whole procedure is, in every sense, an iterative one because it was frequently found that the gross sales of sectors thus determined implied inconceivable value added figures – inconceivable, for example, because the estimate of value added fell outside the range of official value added estimates available to us, or because the gross output–value added ratio was outside the range of official estimates. Such a situation meant that the intermediate sales had to be reviewed and adjusted to make sector accounts consistent one with another.

There were two areas which caused particular difficulties, namely Petroleum (in sector 27), and the Trade, and other transport sectors (40a, b and c). In the case of petroleum, although the foreign trade statistics reveal that there were no imports of crude oil in 1970, crude oil was used by the refinery in 1970. What we deduced had happened was that all the crude oil required by the refinery had been imported in 1969 though the refinery commenced commercial production for the first time in 1970. We therefore assumed that the crude oil used by the refinery was drawn from stocks.

The disaggregation of the total output of Trade, and other transport into Wholesale trade, Retail trade and Other transport was carried out in two stages. First, the total output was disaggregated as between trade and transport in the ratio 7:3. This is the ratio used by the Central Bank to obtain a separate estimate of wholesale and retail trade for the purpose of presenting the table on gross domestic product by industrial origin. In order to disaggregate the trade total as between wholesale and retail trade, it was assumed that all purchases by households and government for consumption purposes were through the retail market and the rest of the transactions took place through the wholesale market. This explains the blank entries shown for intermediate sales by the retail trade industry group. In the case of exports, the trade and transport margin was split between wholesale trade and transport in the proportion 17:3, which was derived from the Central Bank estimates of the value added in trade and transport resulting from merchandise exports. The ratio used for investment was however 7:3. The residual trade and transport margins corresponding to intermediate sales were split between wholesale trade and transport in the same proportion for all industrial groups. These assumptions may give only rough estimates of the separate sales and purchases of the outputs of the three industrial groups 40a, 40b, and 40c but then we need detailed tabulations of censuses of distributive trade and transport to get firmer estimates.

To complete our discussion of the derivation of the $(\mathbf{S} + \mathbf{M}_R^*)$ matrix, we need to emphasise the special role of the diagonal elements in our procedure. It is clear that these can be given any value since row and column sums are affected by the same amount. In most cases they were estimated by applying the input coefficients as before, but they did provide an easy opportunity to take up slack on elements of $\mathbf{M}_R^*$. The situation is this. Intermediate sales for each sector had to be large enough to accommodate the corresponding elements of $\mathbf{M}_R^*$, because intermediate sales include this vector. Thus if intermediate sales do not reasonably accommodate this vector then the diagonal elements could be increased to accommodate the difference. We did not think it appropriate to handle large discrepancies in this way because it implied a new structure for the import content of intermediate sales. However, it was a useful way of removing small discrepancies.

In this way the $(\mathbf{S} + \mathbf{M}_R^*)$ matrix was gradually built up. It is clear that we employed no formal RAS methods, largely because the data on gross outputs and value added were inadequate to sustain these. However, the principle of our procedure was broadly the same as RAS with heavy constraints on each step and a need for frequent backward and forward iteration. The main difference is that whereas with standard RAS procedures one is able to demonstrate the uniqueness of the final solution, we are unable to do this, although we doubt whether the range of feasible solutions from our method is particularly wide. Our attitude on this issue is that, while uniqueness is normally a desirable property, it is probably not worth much if based on initial vectors of, for example, gross output which are known to be subject to large error.

The next stage was to extract the matrix $\mathbf{M}_R^*$ from the matrix $\mathbf{S} + \mathbf{M}_R^*$. As we have repeatedly emphasised, the row controls represented by $\mathbf{M}_R^*$ are available from the previous sections. We also have available an equivalent of the $\mathbf{M}_R^*$ matrix for 1965 (excluding FEECs of course) which has been derived by summing complementary and competitive import components for each cell of the 1965 input–output matrix. Thus some measure of the import content for each cell of the 1965 $(\mathbf{S} + \mathbf{M}_R^*)$ matrix is readily available, and as a first stage in the iteration this was used to approximate the 1970 matrix $\mathbf{M}_R^*$. A few minor adjustments to this were necessary (e.g. to eliminate cases where the import entry in a cell exceeded the total intermediate sales associated with that cell). Once again this adjustment process was heavily constrained by the need to add to the row control for total intermediate imports.

Having compiled the $\mathbf{M}_R^*$ and $(\mathbf{S} + \mathbf{M}_R^*)$ matrices, the $\mathbf{S}$ matrix is obtained simply by deducting the former from the latter. The (i, j)th element of this matrix shows the purchase by the jth industry of the ith industry's product, exclusive of all imports purchased by the former.

The results of this exercise are set down in the following two tables. Table A.16 presents the matrix $\mathbf{S}$ while Table A.17 presents the matrix $\mathbf{M}_R^*$. Looking first at Table A.16, the first 48 rows and columns constitute the matrix $\mathbf{S}$. The remaining rows and columns summarise the other entries set down in our schematic Table A.15 above. The 48 rows (labelled 1 to 41e) show the detail of the sales, both intermediate (first 48 columns) and final of each of our 48 production sectors. The 49th row and columns are merely the summation of the previous 48 and it will be seen that the intersection of the 49th row with the 49th column shows the total intermediate sales of 4358 as recorded in our summary Table A.1.

Row 50 shows the gross value added generated by each of our 48 sectors (totalling 10 295), the value added of domestic servants (100) and the value added generated by government (1275). Since, in deriving the figures, non-traditional exports have been valued inclusive of the FEECs paid to exporters, which are, in effect, subsidies, we need to deduct these to arrive at a figure for gross domestic product. This adjustment is made to the 10 295 shown in column 49 and having reduced this by the 197 of FEEC rebates, we are left with the figure of 10 098 as shown in our summary Table A.1.

Our value added figures differ from all of the various official estimates in some respect or another, but we would argue that by deriving them by way of the constrained iteration described above, our estimates are probably a better approximation to reality than any of the official estimates.

Row 51 records the c.i.f. value of imports and sums to the same total of 2521 as that recorded in Table A.9 above. However, intermediate imports are now classified by using sector rather than by type of import as in Table A.9. The final demand uses of imports shown at the intersection of row 51 and columns 50 to 55 inclusive, merely repeat the information already shown in Table A.6 above. Similarly, row 52 records the import duties on final demand imports as presented in Table A.6. Exactly similar comments apply to row 53, while row 55 merely reproduces the information on indirect taxes set down in Table A.13 above (the duties in this table being already classified by use rather than by type of good).

Table A.16 *Inter-industry transactions matrix* (**S**) *for Sri Lanka (together with related vectors), 1970 (Rs million*

	1	2	3	4	5	6	7	8	9	10a	10b	11	12	13	14	15	16	17	18	19	20	21	22	23	24	25	26	27
	Tea	Rubber	Coconuts	Paddy	Livestock	Fishing	Logging and firewood	Other agriculture	Mining and quarrying	Rice milling	Flour milling	Dairy products	Bread	Other bakery products	Carbonated beverages	Desiccated coconut	Other processed food	Distilling	Tobacco	Textiles	Wood products	Paper	Leather	Rubber	Chemicals	Oils and fats	Coconut fibre and yarn	Petroleum and coal
1 Tea																												
2 Rubber																								8				
3 Coconuts																234	4	1									8	
4 Paddy				70						1012												2						
5 Livestock												18					2						8					
6 Fishing																	5											
7 Logging and firewood	11	1							2				3								15							
8 Other agriculture					1			94		2				1					34	1	4	2						
9 Mining and quarrying																						1						
10a Rice milling																												
10b Flour milling													8															
11 Dairy products																												
12 Bread																												
13 Other bakery products																												
14 Carbonated beverages																												
15 Desiccated coconut														1												187		
16 Other processed food					11								1					1										
17 Distilling																		22							1			
18 Tobacco																												
19 Textiles																				19								
20 Wood products	15																			2	60				3			
21 Paper	22	4														1			4	2		8	1	2	14			
22 Leather										1													8	1				
23 Rubber																							2					
24 Chemicals	14	9	5	32				42					2							2		3	1	2	13			
25 Oils and fats					19									4			13								18	3		
26 Coconut fibre and yarn																											1	
27 Petroleum and coal	6	2				2			1	3						1				1	1	1		1	1	1	2	
28 Structural clay products																												
29 Ceramics														1														
30 Cement																												
31 Basic metals																												
32 Light engineering	34	8	4	3		1	2	3	5	5		1		4	1				2	4		4	1		5		1	
33 Transport equipment																												
34 Machinery, other equipment																												
35 Other manufacturing																												
36 Construction									1																			
37 Electricity	6	1							3	3		1		1	1					4	1	2	1	1	2	2		
38 Road passenger transport																												
39 Rail transport	10								2	12											1							
40a Wholesale trade	25	7	5	4	3	3	1	7	3	17	1	2	13	6	1	22	5	2	12	17	26	7	3	3	17	12	1	
40b Retail trade																												
40c Other transport	15	3	3	2	2	2	1	4	1	9		1	7	3		11	2	1	6	8	13	4	2	2	8	6	1	
41a Communication	5	1	1	2																								
41b Hotels and restaurants																												
41c Professional services	1																											
41d Dwellings																												
41e Other services	5	2	6	9		1				4																		
49 Total intermediate	169	38	24	122	36	9	4	150	18	1068	1	23	34	21	3	269	31	27	58	60	122	34	27	20	82	211	14	
50 Gross value added	587	320	529	977	219	246	126	1030	95	36	18	9	48	28	8	2	28	42	135	127	113	82	20	27	126	5	70	
51 Imports c.i.f.	75	12	10	29	5	4		44	3	3	13	40	105	16	3		18	4	5	125	2	23	4	3	48	1		
52 Import duties	6	1	1	2	4	1		8		1			2	4			9		1	7		3	1		6			
53 FEECs on imports	14	1	1		2			1	2	1		5		4			7	1	2	32		12	1	2	26			
54 FEEC rebates, exports								−46	−10	−1							−3			−5			−2		−5		−25	
55 Other indirect taxes (net)	13	2	12	3				3					11				35		210	1		3	1	1	8			
56 Gross output	864	374	577	1133	266	260	130	1190	108	1109	31	77	200	73	14	271	125	74	411	347	237	157	52	53	291	217	59	
	1	2	3	4	5	6	7	8	9	10a	10b	11	12	13	14	15	16	17	18	19	20	21	22	23	24	25	26	

Finally, turning to the columns, we only need to note that columns 50 to 55 inclusive repeat the detail already set down in Table A.6 above.

In Table A.17 the final column repeats the information on the disaggregation of total imports by type as set down in the last column of Table A.9. The columns headed $\mathbf{m}_c^*$, $\mathbf{m}_g^*$, $\mathbf{m}_K^*$ and $\mathbf{m}_{\Delta s}^*$ are the appropriate columns of Table A.9 plus the FEECs and duties applicable to each type of import. Similarly the column headed $\mathbf{m}_R^*$ is the fifth column of Table A.9 supplemented by import duties and FEECs. The total of the import duties and FEECs included in each of these columns are shown at the base of the column and agree with the totals in Tables A.12 and A.11 respectively.

The 49th row of the matrix analyses total intermediate imports (including duties and FEECs) of 1405 according to the sector using the imports. The matrix $\mathbf{M}_R^*$ which consists of the first 48 rows and columns of the table (labelled 1 to 41e) provides a similar analysis but for each category of import taken separately.

29 Ceramics	30 Cement	31 Basic metals	32 Light engineering	33 Transport equipment	34 Machinery, other equipment	35 Other manufacturing	36 Construction	37 Electricity	38 Road passenger transport	39 Rail transport	40a Wholesale trade	40b Retail trade	40c Other transport	41a Communication	41b Hotels and restaurants	41c Professional services	41d Dwellings	41e Other services	49 Total intermediate sales	50 Private consumption	51 Government consumption	52 Gross domestic capital formation	53 Additions to stock	54 Exports	55 Total final sales	56 Gross output	
																			Σ	c	g	k	ΔS	x		Σ	
															2				2	76	2	31	–86	839	862	864	1 Tea
																			8			22	3	341	366	374	2 Rubber
															6				253	289	4	29		2	326	577	3 Coconuts
																			1084				49		49	1133	4 Paddy
															4				32	230	4				234	266	5 Livestock
															4				9	248	3				251	260	6 Fishing
							3								11				48	82					82	130	7 Logging and firewood
															20				159	916	9			106	1031	1190	8 Other agriculture
2	16	1				1	56								1				80	9				19	28	108	9 Mining and quarrying
															15				15	1020	18		56		1094	1109	10a Rice milling
																			13	15				3	18	31	10b Flour milling
															2				2	72	3				75	77	11 Dairy products
															4				4	194	2				196	200	12 Bread
															2				2	70				1	71	73	13 Other bakery products
															4				4	7			3		10	14	14 Carbonated beverages
																			188					83	83	271	15 Desiccated coconut
															12				25	56	3		34	7	100	125	16 Other processed food
																			23	51					51	74	17 Distilling
																				411					411	411	18 Tobacco
	1										1				3				24	257	5		50	11	323	347	19 Textiles
			1	4		1	82				5								173	54	2	8			64	237	20 Wood products
	1				2	2			1	1	1	4		2	1			2	75	75	7				82	157	21 Paper
				1															11	35				6	41	52	22 Leather
				1					15				27						45	7				1	8	53	23 Rubber
			3	1		1	11								1	10			152	127				12	139	291	24 Chemicals
																			57	86				74	160	217	25 Oils and fats
																			1					58	58	59	26 Coconut fibre and yarn
1	1	1	1		1		1	1	12	2	3	1	6		1	1		1	226	55	1		–69	57	44	270	27 Petroleum and coal
							42												42							42	28 Structural clay products
							18								1	1			22	7					7	29	29 Ceramics
	18						100												118							118	30 Cement
			32	1	2		24												59							59	31 Basic metals
	9	5	28	1		3	83	7	27	8	5	3	34		1			1	306	158	23		–35	2	148	454	32 Light engineering
			5																5	21		13	12		46	51	33 Transport equipment
																						13	80		93	93	34 Machinery, other equipment
											1					5		2	8	30				1	31	39	35 Other manufacturing
										7				3			42	5	58		92	1595			1687	1745	36 Construction
1	5		3						1	1	8	5		2				1	59	27	28				55	114	37 Electricity
														1				3	4	344					344	348	38 Road passenger transport
							7							1					35	108				1	109	144	39 Rail transport
1	5	1	36	5	7	3	131	5	22	13	7	3	19	5	9	7		4	518			108		172	280	798	40a Wholesale trade
																				769	39				808	808	40b Retail trade
1	2	1	19	2	3	2	68	2	11	7	3	1	10	3	4	3		2	266	385	20	46		30	481	747	40c Other transport
			2				3			1	10	10	3	8		10		20	77	16	30			7	53	130	41a Communication
																				198				14	212	212	41b Hotels and restaurants
							2				1					1		12	17	208	1			10	219	236	41c Professional services
																				690					690	690	41d Dwellings
							4		3	1	5	2	2	3		1			49	198	6			256	460	509	41e Other services
6	58	9	130	16	15	13	635	15	92	41	50	29	101	28	113	39	42	53	4358	7601	302	1865	97	2113	11978	16336	49 Total intermediate
6	40	17	192	8	38	20	979	94	219	93	683	740	609	97	107	185	633	335	10295	100	1275				1375	11670	50 Gross value added
4	8	20	80	16	25	5	65	3	20	17	5	1	27	5		7		121	1024	1091	43	328	35		1497	2521	51 Imports c.i.f.
		2	8	2	2	1	7	2	5	5	1		4			2		3	101	120	4	71	2		196	297	52 Import duties
2	5	11	44	9	13		36		10	6	2		11			3		14	280	109		178	19		306	586	53 FEECs on imports
			–1										–12		–8			–56	–197					–197	–197	–394	54 FEEC rebates, exports
[illegible]	7		1				23		2	–18	57	38	7				15	39	475	–110	26			327	243	718	55 Other indirect taxes (net)
9	118	59	454	51	93	39	1745	114	348	144	798	808	747	130	212	236	690	509	16336	8911	1649	2442	153	2243	15398	31734	56 Gross output
9	30	31	32	33	34	35	36	37	38	39	40a	40b	40c	41a	41b	41c	41d	41e	Σ	c	g	k	ΔS	x			

Stage 4 The disaggregation of household consumption

We have already discussed the aggregate for all households of expenditure on domestic commodities of different types, imports, indirect taxes and so on. In this section, we turn to the disaggregation of households according to two characteristics, namely location and income level. Under the heading location, we have disaggregated households into urban, rural and estate households. Under the heading of income level we have disaggregated households by the following six classes of household income level per month; Rs 0–199, 200–399, 400–599, 600–799, 800–999 and 1000+. The reasons for this type of classification are fully rehearsed in Chapter 3.

As in the case of the aggregate figures for households the main source of our information was the four rounds of the SES 1969/70, and Table A.18 below summarises the coverage of the survey in respect of each of the eighteen categories of households.

Table A.17 *The import matrix ($\mathbf{M}_R^*$) for Sri Lanka (together with related vectors), 1970 (Rs million)*

	1 Tea	2 Rubber	3 Coconuts	4 Paddy	5 Livestock	6 Fishing	7 Logging and firewood	8 Other agriculture	9 Mining and quarrying	10a Rice milling	10b Flour milling	11 Dairy products	12 Bread	13 Other bakery products	14 Carbonated beverages	15 Desiccated coconut	16 Other processed food	17 Distilling	18 Tobacco	19 Textiles	20 Wood products	21 Paper	22 Leather	23 Rubber	24 Chemicals	25 Oils and fats	26 Coconut fibre and yarn	27 Petroleum and coal
1 Tea																												
2 Rubber																												
3 Coconuts																												
4 Paddy																												
5 Livestock																							1					
6 Fishing																												
7 Logging and firewood																												
8 Other agriculture					1			17		2							5		4	22								
9 Mining and quarrying	4																											
10a Rice milling																												
10b Flour milling											12		106	8			2				1							
11 Dairy products												42		2														
12 Bread																												
13 Other bakery products																												
14 Carbonated beverages																												
15 Desiccated coconut																												
16 Other processed food					8							2	1	7	2		15	2										
17 Distilling																									4			
18 Tobacco																												
19 Textiles						2			1	1										129		1	1	1	1			
20 Wood products	17																		3									
21 Paper	8											1		4						4		26			5			
22 Leather																							2					
23 Rubber																								1				
24 Chemicals	50	11	10	30				35	1					2	1		5	1		7	1	10	2	2	54			
25 Oils and fats					2												5								10			
26 Coconut fibre and yarn																												
27 Petroleum and coal	10	1				1			1	2										1					2	1		
28 Structural clay products																												
29 Ceramics																	2	1							3			
30 Cement																												
31 Basic metals																												
32 Light engineering	6	2	2	1		2		1	2		1			1				1	1			1		1	1			
33 Transport equipment																												
34 Machinery, other equipment																												
35 Other manufacturing																				1								
36 Construction																												
37 Electricity																												
38 Road passenger transport																												
39 Rail transport																												
40a Wholesale trade																												
40b Retail trade																												
40c Other transport																												
41a Communication																												
41b Hotels and restaurants																												
41c Professional services																												
41d Dwellings																												
41e Other services																												
Σ Total intermediate	95	14	12	31	11	5		53	5	5	13	45	107	24	3		34	5	8	164	2	38	6	5	80	1		
Imports c.i.f.	75	12	10	29	5	4		44	3	3	13	40	105	16	3		18	4	5	125	2	23	4	3	48	1		
Duty	6	1	1	2	4	1		8		1			2	4			9		1	7		3	1		6			
FEECs	14	1	1		2			1	2	1		5		4			7	1	2	32		12	1	2	26			

Table A.18 *Socio-Economic Survey, 1969/70 – numbers of households sampled (rounds 1–4)*

Income groups (Rs household/month)	Urban	Rural	Estates	Total
0–100 } 100–199 }	845	1615	1234	3694
200–399	1597	1391	665	3653
400–599	722	441	79	1242
600–799	336	136	15	487
800–999	205	40	3	248
1000+	332	34	4	370
Total	4037	3657	2000	9694

28	29	30	31	32	33	34	35	36	37	38	39	40a	40b	40c	41a	41b	41c	41d	41e	Σm_r^*	m_c^*	m_g^*	m_k^*	$m_{\Delta S}^*$				
Structural clay products	Ceramics	Cement	Basic metals	Light engineering	Transport equipment	Machinery, other equipment	Other manufacturing	Construction	Electricity	Road passenger transport	Rail transport	Wholesale trade	Retail trade	Other transport	Communication	Hotels and restaurants	Professional services	Dwellings	Other services	Total intermediate	Private consumption	Government consumption	Gross fixed capital formation	Additions to stocks	Less FEECs	Less Duties	Imports c.i.f.	
																												1 Tea
																												2 Rubber
																												3 Coconuts
																												4 Paddy
																				1	1						2	5 Livestock
																												6 Fishing
																												7 Logging and firewood
																				51	147				-10	-10	178	8 Other agriculture
		1																		5							5	9 Mining and quarrying
																					359					-6	353	10a Rice milling
																				129	111					-3	237	10b Flour milling
																				44	23				-8	-4	55	11 Dairy products
																												12 Bread
																					1						1	13 Other bakery products
																												14 Carbonated beverages
																												15 Desiccated coconut
																				37	299				-13	-49	276	16 Other processed food
																				4	12				-1	-11	4	17 Distilling
																					1						1	18 Tobacco
							1													138	162	1			-80	-22	199	19 Textiles
							1													18					-6	-1	11	20 Wood products
		2								1	2	4	1				5		5	71	4				-15	-7	53	21 Paper
																				2						-1	1	22 Leather
				2			1			4				15						23	10	1			-10	-6	18	23 Rubber
	3	1		1			1	3												231	29	7			-41	-16	210	24 Chemicals
																				17					-5	-2	10	25 Oils and fats
																												26 Coconut fibre and yarn
	1	3				2		2	5	27	20	2		14			1		4	100	35	1			-32	-29	75	27 Petroleum and coal
								4												4					-2		2	28 Structural clay products
	2			1	2			4												15	10	1			-7	-5	14	29 Ceramics
		6						29												35					-12	-3	20	30 Cement
			29	69	6	3	1	55												163					-52	-6	105	31 Basic metals
			4	42	9		1	11		3	6			2	1		1		1	104	47	6	108	84	-93	-54	202	32 Light engineering
				2	10															12	13	3	190		-65	-32	121	33 Transport equipment
				10		35														45			279	-28	-105	-23	168	34 Machinery, other equipment
				5								2					5		3	16	14	1			-9	-6	16	35 Other manufacturing
																												36 Construction
																												37 Electricity
																												38 Road passenger transport
																												39 Rail transport
																												40a Wholesale trade
																												40b Retail trade
														11						11	16	1			-5		23	40c Other transport
															4					4							4	41a Communication
																												41b Hotels and restaurants
																			28	28							28	41c Professional services
																												41d Dwellings
																			97	97	26	24			-15		132	41e Other services
	6	13	33	132	27	40	6	108	5	35	28	8	1	42	5		12		138	1405	1320	46	577	56	-586	-297	2521	Σ Total intermediate
	4	8	20	80	16	25	5	65	3	20	17	5	1	27	5		7		121	1024	1091	43	328	35			2521	Imports c.i.f.
			2	8	2	2	1	7	2	5	5	1		4			2		3	101	120	3	71	2			297	Duty
	2	5	11	44	9	13		36		10	6	2		11			3		14	280	109		178	19			586	FEECs

The data required for each of the 18 household groups was identical to that produced for households in the aggregate as shown in Table A.6 (this section can be viewed as a disaggregation of column 1 of that table). The methods of compiling these data are described below.

Table A.2 above has already presented the classification converter built up in relation to the aggregate data as described in Stage 1 above. This was used in conjunction with the SES information on expenditures on each of the 30 commodity groups by urban, rural and estate households (Table A.19) to produce detailed estimates of consumption comparable to those shown in Table A.6. These estimates also incorporate the same upward adjustment in respect of alcohol and tobacco consumption as that applied to the aggregate figures. The full results are as shown in Tables A.20(a) and A.20(b) below. The first of these shows household consumption by production activity while the second shows consumption by commodity group.

At a later stage (Stage 8) we need to return to these figures since, as we demonstrate there, the *income* figures of the SES are substantially understated. This means that the income classes shown in Table A.18 and used in Table A.20 are in error and require amendment. This would be a simple matter if the understatement applied equally over all income classes but unfortunately it is our con-

Table A.19 *Consumers' expenditure by location of household, 1970 (Rs million)*

	Urban	Rural	Estate	All-island
Rationed rice	12	54	5	71
Unrationed rice	126	636	77	839
Wheat flour	16	93	67	176
Other grains and cereals	80	203	13	295
Condiments	102	345	52	498
Pulses	18	67	20	105
Coconuts	55	209	28	292
Vegetables and fruits	118	382	45	545
Meat	52	72	15	139
Fish	129	358	35	522
Milk and milk products	77	149	21	245
Oils, fats, including butter	31	79	16	127
Tea	17	56	7	80
Sugar	77	280	33	390
Other food and beverages	34	126	21	181
Meals away from home	54	141	5	200
Toddy	8	36	6	50
Other alcoholic beverages	53	156	24	233
Traditional tobacco	11	97	19	127
Modern tobacco	115	231	18	365
Clothing and footwear	144	442	81	667
Rent, rates and water charges	264	408	35	707
Fuel and light	72	203	26	301
Consumer durables	64	146	9	219
Household operation (services)	76	111 }	24	325
Household operation (goods)	26	88 }		
Personal care and health	61	165	17	243
Transport and communications	193	403	33	629
Recreation	86	172	14	271
Miscellaneous	17	46	4	67
Total	2188	5954	769	8911

clusion that the understatement applies differentially to different categories of income. The necessary adjustment is therefore extremely cumbersome.

Stage 5 The disaggregation of government consumption

The total of government current expenditures of all types has already been discussed in Stage 1 and analysed by supplying-industry, imports, etc. in Table A.6. We have also noted that government generates 1275 m. of value added. In this section we discuss the disaggregation of government current expenditures, including value added expenditures, by purpose. The first disaggregation, into expenditures on goods and services on the one hand, and transfer payments on the other has already been discussed in Stage 1. This distinction is well established in economic analysis and its importance from the point of view of studying the impact on the economy of government expenditures is clear in that the first category of expenditures generates direct demands on resources and the second is primarily redistributional. Within each of the two broad categories of expenditures we attempted some further disaggregation by purpose giving the complete classification as shown in Table 3.9 of Chapter 3.

The main source of information for this was Table 36 of the CBR. In the case

Table A.20(a) *Consumers' expenditure by location, household income group and activity (Rs million)*

Production activity	Urban						Rural						Estate						Total
	0–199	200–	400–	600–	800–	1000+	0–199	200–	400–	600–	800–	1000+	0–199	200–	400–	600–	800–	1000+	(as in Table A.6)
1 Tea	2.1	5.2	2.9	1.5	0.9	1.8	19.5	22.7	8.3	2.8	1.1	1.1	3.1	2.4	0.4	0.1	–	–	76
2 Rubber	–	–	–	–	–	–	–	–	–	–	–	–	–	–	–	–	–	–	–
3 Coconuts	7.5	20.8	11.0	5.3	3.3	5.4	70.4	82.3	33.6	12.9	3.7	3.7	15.5	11.5	1.6	0.3	0.1	0.1	289
4 Paddy	–	–	–	–	–	–	–	–	–	–	–	–	–	–	–	–	–	–	–
5 Livestock	5.0	19.9	16.2	9.8	8.1	20.6	20.6	48.2	32.2	15.6	4.6	6.6	9.4	9.8	2.2	0.6	0.1	0.5	230
6 Fishing	7.0	21.5	13.0	6.6	4.4	8.6	44.2	73.2	32.3	11.9	3.4	5.1	8.1	6.9	1.2	0.3	0.1	0.1	248
7 Logging and firewood	2.6	6.1	3.7	2.1	1.6	3.6	17.7	22.6	9.4	3.3	1.1	1.1	3.5	2.9	0.5	0.1	0.0	0.1	82
8 Other agriculture	20.8	63.2	39.3	21.4	15.4	31.3	195.4	250.7	110.0	41.1	16.5	16.5	45.8	38.3	6.7	1.8	0.2	0.6	916
9 Mining and quarrying	0.2	0.7	0.4	0.2	0.1	0.2	2.0	2.5	1.1	0.4	0.1	0.1	0.5	0.5	0.1	0.0	0.0	0.0	9
10a Rice milling	25.5	61.2	30.9	15.7	9.7	16.4	273.3	301.5	119.7	39.5	12.7	12.3	53.5	40.0	6.2	1.1	0.8	0.2	1020
10b Flour milling	0.2	0.5	0.3	0.1	0.1	0.1	3.3	3.0	1.1	0.4	0.1	0.1	2.9	2.4	0.4	0.0	0.0	0.0	15
11 Dairy products	1.3	5.8	4.6	2.8	2.4	5.6	7.1	17.3	10.0	5.1	1.7	2.1	2.6	2.7	0.6	0.2	0.0	0.1	72
12 Bread	6.8	19.1	10.8	5.4	3.5	6.7	44.0	53.3	21.3	9.3	2.7	2.7	4.3	3.2	0.6	0.1	0.1	0.2	194
13 Other bakery products	2.2	6.1	3.5	1.9	1.3	2.6	15.7	19.3	7.8	3.3	1.1	1.1	2.1	1.7	0.3	0.1	0.0	0.1	70
14 Carbonated beverages	0.1	0.4	0.2	0.2	0.1	0.3	1.5	1.9	0.8	0.3	0.2	0.2	0.4	0.3	0.1	0.0	0.0	0.0	7
15 Desiccated coconut	–	–	–	–	–	–	–	–	–	–	–	–	–	–	–	–	–	–	–
16 Other processed food	1.4	4.0	2.4	1.3	0.9	1.8	11.9	15.7	6.7	2.4	0.9	0.9	2.9	2.5	0.4	0.1	0.0	0.0	56
17 Distilling	0.4	2.9	2.0	1.4	0.8	4.0	6.7	14.5	8.1	2.4	1.0	1.0	2.5	2.6	0.5	0.2	0.0	0.0	51
18 Tobacco	8.7	33.0	24.7	13.2	8.6	18.2	62.2	117.2	62.5	20.9	6.7	6.7	13.6	11.9	2.2	0.6	0.2	–	411
19 Textiles	3.3	14.4	11.2	8.1	6.1	12.4	32.4	68.2	37.5	18.7	6.8	6.8	14.2	13.2	2.5	0.7	0.3	0.4	257
20 Wood products	0.4	2.4	2.5	1.5	1.6	7.4	4.0	10.8	9.0	5.4	1.4	5.4	0.6	1.1	0.3	0.1	–	0.1	54
21 Paper	0.8	4.2	4.9	3.6	3.3	7.9	5.7	17.1	11.4	6.7	2.4	4.3	0.7	1.1	0.6	0.4	0.1	0.0	75
22 Leather	0.5	2.0	1.5	1.1	0.8	1.7	4.4	9.3	5.1	2.6	0.9	0.9	1.9	1.8	0.3	0.1	0.0	0.1	35
23 Rubber	0.1	0.3	0.3	0.2	0.2	1.1	0.7	1.4	0.9	0.6	0.4	0.5	0.2	0.2	0.0	0.0	0.0	0.0	7
24 Chemicals	2.8	8.9	6.2	4.3	3.5	9.8	19.6	32.0	16.7	7.2	3.1	4.2	3.9	3.5	0.9	0.2	0.0	0.2	127
25 Oils and fats	1.9	6.0	4.4	2.6	2.0	4.4	15.0	20.3	12.9	3.2	1.1	1.1	5.6	4.3	0.8	0.1	0.1	0.1	86
26 Coconut fibre and yarn	–	–	–	–	–	–	–	–	–	–	–	–	–	–	–	–	–	–	–
27 Petroleum and coal	1.6	3.8	2.4	1.5	1.1	3.4	10.9	14.5	6.4	2.7	1.2	1.3	2.2	1.8	0.3	0.1	0.0	0.1	55
28 Structural clay products	–	–	–	–	–	–	–	–	–	–	–	–	–	–	–	–	–	–	–
29 Ceramics	0.1	0.5	0.4	0.3	0.2	0.7	0.9	1.5	0.9	0.4	0.2	0.4	0.2	0.2	0.1	0.0	0.0	0.0	7
30 Cement	–	–	–	–	–	–	–	–	–	–	–	–	–	–	–	–	–	–	–
31 Basic metals	–	–	–	–	–	–	–	–	–	–	–	–	–	–	–	–	–	–	–
32 Light engineering	1.9	8.2	7.5	5.2	5.0	19.9	15.0	33.4	23.3	13.7	5.3	11.8	2.8	3.4	1.0	0.4	0.1	0.3	158
33 Transport equipment	0.1	0.9	1.0	0.6	0.6	2.9	1.5	4.2	3.5	2.1	0.6	2.1	0.2	0.4	0.1	0.1	0.0	0.0	21
34 Machinery, other equipment	–	–	–	–	–	–	–	–	–	–	–	–	–	–	–	–	–	–	–
35 Other manufacturing	0.7	2.0	1.4	0.8	0.6	1.5	5.4	8.1	3.8	1.6	0.6	0.6	1.4	1.2	0.2	0.1	0.0	0.0	30
36 Construction	–	–	–	–	–	–	–	–	–	–	–	–	–	–	–	–	–	–	–
37 Electricity	0.8	2.0	1.2	0.7	0.5	1.2	5.8	7.5	3.1	1.1	0.4	0.4	1.2	1.0	0.2	0.0	0.0	0.0	27
38 Road passenger transport	4.3	14.2	12.7	10.6	9.8	54.0	35.3	68.3	41.9	30.9	19.9	24.2	7.3	7.2	1.8	0.8	0.2	0.9	344
39 Rail transport	1.3	4.5	4.0	3.3	3.1	17.0	11.1	21.5	13.2	9.7	6.2	7.6	2.3	2.3	0.6	0.3	0.1	0.3	108
40a Wholesale trade	–	–	–	–	–	–	–	–	–	–	–	–	–	–	–	–	–	–	–
40b Retail trade	16.7	52.9	34.9	20.4	14.9	34.9	138.0	207.7	99.8	40.5	14.1	17.2	37.2	32.1	5.8	1.3	0.3	0.6	769
40c Other transport	8.4	26.4	17.4	10.2	7.4	17.4	69.3	104.0	49.8	20.2	7.0	8.5	18.8	16.2	2.9	0.6	0.1	0.3	385
41a Communication	0.2	0.7	0.6	0.5	0.5	2.5	1.6	3.2	2.0	1.4	0.9	1.1	0.3	0.3	0.1	0.0	0.0	0.0	16
41b Hotels and restaurants	5.4	17.6	10.7	6.3	4.6	8.4	26.6	57.4	33.6	12.6	4.2	5.6	2.0	2.4	0.4	0.1	0.0	0.1	198
41c Professional services	4.2	14.3	10.1	7.1	5.8	15.9	30.9	52.4	27.9	12.3	5.3	6.9	6.6	6.1	1.6	0.4	0.1	0.3	208
41d Dwellings	15.2	48.4	46.0	33.3	27.1	88.5	91.8	143.9	91.8	35.9	20.0	16.0	15.6	11.8	2.5	0.8	0.3	1.4	690
41e Other services	2.1	11.6	12.4	8.0	7.0	19.4	15.8	46.2	28.9	17.3	11.2	8.8	3.2	3.8	1.3	0.7	0.1	0.1	198
Domestic servants	2.0	6.7	5.0	3.6	3.2	10.4	12.9	22.6	13.2	6.1	3.0	4.8	2.8	2.5	0.6	0.2	0.1	0.2	100
Customs duties	2.1	7.5	5.2	3.3	2.6	8.6	18.6	30.5	16.6	7.6	3.0	4.6	4.4	4.1	0.8	0.2	0.0	0.1	120
Indirect taxes/subsidies	16.5	–21.3	–5.2	0.0	0.6	11.8	–147.0	–86.8	–10.4	–1.1	0.9	2.6	–28.7	–10.6	–0.5	0.2	0.0	0.1	–312
Imports	25.4	68.2	39.6	22.1	15.5	37.1	238.1	289.1	128.4	48.9	17.5	19.9	72.6	56.6	9.3	1.7	0.3	0.7	1091
Government food profits	5.1	14.7	8.1	4.0	2.5	4.1	44.7	58.3	25.4	8.6	2.8	2.8	9.8	8.4	1.5	0.2	0.1	0.1	201
FEECs	1.6	6.0	4.7	3.3	2.7	8.6	14.3	26.8	15.0	7.9	3.4	4.3	4.7	4.4	0.9	0.3	0.1	0.2	109

Table A.20(b) *Consumers' expenditure by location, household income group and commodity type* (Rs million)*

Consumer commodity	Urban							Rural		
	0–199	200–399	400–599	600–799	800–999	1000+	Total	0–199	200–399	400–599
1 Outside ration rice	16.2	47.5	25.7	13.7	8.5	14.5	126.1	197.3	260.3	114.5
2 Wheat flour	2.5	6.5	2.9	1.5	0.8	1.6	15.9	38.9	34.6	12.9
3 Other grains and cereals	10.4	29.1	16.6	8.4	5.4	10.2	80.1	67.3	80.6	32.7
4 Condiments	13.1	36.8	20.7	10.7	7.2	13.5	101.9	113.6	138.2	58.4
5 Pulses	2.4	6.5	3.7	1.8	1.2	2.2	17.7	20.9	27.6	11.7
6 Coconuts	7.6	20.8	11.2	5.6	3.7	5.9	54.8	71.7	82.9	33.9
7 Vegetables, fruits and other nuts	11.6	37.4	24.9	13.7	10.1	20.5	118.1	113.6	149.7	68.9
8 Meat	3.5	13.1	10.4	6.4	5.0	14.0	52.3	12.0	25.3	19.9
9 Fish	14.7	45.7	27.4	14.0	9.3	18.3	129.4	92.7	154.3	67.8
10 Milk and milk products	4.4	19.6	15.8	9.4	8.3	15.4	76.8	23.9	59.9	33.9
11 Oils, fats, including butter	2.7	8.9	6.2	3.8	2.9	6.5	31.0	22.4	29.9	18.7
12 Tea	2.5	5.9	3.3	1.8	1.2	2.2	16.9	17.9	25.3	7.0
13 Sugar	10.2	29.7	16.2	7.9	5.0	8.1	77.0	86.7	115.2	50.2
14 Other food and beverages	3.1	9.5	6.2	4.1	3.3	8.1	34.2	38.9	50.7	21.0
15 Meals away from home	5.5	17.8	10.8	6.4	4.6	8.6	53.6	26.9	57.6	33.9
16 Toddy	1.3	4.2	1.7	0.5	0.4	0.0	8.0	12.0	13.8	7.0
17 Other alcoholic beverages	1.8	13.6	9.1	6.6	3.7	18.3	53.2	31.4	66.8	37.4
18 Traditional tobacco	3.1	5.3	1.7	0.5	0.2	0.0	10.8	40.4	39.2	11.7
19 Modern tobacco	7.3	33.8	27.4	15.0	10.1	21.5	115.1	34.4	99.1	63.1
20 Clothing and footwear	8.5	37.4	29.0	21.1	15.9	32.3	144.2	83.7	177.4	97.0
21 Rent, rates and water charges	15.4	49.3	46.8	34.1	27.7	90.5	263.8	94.2	147.4	93.5
22 Fuel and light	9.4	22.5	13.7	7.9	5.6	12.9	72.1	64.3	82.9	35.1
23 Consumer durables	1.5	10.1	9.9	6.1	6.6	30.2	64.5	16.4	43.8	36.2
24 Household operation	6.5	22.0	17.4	11.9	10.4	33.9	102.2	40.4	71.4	42.1
25 Personal care and health	5.3	17.2	11.6	7.6	5.8	13.5	61.0	41.8	66.8	32.7
26 Transport and communications	7.8	26.1	23.2	19.3	18.0	98.6	193.0	64.3	124.4	77.1
27 Recreation	2.9	13.1	17.4	12.7	11.8	28.0	85.9	20.9	62.2	40.9
28 Miscellaneous	0.5	4.2	3.7	1.8	1.2	5.4	16.8	6.0	16.1	9.3
Total	181.7	593.4	414.5	254.2	193.7	538.7	2176.0	1494.6	2303.7	1168.6

* All-island expenditures are shown in Table 5.2.

of current expenditure on goods and services, this source is reconciled with the total already shown in Table A.3 by adding imputed pension contributions, imputed rents, local government expenditures, advance account wages, and the statistical discrepancy and subtracting the gross payments of trading enterprises. Since our work is constrained to the Table A.3 total, we need to spread these adjustment items between the individual heads of expenditure as identified in Table 36 of the CBR, and this was done as follows. Imputed pension contributions were allocated using information on wage and salary payments by broad groups of departments as supplied by the Central Bank social accounts division. Advance account wages were assumed to relate entirely to the category 'other economic services' and imputed rents were assumed to relate entirely to civil

600–799	800–999	1000+	Total	Estate 0–199	200–399	400–599	600–799	800–999	1000+	Total	Consumer commodity
38.1	12.6	12.7	635.6	36.3	33.6	5.9	1.0	0.1	0.2	77.1	1 Outside ration rice
4.9	0.8	0.9	93.0	34.5	27.6	4.3	0.4	0.1	0.1	67.0	2 Wheat flour
14.3	4.0	4.0	203.0	6.5	4.8	0.9	0.2	0.1	0.3	12.7	3 Other grains and cereals
20.8	6.8	6.8	344.7	23.4	23.2	3.9	0.7	0.1	0.3	51.5	4 Condiments
4.0	1.2	1.4	66.8	10.4	8.2	1.3	0.2	0.0	0.0	20.2	5 Pulses
12.4	4.2	4.2	209.4	14.7	11.1	1.7	0.3	0.1	0.1	28.0	6 Coconuts
26.7	11.4	11.3	381.7	21.9	18.1	3.6	0.7	0.1	0.3	44.7	7 Vegetables, fruits and other nuts
8.9	2.2	3.8	72.0	6.1	6.3	1.4	0.4	0.1	0.4	14.7	8 Meat
25.2	7.2	10.8	358.1	16.9	14.6	2.6	0.6	0.1	0.2	35.0	9 Fish
17.8	5.8	7.3	148.6	8.6	9.2	2.1	0.5	0.1	0.3	20.8	10 Milk and milk products
4.9	1.6	1.6	79.3	8.3	6.3	1.2	0.2	0.1	0.2	16.3	11 Oils, fats, including butter
3.0	1.8	1.2	56.2	3.6	2.9	0.5	0.1	0.0	0.0	7.0	12 Tea
16.8	5.6	5.7	280.2	15.8	14.0	2.5	0.4	0.1	0.2	33.0	13 Sugar
7.4	3.8	3.8	125.6	10.4	8.6	1.4	0.3	0.1	0.1	20.9	14 Other food and beverages
12.4	4.2	5.7	140.6	2.2	2.5	0.4	0.1	0.0	0.1	5.3	15 Meals away from home
3.0	0.0	0.0	35.8	3.2	2.2	0.3	0.1	0.0	0.0	5.8	16 Toddy
10.9	4.6	4.7	155.8	11.1	10.2	1.9	0.4	0.1	0.2	23.9	17 Other alcoholic beverages
4.0	1.0	0.9	97.1	10.8	7.3	0.6	0.1	0.0	0.0	18.8	18 Traditional tobacco
20.8	7.0	7.1	231.4	8.3	7.0	2.0	0.7	0.1	0.3	18.4	19 Modern tobacco
8.5	17.7	17.7	441.9	37.0	34.3	6.5	1.7	0.6	0.9	81.0	20 Clothing and footwear
6.6	20.5	16.3	408.4	16.5	13.0	2.5	1.4	0.4	1.2	35.0	21 Rent, rates and water charges
2.4	4.0	4.0	202.6	12.9	10.8	1.7	0.3	0.1	0.2	26.0	22 Fuel and light
1.8	5.8	21.9	145.9	2.5	4.4	1.2	0.5	0.0	0.3	9.0	23 Consumer durables
9.8	9.8	15.8	199.2	10.1	9.8	2.2	0.6	0.2	0.6	23.5	24 Household operation
3.4	5.0	4.9	164.7	7.5	7.0	2.0	0.5	0.0	0.2	17.2	25 Personal care and health
6.4	36.3	44.3	402.8	13.3	13.0	3.2	1.5	0.3	1.3	32.6	26 Transport and communications
3.7	8.4	15.3	171.5	4.7	5.4	2.1	0.7	0.2	0.5	13.5	27 Recreation
5.9	7.0	1.4	45.8	1.8	1.9	0.3	0.1	0.0	0.0	4.1	28 Miscellaneous
4.6	200.7	235.6	5900.0	359.4	317.3	60.2	14.7	3.1	8.5	763.2	Total

administration. Finally, the statistical discrepancy was spread *pro rata* over all the categories.

As already noted, our estimates of the cost structure of government expenditure made use of the structure for aggregate expenditure as described in PMC, but with some adjustments for changes in relative prices. The working papers underlying PMC provided detailed information on the cost structures of health and education, and local government expenditures. The residual supplies from each of our 48 productive sectors after accounting for these three categories of expenditure were concentrated in construction, electricity and services. These residual amounts were allocated largely in proportion to column totals and the final matrix of expenditures on goods and services was then as shown in Table A.21 below.

Table A.21 *Government current expenditure, 1970 (Rs million)*

Sector	Civil Administration	Defence	Education	Health	Housing and other social services	Agriculture irrigation and land development	Roads and highways	Other community services	Local government	Total as on Table A.6
1 Tea				1.7						
2 Rubber										
3.Coconuts				4.2						
4 Paddy										
5 Livestock				3.6						
6 Fishing				3.0						
7 Logging and firewood										
8 Other agriculture				9.5						
9 Mining and quarrying										
10 Milling				17.1				0.8		
11 Dairy products				3.2						
12 Bread				2.3						
13 Other bakery products										
14 Carbonated beverages										
15 Desiccated coconut										
16 Other processed food				3.2						
17 Distilling										
18 Tobacco										
19 Textiles	0.8	0.4	1.2	0.5	0.8			0.8	0.1	
20 Wood products	0.4	0.4	0.2						0.5	
21 Paper	0.6	0.6	2.2		0.1			0.2	3.5	
22 Leather										
23 Rubber			0.1	0.1						
24 Chemicals				15.7					4.0	
25 Oils and fats										
26 Coconut fibre and yarn										
27 Petroleum and coal									1.2	
28 Structural clay products										
29 Ceramics										
30 Cement										
31 Basic metals										
32 Light engineering			2.0	0.3	0.2	1.1	0.4	0.6	0.2	
33 Transport equipment										
34 Machinery, other equipment										
35 Other manufacturing										
36 Construction	4.0	1.0	9.0	2.6	17.0	11.4	17.0	18.0	12.4	
37 Electricity	3.0	2.0	5.0	1.1					17.4	
38 Road passenger transport										
39 Rail transport										
40 Trade, and other transport			22.0	6.8		11.4		4.0	15.1	
41 Services	0.6	0.6	19.0	6.5	0.7	2.0	0.6	1.6	5.4	
Total intermediate inputs (domestic)	9.4	5.0	58.7	80.4	18.8	25.9	18.0	26.0	59.8	302.0
Wages, salaries and imputed pension contributions	350.8	97.7	474.9	179.9	6.0	49.6	6.1	42.5	68.0	1275.5
Indirect taxes	25.5		2.0	1.0						28.5
Imports	0.9	1.5	15.9	12.4	1.1	1.9	1.4	2.4	5.2	42.7
Total current expenditure	386.6	104.2	551.5	273.7	25.9	77.4	25.5	70.9	133.0	1648.7

For transfer payments, the disaggregation into the ten categories listed in Chapter 3 was based upon detailed information on transfer payments as tabulated by the Central Bank, social accounts division. There is a problem of reconciliation with the figures in CBR Table 36 as shown in Table A.22 below.

Table A.22 *Transfer payments*

	CBR (Table 36)	*Central Bank tabulations*
Total transfer payments	1256.6 (inc. pensions)	862.2
Plus pension payments		182.9
		1045.1
Less food subsidies included above	573.8 (gross)	339.5 (net)
Balance = transfers in our treatment	682.8	705.6

We have not been able to explain the difference between the last two numbers and this difference remains in our accounts as a statistical discrepancy.

Having once identified the total transfer payments of different types we are left with the task of disaggregating each of these totals according to the institutions receiving the transfer. This next part of the story is taken up in Stage 8, which is the third of a group of sections dealing with the balancing of institution current accounts.

Stage 6 The balance of payments

Foreign trade and other external transactions statistics are among the firmest figures available for Sri Lanka. This is perhaps not surprising in view of the stringent foreign exchange controls which operate in response to the severe pressure on import capacity brought about by limited export earnings on the one hand and substantial consumer imports to underpin living standards on the other. However, even in this area there are conflicts among the figures, with different estimates produced by the balance of payments division of the Central Bank on the one hand, and by the Customs Department on the other. The problem is further complicated by lack of consistency with data from the Petroleum Corporation on imports of petroleum products and the Food Commissioner on consumer imports of rice, wheat and sugar. And of course there is the inevitable residual problem of smuggling and dishonest invoicing which one suspects must exist to a degree. However, there is little or nothing we can do about that.

Our basic balance of payments figures are taken from the CBR for 1972, Table 44. The detail there is summarised in Table A.23. The table shows a trade deficit of 277.7 m. which is increased by net factor income payments of 141.8 m. to 419.5 m. The private transfers account shows a further deficit of 5.5 m. thus giving a total current account deficit of 425 m. What is shown as official transfers in Table 44 of the CBR is the value of grants received by Government from abroad. Imports financed by this inflow are recorded under the trading account of the balance of payments. It is therefore conceptually more correct to show this item of official transfer under the capital account. The total current account deficit of 425 m. is financed mainly by international borrowing (350 m.) and the balance of 75 m. by grants under commodity aid and other outright grants.

Table A.23 *Balance of payments, 1970 (Rs million)*

		Receipts (exports)	*Payments (imports)*	*Balance*
Trade: Merchandise		2016.6	2332.4	−315.8
Services		226.9	188.8	+38.1
Goods and services		2243.5	2521.2	−277.7
Factor services		9.8	151.6	−141.8
Private transfers		17.9	23.4	−5.5
Current account				−425.0
Exports (excluding duties)	1916.3			
Duties	327.2			
Net capital receipts	425.0			
	2668.5			
Imports	2521.2			
Net factor income paid abroad	141.8			
Net private transfers to abroad	5.5			
	2668.5			

The trade items in the table have already been discussed in detail elsewhere in this appendix: exports in Stage 1 and Table A.6 and imports in Stage 2 and Tables A.7, A.8, and A.9.

The figures in Table A.23 are not easily reconciled with the summary national income statistics given in Table 9 of the CBR. This is partly because the latter do not take account of subsequent revisions of the balance of payments data. Thus, the CBR Table 9 data are based on 1970 figures given in the 1970 Annual Report, rather than that for 1972 which is used for our Table A.23. Secondly, the summary Table 9 seems to involve a semantic error whereby trade receipts and expenditures from goods and services are confused with trade in goods and services plus non-factor service payments. What the Central Bank calls non-factor services is really merchandise services. The implication is that net private transfers from abroad are left out of the reckoning in the summary table and the residual error is accordingly overstated by this amount. In estimating expenditure on GNP at market prices both the net factor incomes as well as net private transfers to abroad have to be deducted from total expenditure on GDP at market prices.

In terms of our accounting scheme as summarised in Table A.1 the non-trade items in Table A.23 are dealt with as follows. Net factor service payments of 142 m. breaks down into 29 m. of interest payments on the national debt (recorded in column 4 of Table A.1 at the intersection with row 7), and 113 m. of private factor payments (recorded at the intersection of row 1 and column 7). The 18 m. of private transfer receipts is deemed to be a receipt by households and is consequently shown in the household account (row 3) at the intersection with the rest of the world account (column 7). Finally, of the 23 m. of private transfer payments, 7 m. is identified from the government accounts as being paid by government and the remaining 16 m. is assumed to be paid by firms. Both of these components are recorded in row 7 of Table A.1.

Stage 7 The balance of the government accounts

We have already discussed most items of government revenue and expenditure; the only items not so far discussed are direct taxation and transfer payments to the government.

Direct taxes are relatively straightforward since, having already dealt with export duties, all that remains is income tax, profits tax and some small related items, notably the rice-subsidy tax. The total of these various items from ERE is 445 m. and we have calculated that 236 m. of this was paid by companies, including public corporations, and that the remaining 209 m. was paid by individuals. This calculation was based on data on the taxable incomes of companies both resident and non-resident as produced by the department of inland revenue and the tax rates applying to these incomes as set down in the booklet *The New Tax Structure, 1969–70*, published by the Inland Revenue. This yielded a figure for tax paid by private companies; tax payments of public companies were calculated using the profits figures as set down in the CBR and appropriate tax rates and amount to 79 m. The residual of tax after deducting these two items was assumed to be paid by households. The question as to the allocation of the total of household income taxes as between different categories of households is taken up in the next section.

Details of the *transfer receipts* of the central government are set down under heads 5, 6, 7 and 8 of the Estimates and sum to 180 m. The most important items are social security contributions, and interest, rent and dividend receipts, mainly from public bodies. The detail given in the ERE together with the summary information in the CBR (Table 36) was used to derive the allocation by paying sector which is set down in Table A.24 below.

Table A.24 *Central government – transfer receipts (Rs million)*

Households	221.1	(includes 182.9 of imputed pension contribution (see p. 124))
Companies (public and private)	139.8	
Local government	1.6	
Rest of the world	0.2	
	362.7	

All of these items are accounted for in row 4 of Table A.1 at the intersection with the columns corresponding to the paying sectors, and consequently we are now in a position to provide a full statement of the entries in row 4 of this table.

The full statement of government current receipts and payments is then as shown in Table A.26.

Stage 8 The balance of all other institutions' accounts and the factor accounts

This final stage of Appendix 1 brings together the institution and factor accounts. Although we have independent estimates of the distribution of the value added generated by each production activity among the factors of production employed, these are deficient in a number of respects. We shall therefore deal with the estimation of the unadjusted factor incomes matrix and then proceed to balance the institutions accounts by way of some rather crucial assumptions about the biases in the unadjusted factor payments and about the ownership of capital for the different non-governmental institutions.

Table A.25 *Full summary of entries in row 4 of Table A.1 (Rs million)*

	Column (2) Firms	Column (3) Households	Column (4) Government	Column (5) Capital a/cs	Column (6) Production	Column (7) Rest of world
Indirect taxes and FEECs (from Table A.14)	–	119	29	270	856	130
Income and profits tax	236	209				
Transfer receipts (Table A.24)	140	221				
Transfer receipts of local government		18				
FEECs on debt interest paid*			14			
Transfers to local government			59			
FEECs on debt repayments etc.				44	–	
Total as in row 4 of Table A.1	376	567	104	314	856	130

Table A.26 *The government budget, 1970 (Rs million)*

Receipts		*Payments*	
Indirect taxes including some FEECs and export duties)	1404	Current expenditure on goods and services (inc. wages and salaries)	1649
Direct taxes	445	Transfer payments	578
Transfer receipts	440	Intra-government payments*	75
FEECs on debt payments, etc.	57	Balance = government saving	43
	2346		2346

* Excluding imputed rents on government buildings and duties on government imports both of which are included in the first item.

The construction of the unadjusted factor incomes matrix (**V** *)*

Let us define element VP_{ij} as the payment received by the ith factor in the jth production activity. We have distinguished 9 labour factors according to occupational groups and 3 capital factors according to ownership of private housing, other private capital and public capital (see Chapter 3). The production activities number 48 and have been described in Chapter 3. Thus the matrix **VP** is of order 12 × 48. In addition there are two other 'employing activities' but these are contained within the institutions current account. These are employment in government establishments *excluding* enterprises already classified under production activities, and the employment of domestic servants in private households. These will be recorded in the matrix **VI**, a 12 × 6 matrix, the typical element of which, namely VI_{ij}, shows the value added payment direct from the jth institution to the ith factor. The fourth and fifth columns (institutions) of this matrix relate to private firms and public corporations respectively and will be null vectors since factor payments by these institutions are made via production activities. The first three columns of **VI** correspond to the three household sectors (urban, rural and estate) and the last column relates to the government. There are no payments to capital recorded in this matrix and so rows 10–12 also contain zero entries. The matrices **VP** and **VI** can be combined as partitions of the matrix **V** having dimensions (12 X 54). **V** shows factor incomes by each of the 54 production activities or institutional sectors which make factor payments.

The purpose of this sub-section is to document the various sources and specify the approximations which lie behind the filling in of the **V** matrix or, in other words, the disaggregation of the total value added from production activities (10 098 m.), *plus* employment by private households (100) *plus* government employment (1275 m.). See row 1 of Table A.1.

We begin with the main source of information about factor payments for 1970 which is the *Socio-Economic Survey, 1969–70.* This classifies income receivers who are members of households* to their industries of principal employment. Post-tax factor incomes are then attributed to those same industries. According to the SES these incomes consist of profits (net income) of unincorporated businesses; wages and salaries; rents, interest and dividends; pensions and other transfers; and other periodic cash receipts. It does not have data on corporate profits.

*A household is defined in the summary as 'a group of two or more persons related or unrelated, who combine to occupy the whole or part of the housing unit and provide themselves with food and other essentials for living'. Boarders were included provided there were no more than three domestic servants occupying the same premises and taking household meals but lodgers were excluded. *Preliminary Report of the Socio-Economic Survey 1969/70, Department of Census and Statistics*, p. 128. This report is subsequently referred to as SES(2).

No more reliable source than the SES exists as a basis for distributing the value added for each industry among factors of production and it is therefore used as the basis of our methodology. Special tabulations from the full four rounds of the SES, (SES(4)), have been used where available but in certain cases, data for aggregates of industries from SES(4) have been distributed among the individual industries by using the appropriate detail given in the preliminary report of the survey, i.e. SES(2). This occurs where a re-computation of figures calculated prior to the availability of SES(4) data is not thought to be worthwhile, given other sources of error.

When writing the report on which this book is based we had to rely more heavily on SES(2) data than is now the case. The lack of statistics at a sufficiently disaggregated level combined with the use of SES(2) data meant that we were dubious about the accuracy of our estimates of the factor incomes matrix. This continues to be the case partly because of the difficulties which we still face of matching some parts of the SES industrial divisions to the SAM production activities and partly for other reasons which are discussed fully below. The two classifications are compared in Table A.27a. The disaggregation of SES minor divisions, where this was necessary, was achieved using the estimates of value added from the SAM together with figures on productivity based on those given in UNDP Volume IV. Details of the procedure applied to both the manpower matrix and manpower incomes matrix are given later in Appendix 2.

The correspondence between the SES income categories and classification of factor payments in our approach is given below in Table A.27b. However, our approach also requires data on the following additional components of gross income received which are not included in the SES data.

(i) Direct taxes paid by industry of employment.
(ii) The value of non-monetary factor payments by industry of employment.
(iii) The net value of home-grown produce since this is part of the gross output and hence value added of the relevant production activities.
(iv) Net-rental value of owner-occupied housing. (This affects only activity 41d.)

Having added to the SES data to take account of these omissions (in a manner to be described shortly), we can compare the set of value added totals which emerge with those which emerged from our Stage 3 above. This is done in Table

Table A.27(a) *The matching of the SAM and SES industrial classifications*

SAM classification		SES minor industrial divisions
1	Tea	02
2	Rubber	03
3	Coconuts	04
4	Paddy	00
5	Livestock	05
6	Fishing	08
7	Logging and firewood	07
8	Other agriculture	01 and 06
9	Mining and quarrying	Major division 1
10a–13, 15, 16, 25		20 Food industries
14, 17		21 Beverage industries
18	Tobacco	22
19	Textiles	23
20	Wood products	24
21	Paper	25–6
22	Leather	27
23	Rubber	28
24	Chemicals	29
27	Petroleum and coal	30
28–30		31
31	Basic metals	32
32	Light engineering	33
33–34		34
26, 35	Other manufacturing	35 Other manufacturing
36	Construction	Major division 5
37	Electricity	part 40
38–39, 40c		70
40a	Wholesale trade	60
40b	Retail trade	61
41a	Communication	71
41b	Hotels and restaurants	62–3
41c	Professional services	92–5
41d	Dwellings	–
41e	Other services	96–9
	Domestic service	–
	Public administration	–

A.28 in which the first four columns record direct estimates of factor payments built up from the SES data and the government accounts; column 6 records the SAM data on value-added (from Table A.16); and column 5 records the discrepancy between column 6 and the sum of columns 1 to 4. It will be seen that this discrepancy is quite large both for some individual sectors and in the aggregate.

Tables A.29 and A.30 show the detail underlying the figures for labour and capital respectively as presented in Table A.28. The next few paragraphs discuss the definition of the component items in these three tables and our method of quantifying them.

The *factor payments received by labour* exclude the incomes of those who are self-employed or are owners of unincorporated businesses since these are classified under 'other private capital'. Hence '*labour*' includes all post-tax wages and salaries of those whose principal employment status is that of an employee, as well as direct tax payments, non-money factor payments and the value of home-

Table A.27(b) *The matching of the SAM and SES income payments classifications*

SES income classifications	SAM factor payment
Wages and salaries Free goods and services (excluding housing from employers	Labour
Profits (unincorporated business net income)	Other private non-corporate capital
Net rental value Free housing	Private housing
Rents, interest and dividends Pension and other transfers Other periodic cash receipts	Transfer payments
No equivalent	Corporate business surpluses

grown produce. As Table A.29 shows, the total value of these four component elements of 'labour' receipts is 4131, 149, 55 and 306 respectively.

The Table A.29 figures for *wages and salaries* were taken direct from the SES(4) except that, in the service sector, statistics from the Government accounts recording the payments to government employees were adopted in preference to the SES estimates.

Direct taxes paid by employees were obtained by distributing the control total of 149 m., among non-agricultural production activities according to post-tax wages and salary receipts. This procedure will produce estimates of direct taxes which are biased upwards in the case of low paying industries and vice versa. However, skews in the industrial distribution of paid taxes relating to variations between industries in average incomes and in the shapes of earned income distributions are hardly worth worrying about given other sources of error. The 149 m. of payments by employees when added to payments of 43 m. and 17 m. respectively by own account workers and employers (both accounted for in Table A.30 as capital receipts), give the total of personal direct tax payments of 209 identified in Stage 7. Direct taxes by the self-employed were distributed among production activities according to post-tax profits given in the SES.

The figures for *non-money factor payments* in Table A.29 are based on the SES(4) which shows a total of 102 m. for 1969/70. Of this, 47 m. is free housing and so is properly treated as part of our capital entry – private housing – and is incorporated in Table A.30. The balance of 55 m., shown in Table A.29, consists of goods and services provided free by employers or received from sources without payment; the amount of transfers, as opposed to payment in kind for labour services, which this figure includes has been assumed to be nil. The SES disaggregates the total of 55 m. according to rural, estate and urban. The breakdown by production activity shown in Table A.29 then assumes that the rural and estate element went wholly to employees in agriculture and in proportion to numbers of employees, while the urban element went to manufacturing, trade and domestic services and in proportion to post-tax wages and salaries.

The Table A.29 and A.30 figures for *home-grown produce* are again based on the SES(4) which records a total of 636 m., of which only 14 m. is non-agricultural produce. The latter was distributed among manufacturing industries 12, 13, 18 and 19 according to value added; the detail available in the classification of home-grown produce enabled the balance of 622 m. to be allocated to

Table A.28 *Unadjusted factor payments by production activity (Rs million)*

Production activity	Labour	Capital			SAM data	
		Housing	Other private	Public	Residual = (6) – [(1) + (2) + (3) + (4)]	Value added
	(1)	(2)	(3)	(4)	(5)	(6)
1 Tea	465	–	24	–	98	587
2 Rubber	151	–	50	–	119	320
3 Coconuts	107	–	52	–	370	529
4 Paddy	333	–	789	–	–145	977
5 Livestock	33	–	52	–	134	219
6 Fishing	47	–	84	–12	127	246
7 Logging and firewood	49	–	70	–	7	126
8 Other agriculture	144	–	214	–	626	984
9 Mining and quarrying	15	–	12	3	52	85
10a Rice milling	6	–	3	0	27	36
10b Flour milling	3	–	1	0	13	17
11 Dairy products	4	–	2	0	3	9
12 Bread	19	–	9	–	20	48
13 Other bakery products	10	–	4	–	14	28
14 Carbonated beverages	1	–	1	–	6	8
15 Desiccated coconut	1	–	0	–	1	2
16 Other processed food	10	–	5	11	–1	25
17 Distilling	3	–	3	–	36	42
18 Tobacco	26	–	19	–	90	135
19 Textiles	88	–	45	4	–15	122
20 Wood products	120	–	40	1	–48	113
21 Paper	40	–	5	4	33	82
22 Leather	9	–	2	0	7	18
23 Rubber	17	–	0	5	5	27
24 Chemicals	23	–	6	0	92	121
25 Oils and fats	1	–	0	–3	7	5
26 Coconut fibre and yarn	30	–	12	–	3	45
27 Petroleum and coal	8	–	0	39	35	82
28 Structural clay products	20	–	5	–	7	32
29 Ceramics	14	–	4	3	–5	16
30 Cement	4	–	1	27	8	40
31 Basic metals	11	–	2	2	2	17
32 Light engineering	13	–	9	–5	174	191
33 Transport equipment	8	–	2	–	–2	8
34 Machinery, other equipment	9	–	2	–	27	38
35 Other manufacturing	6	–	12	–1	3	20
36 Construction	172	–	30	–8	785	979
37 Electricity	36	–	3	28	27	94
38 Road passenger transport	112	–	16	–34	125	219
39 Rail transport	69	–	10	–	14	93
40a Wholesale trade	103	–	60	16	504	683
40b Retail trade	172	–	391	17	160	740
40c Other transport	230	–	34	0	333	597
41a Communication	67	–	5	1	24	97
41b Hotels and restaurants	24	–	44	–	31	99
41c Professional services	61	–	47	–	77	185
41d Dwellings	0	633	0	–	0	633
41e Other services	208	–	116	72	–117	279
All production activities	3104	633	2297	174	3890	10098
Public administration	1275	–	–	–	–	1275
Domestic service	100	–	–	–	–	100
Σ Employing activities	4479	633	2297	174	3890	11473
Activities n.e.s.	162	–	84	–	–246	–
Grand total	4641	633	2380	174	3645	11473

activities 3–8 directly. Home-grown produce under each activity was then split between labour (Table A.29) and capital (Table A.30), in proportion to the SES numbers of employees (labour) on the one hand, and own account workers plus employers (capital) on the other. (SES(2) Table 27.0)

Turning to the remaining capital payment items, one item in Table A.30, namely *private housing*, is extremely straightforward since the value added already calculated for our sector 41d, 'Dwellings', accrues entirely to this particular factor and no further calculations are necessary.

As noted earlier, the term 'profits' in the SES refers to the net income from unincorporated businesses, or *other private non-corporate capital* in our terminology. These SES profit figures are shown in column 1 of Table A.30. To ensure consistency with our own definition of value added, we need to increase these figures to take account of direct tax payments and income in the form of home grown produce. These adjustments were done using the methods just described

Table A.29 *Unadjusted returns to labour (Rs million)*

Production activity	Post-tax wages and salaries (1)	Direct taxes (2)	Non-money factor payments excluding housing (3)	Home-grown produce consumed (4)	Total (5)
1 Tea	450.5	0	14.2	0	464.7
2 Rubber	142.3	0	8.7	0	151.0
3 Coconuts	45.0	0	2.9	59.0	106.9
4 Paddy	199.3	0	10.9	123.0	333.2
5 Livestock	2.2	0	4.7	26.0	32.9
6 Fishing	41.2	0	0.8	5.0	47.0
7 Logging and firewood	3.2	0	0.2	46.0	49.4
8 Other agriculture	99.1	0	4.0	41.0	144.1
9 Mining and quarrying	16.9	0.8	0	0	17.7
10a Rice milling	5.8	0.3	0	0	6.1
10b Flour milling	3.0	0.2	0	0	3.2
11 Dairy products	3.7	0.2	0	0	3.9
12 Bread	16.8	0.8	0.2	1.0	18.8
13 Other bakery products	8.2	0.4	0.1	1.0	9.7
14 Carbonated beverages	0.9	0.0	0	0	0.9
15 Desiccated coconut	0.8	0.0	0	0	0.8
16 Other processed food	9.5	0.5	0.1	0	10.1
17 Distilling	3.2	0.2	0.1	0	3.5
18 Tobacco	22.4	1.1	0.2	2.0	25.7
19 Textiles	81.2	4.0	0.6	2.0	87.8
20 Wood products	113.4	5.6	0.8	0	119.8
21 Paper	37.8	1.9	0.4	0	40.1
22 Leather	8.1	0.4	0.1	0	8.6
23 Rubber	15.8	0.8	0.3	0	16.9
24 Chemicals	22.0	1.1	0.3	0	23.4
25 Oils and fats	0.7	0.0	0	0	0.7
26 Coconut fibre and yarn	28.5	1.4	0	0	29.9
27 Petroleum and coal	7.7	0.4	0.1	0	8.2
28 Structural clay products	18.6	0.9	0.1	0	19.6
29 Ceramics	13.6	0.7	0.1	0	14.4
30 Cement	3.7	0.2	0	0	3.9
31 Basic metals	10.2	0.5	0.2	0	10.9
32 Light engineering	12.1	0.6	0.1	0	12.8
33 Transport equipment	7.3	0.4	0.2	0	7.9
34 Machinery, other equipment	8.3	0.4	0.2	0	8.9
35 Other manufacturing	6.1	0.3	0.1	0	6.5
36 Construction	164.3	8.1	0	0	172.4
37 Electricity	33.9	1.7	0	0	35.6
38 Road passenger transport	106.6	5.3	0	0	111.9
39 Rail transport	65.9	3.3	0	0	69.2
40a Wholesale trade	96.7	4.8	1.2	0	102.7
40b Retail trade	162.8	8.0	1.7	0	172.5
40c Other transport	219.7	10.8	0	0	230.5
41a Communication	64.1	3.2	0	0	67.3
41b Hotels and restaurants	22.2	1.1	0.3	0	23.6
41c Professional services	58.0	2.9	0	0	60.9
41d Dwellings	–	–	–	0	0.0
41e Other services	198.0	9.8	0	0	207.8
All production activities	2660.8	82.8	53.9	306.0	3103.5
Public administration	1217.5	57.5	–	–	1275.0
Domestic servants	95.3	3.7	1.0	–	100.0
Σ Employing activities	3973.6	144.0	54.9	306.0	4478.5
Activities n.e.s.	157.4	5.0	–	–	162.4
Grand total	4131.0	149.0	54.9	306.0	4640.9

and the resulting figures which need to be added in are shown in columns 2 and 3 of Table A.30.

Public capital receipts are merely the surpluses of public corporations as given in the government accounts (e.g. CBR, 1970, Table II(C)2). In 1970 these summed to 174 m.

Table A.30 *Unadjusted returns to capital*

Production activity	SES profits (1)	Direct taxes (2)	Home-grown produce consumed (3)	Sub-total other private capital (4)	Private housing (5)	Public capital (6)	Total excluding 'residual' (7)
1 Tea	24.4	0	0	24.4	–	0	24.4
2 Rubber	50.1	0	0	50.1	–	0	50.1
3 Coconuts	17.1	0	35.0	52.1	–	0	52.1
4 Paddy	694.4	0	95.0	789.4	–	0	789.4
5 Livestock	7.0	0	45.0	52.0	–	0	52.0
6 Fishing	70.8	0	13.0	83.8	–	–11.8	72.0
7 Logging and firewood	3.2	0	67.0	70.2	–	0	70.2
8 Other agriculture	145.7	0	68.0	213.7	–	0	213.7
9 Mining and quarrying	11.4	0.7	0	12.1	–	3.3	15.4
10a Rice milling	2.6	0.2	0	2.8	– }	0.2	4.4
10b Flour milling	1.3	0.1	0	1.4	–		
11 Dairy products	1.7	0.1	0	1.8	–	0.1	1.9
12 Bread	7.5	0.5	1.0	9.0	–	0	9.0
13 Other bakery products	3.7	0.2	0	3.9	–	0	3.9
14 Carbonated beverages	0.9	0.1	0	1.0	–	0	1.0
15 Desiccated coconut	0.3	0.0	0	0.3	–	0	0.3
16 Other processed food	4.3	0.3	0	4.6	–	11.1	15.7
17 Distilling	3.2	0.2	0	3.4	–	0	3.4
18 Tobacco	14.7	0.9	3.0	18.6	–	0	18.6
19 Textiles	39.8	2.4	3.0	45.2	–	4.0	49.2
20 Wood products	37.4	2.3	0	37.7	–	1.3	41.0
21 Paper	4.5	0.3	0	4.8	–	4.2	9.0
22 Leather	1.5	0.1	0	1.6	–	0.2	1.8
23 Rubber	0.3	0.0	0	0.3	–	5.4	5.7
24 Chemicals	6.0	0.4	0	6.4	–	0.4	6.8
25 Oils and fats	0.3	0.0	0	0.3	–	–2.6	–2.3
26 Coconut fibre and yarn	10.8	0.7	0	11.5	–	0	11.5
27 Petroleum and coal	0.1	0.0	0	0.1	–	39.0	39.1
28 Structural clay products	4.8	0.3	0	5.1	–	0	5.1
29 Ceramics	3.5	0.2	0	3.7	–	3.0	6.7
30 Cement	0.9	0.1	0	1.0	–	27.4	28.4
31 Basic metals	2.3	0.1	0	2.4	–	2.2	4.6
32 Light engineering	8.6	0.5	0	9.1	–	–4.8	4.3
33 Transport equipment	1.9	0.1	0	2.0	–	0	2.0
34 Machinery, other equipment	2.1	0.1	0	2.2	–	0	2.2
35 Other manufacturing	11.7	0.7	0	12.4	–	–0.5	11.9
36 Construction	27.9	1.7	0	29.6	–	–7.8	21.8
37 Electricity	0.9	0.2	0	3.1	–	28.3	31.4
38 Road passenger transport	15.4	0.9	0	16.3	–	–34.2	–17.9
39 Rail transport	9.5	0.6	0	10.1	–	0	10.1
40a Wholesale trade	56.6	3.5	0	60.1	–	15.7	75.8
40b Retail trade	368.8	22.6	0	391.4	–	17.0	408.4
40c Other transport	31.7	1.9	0	33.6	–	0.1	33.7
41a Communication	4.3	0.3	0	4.6	–	0.6	5.2
41b Hotels and restaurants	41.1	2.5	0	43.6	–	0	43.6
41c Professional services	44.0	2.7	0	46.7	–	0	46.7
41d Dwellings	–	–	–	–	633.0	–	633.0
41e Other services	109.0	6.7	0	115.7	–	71.8	187.5
All production activity	1911.5	55.2	330.0	2296.7	633.0	173.5	3103.3
Public administration	–	–	–	–	–	–	–
Domestic servants	–	–	–	–	–	–	–
Σ Employing activities	1911.5	55.2	330.0	2296.7	633.0	173.5	3103.3
Activities n.a.d.	78.8	4.8	–	83.6	–	–	83.6
Grand total	1990.3	60.0	330.0	2380.3	633.0	173.5	3186.9

The final and major item which should appear in Table A.30 is *corporate business capital* for which there is no SES coverage. Since there is no satisfactory alternative source of direct estimates of these items, we are forced to regard it as the 'residual' of our system. Its magnitude at this stage is shown in column 5 of Table A.28, but in a later part of this appendix we will show that this magnitude is not credible given information from other parts of the system. However, before moving on to this we need to consider two statistical factors which may influence the size of the residual as presently calculated and so prevent it from being a genuine indicator of the size of corporate surpluses.

The first of these factors is the different *timing* of the SAM estimates which mostly relate to the calendar year 1970 and the SES which was conducted in four rounds beginning on 1 November 1969, but with the reference period for the income question being the previous twelve months.

If the response was even throughout the survey period only about 30 per cent of the recorded income would relate to 1970. In the presence of price and wage inflation this lag could be a cause of significant downward bias in all but incomes from government employment (which are taken from the government accounts in preference to the SES). Unfortunately the relevant price indices covering this period are generally based on unreliable samples and they show only small increases in non-government wages and salaries (see CBR, 1972).

The second factor is the *underenumeration of the population* of Sri Lanka by the SES which stems mainly from the exclusion of single person households, professional boarding houses with three or more boarders, all institutions (hospitals, schools, convents, etc.) and those with no fixed abode. The provisional intercensal estimate of the 1970 population was 5.38 per cent above the estimated population covered by the survey. We have chosen not to gross up the employment and income figures using a single factor as has been done in the expenditure side of the accounts. This is partly for the reason that while those excluded must consume they do not necessarily receive income from employment; but mainly because even this crude adjustment would not obviate the need, as far as we can estimate, for a further more substantial grossing up across the factor incomes matrix. The underenumeration is hence captured in our overall balancing of the factor and non-government institutions accounts rather than catered for separately.

The payment of factor incomes to institutions

Subject to these qualifications about corporate profits, we have now reached the stage where we have detail on the different categories of factor payments disaggregated by production sector. In other words, we have the data needed to complete the **VP** matrix except for the *occupational detail* of payments to labour. It is one of our remaining tasks to generate this detail but we will put this on one side, returning to it on p. 171, and turn now to the *institutional* detail of factor receipts.

The starting point for this is the summary table, A.31, which was constructed as follows. The total of the first column was taken directly from Table A.29 and the detail in that column was built up from the detail available in the SES. The total for private housing in column 2 is from Table A.30 with most of the detail coming from the SES. The payments here are of three types namely imputed rents on owner occupation, housing subsidies to employees and net rents on private accommodation. The SES(4) indicates that urban, rural and estate sectors receive 132 m., 319 m. and 0.4 m. respectively of the total *plus* 6 m., 11 m. and 30 m. respectively of free housing making a total for the household institutions of 498 m. The remaining part of the total of 633 m. was assumed to be attributable to private corporations. The total of column 3 is taken from Table A.30 with the detail in that column being constructed using the same methods as those underlying Table A.30. Finally, in columns 4 and 5 of Table A.31 all the returns to private corporate and public capital go to the relevant corporate institutions.

Thus in Table A.31, we can show the institutional incomes which derive from the existing ownership of factors of production. In addition institutions engage in transfers of income among themselves and receive non-factor payments from abroad. In the following paragraphs these payments are brought into the story to

Table A.31 *Payment of unadjusted factor incomes to institutions*

	Labour	Capital				Total
		Private housing	Other private		Public	
			Non-corporation	Corporation		
	(1)	(2)	(3)	(4)	(5)	(6)
Urban households	1416.4	137.1	423.8	0	0	1977.3
Rural households	2675.4	329.8	1937.6	0	0	4942.8
Estate households	549.2	30.8	19.1	0	0	599.1
Private corporations	0	135.3	0	3531.9	0	3667.2
Public corporations	0	0	0	0	173.5	173.5
Government	0	0	0	0	0	0
Total	4641.1	633.0	2380.5	3531.9	173.5	11 360.0

obtain our estimates of institutional *disposable* incomes. At the same time we can move towards a proper balancing of those institutional accounts which, for the moment, remain unbalanced.

The balance of the government account from Stage 7 is 43 m. This, together with a net capital transfer from abroad of 425 m. (see Stage 6) is available to finance total capital expenditure of 2640 m. (the sum of the entries in column (3) of Table A.6 plus FEECs on debt repayments). The balance of 2172 m. must be financed by the combined savings of the public corporations and the private sector (households plus private companies).

Table A.32 below sets down a table similar to our summary Table A.1 but differing from it in two respects. First the household current account of Table A.1 has been disaggregated into separate current accounts for urban, rural and estate households. Second, symbols rather than numbers are shown in those cells of the matrix which have yet to be finalised and, in particular, those relating to the payment from production accounts to factors and the payment of factor incomes to institution current accounts.

The public corporation account in row and column 8 is readily completed. Income totals 411 m. of which 174 m. is profits before tax as calculated from information in the CBR and 237 m. is transfer receipts from government of which the major components are interest on that part of the national debt held by the Central Bank and other public financial corporations, and government grants to universities.* Expenditure is 104 m. of which 79 m. is taxation and the rest is a transfer payment to the government. This leaves net savings by the public corporations of 307 m.

Thus we deduce that 1865 (2172–307) is the necessary saving of the private sector if the institutions combined capital account is to balance out as it must. The analysis of Table A.32 is directed towards achieving this balance.

Most of the numerical values shown in Table A.32 are from estimates already discussed but this is not true of the following six items ((i) to (vi) as indicated in the table).

(i) The total figure of 100 estimated as household expenditure on domestic servants has been split between urban, rural and estate households in proportion to the expenditure of these households under the heading 'household operations: services'.

(ii) These figures refer to pensions paid by the private sector. The total

*Both of these categories of institution are included in our definition of public corporations. Hence, the figures which we show for the income and savings of public corporations need to be interpreted with care.

amount is chosen to complement the figures for government pensions and so to make total pension receipts correspond to the figures given in the SES(4) tabulations (urban: 114, rural: 116 and estate: 6).

(iii) Government transfers to households are made up as shown in Table A.33 below. For each item the total figure is available from the government accounts. For pensions, the disaggregation uses the ratios of pension receipts in the SES. For public assistance and other, the disaggregations are modified guesses based on population. Scholarships are split between urban and rural households in the ratio of their population in the age group 15 to 24 years. The disaggregation of receipts of debt interest is a guess.

(iv) The total figure of remittances received from abroad of 18 m. has been spread equally between the three types of households.

(v) This figure is mainly debt interest paid by the government on debt held by the Central Bank, plus 33 m. transferred by government to the university.

(vi) The total of the three entries here (567 m.) has already been analysed in the second column of Table A.25 and in Table A.6. The further disaggregation of these tax and transfer payments by category of household is as shown in Table A.34 below. For the local government item the split of the total is based on population. For the income tax total Government receipts are disaggregated in proportion to incomes received by the highest income group (Rs 1,000+/month) as revealed by the SES.

Thus to the unadjusted estimates of factor incomes discussed earlier we must add the relevant parts of items (i) to (vi) discussed above and shown in Table A.32. It then remains to consider the other transfers between institutions before moving on to the balancing exercise.

Transfers between household sectors and from households *to* corporations have been assumed to be nil. Unfortunately there is no information on the flows of remittances between different categories of households. Transfers *from* the corporate business sector in the form of pensions have been dealt with as item (ii) above.

Information on household receipts of the *distributed returns on private capital* – the major transfer item not yet discussed – is limited by the definition of 'rents, interest and dividends' adopted in the SES. We have chosen to treat private corporations as the ultimate recipient of the *retained* surpluses of incorporated business *and* rents on private housing. In principle, 'rents, interest and dividends' should match the amount of the surpluses *distributed* to households except that they will be net of any direct tax deducted at source. We have ignored this last factor in view of the considerable scaling to which the SES figures are subjected below. All direct tax payments by households have in fact been recorded in the accounts, but in the construction of the unadjusted factor incomes matrix those were allocated to labour and the owners of unincorporated business income. The sectoral breakdown of rents, interest and dividends given in the SES is: urban 68 m., rural 32 m., and estate 1 m. These figures in conjunction with the private pension figures just discussed give the totals for private corporations transfer to households shown in Table A.35 below.

In Table A.35 we show the composition of institutional incomes, summarising the results of our calculations so far. These are all derived from Tables A.31–33. It remains to see whether the income totals can be reconciled with the expenditure data already derived.

Table A.32 *Social-accounting matrix for Sri Lanka with some disaggregation of institution current accounts and factor accounts (preliminary)*

		Factor accounts			Institutions current accounts		
			Capital		Households		
		Labour	Private	Public	Urban	Rural	Estate
		(1)	(2)	(3)	(4)	(5)	(6)
Factor accounts	(1) Labour	0	0	0	38(i)	56(i)	6(i)
	(2) Capital: Private	0	0	0	0	0	0
	(3) Public	0	0	0	0	0	0
Institutions current accounts	(4) Households: Urban (U)	a_U	b_U	0	0	0	0
	(5) Rural (R)	a_R	b_R	0	0	0	0
	(6) Estate (E)	a_E	b_E	0	0	0	0
	(7) Private	0	$9812 - \alpha - b$	0	0	0	0
	(8) Public corporations	0	0	174	0	0	0
	(9) Government	0	0	0	368(vi)	195(vi)	4(vi)
	(10) Institutions combined capital	0	0	0	s_U	s_R	s_E
	(11) Production accounts	0	0	0	1871	5130	627
	(12) Rest of world	0	0	0	207	741	143
	Total	$\alpha + 1375$	$9812 - \alpha$	174	$s_U + 2484$	$s_R + 6095$	$s_E + 780$

The balancing adjustment of the 'factors to institutions' and factor incomes matrices

As already noted, Table A.32 also includes symbols in those cells of the matrix which remain to be filled. These symbols are as follows:

α is total wage payments from production activities

Since value added by production activities is known to be 10 098 it follows that with returns to public capital of 174, returns to private capital must be $9924 - \alpha$. The further notation is:

a_U, a_R, a_E labour incomes from production activities paid to the three types of household

b_U, b_R, b_E returns on non-corporate capital paid direct to households (summing to 'b')

c_U, c_R, c_E returns on corporate business capital paid to households

s_U, s_R, s_E savings of households

s_B profits retained by the private business sector

From this and the accounting balance of Table A.32 we can obtain the following identities:

$$s_U + 2484 = 133 + a_U + b_U + c_U \text{ (i.e. row and column 4)}$$

$$s_R + 6095 = 173 + a_R + b_R + c_R \text{ (row and column 5)}$$

$$s_E + 780 = 13 + a_E + b_E + c_E \text{ (row and column 6)}$$

$$c_U + c_R + c_E + s_B + 341 = 9869 - \alpha - b_U - b_R - b_E \text{ (row and column 7)}$$

$$a_U + a_R + a_E = 1375 + \alpha \text{ (row and column 1)}$$

			Institutions combined capital	Production accounts	Rest of world	Total
Private corporations	Public corporations	Government				
(7)	(8)	(9)	(10)	(11)	(12)	
0	0	1275	0	α	0	$\alpha + 1375$
0	0	0	0	$9924 - \alpha$	−113	$9812 - \alpha$
0	0	0	0	174	0	174
$c_U + 36^{(ii)}$	0	$91^{(iii)}$	0	0	$6^{(iv)}$	$133 + a_U + b_U + c_U$
$c_R + 16^{(ii)}$	0	$151^{(iii)}$	0	0	$6^{(iv)}$	$173 + a_R + b_R + c_R$
$c_E + 1^{(ii)}$	0	$6^{(iii)}$	0	0	$6^{(iv)}$	$13 + a_E + b_E + c_E$
0	0	57	0	0	0	$9869 - \alpha - \beta$
0	0	$237^{(v)}$	0	0	0	411
272	104	0	314	856	130	2241
s_B	307	43	0	0	425	$775 + s$
0	0	302	1962	4358	2113	16 336
16	0	79	364	1024	–	2573
$s_B + c + 341$	411	2241	2640	16 336	2574	

and by summing all five equations we arrive at

$$s_U + s_R + s_E + s_B = 1863$$

which is our earlier estimate of private savings (subject to a rounding error of 2).

The estimates of household incomes given in Table A.35 are difficult to reconcile with the above identities. They are: urban 2178, rural 5148, estate 613. Since the figures are estimates of the right-hand side of the first three identities above they imply negative savings by each type of household (see Table A.36).

Given our earlier conclusion that the total of private savings must be of the order of 1865, to finance the known investment total, the negative household savings shown above implies private business savings of 1865 + 1422, or 3287. This last figure seems quite unrealistic and consequently suggests that incomes in the SES have been seriously underrecorded. We have proceeded on this assumption and now turn to a suggested reconciliation.

It was observed earlier that the SES categories of income do not match directly with those from the SAM. As a result we needed to distinguish factor income receipts from transfer payments and impute values to non-monetary components of income. It is now necessary to go one step further and to decide which of the SES incomes are most likely to be a cause of the underrecording of household income suggested by Table A.36.

The pension figures* given in the SES(4) tabulations are assumed correct. The net rental value of owner-occupied housing and the imputed value of free housing are also accepted without modification. The unspecified 'other periodic cash receipts' recorded in the SES are not used to build up the estimates of income

*The SES figures, which we have taken to represent pensions only, in fact include 'other transfers'. These cannot be deducted because the two types of income are aggregated at the primary data source. We have assumed the additional amounts are negligible.

Table A.33 *Government transfers to households*

	Pensions	Public Assistance	Scholarships	Debt Interest	Other	Total
Urban	78	6	5	1	1	91
Rural	100	30	17	1	3	151
Estate	5	0	0	0	1	6
Total	183	36	22	2	5	248

Table A.34 *Household tax plus transfer payments*

	Urban	Rural	Estate	Total
Import duties	31	82	7	120
Indirect taxes	76	178	23	277
Subsidies	–101	–421	–66	–588
Surpluses	39	142	20	201
FEECs	27	73	9	109
Transfer payments to local government	3	13	2	18
Income tax plus transfer payments to central government	293	128	9	431
Total	368	195	4	567

Table A.35 *Preliminary tabulations of the sources of non-government institutional incomes (Rs million)*

Receiver / Source of income	Households Urban	Households Rural	Households Estate	Corporations Private	Corporations Public
Labour	1416	2675	549	–	–
Private capital					
Private housing	137	330	31	135	–
Other non-corporate	424	1938	19	2	–
Other corporate	–	–	–	3532	–
Public capital	–	–	–	–	174
Transfers from:					
Urban households	0	0	0	0	0
Rural households	0	0	0	0	0
Estate households	0	0	0	0	0
Private corporations	104	48	2	0	0
Public corporations	0	0	0	0	0
Government	91	151	6	57	237
Abroad	6	6	6	0	0
Total	2178	5148	613	3724	411

Table A.36 *Income, payments and implied savings by sector*

	SES income	Payments (as in the equations above)	Implied savings
Urban	2178	2484	−306
Rural	5148	6095	−947
Estate	613	780	−167
Total	7937	9359	−1422

flows appearing in the SAM simply because they cannot be identified. To the extent that they are encapsulated by our estimates they will relate to the numerical components of the totals of rows 4, 5 and 6 of Table A.32.

This leaves the SES figures which make up the unadjusted *factor incomes* paid to labour and to other private non-corporate capital and the unadjusted *transfer payment* of private corporate capital returns distributed to households as being the major potential sources of downward bias in our household income figures. Reorganising the household section of Table A.35 and adding entries for savings and expenditures, we obtain Table A.37. In this table we have further separated out those parts of labour income received by households in the form of non-money factor payments and home-grown produce plus income from domestic services. To adjust these would be incompatible with their treatment in the consumption side of the accounts.* Pensions paid by private corporations are also assumed firm.

Finally, to be consistent with the government accounts we must regard incomes from employment in public administration and all direct taxes paid as being correct. It should be noted that the exclusion of public administration incomes will have, by far, the most significant impact upon the adjustment factors x, y and z. These factors are expected to exceed unity and represent the corrections required to incomes (subject to the above exceptions) from labour, non-corporate business capital and 'rents, interest and dividends' respectively.

Table A.37 also shows (unknown) savings and (known) expenditures for each

*The home-grown produce component of other private capital returns should also be excluded for the same reason but would create non-linearities in the balance equations to be solved later i.e. terms in xy and zy. Given the crudity of the exercise we have not therefore corrected for this 'known' element of non-corporate returns. A similar effect arises in the case of direct taxes and this has also been ignored.

Table A.37 *Distribution of household income by source (adjusted)*

Income/expenditure	Urban	Rural	Estate
Labour excluding public administration etc.	$799x$	$1546x$	$492x$
Other private non-corporate capital	$424y$	$1938y$	$19y$
Transfers from private corporations excluding pensions	$68z$	$32z$	z
Private housing	137	330	31
Labour incomes excluded above	637	1129	57
Transfers from government	91	151	6
Transfers from abroad	6	6	6
Pensions paid by private corporations	36	16	1
Total assuming $x = y = z = 1$	2178	5148	613
Savings	S_U	S_R	S_E
Expenditure	2484	6095	780

type of household. The balance of the household income accounts as in Table A.37 gives us the identities shown below in which the new income entries are substituted into the earlier statement of the same identities.

$$\left.\begin{aligned} s_U + 1557 &= 779x + 424y + 68 \\ s_R + 4463 &= 1546x + 1938y + 32 \\ s_E + 679 &= 492x + 19y + z \end{aligned}\right\} \quad (1)$$

From this point on we need to involve guesswork to a far greater degree than has previously been necessary if we are to be able to complete the story and identify the degree of underrecording of income indicated by the x, y and z coefficients. In what follows we present the results of logically following through one set of *plausible* assumptions. Alternative sets of plausible assumptions might possibly produce somewhat different results. However, we would stress again the need for statisticians and economists to chance their arms with assumptions of this kind if data inconsistencies of the type discussed in this section, and present in most developing countries in one form or another, are to be eliminated, thereby opening the way for the analytical use of data. We begin by attempting to estimate the distribution of ownership of private capital in Sri Lanka. The figures in Table A.38 show the results of this exercise and are not to be taken seriously in their own right. However they do provide a means of finding the factors x, y and z in Table A.37 which provide sensible estimates of income and hence of savings. To derive the sectoral breakdown of Table A.38 it has been assumed that the value of owner-occupied housing in each sector is proportional to the net imputed rental values of housing shown earlier. Similarly, ownership of non-corporate business capital plus other household capital is assumed proportional to non-corporate returns in Table A.35. Ownership of corporate business capital is assumed to be proportional to rent, interest and dividend payments in Table A.37. These are of course very crude assumptions. Equally crude is the assumption which completes the table that stocks of the three types of capital distinguished are proportional to investment in them as revealed by the 1966/67 *Survey of Private Investment* (Central Bank of Ceylon, 1970), with housing divided in value between owner-occupation and rented according to the ratio given by the SES. Clearly the crudity of some of these assumptions could be tempered significantly given rather more thorough research than we had opportunity for.

Crude as they are, the figures in Table A.38 give a rough guide to the percentage distribution of ownership of private capital as between Urban, Rural and

Table A.38 *The ownership of private capital*

Percentage shares of private capital	Urban	Rural	Estate	Total
Non-corporate business capital plus other household capital	5.9	27.1	0.3	33.3
Corporate business capital and rented houses	23.8	11.2	0.4	35.4
Owner-occupied houses	9.1	22.1	0.1	31.3
Total	38.8	60.4	0.8	100.0

Estate Households of 38.8 : 60.4 : 0.8. We now assume that savings by the three household types are in the same ratio; i.e. that savings are *proportional* to the ownership of wealth. Thus if K denotes private wealth and s is household savings, then $s = \mu K$, and our three balance equations for households become:

$$\left.\begin{aligned} 0.388\,\mu K + 1577 &= 779x + 0.059\lambda_1 K + 0.238\lambda_2 K \\ 0.604\,\mu K + 4463 &= 1546x + 0.271\lambda_1 K + 0.112\lambda_2 K \\ 0.008\,\mu K + 679 &= 492x + 0.003\lambda_1 K + 0.004\lambda_2 K \end{aligned}\right\} \quad (2)$$

where λ_1 can be interpreted as the rate of return on non-corporate business capital and other household capital (excluding houses), and λ_2 can be similarly interpreted as the rate of return on corporate business capital and houses to rent. Note that from the point of solving equations (1), the new set have merely transformed the y and z variables. The more significant step has been to reduce s_U, s_R and s_E to known proportions of total household savings μK.

For completeness we must now recognise that household savings plus corporate retained profits must add to 1863 to balance our accounts. Accordingly,

$$\mu K + 0.354\rho K = 1863$$

where the 1863 is the figure calculated earlier for the volume of private savings necessary to finance known investment: μK, as before, is household savings (as yet unknown); 0.354 is the share of the total capital stock in the form of corporate business capital and rented houses (from Table A.38); and ρ is the retained profits of the year expressed as a proportion of that corporate capital stock. It follows that the retentions ratio can be written as:

$$\frac{\rho}{\rho+\lambda_2}$$

It is clear from the three balance equations above that the solution for the *relative* values of λ_1 and λ_2 is not affected by the value of K. Hence, we can take an arbitrary numerical value for K. For ease of interpretation of the results let us assume a value for K of 35 000 m., which in conjunction with a national income figure of 11 360 m. implies a capital–output ratio of about 3:1.

This leaves us with three equations in four unknowns, x, λ_1, λ_2 and ρ (or x, y and z and μK if we solve the other set based on equations (1) and our estimates of sector shares in household savings). To remove the surplus degree of freedom we now assume that the retained profits of corporate businesses are just sufficient to finance business sector investment. We have already estimated the latter as 526 and so the implied value of ρ is given by

$$0.354\rho K = 526$$

Substituting $K = 35\,000$ m. we obtain $\rho = 0.042$ and hence $\mu = 0.038$. Substituting for μK and K, equations (2) can now be solved to yield:

$$x = 1.3302$$

$$\lambda_1 = 0.3190$$

$$\lambda_2 = 0.0477$$

Returning to equations (1), s_U, s_R, s_E, y and z are all obtained directly using the coefficients of equations (2) and the above solutions for λ_1, λ_2 and μK.

The savings of the three sectors and adjustment factors y and z are:

$s_U = 519 \quad y = 1.5615$

$s_R = 807 \quad z = 5.8474$

$s_E = 11$

Total 1337

The estimates for z and λ_2 will of course be rather sensitive to errors in the data, given the relatively small share of income initially attributed to rent, etc.

Subject of course to the assumptions which underlie their construction, the conclusions of this exercise are as follows. First, the SES appears to understate all three income categories (earned income, profits, and rent, etc.). However, the consequent adjustment for the relevant part of earned income (33 per cent) is substantially lower than that for profits (56 per cent) and for the small rent item where the SES entry has to be multiplied by a factor of 5.8. Secondly, our assumption about retained earnings being adequate to finance business investment is likely, if anything, to *understate* the need for household savings. Thus, the adjustment factors just referred to are potentially too low. Thirdly, the rate of return on business capital is only about one seventh of that on other capital. Finally, the retentions ratio of the business sector is of the order of 47 per cent $\left(\frac{\rho}{\rho + \lambda_2}\right)$.

Having conducted this exercise, we are able to use our estimates of the x, y and z coefficients to complete Table A.37 and to construct the balance of the institutions account shown in Table A.39, which contains the adjusted figures comparable to those shown in Table A.35.

Finally, bringing together the various component estimates deriving from the

Table A.39 *Adjusted tabulation of the sources of non-government institutional income*

Receiver / Source of income	Households			Corporations	
	Urban	Rural	Estate	Private	Public
Labour	1673	3185	711	–	–
Private capital					
Private housing	137	330	31	135	–
Other non-corporate	662	3026	30	–	–
Other corporate	–	–	–	1266	–
Public capital	–	–	–	–	174
Transfers from:					
Urban households	0	0	0	0	0
Rural households	0	0	0	0	0
Estate households	0	0	0	0	0
Private corporations	434	203	7	0	0
Public corporations	0	0	0	0	0
Government	91	151	6	57	237
Abroad	6	6	6	0	0
Total income	3003	6901	791	1458	411
– Savings	519	807	11	526	307
= Expenditure	2484	6095	780	932	104

procedure described above, we can fill in the algebraic elements of the matrix shown in Table A.32 and thus reproduce it as Table A.40.*

*The major difference between Table A.40 and Table A.36 of our original report stems from our reclassification of the institution 'Private business sector'. Only distributed profits of corporations are paid out to households in column (8); the 'profits' of unincorporated businesses are paid out not as a transfer but direct from the factor 'other private capital' in column (3).

Disaggregating the returns to employee labour and non-corporate capital according to occupation

We have dealt so far with aggregate returns to employee labour and non-corporate capital, the latter being the net income of self-employed workers and employers of unincorporated businesses. To help us disaggregate these incomes according to the principal occupation of the income receiver the following additional information is currently available.

(1) A money incomes matrix (**MI**) whose *ij*th element shows the income received by those in occupation *i* working in industry *j*. This includes *all* money incomes including transfers and is based on SES(4) tabulations.

(2) A matrix **MT** whose *ij*th element gives the income received by those in occupation *i* in the form of income type *j* (e.g. wages and salaries, SES profits, etc.). Unfortunately, this is not available by industry detail. We have already used the corresponding industry–income type matrix to construct estimates given earlier in Stage 8. Let us denote this **IT** with rows corresponding to industries. We have SES(2) data for **MT** and SES(4) data for **IT**.

(3) A matrix **IS** of money income receipts by industry *i* and employment status *j*, based on SES(4) data but with slightly less industrial detail than that used earlier.

In principle the tabulation of the employee incomes and non-corporate incomes by both industry and occupation would be possible by resorting to the SES returns but it seemed unreasonable to multiply our data requirements at this level given the problems encountered at earlier stages. However, there are several obstacles in the way of deriving occupational breakdowns by employment status using only the existing tabulations. In particular,

(*a*) industries and occupations are mixed with respect to employment status making it difficult to combine **IS** and **MI** in order to obtain the appropriate occupational breakdown of factor payments;

(*b*) the occupational structure of wage employment in a given industry may differ considerably from that for self-employment;

(*c*) there is no occupational breakdown of non-money factor payments Hence we have chosen not to use **IS**.

We have therefore proceeded by testing the assumption that the occupational structure of the payments to employee labour and the self-employed in each industry are identical by calculating what this implies for the occupational structure of aggregate returns to employee labour and returns to self-employment. These have then been compared with the SES data in Item (2) above. Since they are not too far out and since adjusting for the disparity would be an undue 'tampering' compared to the regrettable crudity of our calculations of underrecording in the previous section we reproduce here only a single table (Table A.41) based on **MI** giving the occupational structure to be applied to *both* sets of factor payments. With regard to point (*c*) above we have assumed that the distribution of non-money factor payments among different occupational categories within each employment status is the same as that for money income.

Finally we should emphasise that we have ignored the position of multiple job holding by attributing all factor payments received by the individual, first, to the industry of his principal employment; and second, to his principal occupation within that activity.

Table A.40 *Social-accounting matrix for Sri Lanka with disaggregation of institutions' current accounts and factor accounts (final) (Rs million)*

		Factor accounts				Institutions current accounts	
			Capital			Households	
		Labour	Private housing	Other private	Public	Urban	Rural
		(1)	(2)	(3)	(4)	(5)	(6)
Factor accounts	(1) Labour	0	0	0	0	38	56
	(2) Capital: Housing	0	0	0	0	0	0
	(3) Other private	0	0	0	0	0	0
	(4) Public	0	0	0	0	0	0
Institutions current accounts	Households:						
	(5) Urban	1673	138	662	0	0	0
	(6) Rural	3185	330	3026	0	0	0
	(7) Estate	711	31	30	0	0	0
	(8) Private business sector	0	135	1266	0	0	0
	(9) Public corporations	0	0	0	174	0	0
	(10) Government	0	0	0	0	368	195
	(11) Institutions combined capital	0	0	0	0	519	807
	(12) Production activities	0	0	0	0	1871	5103
	(13) Rest of world	0	0	0	0	207	741
	Total	5569	633	4984	174	3003	6901

Estate	Private corporations	Public corporations	Government	Institutions combined capital	Production activities	Rest of the world	Total
(7)	(8)	(9)	(10)	(11)	(12)	(13)	
6	0	0	1275	0	4194	0	5569
0	0	0	0	0	633	0	633
0	0	0	0	0	5097	–113	4984
0	0	0	0	0	174	0	174
0	434	0	91	0	0	6	3003
0	203	0	151	0	0	6	6901
0	7	0	6	0	0	6	791
0	0	0	57	0	0	0	1458
0	0	0	237	0	0	0	411
4	272	104	0	314	856	130	2241
11	526	307	43	0	0	425	2640
627	0	0	302	1962	4358	2113	16 336
143	16	0	79	364	1024	–	2573
791	1458	411	2241	2640	16 336	2573	

Table 41(a) *Payments to labour (employee labour plus self-employment) by occupational group (as percentage of row totals) – urban sector*

Production activity \ Occupation	Occupation unspecified	Professional technical and related workers	Adminis-trative, executive and managerial workers	Clerical workers	Sales workers	Agricul-tural workers	Miners, quarrymen and related workers	Transport and com-munication workers	Craftsmen, production process workers and labourers	Service, sports and recreation workers
1 Tea		8.8	38.2	18.4		29.6			5.0	
2 Rubber			51.1	12.8		36.1				
3 Coconuts			24.4			70.7			0.7	4.2
4 Paddy						99.5		0.5		
5 Livestock						64.6			35.4	
6 Fishing		0.9	0.4	2.5	0.8	94.4			1.0	
7 Logging and firewood				38.8	17.7	21.6			21.9	
8 Other agriculture			2.2	1.3	58.7	36.0		0.7	0.5	0.6
9 Mining and quarrying					15.4		55.4		29.2	
10a Rice milling	0.2		25.6	9.4	20.5	0.4		2.6	38.1	3.2
10b Flour milling	0.2		25.6	9.4	20.5	0.4		2.6	38.1	3.2
11 Dairy products	0.2		25.6	9.4	20.5	0.4		2.6	38.1	3.2
12 Bread	0.2		25.6	9.4	20.5	0.4		2.6	38.1	3.2
13 Other bakery products	0.2		25.6	9.4	20.5	0.4		2.6	38.1	3.2
14 Carbonated beverages				56.5	12.5			11.3	19.7	
15 Desiccated coconut	0.2		25.6	9.4	20.5	0.4		2.6	38.1	3.2
16 Other processed food	0.2		25.6	9.4	20.5	0.4		2.6	38.1	3.2
17 Distilling				56.5	12.5			11.3	19.7	
18 Tobacco			4.3	13.0	16.5			2.6	58.6	5.0
19 Textiles		1.0	6.4	9.4	2.5			1.7	78.1	0.9
20 Wood products			6.9	1.7	5.7			1.4	84.3	
21 Paper	0.7	14.5	8.7	15.8	8.7			1.4	48.1	2.1
22 Leather		5.1	9.2	30.1	20.8				34.8	
23 Rubber		5.2	21.4	40.5	7.3	1.0		1.6	21.8	1.2
24 Chemicals		26.9	22.6	11.7	7.4				28.5	2.9
25 Oils and fats	0.2		25.6	9.4	20.5	0.4		2.6	38.1	3.2
26 Coconut fibre and yarn			24.4			70.7			0.7	4.2
27 Petroleum and coal			23.5	53.8	2.9				19.8	
28 Structural clay products		6.3	8.7	11.8	42.7				27.9	2.6
29 Ceramics		6.3	8.7	11.8	42.7				27.9	2.6
30 Cement		6.3	8.7	11.8	42.7				27.9	2.6
31 Basic metals		22.4	50.2	11.9					15.5	
32 Light engineering		9.9	16.1	10.2	10.7				53.1	
33 Transport equipment		11.7	16.3	11.6	7.0			1.9	48.9	2.6
34 Machinery, other equipment		11.7	16.3	11.6	7.0			1.9	48.9	2.6
35 Other manufacturing			10.6	10.6	17.3			1.7	58.3	1.5
36 Construction		11.8	1.1	7.1	3.3	0.3		1.0	73.2	2.2
37 Electricity		24.1	1.2	16.4	8.2			5.0	43.7	1.4
38 Road passenger transport		6.3	15.1	17.4	0.8	0.2		37.4	19.7	3.1
39 Rail transport		6.3	15.1	17.4	0.8	0.2		37.4	19.7	3.1
40a Wholesale trade		1.1	25.8	29.5	28.1	0.7		1.7	11.8	1.3
40b Retail trade		0.2	8.6	6.3	80.9	0.3		0.6	2.7	0.4
40c Other transport		6.3	15.1	17.4	0.8	0.2		37.4	19.7	3.1
41a Communication		2.5	3.0	21.9	4.7			63.8	3.3	0.8
41b Hotels and restaurants		0.4	14.8	8.8	46.2			1.2	2.9	25.7
41c Professional services		58.1	12.4	14.1	5.7				6.2	3.5
41d Dwellings										
41e Other services	0.2	33.3	14.6	19.7	7.7		0	2.2	8.3	14.0
Domestic service										100.0
Public administration		44.7	9.3	24.5	0.1	0.2		2.3	9.3	9.6
Unspecified	71.0	0.9	3.1	3.7	3.9	0.1		0.2	16.5	0.6

rural sector

Production activity \ Occupation	Occupation unspecified	Professional technical and related workers	Adminis-trative, executive and managerial workers	Clerical workers	Sales workers	Agricul-tural workers	Miners, quarrymen and related workers	Transport and com-munication workers	Craftsmen, production process workers and labourers	Service, sports and recreation workers
1 Tea			3.0	0.8		88.3		1.3	1.7	4.9
2 Rubber					0.2	99.0			0.8	
3 Coconuts			7.0	0.9	1.0	81.3			2.7	7.1
4 Paddy		0	0.3	0	0.3	98.9		0.4	0.1	0
5 Livestock						93.1			6.9	
6 Fishing				2.7		90.8			5.0	1.5
7 Logging and firewood						71.9			28.1	
8 Other agriculture		0.1			0.6	96.6			1.7	1.0
9 Mining and quarrying			5.7		4.9		49.1		40.3	
10a Rice milling		3.0	4.6		14.9	13.9		0.6	57.3	5.7
10b Flour milling		3.0	4.6		14.9	13.9		0.6	57.3	5.7
11 Dairy products		3.0	4.6		14.9	13.9		0.6	57.3	5.7
12 Bread		3.0	4.6		14.9	13.9		0.6	57.3	5.7
13 Other bakery products		3.0	4.6		14.9	13.9		0.6	57.3	5.7
14 Carbonated beverages					23.7	76.3				
15 Desiccated coconut		3.0	4.6		14.9	13.9		0.6	57.3	5.7
16 Other processed food		3.0	4.6		14.9	13.9		0.6	57.3	5.7
17 Distilling					23.7	76.3				
18 Tobacco						11.9	8.1		80.0	
19 Textiles		1.6	3.8	1.5					92.7	0.4
20 Wood products			1.2	4.9	4.1	3.6		0.9	83.5	1.8
21 Paper				35.4					45.7	18.9
22 Leather				39.3					60.7	
23 Rubber	4.8			25.3					69.9	
24 Chemicals		3.7		8.2	5.5	2.3			80.3	
25 Oils and fats		3.0	4.6		14.9	13.9		0.6	57.3	5.7
26 Coconut fibre and yarn			7.0	0.9	1.0	81.3			2.7	7.1
27 Petroleum and coal								69.3	30.7	
28 Structural clay products								4.8	92.9	2.3
29 Ceramics								4.8	92.9	2.3
30 Cement								4.8	92.9	2.3
31 Basic metals					15.1				84.9	
32 Light engineering									100.0	
33 Transport equipment				15.0					85.0	
34 Machinery, other equipment				15.0					85.0	
35 Other manufacturing			7.3						92.7	
36 Construction		4.5	1.6	3.5	1.0			5.1	82.7	1.6
37 Electricity				11.6		3.8		8.1	76.5	
38 Road passenger transport	0.5	1.7	3.1	5.1		1.8		61.5	25.6	0.7
39 Rail transport	0.5	1.7	3.1	5.1		1.8		61.5	25.6	0.7
40a Wholesale trade			25.6	20.3	33.9	1.2			13.5	5.5
40b Retail trade			5.8	3.9	85.8			0.5	2.5	1.5
40c Other transport	0.5	1.7	3.1	5.1		1.8		61.5	25.6	0.7
41a Communication				33.9	0.7			57.5	7.9	
41b Hotels and restaurants			4.8	3.7	50.7				4.3	36.5
41c Professional services		56.9	1.7	10.1				3.3	16.3	11.7
41d Dwellings										
41e Other services		15.0	2.2	13.1	7.6	0.5		1.7	15.9	44.0
Domestic services										100.0
Public administration		50.6	2.3	21.8	0.3	0.7	0.4	4.5	9.5	9.9
Unspecified	67.2	0.3		1.2	0.4	1.3	0.0		28.6	1.0

Table A.41(c) *Payments to labour (employee labour plus self-employment) by occupational group (as percentage of row totals) – estate sector*

Production activity \ Occupation	Occupation unspecified	Professional technical and related workers	Adminis-tative, executive and managerial workers	Clerical workers	Sales workers	Agricul-tural workers	Miners, quarrymen and related workers	Transport and com-munication workers	Craftsmen, production process workers and labourers	Service, sports and recreation workers
1 Tea		0.3	1.8	3.6		92.1		0.3	1.1	0.8
2 Rubber		1.0		1.8	0.7	93.8			1.1	1.6
3 Coconuts			6.0	6.3		78.1		1.7		7.9
4 Paddy								100.0		
5 Livestock						100.0				
6 Fishing					100.0					
7 Logging and firewood										
8 Other agriculture			16.1			61.5		10.3		12.1
9 Mining and quarrying										
10a Rice milling		20.3			11.2	2.4		20.1	46.0	
10b Flour milling		20.3			11.2	2.4		20.1	46.0	
11 Dairy products		20.3			11.2	2.4		20.1	46.0	
12 Bread		20.3			11.2	2.4		20.1	46.0	
13 Other bakery products		20.3			11.2	2.4		20.1	46.0	
14 Carbonated beverages										
15 Desiccated coconut		20.3			11.2	2.4		20.1	46.0	
16 Other processed food		20.3			11.2	2.4		20.1	46.0	
17 Distilling										
18 Tobacco									100.0	
19 Textiles		5.2							94.8	
20 Wood products									100.0	
21 Paper										
22 Leather										
23 Rubber										
24 Chemicals										
25 Oils and fats		20.3			11.2	2.4		20.1	46.0	
26 Coconut fibre and yarn			6.0	6.3		78.1		1.7		7.9
27 Petroleum and coal										
28 Structural clay products										
29 Ceramics										
30 Cement										
31 Basic metals									100.0	
32 Light engineering										
33 Transport equipment									100.0	
34 Machinery, other equipment									100.0	
35 Other manufacturing									100.0	
36 Construction		32.7		10.5		8.2			48.6	
37 Electricity									100.0	
38 Road passenger transport								81.0	7.2	11.8
39 Rail transport								81.0	7.2	11.8
40a Wholesale trade					100.0					
40b Retail trade			6.4	5.1	83.2	2.3			3.0	
40c Other transport								81.0	7.2	11.8
41a Communication								100.0		
41b Hotels and restaurants									12.1	87.9
41c Professional services		100.0								
41d Dwellings										
41e Other services		1.8	2.0	1.1				2.0	12.6	80.5
Domestic service										100.0
Public administration		82.7		9.4					4.2	3.7
Unspecified	62.7								37.3	

Table 41(d) Payments to labour (employee labour plus self-employment) by occupational group (as percentage of row totals) – all island

Production activity \ Occupation	Occupation unspecified	Professional technical and related workers	Administative, executive and managerial workers	Clerical workers	Sales workers	Agricultural workers	Miners, quarrymen and related workers	Transport and communication workers	Craftsmen, production process workers and labourers	Service, sports and recreation workers
1 Tea		0.5	2.9	3.6	–	89.8		0.5	1.3	1.4
2 Rubber		0.4	1.1	0.9	0.4	95.7		–	0.9	0.6
3 Coconuts		–	8.3	1.4	0.8	80.1		0.2	2.3	6.9
4 Paddy		0	0.3	0	0.3	98.9		0.4	0.1	0
5 Livestock						89.7			10.3	
6 Fishing		0.4	0.2	2.6	0.4	92.3			3.3	0.8
7 Logging and firewood				7.2	3.3	62.6			26.9	
8 Other agriculture		0.1	0.4	0.1	5.2	91.3		0.2	1.5	1.2
9 Mining and quarrying			5.0		6.3		49.9		38.8	
10a Rice milling	0.1	2.6	12.3	3.6	16.9	8.3		2.2	49.5	4.5
10b Flour milling	0.1	2.6	12.3	3.6	16.9	8.3		2.2	49.5	4.5
11 Dairy products	0.1	2.6	12.3	3.6	16.9	8.3		2.2	49.5	4.5
12 Bread	0.1	2.6	12.3	3.6	16.9	8.3		2.2	49.5	4.5
13 Other bakery products	0.1	2.6	12.3	3.6	16.9	8.3		2.2	49.5	4.5
14 Carbonated beverages				20.7	19.6	48.4		4.1	7.2	
15 Desiccated coconut	0.1	2.6	12.3	3.6	16.9	8.3		2.2	49.5	4.5
16 Other processed food	0.1	2.6	12.3	3.6	16.9	8.3		2.2	49.5	4.5
17 Distilling				20.7	19.6	48.4		4.1	7.2	
18 Tobacco			1.0	3.0	12.9	6.2		0.6	75.2	1.1
19 Textiles		1.5	4.5	3.7	0.7			0.5	88.5	0.6
20 Wood products			2.8	4.0	4.5	2.6		1.0	83.8	1.3
21 Paper	0.3	7.1	4.3	25.8	4.2			0.7	46.9	10.7
22 Leather		2.8	5.1	34.2	11.5				46.4	
23 Rubber	1.6	3.4	14.3	35.5	4.8	0.6		1.1	37.9	0.8
24 Chemicals		17.1	13.1	10.2	6.6	1.0			50.3	1.7
25 Oils and fats	0.1	2.6	12.3	3.6	16.9	8.3		2.2	49.5	4.5
26 Coconut fibre and yarn			8.3	1.4	0.8	80.1		0.2	2.3	6.9
27 Petroleum and coal			14.1	32.3	1.8			27.6	24.2	
28 Structural clay products		1.6	2.2	2.9	10.6			3.6	76.7	2.4
29 Ceramics		1.6	2.2	2.9	10.6			3.6	76.7	2.4
30 Cement		1.6	2.2	2.9	10.6			3.6	76.7	2.4
31 Basic metals		10.9	24.4	5.8	7.4				51.5	
32 Light engineering		2.9	4.8	3.0	3.2				86.1	
33 Transport equipment		8.3	11.6	12.6	5.0			1.4	59.3	1.8
34 Machinery, other equipment		8.3	11.6	12.6	5.0			1.4	59.3	1.8
35 Other manufacturing			8.4	3.5	5.7			0.6	81.3	0.5
36 Construction		6.9	1.5	4.6	1.6	0.2		3.9	79.6	1.7
37 Electricity		11.0	0.5	13.7	3.8	2.0		6.6	61.8	0.6
38 Road passenger transport	0.3	3.6	8.1	10.2	0.3	1.1		51.6	23.0	1.8
39 Rail transport	0.3	3.6	8.1	10.2	0.3	1.1		51.6	23.0	1.8
40a Wholesale trade		0.5	25.7	24.7	31.1	1.0		0.8	12.7	3.5
40b Retail trade		0.1	6.9	4.8	83.9	0.1		0.5	2.6	1.1
40c Other transport	0.3	3.6	8.1	10.2	0.3	1.1		51.6	23.0	1.8
41a Communication		0.8	1.0	29.9	2.0			59.6	6.4	0.3
41b Hotels and restaurants		0.1	8.6	5.6	48.9			0.4	3.8	32.6
41c Professional services		58.4	6.7	11.8	2.7			1.7	11.2	7.5
41d Dwellings										
41e Other services	0.1	23.5	8.2	16.0	7.5	0.2		1.9	12.1	30.5
Domestic services										100.0
Public administration	68.7	48.3	5.2	22.8	0.2	0.5	0.3	3.6	9.4	9.7
Unspecified	18.7	0.5	1.3	2.3	1.8	0.8	–	0.1	23.7	0.8

APPENDIX 2

The construction of the manpower matrix

In this second appendix, we turn our attention to one of the crucial *physical* tables underlying the *money flows* matrix described in the previous appendix. This is the table which we have labelled the *manpower matrix* which shows the volume of employment by both industrial and occupational classifications.

A comparison between the SAM and SES classifications of industries has already been given in Appendix 1, Table A.27(a). Unfortunately certain production activities identified separately in the SAM are aggregated at the minor industrial division level of the SES classification. This occurs particularly for food industries 10a–13, 15, 16 and 25. For the manufacturing sector our disaggregation of employment and incomes data given in the SES has used statistics on value added per man in 1968, provided in the course of the UNDP project. See also Divatia and Srivastava (1971). Where SAM activities were aggregated in the SES their respective value added figures (see Appendix 1) were multiplied by the reciprocals of the productivity estimates to obtain employment estimates. These estimates were then scaled (severely so for activities 14 and 17 for which productivity estimates appear double those consistent with the SES) so that their sum accorded with the appropriate SES minor division for employment. The occupational structures of the SAM activities were assumed to be the same as the aggregate SES structure. An identical procedure was followed in constructing the (unadjusted) manpower incomes matrix. The three transportation activities 38, 39 and 40c were identified separately using the value added figures of the SAM and employment figures from the CBR, 1972, Table II(C)8. A common occupational structure was again adopted.

The services sector required extensive reclassification involving the aggregation of parts of different SES minor divisions. In the case of the manpower incomes matrix the statistics for wages and salaries given in the government accounts were substituted for those obtained from the SES (for example, the SES public administration figure was increased by 36 per cent). Otherwise the classification of SES data according to SAM production activities was based on the following principal adjustments:

(i) Income from self-employment recorded against those SES divisions which comprise the government institution in the SAM were excluded from the factor incomes paid out by category. These excluded incomes were attributed to an appropriate production activity (e.g. SES profits recorded against medical, dental, etc. services were classified as professional services in the SAM).

(ii) Parts of SES divisions 92, 93 and 98 allocated to different SAM activities were determined on the basis of a detailed breakdown of the government accounts (for 92 and 93), value added shares and some independent manpower estimates using details from the 1968 manpower matrix.

(iii) Having determined the total employment and total income accruing to employee labour and self-employment for each of the SAM activities 41c, 41e and government, they were disaggregated by occupation. The occupational structures of constituent SES divisions or parts of divisions were weighted according to their contributions to total employment and total incomes in each of the three SAM activities. The two sets of weights differ because the SES incomes data for the government institution was replaced by more reliable figures from the government accounts. In the case of employment weights these simply adopt the redistribution of SES industries without any change in aggregate employment.

Thus the adjustments for underrecording which were estimated in Appendix 1 (Stage 8) apply only to incomes and not to employment. Furthermore, they apply only to factor incomes from production activities not from employment by institutions. Factor incomes generated by government and households are separately adjusted to agree with estimates recorded elsewhere in the SAM.

A final point concerning payments to domestic servants is in order. According to the Preliminary Manpower Matrix for 1968 (UNDP Vol. IV) there were 51 456 maids and related housekeeping service workers not elsewhere specified employed in personal services. The SES(4) records 101.1 thousand employed but only 9.9 thousand income receivers. This is largely due to the exclusion of incomes received by domestic servants in the definition of household income (see SES Preliminary Report, October 1971, Appendix). We might have assumed that all the non-income receivers were domestic servants. This would include no doubt some unpaid family workers in this occupational group but there is no further information to enable us to correct for this. We have assumed a figure of 65 thousand. Payments to domestic servants recorded in the expenditure side of the SES amount to an average of Rs 1.49 per month per household. For all households for the year 1969/70 this would come to about Rs 36 m. An average money income *plus* non-money income of Rs 130 per month for domestic servants would, however, yield an estimate of Rs 100 m. value added contributed by this group of workers. This has been adopted in the consumption sector of the SAM but, as pointed out in Appendix 1 (Stage 1) it is still well below the Rs 337 m. given in the CBR.

The sectoral disaggregation of the manpower matrix and manpower incomes matrix follows the above procedure but uses the sectoral data provided in the SES. In the case of government employment falling under the government institution in the SAM, the sectoral breakdown of employment *and* income also follows that given in the SES. There is no sectoral disaggregation of government wages and salaries available in the government accounts which might otherwise have been used.

Tables A.42(a) to (d) show the manpower matrices for urban, rural and estate sectors and all-island respectively. Tables A.41(a) to (d) have already shown the corresponding sectoral manpower *incomes* matrices in percentage form.

Table A.42(a) *Employed population by industry and occupation – urban sector (000s)*

Production activity	Occupation unspecified	Professional technical and related workers	Adminis-trative, executive and managerial workers	Clerical workers	Sales workers	Agricul-tural workers	Miners, quarrymen and related workers	Transport and com-munication workers	Craftsmen, production process workers and labourers	Service, sports and recreation workers	Total
1 Tea		0.1	0.3	0.7		1.4			0.3		2.9
2 Rubber			0.1	0.1		0.8					1.0
3 Coconuts			0.2			1.4			–	0.2	1.8
4 Paddy						15.6		0.1			15.7
5 Livestock						0.4			0.2		0.6
6 Fishing		0.1	0.1	0.3	0.1	21.0			0.4		21.9
7 Logging and firewood				0.1	0.1	0.2			0.2		0.5
8 Other agriculture			0.1	0.1	0.4	5.0		0.1	0.1	0.1	5.8
9 Mining and quarrying					0.2		0.9		0.7		1.8
10a Rice milling	–		0.1	0.1	0.1	–		–	0.9	0.1	1.3
10b Flour milling	–		0.1	–	0.1	–		–	0.4	–	0.6
11 Dairy products	–		0.1	0.1	0.1	–		–	0.5	–	0.8
12 Bread	–		0.3	0.2	0.4	–		0.1	2.5	0.2	3.7
13 Other bakery products	–		0.1	0.1	0.2	–		–	1.2	0.1	1.8
14 Carbonated beverages				0.1	–			–	0.1		0.2
15 Desiccated coconut	–		–	–	–	–		–	0.1	–	0.2
16 Other processed	–		0.2	0.1	0.2	–		0.1	1.4	0.1	2.1
17 Distilling				0.3	0.1			0.1	0.2		0.8
18 Tobacco			0.1	0.2	0.4			0.1	3.3	0.2	4.3
19 Textiles		0.3	0.3	1.3	0.6			0.2	20.8	0.2	23.6
20 Wood products			0.3	0.2	0.4			0.2	19.2		20.3
21 Paper	0.1	0.7	0.2	0.9	0.3			0.1	4.4	0.1	6.9
22 Leather		0.1	0.1	0.3	0.2				0.9		1.6
23 Rubber		0.2	0.1	0.9	0.2	0.1		0.1	1.2	0.1	2.9
24 Chemicals		0.7	0.3	0.5	0.2				4.1	0.2	6.0
25 Oils and fats	–		–	–	–	–		–	0.1	–	0.1
26 Coconut fibre and yarn			0.1			0.9			–	0.1	1.1
27 Petroleum and coal			0.1	0.7	0.1				0.4		1.3
28 Structural clay products		0.1	–	0.2					0.9	0.1	1.5
29 Ceramics		0.1	–	0.1	0.1				0.7	0.1	1.1
30 Cement		–	–	–	–				0.2	–	0.3
31 Basic metals		0.2	0.2	0.2					0.6		1.1
32 Light engineering		0.1	0.1	0.2	0.1				1.5		2.0
33 Transport equipment		0.1	0.1	0.3	0.2			0.1	1.4	0.1	2.2
34 Machinery, other equipment		0.1	0.1	0.3	0.2			0.1	1.6	0.1	2.5
35 Other manufacturing			0.1	0.3	0.4			0.1	2.0	0.1	3.1
36 Construction		1.1	0.2	1.0	0.2	0.2		0.2	19.3	0.5	22.6
37 Electricity		0.5	0.1	0.5	0.2			0.2	3.3	0.1	4.8
38 Road passenger transport		0.5	0.5	2.4	0.1	–		6.6	4.2	0.6	15.0
39 Rail transport		0.3	0.3	1.5	0.1	–		4.1	2.6	0.4	9.2
40a Wholesale trade		0.1	1.7	6.3	3.2	0.2		0.5	3.9	0.7	16.4
40b Retail trade		0.1	2.6	3.7	67.0	0.3		0.4	3.4	0.5	78.0
40c Other transport		1.1	1.0	5.0	0.2	0.1		13.6	8.6	1.3	30.8
41a Communication		0.1	0.1	1.5	0.1			4.3	0.4	0.1	6.5
41b Hotels and restaurants		0.1	0.7	1.0	2.7			0.1	0.4	3.8	8.9
41c Professional services		3.5	0.3	2.0	0.5				1.2	0.6	8.2
41d Dwellings											
41e Other services	0.2	6.7	2.0	7.4	1.9			1.8	7.6	32.9	60.7
Public administration		38.0	3.3	21.1	0.1	0.1		2.8	15.3	9.8	90.6
Domestic servants										24.6	24.6
Unspecified	0.8	0.8	0.7	2.8	3.5	0.1		0.1	27.7	0.7	37.3
Total	1.2	55.7	17.5	65.3	85.6	47.9	0.9	36.1	170.4	80.4	561.0

... and occupation – rural sector ('000s)

Production activity	Occupation unspecified	Professional technical and related workers	Adminis-trative, executive and managerial workers	Clerical workers	Sales workers	Agricul-tural workers	Miners, quarrymen and related workers	Transport and com-munication workers	Craftsmen, production process workers and labourers	Service, sports and recreation workers	Total
1 Tea			0.5	0.7		92.4		0.8	1.5	2.0	97.9
2 Rubber			0.5		0.4	116.7			1.5		119.0
3 Coconuts			0.8	0.2	0.2	38.1			0.9	3.3	43.5
4 Paddy		0.7	0.4	0.4	0.7	698.0		1.7	1.1	0.4	703.3
5 Livestock						5.6			1.0		6.6
6 Fishing				0.5		26.6			1.3	0.4	28.8
7 Logging and firewood				0.5		3.4			2.2		6.0
8 Other agriculture		0.5			0.7	208.7			3.1	1.7	214.7
9 Mining and quarrying			0.5		0.8		10.9		7.3		19.4
10a Rice milling		0.1	0.1		0.4	0.5		–	2.5	0.2	3.8
10b Flour milling		–	0.1		0.2	0.3		–	1.3	0.1	1.9
11 Dairy products		0.1	0.1		0.3	0.3		–	1.6	0.1	2.5
12 Bread		0.3	0.3		1.2	1.4		0.1	7.3	0.5	11.1
13 Other bakery products		0.1	0.1		0.6	0.7		0.1	3.6	0.2	5.4
14 Carbonated beverages					0.1	0.4					0.5
15 Desiccated coconut		–	–		0.1	0.1		–	0.3	–	0.5
16 Other processed food		0.1	0.2		0.7	0.8		–	4.2	0.3	6.3
17 Distilling					0.3	1.5					1.8
18 Tobacco					1.3	2.2			32.0		35.4
19 Textiles		0.5	1.2	0.5					88.9	0.3	91.4
20 Wood products			0.4	1.2	1.1	2.3		0.4	63.4	1.1	69.8
21 Paper				1.8					5.3		8.0
22 Leather				0.4					1.3		1.7
23 Rubber	0.4			0.4				–	3.0		3.7
24 Chemicals		0.4		0.8	0.4	1.5			6.1		9.1
25 Oils and fats		–	–		–	0.1		–	0.3	–	0.4
26 Coconut fibre and yarn			0.5	0.1	0.1	24.1			0.6	2.1	27.5
27 Petroleum and coal								0.5	1.0		1.5
28 Structural clay products								0.4	10.6	0.2	11.3
29 Ceramics								0.3	7.8	0.1	8.3
30 Cement								0.1	2.1	–	2.2
31 Basic metals					1.0				3.1		4.1
32 Light engineering									6.9		6.9
33 Transport equipment				0.2					1.1		1.2
34 Machinery, other equipment				0.2					1.2		1.4
35 Other manufacturing			0.4						4.9		5.3
36 Construction		2.0	0.5	1.9	0.4			2.2	68.0	1.4	76.4
37 Electricity				0.7		0.7		0.8	7.1		9.4
38 Road passenger transport		0.4	0.3	0.9		0.5		16.8	6.5	0.2	25.7
39 Rail transport		0.2	0.2	0.6		0.3		10.4	4.0	0.1	15.9
40a Wholesale trade			2.6	5.4	9.2	0.5			6.4	1.2	25.3
40b Retail trade			5.6	6.3	140.7			1.3	7.4	2.9	164.2
40c Other transport		0.7	0.7	1.9		0.9		34.7	13.5	0.5	52.9
41a Communication				0.6	0.4			9.4	1.3		16.8
41b Hotels and restaurants			0.7	1.2	15.4				2.6	11.3	31.2
41c Professional services		7.3	0.5	2.2				0.6	3.5	2.1	16.2
41d Dwellings											
41e Other services		8.7	0.8	8.7	1.7	1.0		1.3	16.9	57.6	96.6
Public administration		87.7	1.8	30.4	0.4	1.4	0.7	6.7	24.4	19.6	172.7
Domestic servants										36.2	36.2
Unspecified	6.0	0.8		2.0	0.7	3.5	0.5		81.6	2.0	97.2
Total	6.4	110.2	19.6	75.8	179.3	1234.2	12.1	88.8	523.4	152.0	2401.7

Table A.42(c) *Employed population by industry and occupation – estate sector (000s)*

Production activity \ Occupation	Occupation unspecified	Professional technical and related workers	Adminis-trative, executive and managerial workers	Clerical workers	Sales workers	Agricul-tural workers	Miners, quarrymen and related workers	Transport and com-munication workers	Craftsmen, production process workers and labourers	Service, sports and recreation workers	Total
1 Tea		0.6	0.6	3.8		494.3		0.7	3.7	2.5	506.3
2 Rubber		0.1		0.5	0.6	68.5			0.3	0.8	70.8
3 Coconuts			0.1	0.2		5.7		0.1		0.4	6.5
4 Paddy						0.1		0.1			0.2
5 Livestock						0.3					0.3
6 Fishing					0.1						0.1
7 Logging and firewood											
8 Other agriculture			0.1			1.9		0.1		0.3	2.5
9 Mining and quarrying											
10a Rice milling									0.1		0.2
10b Flour milling									0.1		0.1
11 Dairy products									0.1		0.1
12 Bread		0.1							0.3		0.5
13 Other bakery products									0.2		0.2
14 Carbonated beverages											
15 Desiccated coconut											
16 Other processed food									0.2		0.2
17 Distilling											
18 Tobacco									0.1		0.1
19 Textiles		0.1							1.1		1.2
20 Wood products									0.3		0.3
21 Paper											
22 Leather											
23 Rubber											
24 Chemicals											
25 Oils and fats											
26 Coconut fibre and yarn			0.1	0.1		3.6				0.3	4.1
27 Petroleum and coal											
28 Structural clay products											
29 Ceramics											
30 Cement											
31 Basic metals									0.2		0.2
32 Light engineering											
33 Transport equipment									0.1		0.1
34 Machinery, other equipment									0.1		0.1
35 Other manufacturing									0.1		0.1
36 Construction		0.3		0.1		0.1			0.8		1.3
37 Electricity									0.1		0.1
38 Road passenger transport								0.4			0.4
39 Rail transport								0.2			0.2
40a Wholesale trade					0.1						0.1
40b Retail trade			0.3	0.3	4.9	0.1			0.1		5.7
40c Other transport								0.8	0.1	0.1	0.9
41a Communication				0.1				0.1			0.3
41b Hotels and restaurants									0.1	0.6	0.7
41c Professional services		0.3									0.3
41d Dwellings											
41e Other services		0.1	0.1	0.1				0.1	0.8	4.7	6.0
Public administration		1.8		0.1					0.4	0.3	2.6
Domestic servants										4.2	4.2
Unspecified	0.1								3.2		3.4
Total	0.1	3.5		1.4	5.9	574.9		2.9	12.5	14.0	620.5

Production activity \ Occupation	Occupation unspecified	Professional technical and related workers	Administrative, executive and managerial workers	Clerical workers	Sales workers	Agricultural workers	Miners, quarrymen and related workers	Transport and communication workers	Craftsmen, production process workers and labourers	Service, sports and recreation workers	Total
1 Tea		0.7	1.4	5.3		588.1		1.5	5.5	4.5	607.1
2 Rubber		0.1	0.6	0.6	0.9	186.1			1.8	0.8	190.8
3 Coconuts			1.1	0.4	0.2	45.1		0.1	0.9	3.9	51.7
4 Paddy		0.7	0.4	0.4	0.7	713.7		1.9	1.1	0.4	719.2
5 Livestock						6.3			1.2		7.5
6 Fishing		0.1	0.1	0.8	0.2	47.6			1.7	0.4	50.8
7 Logging and firewood				0.6	0.1	3.6			2.3		6.5
8 Other agriculture		0.5	0.2	0.1	1.1	215.6		0.2	3.2	2.0	222.9
9 Mining and quarrying			0.5		1.0		11.8		8.0		21.2
10a Rice milling		0.1	0.2	0.1	0.6	0.5		0.1	3.5	0.2	5.3
10b Flour milling		0.1	0.1	–	0.3	0.3		–	1.8	0.1	2.7
11 Dairy products		0.1	0.1	0.1	0.4	0.3		0.1	2.2	0.1	3.4
12 Bread		0.3	0.6	0.2	1.6	1.5		0.3	10.1	0.6	15.3
13 Other bakery products		0.2	0.3	0.1	0.8	0.7		0.1	5.0	0.3	7.5
14 Carbonated beverages				0.1	0.1	0.4		–	0.1		0.7
15 Desiccated coconut		–	–	–	0.1	0.1		–	0.5	–	0.7
16 Other processed food		0.2	0.3	0.1	0.9	0.9		0.2	5.8	0.3	8.7
17 Distilling				0.3	0.4	1.5		0.1	0.2		2.6
18 Tobacco			0.1	0.2	1.7	2.2		0.1	35.3	0.2	39.8
19 Textiles		0.9	1.5	1.8	0.6			0.2	110.7	0.5	116.2
20 Wood products			0.7	1.4	1.5	2.3		0.6	82.9	1.1	90.4
21 Paper	0.1	0.7	0.2	2.7	0.3			0.1	10.7	0.9	15.7
22 Leather		0.1	0.1	0.7	0.2				2.2		3.2
23 Rubber	0.4	0.2	0.1	1.2	0.2	0.1		0.1	4.2	0.1	6.6
24 Chemicals		1.0	0.3	1.4	0.6	1.5			10.3	0.2	15.1
25 Oils and fats					0.1	0.1			0.4	–	0.6
26 Coconut fibre and yarn			0.7	0.2	0.1	28.6			0.6	2.4	32.7
27 Petroleum and coal			0.1	0.7	0.1			0.5	1.4		2.7
28 Structural clay products		0.1	–	0.2	0.2			0.4	11.6	0.3	12.8
29 Ceramics		0.1		0.1	0.1			0.3	8.5	0.2	9.3
30 Cement		–	–	–	–			0.1	2.3	–	2.5
31 Basic metals		0.2	0.2	0.2	1.0				3.9		5.4
32 Light engineering		0.1	0.1	0.2	0.1				8.4		8.9
33 Transport equipment		0.1	0.1	0.4	0.2			0.1	2.5	0.1	3.5
34 Machinery, other equipment		0.1	0.1	0.5	0.2			0.1	2.9	0.1	4.0
35 Other manufacturing			0.5	0.3	0.4			0.1	7.1	0.1	8.5
36 Construction		3.4	0.7	3.0	0.6	0.3		2.3	88.0	1.9	100.3
37 Electricity		0.5	0.1	1.2	0.2	0.7		1.1	10.5	0.1	14.3
38 Road passenger transport		0.9	0.8	3.4	0.1	0.5		23.8	10.8	0.9	41.1
39 Rail transport		0.6	0.5	2.1	0.1	0.3		14.7	6.6	0.5	25.4
40a Wholesale trade		0.1	4.3	11.7	12.5	0.7		0.5	10.2	1.9	41.8
40b Retail trade		0.1	8.4	10.2	212.7	0.4		1.8	11.0	3.4	247.9
40c Other transport		1.8	1.7	6.9	0.2	1.0		49.0	22.2	1.8	84.7
41a Communication		0.1	0.1	7.3	0.5			13.8	1.7	0.1	23.5
41b Hotels and restaurants		0.1	1.5	2.2	18.2			0.1	3.1	15.7	40.8
41c Professional services		11.1	0.8	4.2	0.5			0.6	4.7	2.8	24.7
41d Dwellings											
41e Other services	0.2	15.5	3.0	16.2	3.6	1.0		3.3	25.3	95.2	163.3
Public administration		127.1	5.1	51.6	0.5	1.6	0.7	9.5	40.0	29.6	265.7
Domestic servants										65.0	65.0
Unspecified	7.0	1.7	0.7	4.8	4.3	3.6	0.5	0.1	112.5	2.8	137.9
Total	7.8	169.4	38.5	146.4	270.8	1856.9	13.0	127.8	706.3	246.4	3583.2

LIST OF WORKS CITED

Adelman, I. and Morris, C.T. (1971), 'An Anatomy of Patterns of Income Distribution in Developing Nations'. Paper prepared for US Agency for International Development, mimeographed, Washington, DC.

Adelman, I. and Morris C.T. (1967), *Society, Politics and Economic Development: A Quantitative Approach*. Johns Hopkins Press, Baltimore.

Altimir, O. (1975), 'Income Distribution estimates from household surveys and population Censuses in Latin America: An assessment of reliability', Economic Commission for Latin America and Development Research Centre, World Bank (mimeograph).

Bacharach, Michael (1970), *Bi-proportional Matrices and Input–Output Change*, Cambridge University Press.

Balassa, Bela and associates (1971), *The Structure of Protection in Developing Countries*, Johns Hopkins Press for the IBRD and Inter-American Development Bank.

Basevi, G. (1966), 'The US Tariff Structure: Estimate of Effective Rates of Protection of US Industries and Industrial Labor'. *Review of Economic Statistics*, Vol. 48.

Bauer, P.T. (1971), *Dissent on Development: Studies and Debates in Development Economics*, Weidenfeld and Nicolson.

Baxter, R.D. (1868), *National Income: The United Kingdom*, Macmillan, London.

Bell, C.L.G. and Duloy, J.H. (1974), 'Statistical Priorities', Chapter 12 of *Redistribution with Growth*, by Chenery *et al.* (1974).

Bell, C.L.G. and Hazell, P.B.R. (1976), 'A preliminary analysis of the Muda Irrigation Scheme', Development Research Centre, World Bank, Working Papers (mimeograph).

Blitzer, C.R., Clarke, P.B. and Taylor, Lance (1975), *Economy-wide Models and Development Planning*, OUP for World Bank.

Cambridge, Department of Applied Economics (1962–), *A Programme for Growth*, Volumes I to XI, Chapman and Hall, London.

Ceylon, Central Bank of Ceylon (Annual), *Annual Report of the Monetary Board to the Minister of Finance*, Colombo.

Ceylon, Central Bank of Ceylon (1970), *Survey of Private Investment*, Colombo, Central Bank of Ceylon.

Ceylon, Central Bank of Ceylon (1973), *The Determinants of Labour Force Participation in Sri Lanka*, 1973.

Ceylon, Central Bank of Ceylon (1975), *Survey of Sri Lanka's Consumer Finances*, 1973, Colombo.

Ceylon, Department of Census and Statistics (Annual), *Statistical Abstract*, Colombo.

Ceylon, Department of Census and Statistics (1969), *Ceylon Year Book*, Colombo.

Ceylon, Department of Census and Statistics (1971/72), *Report on the Socio-Economic Survey of Ceylon, 1969–70*, Colombo.

Ceylon, *Taxation Inquiry Commission Report* (1968) (Sessional Papers 10–1968), Colombo, Government Press.

Ceylon, Ministry of Planning and Economic Affairs (1966), *Government Policy on Private Foreign Investment*, Colombo.

Ceylon, National Planning Council (1959), *Ten Year Plan* (1958–68) Planning Secretariat, Colombo.

Chenery, Hollis, B., Ahluwalia, Montek, S., Bell, C.L.G., Duloy, John H. and Jolly, Richard (1974), *Redistribution with Growth*, for the IBRD and Institute of Development Studies, University of Sussex by Oxford University Press.

Chenery, H.B. and Syrquin (1975), *Patterns of Development*, 1950–1970, Oxford University Press, 1975.

Clark, Colin (1937), *National Income and Outlay*, Macmillan, London.

Codippily, H.M.A. (1974), *Some Aspects of Income Distribution and Economic Growth with Special Reference to Sri Lanka*, unpublished MA dissertation, University of Warwick.

Copeland, M.A. (1935), 'National wealth and income – an interpretation', *Journal of the American Statistical Association*, Vol. XXX, No. 190, pp. 377–86.

Copeland, M.A. (1937), 'Concepts of national income', in *Studies in Income and Wealth*, Vol. 1 pp. 3–63, National Bureau of Economic Research, New York.

Corden, W.M. (1966), 'The Structure of a Tariff System and the Effective Protective Rate', *Journal of Political Economy*, Vol. 74, pp. 221–37.

Deane, Phyllis (1955), 'The implications of early national income estimates for the measurement of long-term growth in the United Kingdom', *Economic Development and Cultural Change*, Vol. IV, No. 1 pp. 3–38.

Denison, Edward F. (1947), 'Report on tripartite discussions of national income measurement', in *Studies in Income and Wealth*, Vol. 10, pp. 3–22, National Bureau of Economic Research, New York.

Divatia, M.V. and Srivastava, R.K. (1971), *Employment Potential of Industry in Ceylon*, Ministry of Planning and Employment, Colombo.

Gruenbaum, (Gaathon) Ludwig (1941), National Income and Outlay in Palestine 1936, Economic Research Institute of the Jewish Agency for Palestine, Jerusalem.

Hicks, J.R. (1942), *The Social Framework*, 1st edition, The Clarendon Press, Oxford (4th edition, 1971).

International Bank for Reconstruction and Development (IBRD) (1973), *Small Enterprises in Manufacturing: The Emerging Issues*, Mimeo, Washington, DC.

International Labour Office (1971), *Programme of Action for Ceylon: Matching employment opportunities and expectations*, Report and technical papers, ILO, 2 Vols, Geneva.

International Labour Office (1971a), *Report from the Group on Statistical Policy and Organisation*, Colombo (mimeo).

International Labour Office (1973), *Strategies for Employment Promotion*, Geneva.

International Labour Office (1973a), *Employment and Incomes Policies for Iran*, ILO, Geneva.

International Labour Office (1975), *Time for Transition: A mid-term Review of the Second United Nations Development Decade.*

Jayawardena, Lal, 'Sri Lanka' in *Redistribution with Growth* by Chenery, *et al.* (1974).

Johnson, Harry G. (1967), *Economic policies towards less developed countries*, George Allen and Unwin, London.

Jones, Gavin, W. and Selvaratnam, S. (1972), *Population Growth and Economic Development in Ceylon*, Colombo, Marga.

Jones, Gavin, W. and Selvaratnam, S. (1970), 'Urbanisation in Ceylon, 1946–63', *Modern Ceylon Studies: A Journal of the Social Sciences*, Vol. 1, No. 2, July.

Karageorgas, D. (1973), 'The Distribution of Tax Burden by Income Groups in Greece', *Economic Journal*, Vol. 83, pp. 436–47.

Karunaratne, N. (1973), *Techno-Economic Survey of Industrial Potential in Sri Lanka*, DPhil, University of Sussex.

Karunatilake, H.N.S. (1971), *Economic Development in Ceylon* (Praeger Special Studies in International Economics and Development), Praeger.

Karunatilake, H.N.S. (1975), 'The Impact of Welfare Services in Sri Lanka on the Economy', *Central Bank of Ceylon, Staff Studies*, Vol. 5, No. 1.

Keynes, J.M. (1936), *The General Theory of Employment, Interest and Money*, Macmillan, London.

King, Gregory (1696), 'Natural and Political Observations and Conclusions upon the State and Condition of England'. Printed as an appendix to, *An Estimate of the Comparative Strength of Great Britain* (1802), by Sir George Chalmers; and reprinted in *Two Tracts by Gregory King*, Johns Hopkins Press, Baltimore, 1936.

Kuznets, S., 'Economic Growth and Income Inequality', *American Economic Review*, Vol. 45, March 1955.

Levitt, K. (1973), *A System of National Accounts for Trinidad and Tobago*, Report prepared for the Government of Trinidad and Tobago (mimeo).

Lewis, W.A., 'Economic Development with Unlimited Supplies of Labour', *Manchester School of Economic and Social Studies*, May 1954, pp. 139–91.

Little, I.M.D., Scitovsky Tibor and Scott, Maurice F. (1970), *Industry and Trade in Some Developing Countries: A Comparative Study*, OUP for OECD Development Centre, 1970.

Lotz, J.R. (1970), 'Patterns of Government spending in developing countries', *Manchester School of Economic and Social Studies*, pp. 119–44.

McCulloch, J.R. (1837), *A Statistical Account of the British Empire*, 1st edition, Charles Knight, London, (4th edition, 1854).

Mitra, Ashok (1963), 'Underdeveloped Statistics', *Economic Development and Cultural Change*, Vol. XI, No. 3, Part 1, April.

Morawetz, D. (1974), 'Employment Implications of Industrialisation in Developing Countries: A Survey', *Economic Journal*, Vol. 84, No. 335, pp. 491–542.

Myrdal, Gunnar (1956), *Development and Underdevelopment: a note on the mechanism of national and international inequality* (National Bank of Egypt, 50th Anniversary Commemoration Lectures), Cairo, National Bank of Egypt.

Narapalasingham, S. (1970), *On the Construction and Implementation of a planning model for Ceylon*. PhD thesis of the University of Bristol.

Newmarch, W. (1869), 'The progress and present condition of statistical enquiry', *Journal of the Statistical Society of London*, Vol. XXXII, Pt. IV, pp. 359–90.

Organisation for European Economic Co-operation (1950), *A Simplified System of National Accounts*, OEEC, Paris, reprinted 1951.

Organisation for European Economic Co-operation (1952), *A Standardised System of National Accounts*, OEEC, Paris, 1958 edition, 1959.

Oshima, H. (1962), 'The International Comparison of Size Distribution of Family Incomes with Special Reference to Asia', *Review of Economics and Statistics*, November.

Paukert, F. (1973), 'Income Distribution at Different Levels of Development: A Study of Evidence', *International Labour Review*, August.

Paukert, F.J., Skolka and Maton, J. (1974), 'Redistribution of Income, Patterns of Consumption and Employment: A Case Study for the Philippines', WEP Research Working Papers, ILO, Geneva.

Porter, G.R. (1843), *The Progress of the Nation*, 1st edition, John Murray, London: 3rd edition 1851, first published seriatim 1838–42.

Prebisch, R. (1964), *Towards a New Trade Policy for Development*, in Proceeding of the UN Conference on Trade and Development, Vol. 2, pp. 3–64.

Pyatt, Graham (1968), 'On Official Statistics', *Journal of the Royal Statistical Society*, Series A, Vol. 131.

Pyatt, Graham, Bharier, J., Lindley, R.M., Mabro, R.M. and Sabolo, Y. (1973), Mission Working Paper No. XII, 'A Methodology for Macro-Economic Projections', Appendix 12 to *Employment and Incomes Policies for Iran*, ILO (1973a).

Pyatt, Graham and associates (1975), *Swaziland: As Perceived in A Social Accounting Framework*, unpublished mimeo.

Pyatt, Graham and Thorbecke, Erik (1976), *Planning techniques for a Better Future*, International Labour Office, 1976.

Pyatt, Graham and Thorbecke, Erik (forthcoming), 'Planning for Growth Redistribution and Employment', in preparation.

Ranis, G. and Fei, J.C. (1964), *Development of the Labour Surplus Economy: Theory and Policy* (Yale University, Economic Growth Center Publications), Irwin.

Rasaputram, W. (1972), 'Changes in the pattern of income equality in Ceylon', *Marga*, Vol. 1, No. 4.

Roe, A.R., *et al.* (1975), *A Framework of Economic Statistics for the Caribbean Common Market*, Report prepared for the Caribbean Community Secretariat, mimeo.

de Samarasinghe, S.W.R. (1973), *The Monetary and Financial experience of a mixed economy: the case of Ceylon*, 1950–1970, unpublished thesis of the University of Cambridge.

Seers, D. (1961), 'An Accounting System for Projections in a Specialised Exporter of Primary Products', mimeo.

Snodgrass, D.R. (1966), *Ceylon: An Export Economy in Transition* (Yale University Economic Growth Center Publications), Irwin.

Stone, Richard, Champernowne, D.G., and Meade, J.E. (1942), 'The precision of national income estimates', *Review of Economic Studies*, Vol. IX, No. 2, pp. 111–25.

Stone, Richard, ed. (1953–72), *Studies in the National Income and Expenditure of the United Kingdom*, 6 Vols., Cambridge University Press.

Stone, Richard (1970), *Mathematical Models of the Economy and Other Essays*, Chapman and Hall, London.

Stone, Richard (1973), 'Transition and admission models in social demography', *Social Science Research*, Vol. 2, No. 2, pp. 185–230, also in *Social Indicator Models* (eds., K.C. Land and S. Spilerman), Russell Sage Foundation, New York, 1975.

Studenski, Paul (1958), *The Income of Nations*, New York University Press.

Thirlwall, A.P. and Barton, C. (1971), 'Inflation and Growth: The International Evidence', *Banca Nazionale del Lavoro*, September.

Thorbecke, E. and Dambe, G. (1974), 'Agricultural Development and Employment Performance and Planning: A Comparative Analysis', FAO Rome, *Agricultural Planning Studies*, No. 18.

Tinbergen, J. (1937), *An Econometric Approach to Business Cycle Problems*, Hermann *et al.*, Paris.

Tinbergen, J. (1939a), *A Method and its Application to Investment Activity*, League of Nations, Geneva.

Tinbergen, J. (1939b), *Business Cycles in the United States of America, 1919–32*, League of Nations, Geneva.

UK Department of Trade (1975), *Sri Lanka Tea Estates*, HMSO, London.

UK House of Commons Estimates Committee (1966), *The Statistical Service*, 4th Report, Session 1965.

UK Treasury (1941–), *An Analysis of the Sources of War Finance and an Estimate of the National Income and Expenditure in 1938 and 1940*, HMSO, London. The successors to this publication went through a series of titles as follows: 1942–45, as above, with, of course, change of dates; 1946–51, *National Income and Expenditure of the United Kingdom*; 1952, *Preliminary National Income and Expenditure Estimates*; 1953–62 *Preliminary Estimates of National Income and Expenditure*; 1963– , *Preliminary Estimates of National Income and Balance of Payments.*

United Nations (1947), *Measurement of National Income and the Construction of Social Accounts*, Studies and Reports on Statistical Methods, No. 7, United Nations, Geneva.

United Nations, Development Programme (1970), *National Economic Planning and Programming Project*, Colombo.

United Nations Statistical Office (Annual), *Yearbook of National Account Statistics.*

United Nations Statistical Office (1953), *A System of National Accounts and Supporting Tables*, Studies in Methods, Series F, No. 2, United Nationa, New York, Rev. 1, 1960, Rev. 2, 1964.

United Nations Statistical Office (1968), *A System of National Accounts*, Studies in Methods, Series F, No. 2, Rev. 3, United Nations, New York.

United Nations Statistical Office (1971), *Basic Principles of the System of Balances of the National Economy*, Studies in Methods, Series F, No. 17, UN, New York.

United Nations Statistical Office (1972), *A Draft System of Statistics of the Distribution of Income, Consumption and Accumulation*, E/CN, 3/425, 3 February, mimeo.

United Nations Statistical Office (1974), *Statistics of the Distribution of Income, Consumption and Accumulation: Draft Guidelines for the Developing Countries*, E/CN 3/462, 5 July 1974, mimeo.

United Nations, Statistical Office (1975), *Towards a System of Social and Demographic Statistics*, Studies in Methods, Series F, No. 18, United Nations, New York.

van Cleef, ed. (1941a), 'Nationale boekhouding: proeve van een jaaroverzicht Nederland, 1938', *De Economist*, No. 7/8, pp. 415–24.

van Cleef, ed. (1941b), 'Beteekenis en invichtung eener nationale boekhouding', *De Economist*, No. 11, pp. 608–23.

Waterson, Albert (1966), *Development Planning: Lessons of Experience*, OUP, for Economic Development Institute.

Wery, R., Rodgers, G.B. and Hopkins, M.D., 'A Population and Employment Model for the Philippines', *World Employment Programme Research Working Papers*, Geneva, July 1974.

INDEX